A GUIDE to
SCHOLARLY RESOURCES
on the RUSSIAN EMPIRE
and the SOVIET UNION
in the NEW YORK
METROPOLITAN AREA

Members of the Joint Committee on Soviet Studies of the American Council of Learned Societies and the Social Science Research Council

Chair: Loren Graham, *Massachusetts Institute of Technology*
Jeffrey Brooks, *University of Minnesota*
Jane Burbank, *University of Michigan*
Robert Campbell, *Indiana University*
Timothy Colton, *University of Toronto*
Sheila Fitzpatrick, *University of Texas, Austin*
Nancy Shields Kollmann, *Stanford University*
Mary McAuley, *St. Hilda's College, Oxford*
Brian Silver, *Michigan State University*
Michael Swafford, *Vanderbilt University*
William Todd, *Harvard University*

Members of the Bibliography, Information Retrieval and Documentation Subcommittee of the Joint Committee on Soviet Studies of the American Council of Learned Societies and the Social Science Research Council

Chair: Edward L. Keenan, *Harvard University*
Marianna Tax Choldin, *University of Illinois*
Henry Cooper, *Indiana University*
Joseph Dwyer, *Hoover Institution*
Robert Huber, *Social Science Research Council*
Edward Kasinec, *The New York Public Library*
David Kraus, *Library of Congress*
Hugh Olmsted, *Harvard University*
Jason Parker, *American Council of Learned Societies*
Blair Ruble, *Kennan Institute for Advanced Russian Studies*

Members of the Advisory Committee to the Guide

Chair: Edward Kasinec, *The New York Public Library*
Thomas Bird, *Queens College*
Olha Della Cava, *Columbia University*
Marc Raeff, *Columbia University*
Cynthia Whittaker, *Baruch College*

A GUIDE to SCHOLARLY RESOURCES on the RUSSIAN EMPIRE and the SOVIET UNION in the NEW YORK METROPOLITAN AREA

The Social Science Research Council

Sponsored by the
Bibliography, Information Retrieval
and Documentation Subcommittee of
the Joint Committee on Soviet Studies
of the Social Science Research Council and
the American Council of Learned Societies

Compiled by Robert A. Karlowich

M. E. Sharpe, Inc.
Armonk, New York
London, England

Library of Congress Cataloging-in-Publication Data

A guide to scholarly resources on the Russian Empire and the Soviet
    Union in the New York metropolitan area / the Social Science Research
    Council ; compiled by Robert A. Karlowich
        p. cm.
    ISBN 0-87332-619-9
        1. Soviet Union—Library resources—New York Metropolitan Area.
2. Libraries—New York Metropolitan Area—Directories. 3. Research institutes—New York Metropolitan Area—Directories. I. Karlowich, Robert A. II.
Social Science Research Council (U.S.)
    Z2491.G86   1990
    [DK17]
    026.947′00257471—dc20
89-24314
CIP

Printed in the United States of America

∞

MV   10   9   8   7   6   5   4   3   2   1

Contents

List of Entries   vii

Note
Cynthia H. Whittaker   xiii

Foreword
Edward Kasinec   xv

Introduction
Robert A. Karlowich   xvii

A Guide to Scholarly Resources
on the Russian Empire and the Soviet Union
in the New York Metropolitan Area   1

How to Use the Index
Robert A. Karlowich   253

Index   256

List of Entries

A1   American Bible Society *3*

A2   American Geographical Society Collection
       of the University of Wisconsin Library *4*

A3   American Institute of Aeronautics and Astronautics
       Library *6*

A4   American Institute of Physics, Center for History of Physics,
       Niels Bohr Library *8*

A5   American Jewish Committee, Blaustein Library *10*

A6   American Jewish Committee, William E. Wiener
       Oral History Library *11*

A7   American-Jewish Joint Distribution Committee, Archives *13*

A8   American Museum of Natural History, Department
       of Anthropology *14*

A9   American Museum of Natural History, Library *15*

A10   American Numismatic Society *17*

A11   Armenian Missionary Association of America *19*

A12   Astman, Marina *20*

B1   Leo Baeck Institute *20*

B2   Bettmann Archive, Inc. *24*

B3   Brookhaven National Laboratory *24*

B4   Brooklyn Museum, Art Reference Library *25*

B5   Brooklyn Museum *26*

B6   Bund Archives of the Jewish Labor Movement *26*

B7   Byelorussian Congress Committee of America *28*

B8   Byelorussian Folk Dance Company "Vasilok" *29*

B9   Byzantine Catholic Diocese of Passaic,
       Episcopal and Heritage Institute Libraries *29*

C1   Carus Gallery *31*

C2   Chemiakine Metaphysical Arts, Inc. *31*

C3   Citizens Exchange Council *32*

C4   Coalition to Free Soviet Jews, Inc. *33*

C5   Columbia University, The Libraries *34*

C6   Columbia University, Oral History Research Office *37*

C7   Columbia University, Rare Book and Manuscript Library *38*

C8   Columbia University, Boris Bakhmeteff Archive *44*

C9   Columbia University, School of Library Service *47*

C10   Columbia University, W. Averell Harriman Institute *48*

C11	Columbia University, W. Averell Harriman Institute, Institute Reading Room	*49*
C12	Combustion Engineering, Inc.	*50*
C13	Committee for Absorption of Soviet Emigres C.A.S.E. Museum of Russian Contemporary Art in Exile	*51*
C14	Contemporary Russian Art Center of America	*52*
C15	Cory, Constance	*53*
C16	Council on Foreign Relations	*53*
E1	Edison National Historic Site	*55*
E2	Educational Testing Service	*57*
E3	Effect Publishing	*58*
E4	Ex Libris	*59*
F1	Forbes Magazine Galleries	*60*
F2	Freidus, Ella	*61*
F3	Frick Art Reference Library	*61*
F4	Fuld, James J.	*63*
G1	Solomon R. Guggenheim Museum	*64*
H1	Hebrew Union College, Klau Library	*65*
H2	Historical Museum Rodina	*66*
H3	Hoffman, Charles J.	*68*
H4	Holy Trinity Seminary Library	*69*
H5	Huttenbach, Henry R.	*72*
I1	International Film Foundation, Inc.	*73*
I2	International Ladies' Garment Workers' Union, Archives	*73*
I3	International Research & Exchanges Board (IREX)	*75*
I4	Isdebsky-Pritchard, Aline	*76*
J1	Janet Lehr, Inc.	*77*
J2	Jewish Theological Seminary of America	*78*
K1	Victor Kamkin Bookstore, Inc.	*78*
K2	Kerdimun, Boris	*79*
K3	Komar and Melamid Art Studio	*80*
K4	Kosciuszko Foundation	*80*
L1	Lampard, Marie Turbow	*81*
L2	Long, Rose-Carol W.	*82*
M1	Manhattan School of Music	*82*
M2	Metropolitan Museum of Art	*83*
M3	Pierpont Morgan Library	*85*
M4	Morristown National Historical Park	*90*
M5	Museum of Modern Art, Film Stills Archive	*92*
M6	Museum of Modern Art, Film Study Center	*93*
M7	Museum of Modern Art, Library	*94*
N1	National Archives–New York Branch	*96*
N2	National Council of American–Soviet Friendship, Library	*98*
N3	Neizvestny, Ernst	*99*
N4	New Jersey Historical Society	*99*
N5	New Rochelle Historical Association	*101*
N6	New York Academy of Medicine, Library	*101*

N7   New York City Municipal Archives   *102*
N8   New-York Historical Society   *103*
N9   New York Life Insurance Company, Research Center/Archives   *109*
N10   New York Public Library, Berg Collection   *110*
N11   New York Public Library, Jewish Division   *111*
N12   New York Public Library, Miriam and Ira D. Wallach Division of
            Art, Prints and Photographs. Art and Architecture Collection   *114*
N13   New York Public Library, Miriam and Ira D. Wallach Division of
            Art, Prints and Photographs. Photographic Collection   *115*
N14   New York Public Library, Miriam and Ira D. Wallach Division of
            Art, Prints and Photographs. Prints   *116*
N15   New York Public Library, Oriental Division   *119*
N16   New York Public Library, Rare Books and Manuscripts Division   *121*
N17   New York Public Library, Rare Books and Manuscripts Division.
            Arents Collection   *123*
N18   New York Public Library, Rare Books and Manuscripts Division.
            Manuscripts and Archives Section   *124*
N19   New York Public Library, Slavic and Baltic Division   *127*
N20   New York Public Library, Spencer Collection   *142*
N21   New York Public Library, Donnell Library Center,
            Central Children's Room   *144*
N22   New York Public Library, Donnell Library Center,
            Foreign Language Library   *145*
N23   New York Public Library, Donnell Library Center,
            Media Center   *146*
N24   New York Public Library at Lincoln Center, Billy Rose
            Theatre Collection, Performing Arts Research Center   *153*
N25   New York Public Library, Library and Museum
            of the Performing Arts at Lincoln Center, Dance Collection   *156*
N26   New York Public Library, Library and Museum
            of the Performing Arts at Lincoln Center, Music Division   *163*
N27   New York Public Library, Library and Museum
            of the Performing Arts at Lincoln Center, Rodgers and Hammerstein
            Archives of Recorded Sound   *169*
N28   New York Public Library, Mid-Manhattan Library   *170*
N29   New York Public Library, Mid-Manhattan Library,
            Picture Collection   *171*
N30   New York Public Library, Schomberg Center for Research
            in Black Culture   *172*
N31   New York Theosophical Society   *173*
N32   New York Times, Archives   *173*
N33   New York University, Elmer Holmes Bobst Library,
            Special Collections   *174*
N34   New York University, Elmer Holmes Bobst Library,
            Tamiment Collection   *175*
O1   Olcott Library and Research Center   *177*
O2   Orthodox Church in America, Archives   *178*

P1   Pilsudski Institute of America   *180*
P2   Pleskow, Martin   *182*
P3   Polchaninoff, R.V.   *183*
P4   Polish Institute of Arts and Sciences of America, Inc.,
            Alfred Jurzykowski Memorial Library   *184*
P5   Prelacy of Armenian Apostolic Church of America,
            St. Nerses Shnorhali Library   *186*
P6   Princeton University Library, Firestone Library   *187*
P7   Princeton University Library, Firestone Library,
            Rare Book, Manuscript, and Special Collections   *189*
P8   Princeton University Library, Seeley G. Mudd
            Manuscript Library   *194*
R1   Rabinovich, Alex   *198*
R2   Radio Free Europe/Radio Liberty, New York
            Programming Center   *199*
R3   Reference Center for Marxist Studies, Inc.   *201*
R4   University of Rochester, Rush Rhees Library,
            Nikolai Martianoff Collection   *202*
R5   Rockefeller Archive Center   *203*
R6   Nicholas Roerich Museum   *206*
R7   Ronald Feldman Fine Arts, Inc.   *207*
R8   Russian Boy and Girl Scout Archive   *207*
R9   (Russian) Orthodox Cathedral of the Protection of the Holy Virgin
            (Orthodox Church in America)   *209*
R10   Russian Orthodox St. Nicholas Cathedral   *210*
R11   Russica Book and Art Shop   *211*
S1   St. Vladimir's Orthodox Theological Seminary,
            The Father Georges Florovsky Library   *211*
S2   Joseph Schillinger Collection   *213*
S3   Schwab, George   *214*
S4   Shevchenko Scientific Society, Library and Archives   *215*
S5   Sovart, c/o Livet Reichard Company, Inc.   *217*
S6   Sovfoto/Eastfoto   *218*
S7   Stravinsky-Diaghilev Foundation Collection,
            Parmenia Migel Ekstrom Collection   *219*
S8   St. Basil's College, Library   *220*
S9   St. Nicholas Ukrainian Catholic Church   *220*
S10   Synod of Russian Bishops Outside Russia, Cathedral of the Sign   *221*
T1   Tarassuk, Leonid   *222*
T2   Tatyana Gallery   *223*
T3   Tcherepnin Society   *223*
T4   Tolstoy Foundation   *224*
U1   Ukrainian Museum   *226*
U2   Ukrainian Orthodox Church, The Seminary Library   *227*
U3   Ukrainian Research and Documentation Center   *229*
U4   United Nations, Archives   *230*
U5   United Nations, Dag Hammerskjold Library   *231*

U6   United States Military Academy, Library   *233*
V1   Von Loew, Karl   *234*
Y1   Yeshiva University, Mendel Gottesman Library of
         Hebraica/Judaica   *235*
Y2   Yeshiva Univesity, Archives   *236*
Y3   Yeshiva University Museum   *237*
Y4   YIVO Institute for Jewish Research, Library   *238*
Y5   YIVO Institute for Jewish Research, YIVO Archives   *241*
Y6   YMCA of Greater New York, Archives   *249*
Z1   Zionist Archives and Library   *251*

Note

In 1984 the American Association for the Advancement of Slavic Studies held its annual meeting in New York City. As part of their duties as hosts for the meeting, a group of local scholars decided to prepare a guide to Slavic New York, and Baruch College of the City University of New York agreed to publish the twenty-four–page pamphlet which they compiled.

Recognizing the need for a more comprehensive survey of the resources available for reseachers in the metropolitan area, a number of people—in particular Robert A. Karlowich and Edward Kasinec—undertook to prepare such a guide. The resulting volume confirms the long-held (but until now largely undocumented) view that the New York metropolitan area contains some of the richest and most diverse caches of materials available in North America for Russian and Soviet studies. Researchers in many different fields should find welcome and suggestive assistance in this guide.

Cynthia H. Whittaker
Project Director
Baruch College and the Graduate School
The City University of New York

Foreword

It is a privilege to have been asked to write the foreword to this invaluable—and long overdue—survey of metropolitan New York resources for Russian and Soviet culture. Along with other major metropolitan areas in the United States, among them the San Francisco Bay area, Chicago, Philadelphia, and Washington, D.C., the New York City metropolitan area has one of the nation's greatest collections of human and material resources for the study of the culture of the Eastern Slavs, both in the homeland and in emigration.[1]

The strongest impression that emerges from a close reading of the Karlowich compilation is the great diversity of these resources. They include (aside from the obvious printed materials) Armenian and Church Slavonic manuscripts, twentieth-century graphics by El Lissitsky, letters of Catherine II to Melchior Grimm, nineteenth- and twentieth-century American insurance records relating to the old Russian Empire, and, finally, Ukrainian and Byelorussian textiles and costumes held by museums in the area.

Slavic and East European communities were already well established in the New York City area in the 1840s. In 1898 the local Russian and Jewish communities petitioned the Director of the New York Public Library, Dr. John Shaw Billings, to establish a division in which they might read literature in the language of their homeland. In 1945 the eminent American Slavicist and Chief of the Slavonic Division of The New York Public Library, Avrahm Yarmolinsky, convoked a meeting at which one of the points to be discussed was the coordination of collection development and processing of Russian and Soviet materials in the New York area.[2] Indeed, the activities of this little-known conference foreshadowed some of the collective and cooperative efforts that took place in the compilation of this guide. Present at the meeting were not only representatives of both research and private libraries in New York City, but also representatives of booksellers. This is one of the notable aspects of the work that follows: it brings together many different types of individuals and institutions with resources of all kinds for studies relating to the Russian Empire and the Soviet Union.

One element, however, is not included here: entries on the organized research and teaching programs which also play a prominent role in the overall development of Russian/Soviet and East European studies in the New

York metropolitan area. A recent directory issued by the American Association for the Advancement of Slavic Studies lists more than fourteen organized programs for Russian and Soviet studies in the New York area, some of which, like the courses at Columbia University, date their existence to the very early years of this century.[3] So large are some of the programs (e.g., those in the City University of New York) that they number dozens of faculty members among their researchers and teaching staff.

When seen in this broader context of teaching and research staff, and the ethnic communities themselves, the resources enumerated so carefully and well by Professor Karlowich provide an unparalleled opportunity for research and study of Russian and Soviet culture. We look forward to the appearance of a companion volume surveying Eastern and South Central European resources.

Edward Kasinec
Chair, Advisory Committee
Chief, Slavic and Baltic Division
The New York Public Library

Notes

1. Edward Kasinec, "Lesser-known Collections in the San Francisco Area," *AAASS Newsletter* (February 1982): 6; and, of course, the *Scholar's Guide to Washington, D.C.* for Russian/Soviet Studies (Washington, D.C.: Smithsonian Institution Press, 1983). For previous attempts to survey some of the resources in the New York area see *Russko-iazychnyi N'iu-Iork 1982* (New York: Chalidze Publications, 1982); and *Slavic New York* (New York: Baruch College, 1984).

2. *Special Libraries Conference on Russian Materials, November 17, 1945* (New York: American Russian Institute, 1945), unpublished manuscript.

3. See the *AAASS Directory of Programs in Soviet and East European Studies 1987–89* (Stanford, CA: American Association for the Advancement of Slavic Studies, 1987); also Clarence Augustus Manning, *A History of Slavic Studies in the United States* (Milwaukee: Marquette University Press, 1957).

Introduction

Robert A. Karlowich
Project Managing Director

In one sense, this guide is a first for the New York area. In another, it is a continuation of the pioneering work done by Steven A. Grant and John H. Brown in *The Russian Empire and the Soviet Union: A Guide to Manuscripts and Archival Materials in the United States*, published in 1981.[1] In the present guide we have limited ourselves to the New York metropolitan area, defined more or less as a fifty-mile radius emanating from Fifth Avenue and 42nd Street in Manhattan—site of the central building of the Research Division of The New York Public Library, which, in the aggregate, contains one of the major Slavic and East European collections in the Western world.[2] This guide is a first for New York in its narrower, yet more inclusive goal, but it has also been very dependent on the work of Grant and Brown. Since the Grant and Brown guide is no longer in print, we have reproduced—and updated—many of its entries, for the convenience of those doing research in the New York metropolitan area. I must here thank Messrs. Grant and Brown for granting us permission to quote liberally from their work. It will also be obvious to the user of this guide that, like Grant and Brown, we have a most liberal interpretation of the scope of our entries: the subject matter is limitless, and the geographic area covers not only the countries and nationalities subsumed under the Russian Empire or the Soviet Union at any particular time, but also movements that were continued outside these boundaries—artistic, immigrant, political, etc.

As Edward Kasinec points out in his foreword to this volume, the New York metropolitan area offers rich resources for anyone who has an interest in the area of Slavic and East European studies. On subjects ranging from art to Zionism, through ethnography, language, music, numismatics, politics, and religion, the seeker can find something here, and in a variety of languages, to match his or her expertise. Indeed, one can find a great deal of information available in the English language. Among other institutions, the historical societies in New York and New Jersey offer, along with other materials, correspondence from United States ministers in Russia, diaries of travelers, and account books and reports of those carrying on trade with Russia. Impressions of Americans who went to Soviet Russia during the 1920s and 1930s can be found here, and several Jewish institutions have material in English on the present situation of Soviet Jews as well as their early history both in Russia and in the United States. Armenians, Byelorussians, Jews, Poles, Rusyns, and Ukrainians are also represented by their own languages in libraries and archives that hold important collections on their histories and cultures. In fact, some of the major collections in the United States by and about various nationalities of the Soviet Union are represented in the guide. The abundant resources of these holdings in the New York area provide endless possibilities for the scholar or the interested inquirer. It must be emphasized, too, that not the least of the materials are collections of films, photographs, slides, and videotapes, an important part of research today.

If this guide is a first in the specific extent of its coverage, it remains, nonetheless, only a preliminary, limited overview of the riches residing in the New York metropolitan area. Out of more than 300 questionnaires that we sent to prospective entrants, only 153 were returned.[3] Many who did not reply have important collections, and it is to be regretted that, for whatever reasons, they chose not to be included in this guide. But there are undoubtedly collections beyond those 300 that we did not locate, and even now new galleries and museums are opening that will include, in one form or another, materials covering or relevant to the Russian Empire and Soviet Union.[4] Our fifty-mile radius is also an arbitrary limitation, something that gave us a reasonable cutoff point; perhaps, however, it should be extended in the future to cover some significant collections that do not lie too far outside our demarcation. In any case, our hope is that other areas will soon compile their own local guides to similar resources. This guide is, in other words, a probe, an effort not only to bring into focus resources available on our topic, but also to build on our experience and hope for an ever-expanding record of these resources.

Edward Kasinec has pointed out the need to define and list the organized research and teaching programs which are so numerous in the New York metropolitan area. I would add to that list the need to document the existence of any data bases, personal or institutional, that have been compiled and might be useful to the users of a guide such as this. Here we have only reported on one, in the reading room of the Harriman Institute, but there must be more out there. There is still work to be done.

The Entries

The guide does locate and describe a collection, but we should note that the description does not provide any more detail than was supplied by the owner or institution. Most of these descriptions are necessarily brief, even for the larger institutions. When possible, we have appended to the entries bibliographies that cite articles and books describing the holdings in more detail. Efforts to describe Slavic and East European collections and their histories in the United States are beginning to take on the dimensions of an industry, which is good news. In recent years the American Association for the Advancement of Slavic Studies, at its annual and regional conventions, has had at least one panel where book dealers, librarians, scholars, and institutions in these areas are discussed. Some of the papers from these sessions have been published in the professional journals. Robert H. Davis, Jr., librarian in the Slavic and Baltic Division of The New York Public Library, is preparing an article, based on his presentations at such meetings, on the valuable photographic collections in his division and relevant material held in other sections of the library. Ellen Scaruffi, Curator of the Bakhmeteff Archive, Columbia University, has presented lectures on the wealth of historical photographs and iconographic materials in the Bakhmeteff collection. These presentations could not, unfortunately, be reproduced here, but the user should always be aware that the bibliographical listings in the entries are far from exhaustive, and be on the lookout for new descriptions and guides.

Organization of the Guide

The user will see that the entries in the guide are numbered in alphabetical/numerical order, generally by institution, not library. Thus, the Niels Bohr Library is listed under the American Institute of Physics. The index, however, has a listing under Niels Bohr Library, to speed the inquirer to that source. Each entry has its own address, which means that all entries for institutions such as Columbia University and The New York Public Library are not grouped together but treated as individual libraries, although they are listed in alphabetical order under their institutional heading.[5] Whenever possible we listed one contact person, someone who would be able to provide information on use of the collection; occasionally more than one is given, especially if the entry is divided into specialties. The headings listed below then follow in order:

TELEPHONE: Usually the telephone of the contact person or a reference/information desk.

SCHEDULE: Provides hours open. These, of course, change and it is always advisable to call or write ahead before visiting any institution.

ACCESS: Who can use the collection and under what conditions.

FACILITIES: Availability of reading rooms, and whether photocopying and/or photography are permitted.

HISTORY: If the collection is of long duration, a short historical statement is given; otherwise brief background information, if there is any, is incorporated into the holdings statement.

HOLDINGS: This is the main body of the entry and reflects information received in our questionnaire and, in some instances, data supplied in an accompanying brochure or pamphlet on the collection (usually not acknowledged, and never set off in quotation marks). In those instances where it was believed helpful, we have added entries from Grant & Brown and, where possible, have brought them up to date.

SPECIAL FEATURES: If the holdings include a special collection that should be brought to people's attention, we have put it under this heading.

CATALOGS: The information listed here was supplied by the source in order to facilitate access to information.

BIBLIOGRAPHY: Titles listed here are usually those supplied by the source. Sometimes we have obtained titles from others, such as members of the Advisory Committee to the guide, and have added them as well. Titles excluded from the bibliography are publications sponsored or issued by an institution because the work is based on material in its collection; if we had included such titles, some bibliographies would have run to the hundreds of citations. Rather, we have listed only works that describe the collections in full or in part; these include bibliographies, catalogs, art catalogs, exhibition catalogs, and the brochures and pamphlets that we received and used to expand the description of a given entry.

Participants

The guide was sponsored by the Bibliography, Information Retrieval, and Documentation Subcommittee of the Joint Committee on Soviet Studies of the Social Science Research Council and the American Council of Learned Societies. The initial work of compilation of names of individuals and institutions to be queried about their collections was aided by an Advisory Committee to the guide. This same committee also approved the final form of the questionnaire, covering letter, survey description, and news releases announcing the guide. Dr. Margaret Betz was an able assistant for the first six months of the project, helping in many ways to get the guide off and running. Professor Cynthia Whittaker, project director, also gave us valuable working and storage space while Dr. Betz was part of the project. I wish to thank members of the subcommittee, the Advisory Committee, and especially Blair Ruble, formerly staff associate of the Social Science Research Council, for their faith in me as I assured them from time to time that the project would indeed come to an end.

There are many other people who contributed their time and expertise to the guide. Edward Kasinec, chair of the Advisory Committee, supplied many suggestions for entries and helped track some of them down; his knowledge of people and places relevant to this guide is probably unequaled and is certainly reflected in its contents. I must express my appreciation to the following people in particular who provided information for specific entries: Ms. Arevig Caprelian, rare book cataloger at the New-York Historical Society and Columbia University, who described the present situation at St. Nerses Shnorhali Library; Serge Gleboff, Librarian at the Slavic and Baltic Division, New York Public Library, for his help in gathering data on material held by the Synod of Russian Bishops Outside Russia, Cathedral of the Sign; Tatiana Goerner, rare book cataloger at the New-York Historical Society, for supplying much-needed current information on the library there; Zora Kipel, assistant chief of the Slavic and Baltic Division, New York Public Library, who gave admirable assistance in gathering Byelorussian entries, and graciously supplied her ethnic directory[6] for my use; George Simor, librarian at the City University of New York, Graduate Center, who shared with me his data for the Polish Institute of Arts and Sciences in America; Robert Whittaker, professor of Russian literature at Lehman College, who wrote the very informative entry for the Holy Trinity Seminary Library; Ellen Scaruffi, curator of the Bakhmeteff Archives at Columbia University, who helped in many ways with information about resources at Columbia and also provided names of other sources for inclusion in the guide. Susan Cook Summer, original cataloger at Columbia University, reviewed the index and made many useful corrections and enlightened comments. I am indebted to her for her expert observations; if I did not always follow her advice, that does not detract in the least from the value of her contribution.

And, of course, every entry in the guide represents a participant who gave willingly of his or her time, not once but at least twice, and sometimes more, as they corrected printouts describing their holdings. I have made every effort to reproduce accurately the information they sent to me and I am most grateful for their patience and attention and want to take this opportunity to thank them.

Finally, I wish to extend my deepest thanks to my wife, Dorothy Anne Warner, who not only kept the files in good order for this project, but also provided invaluable assistance by carefully proofreading the text several times, catching many errors that inevitably creep into a work of this nature and otherwise might have remained.

Notes

1. Steven A. Grant and John H. Brown, *The Russian Empire and the Soviet Union: A Guide to Manuscripts and Archival Materials in the United States* (Boston: G.K. Hall, 1981), 632 p. Hereafter referred to as Grant & Brown.

2. There are very few exceptions to this rule and they are included because there is some connection to the New York metropolitan area. An example is the Nikolai Martianoff collection, a major part of which has been moved to the University of Rochester. Martianoff was a book dealer and editor who lived and worked in New York City.

3. A very few respondents requested that we not list them. There were also about twenty questionnaires returned by the post office with no forwarding address.

4. For instance, there is now a Lower East Side Tenement Museum, and in 1990 a Holocaust Museum is expected to open.

5. For the New York Public Library, which has the most entries, the sequence is: the central research library at Fifth Avenue and 42nd Street, then Donnell Library Center, followed by the libraries of Lincoln Center and the Mid-Manhattan and Schomburg libraries. These entries include archival departments where relevant.

6. Zora Kipel, comp., *Ethnic Directory of New Jersey* (Union City, NJ: Wm. H. Wise, [1978]), 283 p.

A GUIDE to
SCHOLARLY RESOURCES
on the RUSSIAN EMPIRE
and the SOVIET UNION
in the NEW YORK
METROPOLITAN AREA

A1
AMERICAN BIBLE SOCIETY

1865 Broadway
New York, NY 10023

Peter J. Wosh
Archivist/Records Manager

TELEPHONE   212 408–1495

SCHEDULE   Mon–Fri 9:00 a.m.–4:00 p.m.

ACCESS   Open to the public.

FACILITIES   Reading room; permission can be obtained to photograph or photocopy items.

HOLDINGS   Established in 1816, the American Bible Society was
founded to circulate the Scriptures "without note or comment." Its archive
documents Scripture distribution, translation, and production in the United
States and abroad, especially in countries where the ABS maintained a
presence.

The Foreign Agencies and Corresponding Secretary's files (1816–1951)
contain primarily correspondence between ABS officials and American merchants, missionaries and Protestants throughout Russia. There is also a
small collection of printed Annual Reports of 19th century Bible Societies
in Russia.

Grant & Brown list the following:

"The Russian Bible Society, 1814–21"; "Evangelical Bible Society in Russia, 1848–1902" (incomplete); "EBS in Russia, Estonian Section, 1858–84"
(incomplete); "EBS, St. Petersburg Section, 1878"; and "The Society for the
Distribution of the Holy Scriptures in Russia, 1878–1901" (incomplete).
(The Historical Bible Collection includes a number of Russian Bibles, i.e.,
published works.) Total comprises 5 microfilm reels and 3 linear feet of documents.

Also three manuscripts:

Armenian Gospels (ca. 14th century). Paper, 274 folios, 2 cols., 23 lines.
Illumination: life of Christ, 15 pp., Evangelists' portraits, incipits. (No.
1816);

Church Slavonic. Matthew (ca. 14th century) (1:1–22:21). Parchment, 24
folios, 1 col., 25–27 lines. Illumination: rubrics. (No. 35077);

Kahlossian Matthew plus Decalogue (ca. 1860). Copybook, paper, 92 folios + 2 pp. Translation by Ivan Nadezhdin, in Alaska, with space left for

Church Slavonic parallel text but only the first verse in each chapter entered. (*Note:* This is the language of the Tlingit tribes, whom Russians call Koloshi or Kaliuzhi.) (No. 18020)

CATALOGS   Unpublished internal finding aids.

BIBLIOGRAPHY   See Grant & Brown, pp. 288–289.

A2
AMERICAN GEOGRAPHICAL SOCIETY
COLLECTION OF THE UNIVERSITY OF WISCONSIN LIBRARY

P.O. Box 399
Milwaukee, WI 53201

Reference Librarian

TELEPHONE   414 229–6282, 3984; 800 558–8993

SCHEDULE   Mon–Fri 8:00 a.m.–5:00 p.m.; Sat 8:00 a.m.–noon

ACCESS   Open to the public by permission.

FACILITIES   Reading room; permission can be obtained to photograph or copy items. The Library makes its materials and services available to users throughout the world by regularly fulfilling interlibrary loan and photocopying requests, by responding to telephone and mail inquiries, and by providing skilled bibliographical and reference assistance to faculty, researchers, students, and industry.

HISTORY   The American Geographical Society Collection was established in 1852, when the Society officially obtained a charter. Since that time the collection has expanded without interruption and is divided into 3 sections: Monographs and Periodicals, Maps and Atlases, and Photographs. In August 1978, the Collection was transferred from New York to the University of Wisconsin–Milwaukee, though the American Geographical Society itself remained in New York. At the present time the Collection numbers some 208,460 volumes of books and periodicals, 33,655 pamphlets, 421,903 maps, 6,774 atlases, 71 globes, 98,000 Landsat images and 138,823 photographs and negatives.

HOLDINGS   The American Geographical Society Collection is a major reference and research library, considered to be outstanding among the world's leading geographical libraries. The comprehensiveness of its serials, monographs, maps, atlases and pamphlet holdings as well as remarkably easy access to this literature through its extensive research catalogues and through its monthly bibliography (see below under CATALOGS and BIBLIOGRAPHY) make this collection indispensable for research in geography, cartography and related fields.

The scope of the collection is broad, encompassing all aspects of geography and selected facets of related disciplines such as economics, demography, regional science, urban studies, history, anthropology, archaeology, sociology, geology, soil science, oceanography, and meteorology. The materials collected range from the early travel narratives to the scientific results of polar and oceanographic expeditions and to the technical reports and discussion papers on quantitative techniques that characterize much of contemporary research. In keeping with the concerns of modern geography, emphasis has been placed on collecting materials on population, resources, urbanization, environmental quality, cultural diversity, and man's role as a builder and despoiler of nature.

One of the strengths of the collection since its founding in 1852 has been an unusually complete set of geographical periodicals, built up through an extensive program of exchanges maintained with numerous institutions, supplemented by its subscription arrangements, making the Library rank first in the United States in its holding of geographical periodicals. These are complemented by a selection of early and contemporary government documents that include census reports, topographic, hydrographic, and geological survey reports, and a working collection of encyclopedias, dictionaries, directories, yearbooks and related reference material.

Where materials from and about the Russian Empire and Soviet Union are concerned, the Library does not make any special distinction, but for this guide the following estimate of holdings was given:

	Monographs	Periodicals	Maps	Atlases
USSR	2,900	1	9,000	110
Poland	480	7	2,500	75

Some rare titles reported in the Collection are:

L'Academie Impériale des Sciences de St. Petersbourg. *Atlas Russien. . . .* St. Petersburg, 1745.

William Tooke. *View of the Russian Empire. . . .* London, 1799.

Atlas Climatologique de l'Empire de Russie. 1900.

T. H. Engelbrecht. *Landwirtschaftliches Atlas des russischen Reiches in Europa und Asien.* Berlin, 1916.

Atlas Mira. Moscow, 1954.

From the ASG Photographic Collection:

Louise Boyd collection of photographs of the Polish countryside taken in the 1930s (ca. 2,000).

Professor Theodore Shabad's collection of monographs, periodicals, maps, and some photographs was recently donated to the Collection and is now being processed for use.

CATALOGS   The Research Catalogue was devised in 1923 as a classed (hierarchical) catalogue by John Kirkland Wright. It allows ready access on a regional and topical basis not only to books but also to periodical articles, government documents, pamphlets, technical reports, and the like. Cards in the Research Catalogue are arranged in accordance with the Regional and Systematic Classification schemes utilized by the Library. The Regional Sections of the Catalogue are presently divided into 54 major regions, most of which are further subdivided into smaller geographical/political regions. A subject approach is provided by the Topical Sections of the Research Catalogue. American Geographical Society of New York. *Research Catalogue.* Boston: G.K. Hall, 1962. 15v. and map suppl.; *idem., Supplement 1–2.* Boston: G.K. Hall, 1972–78. 6v.

BIBLIOGRAPHY   *Current Geographical Publications. Additions to the Research Catalogue of the American Geographical Society.* V. 1–, New York: The Society, 1938– (monthly except July and August); "The American Geographical Society Collection/The University of Wisconsin–Milwaukee Library." Double-sided, 8½ x 11 information sheet. Undated.

A3
AMERICAN INSTITUTE OF AERONAUTICS
AND ASTRONAUTICS LIBRARY

555 West 57th Street
New York, NY 10019

Barbara Lawrence
Administrator

TELEPHONE	212 247–6500
SCHEDULE	Mon–Fri 9:00 a.m.–5:00 p.m.
ACCESS	Serves the aerospace community at large, but is open to the public.
FACILITIES	Reading room; photocopying and photography available for a fee.

HISTORY   The American Institute of Aeronautics and Astronautics Library was established in 1936, a few years after the Institute itself was founded. The library provided bibliographies, book reviews, and abstracts for publication in the society journal, *Aeronautical Engineering Review*, as well as a free lending service to members. In 1962, the Institute's Technical Information Service received a contract from NASA, which has been renewed ever since. The contract has made possible a major expansion of the Institute's abstracting and indexing product, *International Aerospace Abstracts* (IAA) and a concomitant expansion of the AIAA Library's acquisitions role. This resulted in a larger membership and broader interests. The AIAA Library complements the IAA and Aerospace Database (see below) announcement and retrieval functions so that professionals, students and amateurs are all served.

HOLDINGS   The focus of the collection is scientific and technical literature in aerospace and supporting technologies. The collection also includes appropriate literature in chemistry, materials, engineering, geosciences, mathematics, computer sciences, physics, and even social science. The full spectrum of published literature is collected: journals, other serials, preprints, conference volumes, books, and theses. Microfiche for AIAA papers and other items in IAA are created (subject to copyright permissions), and the collection includes microfiche of NASA reports. There are 1,600 serials titles, with current subscriptions for 1,200 journals. Books, many of foreign origin, number 28,000. The collection of papers is extensive, 800,000, and there are at least 750,000 microfiche. Over 50 percent of the nearly one million items in IAA were published outside the United States. Close to 20 percent of the items in IAA are of Soviet-bloc origin; 12 percent are from the Soviet Union.

Material covering the area of this guide can be determined through the Aerospace Database, which is the electronic version of IAA and Scientific and Technical Aerospace Reports (STAR), available through Dialog; by telephone, write-in, or in-person visits to the Library; through a microfiche subscription service to all Soviet accessions. Holdings are extensive enough so that the Library of Congress relies on the AIAA Library for certain Soviet materials.

CATALOGS   Title and author catalog only. IAA is the subject access tool. Shelving is according to acquisition, not subject organization. Books and journals are included in databases of the NASA library network system, called NALNET. Publications based on the NALNET databases include book and journal holdings lists, and are available only to government agency libaries.

BIBLIOGRAPHY   Barbara Lawrence. "The American Institute of Aeronautics and Astronautics Library: Serving a Society and the Aerospace Community." *Sci-Tech Libraries Serving Societies and Institutes*, pp. 7–14. New York: Haworth Press, 1987; American Institute of Aeronautics and Astronautics. *Technical Information Service*. New York: TIS, AIAA, 1986. 10 p.

A4
AMERICAN INSTITUTE OF PHYSICS
CENTER FOR HISTORY OF PHYSICS
NIELS BOHR LIBRARY

335 East 45th Street
New York, NY 10017

Spencer Weart
Director, Center for History of Physics

TELEPHONE	212 661–9404
TELEX	960983

SCHEDULE   Mon–Fri 8:45 a.m.–4:45 p.m.

ACCESS   Open to the public. All unpublished materials, including microfilms, require an approved application for access. Applications may be obtained from the Center by mail before making a visit.

FACILITIES   Reading room, permission can be obtained to photograph or photocopy items.

HOLDINGS   The Niels Bohr Library opened in 1962 and through its non-circulating resources of books, journals, archives and manuscripts, and other materials seeks to document the history of 19th- and 20th-century physics and allied sciences, such as astronomy, in America and throughout the world. More specifically, the Library collects physics monographs and journals, textbooks, laboratory manuals, instrument catalogs and published catalogs, as well as biographies, bibliographies, monographs and journals on history, philosophy, and sociology of science. The American Institute of Physics (AIP) publishes some current technical Soviet journals translated into English.

Currently, the Library holds over 175 collections of records and manuscripts and a large number of individual items of historical interest; it is also the repository for the permanently valuable records of the American Institute of Physics. In addition to the holdings of original materials, the library has a large number of collections on microform, including the Archives for History of Quantum Physics, the Sources for History of Modern Astrophysics, and collections of correspondence. The collection holds scattered correspondence from Russian/Soviet scientists, ca. 1900–1950.

There is also a collection of historical photographs which numbers over 2,000 items, mostly images of individual scientists, but many show groups, laboratories, and apparatus.

The oral history interviews collection includes over 1,500 hours of interviews with some 600 physicists and astronomers. Most of them are transcribed. Among them are some that pertain to Russia and the USSR. They have been described in Grant & Brown and are repeated here with some minor corrections by the Niels Bohr Library:

George Gamow (1904–1968). Includes ca. 20 pages on his early life in Odessa, his work at University of Leningrad, and his leaving Russia in 1933.

Lew Kowarski (b. 1907). Several pages concern his childhood in St. Petersburg, 1907–17.

A. G. Massevitch (b. 1918). Considerable information on her career and education at the University of Moscow through the 1940s, as well as on scientific careers in the Soviet Union. 1 hour.

E. R. Mustel (b. 1911). References to his childhood and astronomical education in Russia.

Leon Rosenfeld (1904–1974). Contains passing references to Soviet nuclear physics in the 1930s.

Stanislav Vasilevskis (b. 1907). Some pages on his childhood and education in Latvia; the Russian impact on Riga, 1907–44; and his departure from Latvia during World War II.

The Library has an extensive vertical file collection, originally assembled as a Biographical-Bibliographical Archive in the mid-1960s. The file now contains information on over 1,300 physicists and astronomers, including well over 100 autobiographies; data from uniform surveys of physicists and astronomers; and miscellaneous material on physics-related institutions in government, academia, and industry.

CATALOGS   Two special card catalogs supplement the author, author/title, and subject card catalogs for books and journals. One lists scientific works by year of publication, the other lists textbooks by year of publication. The oral histories are indexed; manuscripts are described in a preliminary guide; a published guide for all unpublished holdings is in process. The Niels Bohr Library has a collection of finding aids of inventories and guides to papers held elsewhere. The Library also maintains an International Catalog of Sources for History of Physics and Allied Sciences which includes over 2,500 entries on materials in other repositories or in private hands, along with information on materials known to be lost or destroyed. This is an unpublished, in-house computerized list, although the pre-1982 entries are still in a card file. All the information in the catalog and card file will eventually be contributed to the RLIN/AMC system.

BIBLIOGRAPHY   American Institute of Physics. *Center for History of Physics*. Undated, unpaginated brochure; American Institute of Physics. Center for History of Physics. *Resources of the Niels Bohr Library*. Undated, unpaginated brochure; *History Newsletter* V. 1, No. 1–, 1964–. (Semiannual. Published by the Center for History of Physics. Current subscription available on request). See Grant & Brown, p. 289.

A5
AMERICAN JEWISH COMMITTEE
BLAUSTEIN LIBRARY

165 East 56th Street
New York, NY 10022

Cyma M. Horowitz
Director

TELEPHONE   212 751–4000 Ext. 294

SCHEDULE   Mon–Fri 9:30 a.m.–5:30 p.m.

ACCESS   Open to qualified scholars and researchers. Permission must be obtained to use the collection.

FACILITIES   Reading room; photocopying and photography permitted.

HOLDINGS   There are about 7 standard library shelves devoted to Jews in Russia and Ukraine, numbering some 300 volumes of books, pamphlets, and communications and memorandums by the American Jewish Committee to various bodies and organizations. Subjects covered are anti-semitism, communal organization, emigration, human rights, political and social conditions, dealing mostly with the period from the early 1900s to the present. Material is primarily in the English language but includes French, German, Yiddish and Russian. There are also 2 drawers of vertical file materials under the heading "Russia" with subheadings such as, "Human Rights," "Jews—Emigration," "Anti-semitism," etc. Material consists of such items as articles, pamphlets, and other relevant information, but contains no copies of articles cited in the library's periodical index (see below under CATALOGS). The Library has no belles-lettres.

The Library is also responsible for archival material of the American Jewish Committee up to 1933. Material covering 1934–1973 is the responsibility of the Records Center but is housed at the YIVO Institute for Jewish Research, 1048 Fifth Avenue, New York, NY 10028. All material covering 15 years prior to the present is closed to the public. There are indexes covering the Soviet Union. The Library's holdings of this material measure approximately 16 feet. On the basis of each research request, material in the chronological files, committee minutes, and overlapping subject areas can be investigated. See below under BIBLIOGRAPHY for inventory.

CATALOGS   There is a dictionary catalog. There is also an up-to-date periodical index compiled by the Library of selected articles from about 25 important Jewish periodicals; subject headings are coordinated with the dictionary catalog.

BIBLIOGRAPHY   Louise Renee Rosenberg. *Jews in the Soviet Union: An Annotated Bibliography, 1967–1971.* New York: American Jewish Committee, 1971. 59 p.; Louise R. Fluk. *Jews in the Soviet Union: An Annotated Bibliography,* [January 1964–September 1974]. New York: American Jewish Committee, [1975]. 44 p.; Sylvia Orenstein. *Source Book on Soviet Jewry: An Annotated Bibliography,* [1971–1980]. New York: American Jewish Committee, [1981]. 116 p. (All three bibliographies were compiled from titles in the Blaustein Library); Cyma Horowitz. "A Major Library." *News and Views: Reports from the American Jewish Committee* 6:1 (Autumn 1983): 32D–32F; Seymour J. Pomrenze. *Inventory of Records of the American Jewish Committee, 1906–80.* New York: The American Jewish Committee, 1981. 7 p. (Produced and distributed on demand by University Microfilms International, Ann Arbor, Michigan 48106.)

A6
AMERICAN JEWISH COMMITTEE
WILLIAM E. WIENER ORAL HISTORY LIBRARY

165 East 56th Street
New York, NY 10022–2746

Irma Kopp Krents
Director

TELEPHONE   212 751–4000

SCHEDULE   Mon–Fri 9:30 a.m.–5:30 p.m.

ACCESS   Open for scholarly research only. Call for appointment.

FACILITIES   Reading space available on appointment. No photo-copying or photography.

HOLDINGS   Grant & Brown make the following statement about the Library:

Established in 1969, the Library has a rapidly expanding collection of oral history materials, currently numbering about 600 memoirs, representing hundreds of taped hours and over 61,000 transcribed pages. Holdings concern American Jews, many of whose pasts are traceable to Eastern Europe. Individual items are often parts of larger projects, which are designated in abbreviated form in parentheses after the individuals' names. The cited Russian/Soviet-related parts of memoirs may frequently be minimal.

Grant & Brown also cite 102 entries for oral histories of individuals who were born in Russia, Byelorussia, Ukraine, Poland, the Baltic states, and the United States. Each entry indicates whether it is open to researchers or, if closed, when it will be open.

A two-year oral history project, mentioned by Grant & Brown, to interview recent Soviet Jewish emigres to the United States was completed in 1981 (see BIBLIOGRAPHY below). The published catalog contains entries for 178 individuals (about 22 of whom were born before 1917) of varying length and content. Comments are given on Soviet life at various times, including anti-semitism, wartime experiences, prison life, secondary and higher education, daily life, efforts to emigrate and treatment of those who applied for emigration. In addition, information is provided on treatment at the emigre depots in Vienna and Rome and on reasons why some chose the United States over Israel, and impressions and opinions are offered on life in the United States, adjustment by the individual and his or her children to life here, and Jewish life in particular, both in the Soviet Union and the United States. Among those whose biographies or interviews are included are: Joseph Brodsky (b. 1940), Misha Dicter (b. 1945), Lasar Epstein (b. 1886), Leopold Godowsky, Jr. (b. 1900), Boris Goldovsky (b. 1908), Victor H. Gotbaum (b. 1922), Max H. Kampelman (b. 1920), Alfred Kazin (b. 1915), Alexander Kipnis (b. 1891), Jacques Lipchitz (1891–1973), Jan Peerce (b. 1907), Roberta Peters (b. 1930), Jacob S. Potofsky (b. 1894), Tony Randall (b. 1924), GEORGE SCHWAB, Joseph Sisco (b. 1919), Raphael Soyer (b. 1899), Michael Tilson Thomas (b. 1944).

CATALOGS   Book catalog is available for the collection through 1985. An attendant will help for 1986 on.

BIBLIOGRAPHY   Milton E. Krents. *Midpoint in a Decade: A Progress Report of the William E. Wiener Oral History Library, 1974–1975.* [New York]: American Jewish Committee, 1975. 26 p.; *Catalogue, Oral Histories of*

Recent Soviet Emigres in America. [New York]: William E. Wiener Oral History Library of the American Jewish Committee, 1981. 68 p. (now included in the book catalog; see above under CATALOG); Sylvia Rothchild. *A Special Legacy: An Oral History of Soviet Jewish Emigres in the United States.* New York: Simon and Schuster, 1985. 336 p. See Grant & Brown, pp. 289–295 (not reproduced here).

A7
AMERICAN-JEWISH JOINT DISTRIBUTION
COMMITTEE ARCHIVES

See also YIVO INSTITUTE FOR JEWISH RESEARCH,
YIVO ARCHIVES

711 Third Avenue
New York, NY 10017

Denise Bernard Gluck
Archivist

TELEPHONE   212 687–6200

SCHEDULE   Mon–Fri 9:30 a.m.–4:30 p.m. (Open by appointment only)

ACCESS   Permission by application to Archivist.

FACILITIES   Reading room; photocopying and photography permitted depending on material.

HOLDINGS   The Committee was founded in 1914 as a temporary relief organization for Jews in Europe and Palestine. Since then, it has been active in aiding Jewish communities all over the world. The Archives contain the records of the Committee, documenting activities in the Russian Empire and USSR since 1914. The Committee was especially active in the early 1920s, when Agro-Joint worked closely with the Hoover American Relief Administration to establish farming villages in the USSR. Size of collection: approximately 110 file folders.

SPECIAL FEATURES Documents and photos describing famine relief and reconstruction in Ukraine, Lithuania, and Carpathia, 1919–1930.

CATALOGS   Catalog of archives, 1914–1932, 1933–1944, available in Committee office.
BIBLIOGRAPHY   No bibliography reported.

A8
AMERICAN MUSEUM OF NATURAL HISTORY
DEPARTMENT OF ANTHROPOLOGY

Central Park West at 79th Street
New York, NY 10024

Laurel Kendall
Curator

TELEPHONE   212 769–5375

SCHEDULE   Mon–Fri 10:00 a.m.–5:00 p.m.

ACCESS   Open to the public. Scholars of graduate level or above
may submit written requests to study the collection. See also below under
CATALOGS.

FACILITIES   Archive reading room; collection study room. Photocopying and photography permitted.

HISTORY   The Jesup collection (1897–1902) is the result of five
years of research and collection of North Pacific tribes and the Gilyak (Nivkin), Kamchadal (Itel'men), Koryak, Chukchee, Yakut, Yukaghir, Lamut
(Even), Tungus (Evenk or Evenki), and Goldi (Nanai). (*Note:* The names in
parentheses are commonly used today; the AMNH collection is cataloged by
names in use at the turn of the century.) The purpose was to study the cultural and physical relationships of tribes between the two geographical areas
and secondarily, to develop extensive museum collections and ethnographic
records.
    Another significant addition was the George T. Emmons collection, pur-
chased in 1888 and 1894, which includes objects from the Siberian coast.

HOLDINGS   The Siberian collection consists of armor and weapons;
utensils, dishes and pottery; bags and baskets; hunting and fishing imple-
ments; clothing and textiles; tools; boats; dog sleds and harness; horse
saddles and harness; jewelry; charms and amulets; musical instruments;
wood and ivory carvings and other artworks; and games and toys. Other
holdings of the Museum include ethnographic objects from the Armenians,
Georgians, Cossacks, Samoyed, and Russians in Siberia. The ethnographic
objects consist of costumes; jewelry; books; ceramics; religious objects; rugs;
musical instruments; swords and scabbards; a tent; an axe; a net; a table; a
compass; a spear; a sled; a lasso; and oars. The size of the Siberian collection

is approximately 5,300 objects. The Siberian collection is probably the best and most comprehensive collection of its kind outside of the Soviet Union. Representative artifacts of Siberian and other Soviet peoples are on permanent exhibition in the Museum's Hall of Asian Peoples.

CATALOGS   Catalogs are available which list the artifacts and provenance. The object catalogs and collections are available to researchers of graduate level, or individuals demonstrating serious scholarly pursuits, by writing to the Department of Anthropology and obtaining written permission for access.

Further information can be gained from the Accessions files. These files include correspondence, forms, and additional information on the objects. Access to the catalogs, collections, and archives is obtained by writing the Department of Anthropology for permission.

BIBLIOGRAPHY   Franz Boas. "The Jesup North Pacific Expedition." *The American Museum Journal* III: 5 (October 1903): 73–119; Published ethnographic reports of the Jesup Expedition are available in the Museum library and in other libraries in the metropolitan area. Contact the Department of Anthropology Archivist concerning additional notes and records of the Jesup Expedition. William W. Fitzhugh and Aron Crowell. *Crossroads of Continents; Cultures of Siberia and Alaska*. Washington, DC: Smithsonian Institution Press, 1988.

A9
AMERICAN MUSEUM OF NATURAL HISTORY
DEPARTMENT OF LIBRARY SERVICES

Central Park West at 79th Street
New York, NY 10024

Reference Section

TELEPHONE   212 769–5400

SCHEDULE   Mon–Fri 11:00 a.m.–4:00 p.m.; Wed 11:00 a.m.–8:30 p.m.; Sat 10:00 a.m.–3:00 p.m. (academic year). Call to verify hours.

ACCESS   Library may be used only for research by students, faculty, researchers and the general public. Stacks are closed to the public, but requests for specific material may be consulted in the reading room. Request slips must be accompanied with identification (driver's license, faculty or student cards, etc.), which will be returned when all Library material has been returned to the circulation desk. Photocopying is available through the circulation desk and all copying is done by the Library staff at a per exposure charge. Oversized and/or fragile materials may not be photocopied. Because of the uniqueness and rarity of its film collection, film may not be borrowed or rented, but appointments for viewing specific titles may be arranged through the Reference Librarian. The researcher will be charged an hourly viewing fee and short footage segments may be available for reproduction upon payment of film/video duplication costs and use fees. Material from the Rare Book and Manuscript Collection may be requested from the Reference Librarian; two forms of identification are required for use of such material. Permission must be requested in advance from the Reference Librarian for in-depth research use of the Rare Book Room.

HOLDINGS   The Library contains extensive holdings in serials from the Academy of Sciences in Russia and the Soviet Union, as well as those from the various republics and affiliates, the universities of Moscow and Leningrad, and individual institutes for agriculture, mining, etc., and from museums. Subjects include all areas covered by the Museum when possible, i.e., mammalogy, geology, ethnology, ornithology, anthropology, entomology, paleontology, herpetology, ichthyology, mineralogy, invertebrates, systematics, ecology, oceanography, conchology, parasitology, peripheral biological sciences, history of science, museology and bibliography. Monograph holdings are also extensive within the same areas and along with serial holdings go back to the 19th century. However, because the old catalog (see below under CATALOGS) does not have a subject approach, it is difficult to determine even approximately the extent of monograph coverage in these areas. International exchanges with counterpart institutions (including those in Russia) have been carried on since the 19th century.

The Library also has film, photographs and diaries from some of the numerous expeditions undertaken by the Museum over the last century. Among them are some that relate to Russia and its colonies:

1897–1903: The Jesup North Pacific Expedition, which included work among the tribes of Siberia (1899–1902) under the direction of Waldemar Jochelson.

1898: The E. O. Hovey Geological Expedition, which visited Russia and Italy to collect geological specimens and minerals.

1926: The Morden–James L. Clark Asiatic Expedition, which went to India, the Russian Pamirs, Chinese Turkestan, Western Mongolia, Siberia and Peking "to collect Asiatic fauna, especially the 'Ovis Pole' ibex." Photographs were taken. Clark's "Diary of the Morden-Clark Asiatic Expedition" is available in the Rare Book and Manuscript Collection.

1929–1930: The Morden-Graves Asiatic Expedition, under the direction of William Morden and George C. Graves III, which went to Turkestan (Russian Central Asia) and the Amur River to "secure series of long-haired Siberian Tiger as well as other mammals and birds." Films and photographs were made.

CATALOGS   There are two card catalogs with two distinct classification systems: the old class system, unique to the Museum Library; and the Library of Congress classification system. Generally, material published after the mid-1960s may be found in the Library of Congress catalog (also known as the "New Catalog") under subject or author/title. Older material may be accessed through the classed catalog (there is a subject guide to this catalog located at the reference desk) and also by author or title catalogs. The card catalog also includes a section labeled "serial catalog" which contains entries for the library's 18,760 periodical titles, arranged in alphabetical order by title or institution name. A computer printout, arranged alphabetically by serial title, may be used in conjunction with the serial card catalog. The Library's holdings of material in the "Old Catalog" (through the mid-1960s) can also be accessed through the *Research Catalog of the Library of the American Museum of Natural History: Authors*. Boston: G.K. Hall, 1977. 13 volumes; also *Research Catalog of the Library of the American Museum of Natural History: Classed Catalog*. Boston: G.K. Hall, 1978. 12 volumes. About 10,000 serial titles are on line in OCLC. *A Catalog of the AMNH Film Archives* may be consulted at the Reference Desk or ordered from the publisher, Garland Publishing, Inc.

BIBLIOGRAPHY   For a report of the Hovey Geological Expedition, see *Annual Reports*, No. 30, 1898: 47–48; for a report of the Jochelson section of the Jesup North Pacific Expedition, see *American Museum Journal*, 3:5 (October 1903): 90–115. A brief but helpful *Guide to the Library: American Museum of Natural History* is available from the Library.

A10
AMERICAN NUMISMATIC SOCIETY

Broadway at 156th Street
New York, NY 10032

Francis D. Campbell
Librarian

For numismatic objects:
William L. Bischoff, Assistant Curator

TELEPHONE   212 234-3130

SCHEDULE　　　Tues–Sat 9:00 a.m.–4:30 p.m.

ACCESS　　　Open to the public. Visitors intending to make extended use of the collections should write ahead to secure an appointment.

FACILITIES　　　Reading room; photocopy service is available at $.25 per exposure. Requests should be limited to brief articles; items which might be damaged in copying will not be reproduced. Plaster casts (at $2.00 per coin), photographs and color slides of items in the collection can be provided. Information on photography with a detailed rate schedule is available in the leaflet *Photographic Services*, which will be sent on request.

HOLDINGS　　　The American Numismatic Society was founded in 1858, and its principal objective is the collection and preservation of numismatic objects (coins, medals, decorations and paper money) with the attendant responsibilities of documentation, scholarly research, and publication in the discipline. The Society's Library today has one of the world's most comprehensive collections of numismatic literature, numbering some 100,000 items. There are some 260 volumes pertaining to the Russian Empire and Soviet Union, and altogether 900 cataloged pamphlets, periodical articles and books in this field. The library holds 11 of 12 parts published of *Monety Tsarstvovanii, 1700–1890*, compiled by the Grand Duke Georgii Mikhailovich—the largest collection of Russian coins from 1700 to 1890, with the inclusion of important documents. The library also receives some 197 journals with good representation from Eastern Europe. Issues of all journals are analyzed for numismatic content.

There are some 2,000 coins for pre-1917 Russia (including possessions such as Finland and Poland), about 260 for the period since 1917; about 3,000 paper money notes. Medals and decorations: 300 and 180 respectively.

Grant & Brown list two items:

Peter I. License badge, 1705. Copper disk 24.1 mm in diameter, 1.7 mm thick. Issued by the regime, it had to be worn (carried) to show that the bearer had paid the necessary tax to wear a beard or mustache. The object is stored in a vault. Also, a document describing the token.

Russian Veterans' Society of the World War, Inc. Ca. 7 items. Typescript entitled "Information of the Russian (Disabled) Veterans' Society of the World War," 5 pp.; 2 letters from the Veterans' Society president Alexander Elshin to Sawyer Mosser, the ANS librarian; "Declaration" establishing the Order and Cross of the Compassionate Heart, with accompanying illustration; an "Application" for the award of the decorations of the Russian Orders; and a copy of the award certificate of the Order of the Compassionate Heart granted to Elshin, ca. 1933.

CATALOGS　　　*Dictionary Catalogue.* Boston: G.K. Hall, 1962. 7v. [v.7] unnumbered, has title *Auction catalogue*. Suppl. 1–3. Boston: G.K. Hall, 1967–78. 4v. A dictionary card catalog is on the premises.

BIBLIOGRAPHY   The American Numismatic Society. *Guide to User Services: Numismatic Collections, Library, Publication Program*. New York: The Society, n.d. Unpaged leaflet. See Grant & Brown, p. 296.

ARMENIAN APOSTOLIC CHURCH OF AMERICA

See PRELACY OF ARMENIAN APOSTOLIC CHURCH OF AMERICA

A11

ARMENIAN MISSIONARY ASSOCIATION OF AMERICA

140 Forest Avenue
Paramus, NJ 07652

The Reverend Moses B. Janbazian
Executive Director

TELEPHONE   201 265–2607

SCHEDULE   Mon–Fri 8:30 a.m.–4:30 p.m.

ACCESS   Open to the public.

FACILITIES   No reading room; photocopying and photography permitted.

HOLDINGS   Approximately 200–300 volumes and some periodicals on Armenian history.

CATALOGS   No catalogs reported.

BIBLIOGRAPHY   No bibliography reported.

ARMY MUSEUM AND ARCHIVE OF THE RUSSIAN IMPERIAL ARMY

See HISTORICAL MUSEUM RODINA

A12
ASTMAN, MARINA
PRIVATE COLLECTION

112–50 78th Avenue, #6–D
Forest Hills, NY 11375

TELEPHONE   718 544–7040

SCHEDULE   Call to inquire about an appointment.

ACCESS   Not open to the public; inquire about the possibility of studying the collection.

FACILITIES   Reading room; photocopying and photography permitted.

HOLDINGS   Diaries, photographs, copies of original documents inherited from Marina Astman's mother's family. About 10 diaries kept from 1890–1918, handwritten by Professor Astman's grandmother, born von Falz-Fein. Photographs of different estates, especially of Askania Nova, the famous zoological reservation in the south of Russia founded by Friedrich von Falz-Fein. Part of the original collection has been given to the Bakhmeteff Archives at Columbia University (a letter from Alexander III to Professor Astman's great-grandfather, Dimitri Nikolaevich Nabokov; birth and graduation certificates of various members of the Nabokov family). The archives of Professor Astman's uncle, Nicholas Nabokov, are deposited at the Texas University archives in Austin, Texas.

CATALOGS   No catalogs reported.

BIBLIOGRAPHY No bibliography reported.

B1
LEO BAECK INSTITUTE

129 East 73rd Street
New York, NY 10021

Jacqueline Rea
Art Curator

TELEPHONE   212 744–6400

SCHEDULE   Mon–Thur 9:00 a.m.–5:00 p.m.; Fri 9:00 a.m.–3:00 p.m.

ACCESS   Open to the public.

FACILITIES   Reading room; photocopying and photography are permitted unless specifically restricted.

HOLDINGS   Primarily devoted to the preservation of documention and publications relating to the history of German-speaking Jews, there are a small number of archival materials and books dealing with emigration, Jewish life, pogroms; a few art works: portraits, Russian ballet dancers, Jewish life in Poland during World War I by Leonid Pasternak, Ernst Oppler, Hermann Struck.

Grant & Brown list the following holdings:

Julie Braun-Vogelstein (1883–1971). Collection, ca. 1850–1971, ca. 35 ft. Includes 1 letter, 2 June 1912, from Leon Trotskii to Victor Adler, Vienna, handwritten. Concerns personal matters. Unpublished finding aid.

Sam Echt (d. 1975). Collection, ca. 1929 to ca. 1950, ca. 2 in. Jewish community leader in Danzig. Includes materials about a trip to the Soviet Union by a trade delegation from Danzig, 6–15 July 1929: the delegation's summary report, 20 pp., with verbatim notes of discussions with M. Kalinin and others; reports about the delegation's meeting with the German ambassador in Moscow, von Dirksen, and the Polish ambassador, Patek; notes on discussions with A. Mikojan, people's commissar for foreign trade, typed, 8 pp.; notes of a visit with Mr. Tolokonzeff, Presidium member and head of "Maschinenbauwessens," 3 pp.; notes on discussion with Mr. Tschubar (Chubar), chairman of the Council of People's Commissars, 2 pp.; other notes; and several Soviet newspaper clippings, most with German translations.

Emigration 1864–1952. Artificial collection, over 170 items, ca. 900 pp., about half in German. Includes materials on the persecution and situation of Jews in Eastern Europe (e.g., Russia, Lithuania, Poland, and Roumania), much of it generated by organizations founded for their relief. Among the holdings are resolutions, circulars, and reports of several German groups helping Russian Jews. Russian-related items, mostly typed, printed, and mimeographed ephemera, 1882–1929. Unpublished inventory.

Emigration 1881–1914. Artificial collection, 62 items. Similar to immediately preceding collection. Unpublished inventory.

Efraim Frisch (1873–1942). Archives, 1894–1967, ca. 4 ft. Includes the papers of his wife, Fega Frisch, née Lifschitz (1878–1964), born in Grodno. She translated many Russian authors into German. Among her typed translations: "Charakter und Eigentuemlichkeiten der judischen Folklore," by S.A. Anskii, with handwritten corrections, 63 pp., the original of which appeared in St. Petersburg, 3 vols., 1908–11; "Der Weg," "Zwischen Zweien," and "Mikita" by Baruch Hager, each 6 pp.; and letters from Anton Chekhov to his wife, with handwritten corrections, 14 pp. Other translations are of Pushkin, Lermontov, and Tolstoi. There are also critiques of her translations, a diploma from a Grodno girls' high school, and some printed matter with her published translations. (*Note:* Other parts of the collection, Efraim Frisch's papers and the editorial archives of the *Neue Merkur*, 1922–29, which he edited, would hold some related material.) Unpublished finding aid.

Hirsch of Gereuth Family. Papers, 1835–1966, ca. 1 ft. Includes the papers of Baron Moritz Hirsch (1831–1896), German Jewish railroad builder and philanthropist. Photostatic copies, positive, of originals in Vienna archives. After 1869 he was building railroads in Turkey, Russia, and Austria. Among the mainly Jewish causes he supported was the Jewish Colonization Association (ICA), which he established to aid Jewish farmers emigrate from Russia and set up agricultural settlements in South America and Palestine.

Jacob Jacobson (1888–1968). Collection, 18th c.–1960s, 18 ft. Historian and archival curator. Section III, 37–40 and 97, includes items on Koenigsberg (present Kaliningrad): typed copies of records concerning the citizenship rights of Jews in Koenigsberg, 1798 and 1814; election list, contributors' list, accounts, including for the burial society, ca. 1800/1801, handwritten in German and Hebrew; copies of regulations on Jewish given names; requests for birth, marriage, and death certificates, 1847, originals; and typed excerpts from the Findbuch concerning the Jewish question. Section IV contains some material on the Prussian administration of territories gained in the partitions of Poland, including Bialystok and Plock, and on South Prussian Jews.

Jewish Colonization Association (ICA). Records, 1802–92, 7 items. Comprises 7 pertinent reports: handwritten historical summary, ca. 1891–92, 37 pp., of the expulsion of Jews from Russian villages after 1802, with texts of various laws and edicts about Jewish affairs and Jews, 1804, 1807, 1812, 1845, 1848, 1853, and 1882; undated handwritten report, 41 pp., on the magnitude of the Jewish problem and the emigration of over 100,000 Russian Jews to the U.S.; report about prospects of emigration from Russia and negotiations with Baron von Hirsch, written in Koenigsberg, 29 January 1892, signed M. Grodsenski, 16 pp.; report, carbon copy, 23 pp., Koenigsberg, June 1892, with emigration statistics from Russia via Berlin and Hamburg to the U.S. from 1820 to 1890, data on emigration to and from Argentina, 1871–90, and estimates of Jewish population and potential emigration figures, signed M. Grodsenski; undated fragment in German, 3 pp., and 2 Russian reports, 11 pp. and 12 pp. (*Note:* The main body of ICA archival material is in London but currently is inaccessible to scholarly use because of severe water damage.)

Eric Muehsam (1878–1934). Papers, ca. 1896–1968, 2.5 in. Anarchist and writer, murdered in Oranienburg concentration camp. Includes some correspondence and papers of his wife Kreszentia (Zenzl) Muehsam, née Elfinger (1884–1962). After his death she fled to Prague and then, in 1935, to Moscow, at the invitation of Hélène Stassowa of the International Red Help (MOPR). Imprisoned in 1936 and again in 1938, she survived 17 years of prison and hard labor, emigrated to East Berlin in 1955, and died there. Includes 9 letters from her to Erich's family during her Moscow years; correspondence from this family (Charlotte and Leo Landau), Stassowa, Sophie Zinkiowicz, and Hans Muehsam (10 letters, 1 of which was returned by Soviet authorities); and newspaper clippings about Zenzl's experiences under Hitler and Stalin. Unpublished finding aid.

Joseph Roth-Bornstein. Collection, 1917–39, 5 in. Includes materials of Joseph Roth (1894–1939), Austrian journalist and author, and Joseph Bornstein, who was Roth's literary agent during the 1930s. There are loose diaries and notebooks, handwritten, 129 pp., from 1927, concerning Roth's Russian trip the previous year, plus his certification of registration as a correspondent for the *Frankfurter Zeitung*, 1926, in Russian. Unpublished finding aid.

Leopold Schwarzschild (1891–1950). Papers, 1933–62, ca. 7 ft. Political publicist, economist, and journalist. Correspondence, 1941–49; personal documents and photos; and manuscripts, in German and English, of writings on World War II and of his books *The Red Prussian* (a biography of Karl Marx) and *Gog and Magog: The Nazi–Bolshevik Twins*, the printing of the latter by Oxford University Press in 1941 being stopped after Hitler invaded the USSR.

Zosa Szajkowski. Collection, in process. Manuscript, 1,500 pp., and research notes concerning diplomatic efforts of German Jews on behalf of Russian and Polish Jews seeking to emigrate to North and South America, mid-19th c. to ca. 1928.

CATALOGS   There is a card catalog of archival collections. The catalog is being prepared for publication and should be out in 1989. There is also a partial card catalog of the art collection. See also separate entries cited from Grant & Brown above for unpublished finding aids.

BIBLIOGRAPHY   See Grant & Brown, pp. 357–358.

B2
BETTMANN ARCHIVE, INC.

136 East 57th Street
New York, NY 10022

TELEPHONE   212 758–0362

SCHEDULE   Mon–Fri 9:00 a.m.–5:00 p.m.

ACCESS   By appointment.

FACILITIES   No facilities reported. Reproductions are available at specific rates. Telephone before visiting for further information.

HOLDINGS   Bettmann reports no change in its collections or policies since Grant & Brown was published, when it was reported that Russian material is not a specialty but pertinent material in the collections is extensive.

CATALOGS   No catalogs reported.

BIBLIOGRAPHY   See Grant & Brown, p. 297.

B3
BROOKHAVEN NATIONAL LABORATORY
ASSOCIATED UNIVERSITIES, INC.
TECHNICAL INFORMATION DIVISION
RESEARCH LIBRARY

Upton, NY 11973

Marilyn C. Galli
Library Administrator

TELEPHONE   516 282–3485

SCHEDULE   Mon–Fri 8:30 a.m.–5:00 p.m.

ACCESS   By appointment only. Reading room available and photocopying and photography allowed in limited amounts.

HOLDINGS   The Research Library maintains a small collection of Soviet scientific and technical literature for the use of its scientific staff in their research in the fields of nuclear physics, high energy physics, chemistry, nuclear engineering and related fields. No cohesive or specific effort has been made to gather technical documentation. None of the materials is especially noteworthy or rare. However, the periodical collection does provide a convenient source for some materials in the area.

CATALOGS   There are three separate typed lists: (1) "Russian Titles: Receiving" (both in original and translation, with beginning volumes and years noted; 40 titles); (2) "Russian Titles: Not Currently Received" (both in original and translation, holdings are indicated; 29 titles); (3) a list of names of research institutes from which some technical reports and research summaries are received (10 titles).

BIBLIOGRAPHY   No bibliography reported.

B4
BROOKLYN MUSEUM
ART REFERENCE LIBRARY

200 Eastern Parkway
Brooklyn, NY 11238

Deirdre E. Lawrence
Principal Librarian

TELEPHONE	718 638–5000 Ext. 308
SCHEDULE	Wed–Fri 1:30 p.m.–5:00 p.m.
ACCESS	By appointment.
FACILITIES	Reading room; photocopying and photography permitted.

HOLDINGS   The Museum collects mainly in the areas of fine arts and cultural history and the library was developed to support research on the Museum collections. One hundred and fifty titles are concerned with research material on the art and history of the Russian Empire.

CATALOGS   Card catalog and RLIN.

BIBLIOGRAPHY   No bibliography reported.

B5
BROOKLYN MUSEUM
COSTUME COLLECTION

200 Eastern Parkway
Brooklyn, NY 11238

Elizabeth Ann Coleman
Curator of Costumes and Textiles

TELEPHONE   718 638–5000

SCHEDULE   Mon, Wed–Sun 10:00 a.m.–5:00 p.m.

ACCESS   Open to the public; permission can be obtained to study collection.

FACILITIES   Reading room; photography can be arranged.

HOLDINGS   In 1931, the Brooklyn Museum acquired a portion of the collection of 18th- and 19th-century Russian peasant costumes and Russian peasant textile art which had been assembled by Mme N.L. de Shabelsky between about 1880 and 1900. The collection includes several hundred pieces: decorative towel ends, bed linen edgings, laces, and a dazzling array of costume items. The collection has been described as the most important such grouping outside the Soviet Union. (Other pieces from the de Shabelsky collection are in the Museum of Fine Arts in Boston, and the Cleveland Museum of Art.)

CATALOGS   No catalogs.

BIBLIOGRAPHY   *Pearls Among the Gold: Russian Women's Festive Dress. February 25 to June 29, 1987, The Brooklyn Museum.* Unpaged brochure; *Old Russian Art.* Exhibition Catalogue, 1930–31. Unpaged.

B6
BUND ARCHIVES OF THE JEWISH LABOR MOVEMENT

25 East 21st Street
New York, NY 10010

Benjamin Nadel
Director

TELEPHONE   212 473–5101

SCHEDULE   Mon–Fri 10:00 a.m.–5:00 p.m.

ACCESS   Open to researchers and scholars upon written request.

FACILITIES   Reading room; limited photocopying.

HISTORY   Established in 1899 in Geneva, Switzerland, to serve as
the archive–library of the then illegal social democratic Jewish Labor Bund
of Russia, Poland and Lithuania. Moved to Berlin in 1919; transferred to
Paris in 1933. After World War II brought to United States. Opened in New
York in 1952. One of the rarest immigrant collections, exceptional because
of its age, comprehensiveness, and the founders' intention to preserve the
present for the future.

HOLDINGS   Pamphlets, leaflets, periodicals, newspapers, posters,
books, manuscripts of the Jewish Labor Bund and Russian Revolutionary
Movement up to 1917; selected printed materials on Communism and
Soviet Russia. Subjects include: the Russian Social Democratic movement,
from "Osvobozhdenie Truda" and "Soiuz Russkikh S.D." to the Mensheviks
and Bolsheviks; the Populist movement in Russia and particularly the Yiddish literature of the Socialist Revolutionaries; the Polish Socialist Party
and its Jewish sections (the Social Democrats of Poland and Lithuania;
"Proletariat" and other groups of the Polish labor movement); Poale Zion,
Socialist Territorialists, and other Russian–Polish Zionist groups; the Latvian Social Democratic Party; the Georgian, Armenian, Ukrainian Social
Democratic parties; anarchists, particularly Jewish anarchists; revolutionary
movements in the universities and high schools in Russia; the 1905 revolution in Russia; pogroms and Jewish self-defense groups; Russian, Polish,
and Jewish communists in Russia and other Eastern European countries; international socialist labor movement, Second and Third Internationals; the
trade union movement in independent Poland (1919–1939); Jewish political
parties in independent Poland; cultural movements among Jews, particularly "Cisho" (Central Yiddish School Organization in Poland); statistics on
the economic situation of Jews in Eastern Europe; biographies of writers
and communal leaders; information on the annihilation and resistance of
Jews in Europe during World War II.

Also collection of materials relating to American Jewish history, particularly to trade unionism, socialist and communist movements, and Yiddish
culture. Documents, publications, protocols, and correspondence from the
development of the INTERNATIONAL LADIES' GARMENT WORKERS'
UNION and its various locals; of the Amalgamated Clothing and Textile
Workers of America, its main office and various branches; of the United
Hebrew Trade; of the Workmen's Circle; and of the Jewish Labor Committee. The Archives also have a rare and extensive collection of the
Yiddish-language labor press in the U.S. as well as considerable holdings in

the radical and labor-related literary Yiddish avant-garde press dating from the 1880s to the present.

Papers of the Foreign Committee of the Bund 1899–1919, papers of the Mensheviks in emigration 1920s–1960s.

Size of collection: over 1,200 linear feet shelved in over 6,000 files and containers.

CATALOGS   Card catalogs of books, pamphlets and press. In-house guide of archival materials.

BIBLIOGRAPHY   Norma Fain Pratt. "Archival Resources and Writing Immigrant American History: The Bund Archives of the Jewish Labor Movement." *Journal of Library History* 16:1 (Winter 1981): 166–176. Selected bibliography published in Bund Archives *Bulletin*, New Series, from 1979.

B7
BYELORUSSIAN CONGRESS COMMITTEE OF AMERICA
NEW JERSEY HEADQUARTERS

10 Colfax Street
South River, NJ 08882

Vitali Cierpicki
Vice-President

TELEPHONE   201 257–6844

SCHEDULE   To be arranged between the institution and the re-searcher.

ACCESS   Permission must be obtained to use the collection.

FACILITIES   There is no reading room, but permission may be obtained to photocopy or photograph items.

HOLDINGS   Brought from Byelorussia, the purpose of collection is to preserve historical documents concerning Byelorussia and its people. Collection includes Byelorussian periodicals, newpapers, books and maps. One volume of the "Statutes of Grand Duchy of Lithuania (Byelorussia)."

CATALOGS   No catalogs.

BIBLIOGRAPHY   Hand-written bibliography of the churches in the BSSR (Byelorussia) until World War II.

B8
BYELORUSSIAN FOLK DANCE COMPANY "VASILOK"
KRECHEUSKI FOUNDATION

166–34 Gothic Drive
Jamaica, NY 11432

Alla O. Romano	Victar Tur
Director	Manager

TELEPHONE   No telephone reported.

SCHEDULE   No established hours.

ACCESS   By appointment.

FACILITIES   Location is a dance hall. There is a reading room and permission can be obtained to photocopy or photograph items.

HOLDINGS   Goal of the company is to study and preserve Byelorussian folk dances, music, and folk art. There is a collection of books on Byelorussian folk dancing (choreography and history), folk costumes, embroidery and weaving designs, as well as folk music tapes. The collection also includes folk costumes from various regions of Byelorussia, some dating back to the beginning of the century.

CATALOGS   No catalog reported.

BIBLIOGRAPHY   No bibliography reported.

B9
BYZANTINE CATHOLIC DIOCESE OF PASSAIC
EPISCOPAL AND HERITAGE INSTITUTE LIBRARIES

445 Lackawanna Avenue
West Patterson, NJ 07424

Most Reverend Michael J. Dudick
Director

TELEPHONE   201 778–9595

SCHEDULE   Mon–Fri 8:00 a.m.–4:00 p.m.

ACCESS   By appointment.

FACILITIES   Reading room; photography and photocopying permitted with some limitations.

HISTORY   The establishment of the Heritage Institute for the Byzantine Catholic Diocese of Passaic in 1971 was a direct result of the Most Reverend Michael J. Dudick's concern for the preservation of the rich cultural and, more especially, religious-cultural, tradition of the people under his spiritual leadership.

HOLDINGS   The collections of the Episcopal and Heritage Institute Libraries reflect the many broad cultural streams in the history of the peoples of Transcarpathia, as well as the large cultural world of Eastern Christianity. There are cases with precious icons, vestments, carvings, paintings, and a uniquely valuable collection of antimensia (portable altar cloths) including those for half the bishops who reigned in Subcarpathian Ruthenia, and from all the Byzantine–Ruthenian bishops in the United States; some date from the beginning of the eighteenth century. Also notable are 19 old Slavonic printed books and manuscripts, representing the rarest portion of the libraries' holdings. The collections as a whole number several hundred items and also contain books from the nineteenth and twentieth centuries in Russian, Ukrainian, and Hungarian, relating to Carpatho-Ruthenians in Europe and the United States. There is an exceptionally large number of edificatory, homiletic and service books in Church Slavonic published in Galicia of the nineteenth and early twentieth centuries. The 17th- and 18th-century books are all exceedingly rare and the Ruthenian texts may be among the largest collections in the United States, comparing favorably with the holdings of old Ruthenian books held by such research libraries as the Library of Congress and the Houghton Rare Books and Manuscript Library at Harvard University.

CATALOGS   The collection is in the process of being cataloged.

BIBLIOGRAPHY Bohdan Struminsky, comp. *Byzantine–Ruthenian Antimensia in the Episcopal and Heritage Institute Libraries of the Byzantine Catholic Diocese of Passaic.* Introduction by Edward Kasinec. December, 1980. 55 p.; Bohdan Struminsky, comp. *Old Ruthenian Printed Books and Manuscripts in the Episcopal and Heritage Institute Libraries of the Byzantine Catholic Diocese of Passaic.* Introduction by Edward Kasinec. December, 1980. 21 p.; Edward Kasinec. "The Episcopal and Heritage Institute Libraries." *Eastern Catholic Life* (March 14, 1982): 4; Edward Kasinec. "The Heritage and Episcopal Libraries of the Diocese of Passaic." *Eastern Catholic Life* (June 29, 1980): 3.

C1
CARUS GALLERY

872 Madison Avenue
New York, NY 10021

Dorothea Carus
President and Director

TELEPHONE 212 879–4660

SCHEDULE Tues–Sat 11:00 a.m.–5:00 p.m.

ACCESS Commercial art gallery, open to the public. No reading room, but permission may be obtained to copy or photograph items.

HOLDINGS A limited selection of Russian avant-garde material, 1910–1930: artwork (drawings, watercolors, collages, prints) as well as artists' books and periodicals; approximately 100 items. There is a reference library in the gallery.

CATALOGS None, but announcements are available.

BIBLIOGRAPHY No bibliography reported.

C2
CHEMIAKINE METAPHYSICAL ARTS, INC.

111 Wooster Street
New York, NY 10012

Sarah de Kay

TELEPHONE 212 226–9215

SCHEDULE Open by appointment only.

ACCESS Submit letter detailing research project.

FACILITIES There is no reading room. Photocopying and photography possible, according to proposed use.

HISTORY Personal collection of the artist Mikhail Chemiakin, reflecting his interest in Russian history (especially pertaining to the royal family) and daily life. In the course of his assistance to non-conformist artists of the post-Stalin period, much material on this subject has also been collected.

HOLDINGS   Books, photographs (from the tsarist period to the present). Original works of art (largely 20th-century, but also including 18th- and 19th-century works), lithographs and etchings of the 19th and 20th centuries. Approximately 5,000 items.

SPECIAL FEATURES Rare 17th- and 18th-century books on ceremonies of the royal family; 18th-century portraits of Peter I; life mask of Peter I; death mask of Pushkin; rare photographs of non-conformist artists.

CATALOGS   No catalog, but in the studio there is an appraisal for insurance purposes which lists much of the collection as it stood in 1984.

BIBLIOGRAPHY   No bibliography reported.

C3
CITIZEN EXCHANGE COUNCIL

18 East 41 Street
New York, NY 10017

Michael C. Brainerd
President

TELEPHONE   212 889–7960

SCHEDULE   Mon–Fri 9:00 a.m.–5:00 p.m.

ACCESS   No reading room. No statement on photocopying or photography available.

HISTORY   The Council was established in 1962, in response to the Cuban Missile Crisis, by New Yorker Stephen D. James, with the idea of a massive exchange of American and Soviet citizens to help allay mutual fears and misunderstandings. In 1965 the first group of participants, paying $600 each, went to Moscow and Leningrad for a three-week visit.

HOLDINGS   The Council reports there are no resources for inclusion in the Guide. However, a brochure issued by the Council states that it is beginning a series of videotapes called "The USSR Now and Tomorrow," which is intended for high school use. The tapes will run in twenty-minute segments, and the first film, "Change in the USSR," will compare the USSR of the fifties and of the eighties in several areas. The Council also has other films, filmstrips and videotapes which are distributed to schools and interested community organizations. A nominal rental fee is charged for reproduction and handling.

The Council also sponsors concerts, exhibitions of photography, and lectures in local communities. Most of these are cooperative efforts with other organizations throughout the country.

CATALOGS   No catalogs reported.

BIBLIOGRAPHY *Citizen Exchange Council in the Eighties.* [New York: Citizen Exchange Council, no date.] Unpaginated brochure; *Citizen Exchange Council Communique* [newsletter published by the Council].

C4
COALITION TO FREE SOVIET JEWS, INC.

Formerly THE GREATER NEW YORK CONFERENCE
ON SOVIET JEWRY

Suite 1510
8 West 40th Street
New York, NY 10018

Rena L. Schwarz
Coordinator of Special Projects

TELEPHONE   212 354–1316

SCHEDULE   Mon–Fri 9:00 a.m.–5:30 p.m.

ACCESS   By appointment only. Because of the sensitive and confidential nature of the Coalition's work, it is necessary that the purpose of research and references be provided *prior* to a person's visit.

FACILITIES   Reading room; photocopying and photography permitted. However, requests to photocopy and/or photograph documents will be reviewed on a case by case basis. The same holds true for files: while the researcher will be aided by a staff person, he or she will not have total access to the files.

HISTORY   The Coalition to Free Soviet Jews, begun in 1970, has one major mission and that is achieving freedom for Soviet Jews. This quest for freedom can be divided into two separate categories: (1) freedom of emigration, and (2) religious and cultural freedom for Soviet Jews until such time as they are allowed to emigrate. To achieve these twin missions of freedom for Soviet Jews, the Coalition engages in activities which have three broad objectives: (1) maintaining a high level of public awareness; (2) maintaining pressure on the United States, its governmental agencies and its allies, as well as on the Soviet Union and on Third World countries; and (3) private interventions.

HOLDINGS   News clippings from American Jewish publications as well as the secular and international press. Chronological records and subject files on topics related to Soviet Jewry beginning with 1970. Maintains records on approximately 20,000 refuseniks and activists to keep congressmen, senators, the White House, and the State Department informed.
   A video library is still in its initial stages but covers a variety of sources. Some tapes, such as "Hirelings and Accomplices," were broadcast on television. Other examples include tapes which were made in the last year of refuseniks' appeals; the 1987 U.S. Embassy Passover Seder; and the Moscow Bookfair of October 1987. In general, this is not a lending library, though exceptions are sometimes made. There is a television set and VCR in the office for viewing.

CATALOGS   File organization is divided into two categories: (1) refuseniks and activists, filed alphabetically; (2) issues, filed topically.

BIBLIOGRAPHY   Annual reports published by the Coalition, 1970–.

C5
COLUMBIA UNIVERSITY
THE LIBRARIES

306 Lehman Library
420 West 118th Street
New York, NY 10027

Eugene Beshenkovsky
Slavic and East European Bibliographer

TELEPHONE   212 854–4701

SCHEDULE Mon–Thur 9:00 a.m.–11:00 p.m.; Fri 9:00 a.m.–9:00 p.m.; Sat 10:00 a.m.–7:00 p.m.; Sun 12:00 p.m.–10:00 p.m. Summer schedules and hours between semesters vary. Call the Information Office (212 854–2271, 2272) for details.

ACCESS The collection is intended primarily for use by the faculty, research associates, and student body of all faculties of the university and in particular for scholarly research projects supported or connected with the School of International and Public Affairs and the Department of Slavic Languages. Permission for use may be obtained through METRO application or letter. Reading rooms are available and copying and photography are allowed. The Library Information Office (234 Butler, 212 854–2271, 2272) administers library user privileges. Call 212 854–3533 for recorded hours.

HOLDINGS The Slavic and East Central European collection contains over 500,000 volumes in Russian and other Slavic and East Central European languages in addition to materials in Western languages. There are some 6,000 titles of journals and periodicals, 1,272 newspaper titles and a growing microform collection, estimated at some 9,000 titles. The collection emphasizes history, linguistics, literature and arts, economics, sociology, political science, communism, military history, law, philosophy, geography and library science. In addition to non-Russian languages of the Soviet Union, such as Byelorussian, Ukrainian, Estonian, Latvian, Lithuanian, and Moldavian, the library holds an outstanding collection of over 15,000 volumes of books and pamphlets in forty-seven languages of Soviet Central Asia and the Caucasus. Called the "Soviet Nationalities Collection," it consists of published materials in the Indo-European, Uralic, Altaic, Transcaucasian, and Paleo-Siberian languages, and contains both current and discontinued periodicals.

The Russian language collection is by far the most important and strongest of the Slavic and East Central European holdings, with those in the humanities and history the most extensive and comprehensive. In general the disciplines covered are Russian and Soviet studies, Russian history from earliest times to present, social sciences, communism and the Communist Party, political economy, economic planning and economic geography of the Soviet Union, demography, law, diplomacy and foreign relations, government (pre- and post-1917), political movements and parties (pre- and post-1917), intellectual life, language, literature and folklore, history of thought and culture and Russian civilization. There is also an impressive reference collection. Russian emigre literature is significantly represented, particularly Third-Wave material in literature, both monographs and serials. Columbia has one of the best collections of Russian 19th-century journals and periodicals, as well as a significant collection of Russian pre- and post-revolutionary newspapers. Current subscriptions include one newspaper in the Russian language from each of the individual republics of the Soviet Union. There is a fine collection of materials on Russian art, both religious and secular, including architecture. Avery Library has complete holdings of major Russian/Soviet architectural journals.

As a member of the Research Libraries Group, Columbia has been assigned primary collecting responsibility for, among others, Caucasian languages (including Armenian and Georgian), Russian architecture, and the vernacular languages of Soviet Central Asia. Columbia relies on the other RLG libraries for comprehensive collection development in areas such as Baltic languages, Ukrainian, and Byelorussian.

Avery Library, as the preeminent library of architecture, has collected materials on that subject from all over the world. Only Russia and Russian Architecture are used in the catalog, and approximately one and a half drawers of cards can be found under those headings.

Works on Russian music are less well represented, although in the last ten years or so the collection of compositions by famous Russian/Soviet composers and works about them has grown substantially.

CATALOGS   Older materials can be located in the card catalog. The Union Card Catalog in 325 Butler Library contains records of materials held in departmental libraries of Columbia Libraries. There are also departmental library and distinctive collection catalogs. The Columbia Libraries Information Online (CLIO) makes available, from all library locations, records of materials recently cataloged, on order, or in-process. Records can be located through CLIO by searching for author, title, subject, title words, call numbers, etc. Online access to keyword indexes greatly facilitates the retrieval of information about variant spellings and names appearing in various forms. Terminals for using CLIO are available in public areas in the Libraries. Persons with access to the University's PACX network and persons with dial-in accounts will be able to call up the CLIO data base from their own terminals outside the Libraries. Except for serials, the Soviet Nationalities Collection is completely entered in RLIN in the vernacular languages with the addition of Russian titles. New material continues to be entered.

BIBLIOGRAPHY   "A Guide to Russian Newspapers in Columbia University Libraries." In process, approximately 200 sheets. Manuscript is available for consultation in the office of the Slavic Bibliographer; Avery Architectural Library. *Avery Index to Architectural Periodicals.* 2d. ed. Boston: G. K. Hall, 1973. 15v.; Leonarda Wielawski. "Poland." In *East Central and Southeast Europe; A Handbook of Library and Archival Resources in North America*, pp. 98–102. Edited by Paul L. Horecky and David H. Kraus. Santa Barbara, CA: Clio Press, [1976]; Susan Cook Summer. "The Soviet Nationalities Collection." *Columbia Librarian* XVI:3 (Winter 1987): 5–7.

C6
COLUMBIA UNIVERSITY
ORAL HISTORY RESEARCH OFFICE

Box 20, Room 801
Butler Library
534 West 114th Street
New York, NY 10027

Ronald J. Grele
Director

TELEPHONE   212 854–2273

SCHEDULE   Mon–Fri 9:00 a.m.–5:00 p.m.

ACCESS   Open to the public.

FACILITIES   Reading room. Photocopying available for interviews copyrighted by Columbia University, limit 20 pages.

HOLDINGS   Interviews with various Russian officials or with Americans involved in Russian affairs, or international relations. Some examples are: the Nikita Khrushchev tapes; interviews concerning the history of Radio Liberty; the Alexandra Kollontai Project; and the History of Socialism Project. Approximately 100 interviews, all transcribed, about 6,000 pages. One-fifth of the collection is available for purchase on microfiche; information may be obtained from the Oral History Research Office.

CATALOGS   Elizabeth B. Mason and Louis M. Starr. *The Oral History Collection of Columbia University.* New York: Oral History Research Office, 1979. Available for purchase at $22.50. A Master Biographical Index contains a card file of all personal names mentioned in all 5,000 interviews and is available in the office. The catalog has been entered into the AMC subsystem of RLIN.

BIBLIOGRAPHY   Anne Whitehouse. "Recording the Past: Columbia's Oral History Collection." *Columbia Magazine* (February 1982): 39–43. Annual reports under the heading, *Oral History,* published by the Oral History Research Office (OHRO) discuss work in progress and additions to the collection.

C7
COLUMBIA UNIVERSITY
RARE BOOK AND MANUSCRIPT LIBRARY

Sixth Floor East, Butler Library
534 West 114th Street
New York, NY 10027

Kenneth Lohf
Librarian

TELEPHONE   212 854–5153, 3528

SCHEDULE   Mon–Fri 9:00 a.m.–4:45 p.m. Hours change during vacation periods, summer sessions, and intersessions. Consult appropriate schedules posted in the library, or write to the Librarian for Rare Books and Manuscripts before your visit.

ACCESS   The collections are available for the use of Columbia University faculty and students, those in affiliated institutions and researchers not affiliated with Columbia who are engaged in scholarly or publication projects. Generally, unique materials are available to Metropolitan New York City researchers upon presentation of a METRO referral card and satisfactory identification. Readers are required to register at the Reference Center, and to provide satisfactory identification (student ID, faculty card, driver's license, passport, or the like). Use of rare books and manuscripts will be facilitated by writing well in advance of a visit, which is especially important in the cases of collections restricted or closed by donors.

FACILITIES   Two reading rooms are available: The Corliss Lamont Rare Book Reading Room and the George D. Woods Manuscript Reading Room. Photocopying, microfilming and photographic services are available. The physical condition of the original or donor restriction may limit photocopying, and the librarian on duty will advise the reader in these instances. Readers are not permitted to use their own copying equipment or cameras.

HOLDINGS   The Rare Book Department houses the rare book collections of the Columbia University Libraries in all subject areas except law, art and architecture, health sciences, and East Asian languages and literature. The Manuscript Department is the University's major repository for collections of original papers, letters, manuscripts and documents. Numbering 22,000,000 manuscripts, filed in 2,000 separate collections, the holdings include major original resources in nearly all subjects and academic disciplines.

Outside of the holdings in the BAKHMETEFF ARCHIVE OF RUSSIAN AND EAST EUROPEAN HISTORY AND CULTURE, the following entries were listed in Grant & Brown for the RARE BOOK AND MANUSCRIPT LIBRARY:

American Institute of Pacific Relations (192?–62). Office files, ca. 235,000 items. Primary concerns of the American branch and its international counterpart were the political, economic, and social problems of eastern and southern Asia and the South Pacific, and problems of American foreign policy. The institutes held international conferences, conducted research programs, and published works on these topics. Contains travel letters and reports on conditions in Russia and other countries, 1933–54.

Armenian Manuscripts (Smith Collection, Plimpton Collection, and separate holdings). The Smith Collection holds 2 leaves from a Gospel of John, ca. 12 c. (MS. Armen [1 frag.]) and a miscellany from 1584 and later (MS. Armen. 5). The Plimpton Collection contains a hymnal of 1659 (MS. Armen. 2), four Gospels, 17th c. (MS. Armen. 3), and a phylactery from 1636 (MS. Armen. 4). Separate holdings include a manuscript copy of the ritual of the Armenian church, 1628 (X892.9 Ar 5Q), theological lectures, n.d. (X892.9 L49), and an undated hymnal (X892.9 N35).

Nicolai T. Berezowsky (1893–1954). Papers, 1900–53, 9 boxes, ca. 1,250 letters and 15 vols. Violinist and conductor. Correspondence with Serge Koussevitsky (22 letters), Nicolai Lopatnikoff (72), Vladimir Golschmann, Alexander Gretchaninoff, Artur Rodzinski, Leopold and Olga Samaroff Stokowski, Paul Nordoff, and others. One TLS to him is from the Moscow First Symphony Ensemble (18 December 1930), 1 p.

Louis Cowan Collection (1941–45). 45 items. Collection of Soviet World War II posters. Colorful propaganda works produced by such artists as Mikhail Cheremnykh for TASS, the Soviet Telegraph Agency. An artists' collective would receive war news from TASS, quickly give it a graphic interpretation (usually within 24 hours), and hang the results in display windows of stores. The TASS Windows Collective in Moscow produced a total of 1,250 posters. There is a published brochure describing these posters, exhibited at Columbia's Russian Institute in December 1976, with commentary by Elizabeth Kridl Valkenier.

Malcolm Waters Davis (1889–1970). Papers, ca. 1883–1949, ca. 400 items. Author and international affairs specialist. Correspondence and literary manuscripts. Davis lived in Russia 1916–19. His letters from these years contain observations about the country and particularly the Revolution. He later became associated with the Carnegie Endowment for International

Peace. *Note:* The Manuscript Department also holds the office files of the New York and Paris branches of the Carnegie Endowment for International Peace, ca. 1911–54; ca. 500 vols., 124 cartons, and 900 correspondence files, among which there may well be relevant materials. Time did not permit an examination.

Theodore S. Farrelly (1883–1955). Papers, ca. 1930–55, ca. 1,000 items. Writer. Collection of letters, prints, photos, and other materials relating to Alaska. Farrelly's research, resulting in books and articles, covered much of early Russian colonization in Alaska.

William Averell Harriman Papers on Special Envoy. Working files for the book *Special Envoy to Churchill and Stalin, 1941–1946* (New York: Random House, 1975) by William Averell Harriman (1891–1986) and Elie Abel (b. 1920), Columbia University's dean of journalism. Typescript drafts with handwritten corrections of Harriman's recollections; typed notes; photocopies of American, British, and Soviet (in translation) diplomatic correspondence, memoranda, and reports; speeches and other writings by Harriman; and related background materials. Arranged in numbered folders (rough chronological order), some with subject headings. Some folders are lacking. Files cover 1941–46 and 1951–54. Includes photocopies of letters from Franklin D. Roosevelt, Harry S. Truman, Edward L. Stettinius, Harry Hopkins, Dean Acheson, Charles Bohlen, Joseph Stalin, Vyacheslav Molotov, Andrei Vyshinski, Winston Churchill, and Anthony Eden. An additional 5 letters from Harriman to Abel (1973–74) concern details of writing this book.

Lydia Holubnychny (1929–1975). Papers, ca. 1923–1975, ca. 4,000 items. Sino–Soviet scholar. Include research materials for her dissertation; 5 boxes of Russian and miscellaneous files; a name file index, A–Z, 7 boxes; notes on China, 2 boxes; 2 boxes of bibliography cards; and a box of annotated books.

Herbert Renfro Knickerbocker (1898–1972). Papers, 1914–50, 8,000 items. Foreign correspondent. Notebooks, photos, clippings, 1927–45. Letters from Walter Duranty, Leon Trotskii, and Winston Churchill.

Max Matthasia Laserson (1887–1951). Papers, 1932–46, ca. 1,000 items. Lecturer in legal and political philosophy at Columbia. Correspondence, notes, and drafts related to his published works on international law and politics, especially of Russia.

Mikhail Lermontov (1814–1841). Collection of 3 albums containing poetry and drawings, many by the poet Lermontov. Such albums were kept at home so that friends could record their sentiments. Known as the "Vereshchagina Albums," only 2 actually belonged to the Vereshchagin family, which was distantly related to the Lermontovs. The third belonged to Varvara Lopukhina, a cousin of the Vereshchagins and an early sweetheart of Lermontov. Album I, 1808–22, belonged to Elizaveta Arkadievna Annenkova-Vereshchagina. It contains poems by Russian and French poets. Some of the verses by Russian poets are copies; others are autographs. Many poems have penciled annotations identifying their writers (added later and not to be trusted). Besides verses this album contains many drawings (none of Lermontov). Other poets whose works are identified: N. Vakhrameev, Ivan Dmitriev, Davidov, A. Guselnikov, V.A. Zhukovskii, Popov, Vasilli Kapnist, Princess Nadezhda Pokhuznina, and S. Martinoff. Album II, 1831–33, belonged to Elizaveta's daughter, Alexandra [Alexandrina] Vereshchagina von Hügel (Baroness Karl), 1810–1873, who moved in the same literary circles as her cousin Lermontov. Contains Russian and French poems, also some English poetry, reflecting Russian interest in Lord Bryon and Thomas Moore. One poem has been identified as Lermontov's and there are 9 drawings by him. Other poets: Prince Alexei Khovansky, A.S. Pushkin, E. Baratynsky, Offrosimoff, I. Kozlov, A. Bystren, Karlhof, and Glebov. Album III, 1825–40, was cherished by Lermontov's former sweetheart, Varvara Lopukhina, long after her marriage to Nikolai Bakhmetev, who never lost his jealousy of Lermontov. Her cousin, Alexandrina, eventually gained possession of this album. It contains no verses, only watercolors, ink and pencil drawings, all by Lermontov. A microfilm copy has been made; only with permission of the librarian for rare books and manuscripts can the microfilm (not the originals) be used. The albums are described in Helen Michailoff's article "The Vereshchagina Albums," *Russian Literature Tri-quarterly*, no. 10 (Fall 1974).

John Milton (1608–1674). Letterbook, 1649–59, 1 vol. English poet and secretary to Oliver Cromwell. Copies (in a secretary's hand) of 156 letters written by Milton when he was Cromwell's secretary. All but 10 are in Latin, arranged by the name of the recipient. [Letter] 98 is "Instructions for ye Agent to ye Great Duke of Muscovy" (1657) and no. 99 is "Im[per]atori Duciq[ue] magno Russiae" (To the emperor and grand duke of Russia, i.e., the tsar), ca. 1657. The tsar and grand duke would be Aleksei Mikhailovich.

Robert Minor (1884–1952). Papers, 1907–52, 15,000 items. Journalist, cartoonist, and founder of the American communist movement. Collection of notes, speeches, articles, and clippings. Covers his career as communist writer (including for the New York *Daily Worker*), party policies in the 1930s–50s, and red trials of 1949–53. Extensive clippings on the Russian Revolution and the Spanish Civil War.

Max Rabinoff (1877–1966). Papers, 1908–61, 975 items. Economist and musical impresario. Rabinoff was economic adviser to Estonia, Georgia, and Azerbaijan. He helped develop the Export-Import Bank and promoted trade with Russia. He was connected with the Ballet Russe in 1909–11. The correspondence, printed matter, photos, and oral history interview (transcript, 48 pp.) concern all phases of his life, but especially his introduction of Russian ballet to the U.S. in 1909–11 and the famous ballerina Anna Pavlova.

Carl Remington (1879–1919). Papers, 1899–1905, ca. 100 items. Secretary to the American governor-general of the Philippines. Diaries, scrapbooks, letters, speeches, and reports (the last 2 in copies). Remington was involved in preparations for the arrival of Russian warships in Manila harbor after the battle of Tsushima Straits in 1905. Materials pertain to this event and to the Russo–Japanese War in general.

Geroid Tanqueray Robinson (1892–1971). Papers, 1915–65, 25,575 items. Professor of history and founder of the Russian Institute at Columbia. Letters, lecture notes, and other writings for the major phases of his career. Drafts and proofs of his *Rural Russia Under the Old Regime* (1932). He participated in the Council on Foreign Relations, the Arden Conference, and the Research Program on the Communist Party in the Soviet Union. A letter from Popov in the Ministry of Agriculture, census division, concerns peasant resistance to a census of agricultural supplies, 14 August 1917.

Manuel Rosenberg (1897–1967). Drawings and sketches, ca. 1920–50, 60 of 300 drawings. Chief artist (illustrator and cartoonist) and writer for the Scripps-Howard newspapers. Visited the Soviet Union in 1929 together with other journalists, producing 60 sheets of drawings on the trip. In his file of sketches and caricatures is one of Feodor Chaliapin.

James Shotwell (1874–1965). Papers, 1914–30, ca. 60,000 items. American historian. Individual Russian-related items not ascertained. Correspondence and documents concern the Paris Peace Conference, League of Nations, Locarno Pact, International Labor Organization, and other topics. Shotwell edited the *Economic and Social History of the World War*, 150 vols., 1919–29, which included several important books on Russia.

David Eugene Smith (1860–1945). Papers, ca. 1100–1939, ca. 40,000 items. Mathematics professor. Collected materials about mathematics and science. Many letters from Russian/Soviet scientists concern the history of science and other subjects.

Society for the Prevention of World War III (1945–72). Records, 12 boxes, ca. 5,000 items. Data on trade between Moscow and Bonn and about the Berlin crisis of 1961.

Boris Michael Stanfield (b. 1889). Papers, 1937–57, ca. 4 of 14 boxes, ca. 3,500 items. Columbia economics professor. Mimeographed material, clippings, and periodicals concerning economics, the labor movement, and the USSR (arranged by subject).

Lincoln Steffens (1866–1936). Papers, over 50 boxes. Author and editor. Scrapbook of his 1916–17 lecture tour speaking on Russia contains letters and clippings. Correspondence files, manuscripts, and scrapbooks are available on microfilm for interlibrary loan.

TASS Windows. See under Louis G. Cowan Collection.

Leo Nikolaevich Tolstoi (1828–1910). Correspondence, 1897–1937, 124 letters. Russian writer and religious philosopher. Letters from Tolstoi and members of his family to Aylmer Maude, the English translator of his works. They concern Tolstoi's health, art, censorship, John Ruskin, the "Resurrection" fund, the Dukhobors' banishment to Siberia, Jewish pogroms, Dmitrii Merezhkovsky, peasant misery, famine, the assassination of Alexander II, the doctrine of non-resistance to evil, and Tolstoi's attitudes toward slander and stimulants. Among the correspondents, besides Tolstoi himself (69 letters), are Maria Tolstaia Obolenskaia (6), Alexandra Tolstaia (3), Olga Tolstaia (5), Sergius Tolstoi (11), Tatiana Tolstaia (11), and Mrs. V.G. Tchertkoff (1).

Frank A. Vanderlip, Jr. (1864–1937). Papers, ca. 1890–1937, ca. 80,000 items. American financier. Information on American–Soviet economic relations in the early post-revolutionary years.

World War I—Posters. Ca. 500 items. Most of the posters are from Britain and the U.S. but some are French and Russian. Restrictions.

World War II—Posters. Ca. 700 items. Posters from the U.S., Great Britain, the USSR, Germany, and elsewhere, 1939–49. Restrictions.

World War II—Propaganda. Ca. 175 items. Materials from 1939–45, among them some pieces from the Soviet Union.

World War II—Russian War Posters. Ca. 75 items. Posters issued by TASS from 1939–45 (not TASS Windows as in the Louis G. Cowan Collection). A binder gives translations, authors, and other information for the posters. Restrictions.

Wladimir S. Woytinsky (1885–1960). Papers, 1906–1907, ca. 25 items. Russian-born economist and, in his youth, a radical. Russian and English manuscripts, with corrections, of his *The Soviet of the Unemployed in Petersburg* (1906–1907).

Chan-han Wu (fl. 1920s). Correspondence, 1923–29, 28 items. Chinese student in Germany and USSR in the 1920s, member of the Chinese Communist Party, and Trotskyite. Letters written to his brother Chao Fa Wu. He apparently joined the Chinese Communist Party while in Germany and went to Moscow to study at the Sun Yat-sen University. Letters describe Chinese student life in Moscow during the revolutionary fervor of 1926–29. Also, letters from Wu's companion, Irene Petrashevskaya, in Moscow to Chao Fa Wu, 6 ALS, 1 TLS, 1927–28.

Note: Many collections in the Manuscript Department hold a small amount of Russian-related material (e.g., a calling card with brief signed note of P. Chaikovskii, or the papers of Joseph Schillinger). Time did not permit identification of such scattered holdings.

Since Grant & Brown was published most of the new Russian materials received have gone to the Bakhmeteff Archive; there are just a few scattered items in larger collections outside the Bakhmeteff Archive. There are also many Russian books in the Rare Book collection but there is no inventory for them at present.

CATALOGS   Finding Aid: *Manuscript Collections in the Columbia University Libraries: A Descriptive List.* New York, 1959, is brief and selective.

BIBLIOGRAPHY   "Library Guide; Rare Book and Manuscript Library, George D. Woods Manuscript Reading Room" (Broadsheet, unpaginated, undated); "Library Guide; Rare Book and Manuscript Library, Corliss Lamont Rare Book Reading Room" (Broadsheet, unpaginated, undated). See Grant & Brown, pp. 350–353.

C8
COLUMBIA UNIVERSITY
RARE BOOK AND MANUSCRIPT LIBRARY

BORIS BAKHMETEFF ARCHIVE OF RUSSIAN AND EAST EUROPEAN HISTORY AND CULTURE

Sixth Floor East, Butler Library
534 West 114 Street
New York, NY 10027

Ellen J. Scaruffi
Curator

TELEPHONE   212 854–3986

SCHEDULE   Mon–Fri 9:00 a.m.–4:45 p.m.

ACCESS   Open only to qualified scholars engaged in research, by letter of application sent to Rare Book and Manuscript Library briefly describing the project and providing suitable academic credentials.

FACILITIES   There is a reading room and limited photocopying is allowed, upon consultation with the curator.

HISTORY   Established in 1951 by Professors Philip Mosely, Geroid Robinson, Ernest J. Simmons, and Carl White, Director of Libraries, the purpose of the archive was to collect materials on all aspects of Russian and East European history and culture. The Bakhmeteff Archive has become one of the two most important repositories in the United States for archival and manuscript material relating to Russia and Eastern Europe.

HOLDINGS There are over 2,000 linear feet of material in some 900 collections, containing a total of approximately 1.2 million items. The Archive is particularly strong in the following subject areas: the history and culture of the Russian Empire and the Soviet Union, and of the countries of Eastern Europe, specifically Hungary, Yugoslavia, Poland, Czechoslovakia; the activity of emigres and refugees from these countries, chiefly in Western Europe and the United States; American relations with and views of Russia and Eastern Europe; and American scholarship on Russia and Eastern Europe. The greater part of the Archive's holdings concern 20th-century Russia and the Soviet Union, and the Russian emigre communities in Europe after 1917.

The publication of the Bakhmeteff holdings by G.K. Hall in 1988 (see below under CATALOGS) supersedes the extensive listing in Grant & Brown. The Rare Book and Manuscript Library advises scholars to consult the G.K. Hall publication in their search for material.

Since publication of the G.K. Hall volume, material has continued to come into the collection. The following items give some idea of the range of material the Archive continues to receive:

Bacherac, Alexander (Aleksandr Vasil'evich Bakhrakh, or Bachrach; 1902–). Papers, 1922–1983. Ca. 2,500 (8 boxes; box 8 closed until January 1, 1991). Letters received by Bacherac, emigre writer who was the author of *Bunin v khalate*, discuss 20th-century Russian literature, contemporary Slavic studies, and Russian emigre publishing activities. Correspondents include Boris Bugaev, Ivan Bunin, Kornei Chukovskii, Andre Gide, and Boris Pil'niak. There are over 300 letters by Gleb Struve written from 1964 to 1983. There are both letters and manuscripts by Vladislav Khodasevich, Aleksei Remizov and Marina Tsvetaeva.

Barnum, Frederick Lee. Diary, 1919–1920. 3 v. Barnum was an American doctor and his diary describes his experiences as a physician with the American Red Cross in Siberia in 1919 and 1920 during which time he treated Russian patients and was involved in food distribution.

Columbia University. Department of Slavic Languages. Papers. 1946–1956. 76 items (1 box).

Correspondence of linguist Roman Jakobson with Professor Ernest Simmons. The letters discuss Jakobson's years as a teacher at Columbia University, and Slavic studies in the United States.

DeDaehn, Peter. Papers, 1900–1969. 79 items (1 box). DeDaehn was a colonel in the tsarist Russian army. His account books for the years 1900 through 1969 contain detailed records of daily household expenditures, including everything from doctor, laundry and grocery bills to transportation and the theatre. Correspondence consists of letters from Alexander DeDaehn to his mother describing his social life in St. Petersburg and travels through Russia in 1903. Typed copies of Alexander's letters written in 1904 give an account of his experiences and observations as a Russian soldier in China.

Greiner, Alexander W., 1888–1958. Papers, 1918–1958. Ca. 250 items (1 box). Greiner was born in Riga, graduated from the Moscow Imperial Conservatory of Music and later became a piano salesman for J.F. Muller in Moscow. From 1918 to 1920 he worked as a secretary for the American YMCA's mission to the Soviet Union, and from 1926 until his death in 1958 Greiner was the concert artist manager for Steinway & Sons, piano manufacturers in New York. The correspondence, documents, and photographs relate primarily to Greiner's years spent as a secretary for the American YMCA in the Soviet Union.

Myhockyj, Dmytro, 1878–1957(?). Papers, 1907–1971. Ca. 100 items (3 folders). Myhockyj was a Ukrainian Catholic priest who lived in New York City. There are letters from the Vatican, the Pontifico Seminario di S. Giosafat and the Ukrainian Catholic Diocese of Stamford, CT concerning Myhockyj's career as a priest, the Church's missionary activities, and mass in the vernacular. Other letters are from relatives in the Ukraine and describe their daily life in the 1960s.

Russia. Departament Politsii. Documents 1812–1813. 277 p. Collection of printed imperial decrees, primarily for the year 1813, bound with handwritten documents concerning official appointments, promotions and decorations awarded for military and civil service.

Sapir, Boris, 1902–. Correspondence, 1974–1984. 227 items (1 box). Letters of Sapir to historian Leon Shapiro. Sapir was a Menshevik in the Soviet Union after the Civil War and later active with Menshevik groups in Europe. The correspondence deals primarily with contemporary political events in the United States, Europe and the Middle East. It also contains extensive critical commentary on a wide range of publications including the Russian emigre press, world literature and the social sciences.

Trefusis, Denys, d. 1929. The Stones of Emptiness: A Picture of Soviet Russia, 1928. 216 p. (bound). Photoreproduction. Trefusis was an English businessman who frequently visited Russia between 1908 and 1928. The manuscript records his impressions of the Soviet Union during his travels there in the late 1920s.

CATALOGS   All collections have unpublished finding aids; selected letters, manuscripts, and documents are entered in the local card catalog. All collection level descriptions have been and will continue to be entered into the Archives and Manuscript Control (AMC) of RLIN. *Russia in the Twentieth Century: A Catalog of the Bakhmeteff Archive of Russian and East European History and Culture.* Boston: G.K. Hall, 1987. 187 p.

BIBLIOGRAPHY   Philip E. Mosely. "Columbia's New Treasure-house of

Russian History." *Columbia Library Columns* no. 2 (1953): 17–24; Philip E. Mosely. "Columbia's Dynamic Archive of Russian History and Culture." *Columbia Library Columns* no. 2 (1958): 32–36; Ellen Scaruffi. "The Bakhmeteff Archive of Russian and East European History and Culture." *Columbia Librarian* XVI (Winter 1987): 4–5. See Grant & Brown, pp. 298–343 (not reproduced here).

C9
COLUMBIA UNIVERSITY
SCHOOL OF LIBRARY SERVICE LIBRARY

606 Butler Library
534 West 114th Street
New York, NY 10027

Olha della Cava
Librarian

TELEPHONE   212 854–3543

SCHEDULE   Mon–Thur 9:00 a.m.–11:00 p.m.; Fri 9:00 a.m.–9:00 p.m.; Sat 10:00 a.m.–6:00 p.m.; Sun 12:00 p.m.–10:00 p.m.

ACCESS   Not open to the public, but permission to use the collection may be requested at the Library Information Office, 234 Butler Library.

FACILITIES   Reading room; photocopying and photography permitted.

HISTORY   Supports the curriculum of the Columbia School of Library Service and serves as the library of record in the field of library and information science, as well as in printing history and the allied arts.

HOLDINGS   Primarily books and periodicals dealing with library and information science and history of printing in the Russian Empire and the USSR. The entire collection numbers about 98,000 volumes, of which some 1,000 volumes pertain to the Russian Empire and the USSR.

CATALOGS   *Dictionary Catalog of the Library of the School of Library Service, Columbia University*. Boston: G.K. Hall, 1962. 7v.; First supplement. Boston: G.K. Hall, 1976. 4v.

BIBLIOGRAPHY   No bibliography reported.

C10
COLUMBIA UNIVERSITY
W. AVERELL HARRIMAN INSTITUTE
FOR ADVANCED STUDY OF THE SOVIET UNION

International Affairs Building, 12th Floor
420 West 118th Street
New York, NY 10027

Peter Charow
Assistant Director

TELEPHONE   212 854–4623

SCHEDULE   Mon–Fri 9:00 a.m.–5:00 p.m.

ACCESS   Open to those engaged in scholarly research. Since
space is limited at the Institute, especially where viewing video tapes is concerned, it is always advisable to inquire ahead about the availability of
material for research topics and to schedule viewing time.

FACILITIES   There are two rooms available for viewing video tapes;
certificate essays can be read in the INSTITUTE READING ROOM (see below under HOLDINGS for details). Copies of tapes have limitations due to
copyright restrictions. Some costs may also be involved in using them. Consult the Institute for details.

HOLDINGS   In addition to the library holdings in the INSTITUTE
READING ROOM, there are two major collections held on the premises of
the Harriman Institute: the certificate essays of students and the video tapes
of Soviet television.

All students of the Institute must submit an essay to qualify for the certificate. It must be an original piece of research, interpretation, or analysis
based on primary source material. Essays generally range in length from forty to four hundred pages. There are now almost six hundred such essays held
by the Institute in a non-circulating collection.

In 1985 the Harriman Institute began recording internal television broadcasts of the Soviet Union through use of a 16-foot dish antenna on the roof
of the International Affairs Building. At first the tapings were intermittent,
but beginning in early 1986, the Institute started complete recording of
Moscow's "Programma II," one of the principal state television networks,
which is beamed across the Soviet Union. The programs cover a wide spectrum of subjects, especially covering politics, economics, social life, news

broadcasts, interviews of various types, and even language instruction. The Institute continues to update its collection of recordings daily.

CATALOGS There is an alphabetic list of the certificate essays. The content of the video tapes is entered into a computer program so that individual topics can be recalled and their locations identified.

BIBLIOGRAPHY *Information Brochure.* New York: The W. Averell Harriman Institute for Advanced Study of the Soviet Union. Undated. 23 p.

C11
COLUMBIA UNIVERSITY
W. AVERELL HARRIMAN INSTITUTE FOR
ADVANCED STUDY OF THE SOVIET UNION

THE HARRIMAN INSTITUTE READING ROOM

International Affairs Building, 12th Floor
420 West 118 Street
New York, N.Y. 10027

Galina Rappaport
Information Manager

TELEPHONE 212 854–4623

SCHEDULE Mon–Fri 9:00 a.m.–5:00 p.m.

ACCESS Permission may be obtained to use the collection.

FACILITIES Reading room; photocopying and photography permitted.

HOLDINGS The Harriman Institute maintains its own Reading Room and is becoming a major reference center for materials on the Soviet Union, housing a core collection of some 5,000 titles of frequently used books, reference materials, and Soviet newspapers, as well as Western and Soviet journals. There are also collections donated by such pioneers in Soviet studies as Geroid T. Robinson, John Hazard, Paul Wohl, and Jesse Clarkson.

CATALOGS Card catalog and on-line access by author, title and subject. Computerized index to Soviet bibliographies. In-depth indexing of the basic reference sources to provide quick access to bibliographic information and to make possible the future publication of The Harriman Institute Guide to Soviet Studies.

BIBLIOGRAPHY *Information Brochure.* New York: The W. Averell Harriman Institute for Advanced Study of the Soviet Union. Undated. 23 p.

C12
COMBUSTION ENGINEERING, INC.

900 Long Ridge Road
Stamford, CT 06904

Mark E. Baxter
Director, Public Affairs

TELEPHONE   203 329–8771, 328–7778

SCHEDULE   Mon–Fri 7:30 a.m.–5:00 p.m.

ACCESS   Not open to the public; no permission may be obtained to study the collection.

FACILITIES   No reading room; items may not photographed or photocopied.

HOLDINGS   Hard copy of Russian resources is not maintained in the library. News releases and media items and articles pertaining to C-E's Soviet Joint Venture are compiled by the communications department.
   Grant & Brown report the following:
   The company maintains records of sales and exports it has made to the USSR. Its activities date from the early 1940s. For information, the researcher should write directly to Combustion Engineering.

CATALOGS   No catalogs reported.

BIBLIOGRAPHY   See Grant & Brown, p. 116.

C13
COMMITTEE FOR ABSORPTION OF SOVIET EMIGRES (C.A.S.E.)
C.A.S.E. MUSEUM OF RUSSIAN CONTEMPORARY ART IN EXILE

80 Grand Street
Jersey City, NJ 07302

Robert A. Frauenglas   Alexander Glezer
Executive Director   Museum Curator

TELEPHONE 201 332–7963

SCHEDULE Mon–Thur 10:00 a.m.–4:30 p.m.

ACCESS Open to the public.

FACILITIES No reading room. Permission to photocopy and photograph items may be obtained.

HISTORY Originated as private collection of Alexander Glezer, much of which was smuggled out of the Soviet Union after Glezer's expulsion in 1975. The Museum was set up (with a branch in a Parisian suburb) to house the works of Soviet unofficial artists, now living in the West or still in the USSR.

HOLDINGS The Museum houses some 550 works of art in its permanent collection, and displays works on loan for special exhibitions.

CATALOGS No catalogs reported.

BIBLIOGRAPHY *Oscar Rabin: Retrospective Exhibition, 1957–1984; Eight One-Man Shows: Evgeni Esaulenko, Valery Gerlovin, Rimma Gerlovina, Vladimir Grigorovich, Leonid Lerman, Marina Popova, Vladimir Yakovlev, Anatoly Zverev. October 20–November 11, 1985; 10 Years Ago: A Retrospective Review of the "Bulldozer" and "Four Hours of Freedom" Exhibitions of 1974. September 15, 1984–October 15, 1984; Two One-Man Shows.*

C14
CONTEMPORARY RUSSIAN ART CENTER OF AMERICA

145 Chambers Street
New York, NY 10007

Margarita Tupitsyn
Curator

TELEPHONE   212 227–1145

SCHEDULE   Open by appointment.

ACCESS   By appointment.

FACILITIES   Permission may be granted for photocopying and photography; reading room available for short period of time.

HOLDINGS   Archives of contemporary Soviet art, including books, magazines, many photographs, documents, as well as a large collection of original paintings, drawings, and sculpture (The Norton Dodge Collection). The Center originated as an exhibition space for contemporary Soviet art and now also serves as an archive, with a collection available for various exhibitions in museums and galleries. Among artists represented: Bulatov, Komar and Melamid, Masterkova, Kabakov, and works by the Apt Art group in Moscow, 1983–86. Rare photographs of performances and art works, manifestos and other artist materials.

CATALOGS   No catalogs; must consult with curator.

BIBLIOGRAPHY   (All of the following entries are for exhibits at the Contemporary Russian Art Center of America unless otherwise indicated.) Margarita Tupitsyn. *Russian New Wave.* December 1981–February 1982; Margarita Tupitsyn. *Henry Khudyakov: Visionary Nonwearables–ESPionage.* May–August 1982; Margaret Betz and Margarita Tupitsyn. *Lydia Masterkova: Striving Upward to the Real.* February–April 1983; Charlotte Douglas and Margarita Tupitsyn. *Gennady Zubkov and the Leningrad Sterligov Group.* April–June 1983; Margarita Tupitsyn. *Come Yesterday and You'll Be First.* City Without Walls, Newark, NJ, September 1983; Margarita Tupitsyn. *Sots Art: Russian Mock Heroic Style.* Semaphore Gallery, New York, NY, January 1984; Norton Dodge, ed., introduction by Margarita Tupitsyn. *Leonid Lamm: Recollections From the Twilight Zone.* Firebird Gallery, Alexandria, VA, May 7–June 8, 1985; Margarita Tupitsyn. *Sots Art.* The New Museum of Contemporary Art, New York, NY, April 12–June 12, 1986.

C15
CORY, CONSTANCE
PRIVATE COLLECTION

45 Tenafly Road
Englewood, NJ 07631

TELEPHONE   201 894–9048

SCHEDULE   Mon–Fri 9:00 a.m.–5:00 p.m.

ACCESS   Not open to the public, but permission may be obtained to study collection.

FACILITIES   No reading room. Photocopying and photography permitted. Projector available.

HISTORY   David Cory visited USSR in 1934, 1970, and 1978. In 1978 served as photographer for Citizen Exchange Committee cruise on Volga River from Rostov to Stalingrad [sic], followed by visits to Moscow, Leningrad, and Tallinn.

HOLDINGS   Collection of 35 mm color slides of 1970 and 1978 visits to USSR; 20 slides from 1970; approximately 700 from 1978.

CATALOGS   No catalogs.

BIBLIOGRAPHY   No bibliography.

C16
COUNCIL ON FOREIGN RELATIONS
LIBRARY

The Harold Pratt House
58 East 68th Street
New York, NY 10021

Virginia Etheridge
Director of Library Services

TELEPHONE   212 734–0400

SCHEDULE   Mon–Fri 9:00 a.m.–5:00 p.m.

ACCESS   The Library was organized to serve the members and staff of the Council, its journal *Foreign Affairs*, and other publications, programs, and visiting fellows. This is still its major function. Its services can also be made available to qualified users who are introduced by members or who are serious students seeking material not readily available elsewhere. Council records more than 25 years old are open for study and reference, provided that each user agrees to not attribute directly or indirectly to any living person any assertion of fact or opinion based upon any Council record without first obtaining the written permission of that person.

FACILITIES   Reading room; permission can be obtained to photocopy items.

HISTORY   The Library began operating in 1930, at which time it had about 3,000 volumes. By 1969 the collection had reached some 55,000 volumes, but by 1972–73 it became necessary to limit the quantity of books and documentation being kept on the premises. An agreement was reached whereby Hunter College would accept materials withdrawn from the Council Library and make them available to members and staff as needed.

HOLDINGS   The Library consists of approximately 40,000 volumes, designed as a compact research collection, restricted to important volumes and documents dealing with diverse issues that make up the study of international relations. It focuses on international relations since 1918, but also includes reference and source materials necessary for understanding pre–World War I diplomatic and economic relations. With the ever-widening scope of the field, the collection must now provide at least selective coverage in a greatly increased number of areas: from atomic weaponry and biography, through economics, energy resources, environment, game theory, history, politics, and external relations of foreign nations, military strategy, political science, regional development, to technology, terrorism and United States foreign policy. The collection is arranged primarily along geographic lines, bringing together all material pertaining to a specific country or region. There is a good basic collection on the Soviet Union.

The principal categories for collection are: documents of international organizations; official publications of the United States and other governments; American and foreign books and pamphlets; some 300 periodicals and 16 newspapers.

SPECIAL   There are more than 400 file drawers of classified clippings from newspapers and periodicals, news releases,
FEATURES   pamphlets, and other miscellaneous publications beginning with 1931. The file contains a great deal of material on the Soviet Union. There are also

9,000 microfilm frames of World War II material.

The Council Archives contain summaries of speakers' remarks at membership meetings, digests of discussions at study and discussion group meetings, papers prepared for such groups, and notes of proceedings of conferences arranged by the Council or in which the Council participated. They also include the War and Peace Studies carried on at the Council in the years 1939–45. The following entries are updates from Grant & Brown:

Records of Meetings. 42 vols., 1920–62. Each volume, loose-leaf binder, contains ca. 500–600 pieces of paper. Includes material relating to the Soviet Union.

Records of Groups. 88 vols., 1922–62. Includes material relating to study groups on the Soviet Union each year since 1944. Materials on the Soviet Union can also be found in records of groups primarily devoted to other subjects.

CATALOGS *Catalog of the Foreign Relations Library*. Boston: G.K. Hall (for the Council on Foreign Relations), 1969. 9v. *First Supplement*. Boston: G.K. Hall, 1980. 3v. Author/subject card catalog, 1968–. A "Table of Contents" is available for the Council Archives which lists the "Groups" by titles, arranged chronologically by program year (September–June), and "Meetings" arranged alphabetically by speaker within each program year, including the title of the speech.

BIBLIOGRAPHY Council on Foreign Relations. *Library*. Undated brochure, 12 leaves (unpaginated). See Grant & Brown, p. 353.

E1
EDISON NATIONAL HISTORIC SITE

Main Street and Lakeside Avenue
West Orange, NJ 07052

Mary B. Bowling
Archivist

TELEPHONE 201 736–0550

SCHEDULE Mon–Fri 9:00 a.m.–4.30 p.m.

ACCESS By appointment only. The Edison Archives are open to persons engaged in specific research projects, whose information needs exceed the usefulness of the numerous available published works on Edison.

Persons wishing to examine materials should contact the Archivist at least two weeks in advance of their expected visits. Users are asked for two pieces of identification, such as academic IDs, drivers' licenses, and passports, and they are required to complete and sign a registration form. Limited, specific requests for reference assistance by mail or phone from individuals who are unable to travel to the site will also be addressed by the staff; ordinarily, not more than one-half hour can be spent on each such request. Because of the damage it causes to fragile historic documents, browsing use of the collection is not permitted.

FACILITIES   Reading room; photocopying and photography by staff member only and physical condition permitting.

HOLDINGS   Along with the site of Edison's West Orange laboratory, the Edison Archives were acquired by the National Park Service, U.S. Department of the Interior, in 1954 and contain approximately 3.5 million items of original material documenting the life, work and enterprises of Thomas Alva Edison (1847–1931). The collection consists of correspondence, memoranda, laboratory notebooks, legal files, Edison's library of some 10,196 volumes, photographs, sound recordings and ephemeral materials.

Since the collection is not arranged or indexed by geographical area, the quantity and nature of all Russian/Soviet-related materials are unknown. However, they certainly exceed what was reported in Grant & Brown. Recent research has led to scattered references to Russian emigres who worked for Edison as well as commercially released Russian sound recordings. There is an unreleased 1908 recording of Tolstoi reading one of his essays in English (with related correspondence), and Russian patent materials. Ongoing archival processing is likely to lead to considerably more.

Grant & Brown report the following:

Incoming correspondence files include ca. 16 letters relating to Edison's inventions and Russia. For example, there are letters from Russian officials or engineers to the Edison Electric Light Co. (New York), inquiring about establishing lighting systems and the costs of certain manufactured items, 1 letter each in 1883, 1885, 1888 and 1890. Ten letters in 1890 and 1 in 1894 are from Julius H. Block, a Moscow importer of machinery and hardware, telling of phonograph demostrations he had given and recommending ways to market phonographs. Edison replied in 1 note to Block, 1894. Grant & Brown further report that the above material could be found under "Electric Light–Foreign–Russia, 1883–1890" and "Phonograph–Foreign–Russia, 1890–1894."

CATALOGS   There are no catalogs for Russian/Soviet-related materials. A number of finding aids exist for various parts of the collection, but no integrated guide has yet been issued, and most of the finding aids cannot be copied for off-site use. The staff will help researchers interpret the existing inventories and catalogs.

BIBLIOGRAPHY   United States Department of the Interior. National Park Service. Edison National Historic Site. *The Edison Archives; Access Policy and Research Procedures*. Ten-page descriptive leaflet [latest revision: Oct. 1986]. For a report on the recording of Tolstoi's voice, see Lev Shilov. "Naidena unikal'naia zapis'" *Vecherniaia Moskva*, August 4, 1988, p. 3. See Grant and Brown, p. 278.

E2
EDUCATIONAL TESTING SERVICE
ETS ARCHIVES 36-B

Rosedale Road
Princeton, NJ 08541

Gary D. Saretzky
Archivist

TELEPHONE   609 734-5744

SCHEDULE   Mon–Fri 8:30 a.m.–4:45 p.m.

ACCESS   Open to the public. Appointments are encouraged, particularly for individuals with complex reference questions. The staff will also respond to mail and telephone requests. Permission required to use some collections. Most internal files are restricted to ETS business use for 25 years after creation; they are then declassified or another review date set.

FACILITIES   Reading room; photocopying and photography permitted.

HOLDINGS   The archives collects materials relevant to the history of Educational Testing Service and, more generally, the history of testing. Several manuscript collections include materials relevant to Soviet education, 1950s–1970s, generated as a result of delegations and exchange programs. Also, some information regarding testing in the Soviet Union by the College Board and ETS. Holdings include U.S./U.S.S.R. Exchange Program in Higher Education, 1974–78; English Examination for Foreign Students, 1926–1961; Henry Chauncey Papers.

Grant & Brown report the following:

Educational Testing Service has been involved in education exchanges with the Soviet Union since the late 1950s. In 1958, for example, Henry Chauncey, president of ETS from 1948 to 1970, was a member of the first official U.S. educational delegation to the USSR. Mr. Chauncey made subsequent trips to the Soviet Union in similar capacities in 1965 and 1976. His papers in the archives include dictated (typed) notes on both the 1958, 312 pp., and 1965, 236 pp., trips. The latter notes are entitled "Interviews with Soviet Educators on Recent Developments and the Current Status of Education in the USSR." Archival files for reports, photographs, tape recordings, and other materials include taped seminars by participants in the 1976 trip (recorded after their return), as well as papers prepared for a Soviet delegation that came to the United States in 1958, notes by Americans who have visited the Soviet Union (Alex Inkeles in 1956 and Edwin Fleishman in 1960), and translations of Soviet educational publications. Many educational officials and institutions in the USSR are mentioned in the holdings. Prominent among them is A.I. Markushevich, former deputy minister of education and vice-president of the Academy of Pedagogical Science.

CATALOGS   Guides to above collections are available for on-site use.

BIBLIOGRAPHY   See Grant & Brown, pp. 274–275.

E3
EFFECT PUBLISHING
(POSSEV–USA)

501 Fifth Avenue
New York, NY 10017

Gabriel Valk
President

TELEPHONE   212 557–1321

SCHEDULE   Mon–Fri 11:00 a.m.–6:00 p.m.

ACCESS   Open to the public. No reading room; no photography or photocopying.

HOLDINGS   Founded in New York in 1981 to fill the need for a center of this type of literature, i.e., "the only source of uncensored information on the Soviet Union by people who have grown up there." Current Russian emigre books offered for sale, also representative in the United States for Possev, and for the retail and wholesale distribution of books published by about 20 houses. Special division for sale of rare books. Corporate records from 1981, tax forms, are all in 12–15 file drawers.

CATALOGS   Two or three commercial catalogs printed each year. Strictly Russian-language materials.

BIBLIOGRAPHY   No bibliography reported.

E4
EX LIBRIS

160A East 70th Street
New York, NY 10021

W. Michael Sheehe   Christoper Edgar
Manager   Russian Bibliographer

TELEPHONE   212 249–2618

SCHEDULE   Tues–Fri 10:00 a.m.–5:00 p.m., Sat 12:00 p.m.–5:00 p.m.

ACCESS   Open to the public.

FACILITIES   No reading room; no photography or photocopying permitted.

HOLDINGS   Ex Libris was founded in 1973 and is a retail business specializing in original and documentary art books and periodicals of the early 20th century. Holdings consist of approximately 200–250 items of books, periodicals, prints, posters; some photographs, letters, and arts and crafts (porcelain). Includes Russian Futurist publications. Constructivist graphic design (notably El Lissitsky and Rodchenko), film posters of the 1920s, materials on Constructivist architecture, early 20th-century poetry.

CATALOGS   No catalogs reported.

BIBLIOGRAPHY   "Constructivism & Futurism: Russian & Other." *Ex Libris* 6 (1977); "Knigi: Books for all Branches of Learning." *Ex Libris* 15 (1987).

FALKOWSKI, EDWARD

See NEW YORK UNIVERSITY
ELMER HOLMES BOBST LIBRARY
TAMIMENT COLLECTION

F1
FORBES MAGAZINE
GALLERIES
62 Fifth Avenue

New York, NY 10011

Margaret Kelly
Curator

TELEPHONE 212 620–5548

SCHEDULE Tues–Wed, Fri–Sat 10:00 a.m.–4:00 p.m.; Thursdays reserved for free guided tours. Appointment must be made beforehand.

ACCESS Open to the public. Reference materials are accessible to post-graduate level students by appointment only.

FACILITIES No reading room. Each photocopy or photograph request will be considered on an individual basis.

HOLDINGS Christopher Forbes, Associate Publisher of *Forbes Magazine*, was the impetus behind the collection and became its first curator when the collection was established in 1972. The collection consists of Faberge jewelry, picture frames, cigarette cases from tsarist collections, including the largest collection in the world of 12 Imperial Easter Eggs, commissioned from Peter Carl Faberge for the last two tsars of Russia, ranging in date from the first, presented by Alexander III in 1885, to the egg presented by Nicholas II in 1916. Approximately 325 objects.

CATALOGS Brochures and catalogs are issued to complement current exhibitions on view at the FORBES Magazine Galleries, including *Faberge: Craftsman, Courtier, Commercant.*

BIBLIOGRAPHY Christopher Forbes, ed. *Masterpieces from the House of Faberge.* New York: Harry N. Abrams, 1984. 192 p. Margaret Kelly. Highlights from the FORBES Magazine Galleries. New York: Forbes, 1985. 96 p.

F2
FREIDUS, ELLA
PRIVATE COLLECTION

Box 181
Cold Spring Harbor, NY 11724

TELEPHONE   516 367–4255

SCHEDULE   Call for an appointment.

ACCESS   Permission may be obtained to study collection.

FACILITIES   Use of home; photocopying and photography permit-
                 ted.

HISTORY   Worldwide agents, patron and collector of paintings
and documents pertaining to David Burliuk and family.

HOLDINGS   Several hundred paintings, books, letters.

SPECIAL   Portrait of the poet Benedict Livshits by Vladimir
FEATURES   Burliuk.

CATALOGS   Catalogs reported available.

BIBLIOGRAPHY   Bibliographies reported available.

F3
FRICK ART REFERENCE LIBRARY

10 East 71 Street
New York, NY 10021

Helen Sanger
Librarian

TELEPHONE   212 288–8700

SCHEDULE   Mon–Fri 10:00 a.m.–4:00 p.m.; Sat 10:00 a.m.–12:00
p.m. (Closed Saturdays in June and July. Closed entire month of August.)

ACCESS   Open to graduate students and adults with a serious interest in art. Identification is necessary for admission.

FACILITIES   Reading room, photocopy service (available Monday to Friday, 10:00 a.m.–3:30 p.m.). No photography permitted.

HISTORY   The library was founded in 1920 by Miss Helen Clay Frick to complement her father's art collection. The Library's holdings relate chiefly to paintings, drawings, sculpture and illuminated manuscripts of Western Europe and the United States, from the 4th century to the early decades of the 20th century.

HOLDINGS   The Library contains some 162,180 books and bound periodicals, which include works on specific schools of painting, sculpture, artists, and reference works. There are also catalogs of private collections and museums, catalogs of exhibitions and bulletins, yearbooks and catalogs of museums and art societies. Also in the collection are close to 58,000 catalogs of art auction sales. A small amount of this material relates to Russian art and art collections dating from the early 20th century.

SPECIAL   The Library holds a unique photograph collection of
FEATURES   paintings, drawings and sculpture consisting of over 353,000 items. Each item is mounted and the verso contains information when available concerning date, source of reproduction, records of exhibitions, a history of collections through which the picture has passed, descriptive notes including records of signatures, color notes and opinions of various authorities as to the correct attribution, and a bibliography of books and articles mentioning, cataloguing or describing the original. A list of sources from which information was obtained is also appended. There is also a similar collection for illuminated manuscripts covering over 66,000 items. However, this material is not mounted and not as extensively treated as the paintings, drawings and sculpture. Also part of these two collections are 59,207 negatives representing photographs taken by the Frick staff or their appointees in various museums, galleries and private collections in Western Europe and the United States. Russian art is not extensively represented in these collections, but that topic and the collection in general are definitely worth consulting as a court of last resort.

CATALOGS   There is a dictionary card catalog with extensive cross indexing. There are special catalogs for art auction sales (with entries by collections, auction house, and date of sale), and for the photograph collection. Since 1985, the book collection has been represented in RLIN. *Original Index to Art Periodicals*. Boston: G.K. Hall, 1983. 12v.

BIBLIOGRAPHY   Hannah Johnson Howell. "The Frick Art Reference Library." *College Art Journal* (Winter 1951–52): 123–126; K. McC. Knox. *The Story of the Frick Art Reference Library: The Early Years.* New York: Frick Art Reference Library, 1979. 149 p.

F4
FULD, JAMES J.
PRIVATE COLLECTION

300 Park Avenue
Room 2100
New York, NY 10022

TELEPHONE   212 909–7710

SCHEDULE   By appointment.

ACCESS   Open to serious researchers.

FACILITIES   No reading room; photography or photocopying of items determined on an individual basis.

HOLDINGS   In addition to signed programs, letters, and autographs of such people in the music and dance world as Leon Bakst, Mikhail Baryshnikov, Fedor Chaliapin, Sergei Diaghilev, Mikhail Fokine, Aleksandr Glazunov, Reinhold Gliere, Mikhail Glinka, Tamara Karsavina, Aram Khachaturian, Aleksei L'vov, Modeste Moussorgskii, Vaslav Nijinsky, Rudolf Nureyev, Anna Pavlova, Sergei Rachmaninoff, and Anton Rubinstein, Mr. Fuld also has in his private collection Russian printed music from 1800, as well as many first editions of important Russian music by Petr Chaikovskii, Alexander Borodin, Nicholas Rimsky-Korsakov, Sergei Prokofiev, Dmitry Shostakovich, Igor Stravinsky and other Russian composers.

CATALOGS   No catalogs.

BIBLIOGRAPHY   See Grant & Brown, p. 354 (not reproduced here).

G1
SOLOMON R. GUGGENHEIM MUSEUM
1071 Fifth Avenue
New York, NY 10028

Librarian

TELEPHONE   212 360–3538

SCHEDULE   Mon–Fri 10:00 a.m.–6:00 p.m.

ACCESS   By appointment.

FACILITIES   Reading room; photocopying and photography permitted depending on the materials.

HOLDINGS   Fine arts, exhibition catalogs and books, periodicals and correspondence of Russian, Soviet and Eastern European 20th-century artists in the Museum's collection.

SPECIAL   Collection of slides of Stage Designs and the Russian
FEATURES   Avant-Garde and Russian Painters and the Stage, 1884–1965 in the Museum's Conservation Department. Complete set of study photographs of George Kostakis collection of 20th-century Russian and Soviet Avant-Garde art, ca. 1905–1980. Strong collection also of Kandinsky materials, whose art was collected from the establishment of the Guggenheim.

Grant & Brown list the following works held by the Museum:

Alexander Archipenko, 4 sculptures and 1 gouache;

Saul Baizermann, 2 sculptures;

Ilya Bolotowsky, 4 paintings and 1 gouache;

Marc Chagall, 8 paintings and 12 works on paper (including 3 prints);

Ilja G. Chashnik, 2 drawings (watercolors);

Wassily Kandinsky, 69 paintings, 52 drawings (watercolors), 12 prints, and 1 book;

Alexander Liberman, 1 sculpture, 1 painting, and 1 print;

Jacques Lipchitz, 2 sculptures;

El Lissitsky, 1 drawing (watercolor) and 2 portfolios of prints;

Kasimir Malewitch, 1 painting;

Antoine Pevsner, 2 sculptures;

Alexander Rodchenko, 4 zinc plates;

Mark Rothko, 1 painting;

Vera Stravinsky, 1 painting;

Adja Yunkers, 2 paintings.

Grant & Brown also state that there are Curatorial Research Files where photographs of each of the works listed above are available for purchase; and there is personal correspondence with the following artists: Archipenko, Bolotowsky, Chagall, Gabo, Goncharova, Kandinsky, Lipchitz, Pevsner, and Stravinsky.

CATALOGS   Dictionary catalog.

BIBLIOGRAPHY   See Grant & Brown, pp. 396–397.

H1
HEBREW UNION COLLEGE—
JEWISH INSTITUTE OF RELIGION
KLAU LIBRARY

1 West 4th Street
New York, NY 10012

Philip E. Miller
Librarian

TELEPHONE   212 674–5300

SCHEDULE   Mon–Thur 9:00 a.m.–5:00 p.m.; Fri 9:00 a.m.–4:00 p.m.

ACCESS   Open to the public.

FACILITIES   Reading room. Photocopying and photography permitted.

HISTORY   The library was founded in 1922 as part of the Jewish Institute of Religion (which merged with Hebrew Union College in 1948).

HOLDINGS   The Library presently has 120,000 volumes including a large history component, of which Russia is a part. Approximately 500 volumes (19th and 20th century imprints) pertain directly to Russian-Jewish history. Some Jewish periodicals in Russian.

CATALOGS   Card catalog.

BIBLIOGRAPHY   No bibliography reported.

H2
HISTORICAL MUSEUM RODINA

American Russian Welfare Society, Inc.
Alexander Avenue
Howell, NJ 07731

Lubov Stellezky
Curator

TELEPHONE   201 363–0876

SCHEDULE   By appointment.

ACCESS   Open to the public by appointment.

FACILITIES   No reading room but a table is available; permission
may be obtained to photograph or photocopy items.

HOLDINGS   The objective of the Museum is to preserve everything
possible that is representative of Russia before the October Revolution.
Mrs. Stellezky reports that the Army Museum and Archive of the Russian
Imperial Army and the Russian Naval Museum are now under her supervision. While the holdings for each collection remain separate, the Museum
has been undergoing some reorganization and therefore was not easily accessible in summer 1988. The following entries for the two separate museums were given in Grant & Brown and are repeated here for the sake of
continuity:

Army Museum and Archive
of the Russian Imperial Army

Like the Russian Naval Museum with which it is housed (see below), the
Army Museum and Archive holds materials in each of its component parts.
In display cases within the museum are documents and memorabilia of the
Imperial Russian Army, from the 18th–20th centuries. Included are photograph albums of Cossacks, the Nikolaevsk Cavalry Academy, the Kadet
Corps, and the Romanov family. On exhibit also are medallions, models of
uniforms, and textual material. Among the latter are decrees signed by
Catherine II, 1785 and 1790, and Anna, 1735.
    The Archive has 37 books, typed and handwritten, of military service
records of all officers of the Russian Imperial Army in all military districts,
1904–14. It also holds the papers of General Schultz, consisting of 10
notebooks from his service in the army in the Russo–Turkish War of

1877–78 and later years.

Miscellaneous collections in the Archive include military orders—printed, typed, or hectographed—from 1908, 1911, 1917–18, particularly for the Caucasian front, and promotions; the "rodoslovnaia kniga" of General Nilov; personal papers of officers on education and military service, 2 feet; a list of officers killed in 1914, 3 books; the career records of Junker Academy graduates, 6 books; military orders and promotions for 1915–16, 2 books; miscellanea on the Kadet Corps, 3 feet; various cavalry charters; a typed history of the Semenovsky regiment; maps; and a collection of newspaper clippings of Boris A. Nikolaev, a captain of artillery.

Russian Naval Museum

The following information comes from an article by John Long in *Slavic Review* (see BIBLIOGRAPHY below):

This museum, created in 1966, is run by the Association of Russian Imperial Naval Officers in America and the American–Russian Welfare Society "Rodina." The museum forms an annex to the "Rodina" main building and itself shares building space with the separate Army Museum and Archive (see above). Organized into 3 divisions—museum, library, and archives—this repository holds a large number of rare and valuable items, mainly connected with the military history of Russia.

In the museum proper are numerous objets d'art, military paraphernalia, ship models, uniforms, weapons models, and medallions, as well as textual materials. Among the paintings are portraits of all Russian monarchs from Peter the Great to Nicholas II and also of most important figures in Russian naval history (e.g., Count F.M. Apraksin, co-founder of the Russian navy with Peter I). Eighteenth-century engravings and lithographs portray people and incidents related to Russian history. The large photograph collection covers such topics as the Russo–Japanese War of 1904–1905, World War I, the Revolution and Civil War, and emigre Russians.

The museum has an impressive documents and autographs collection as well. A manuscript letter to Prince Romodanovsky, December 30, 1715, and an ukaz addressed to Brigadier Francis Lefort, December 1, 1718, are both from Peter I. There are 2 holograph letters of Catherine the Great, one an imperial rescript to Prince Alexei G. Orlov, February 23, 1773, and the other, fragmentary only, to Rear Admiral Prince Nassau-Siegen. A signed letter of Paul I to Eugene of Wuerttemburg is dated October 17, 1796, in French. From Alexander I there are an ukaz to the Lithuanian military-governor General Rimsky-Korsakov, April 21, 1812, and citations issued to Prince Vorontsov and Peter Nadgoft for service against Napoleon I. The signatures of Nicholas I and Alexander II also appear on documents in the museum collections.

Other items include an incomplete letter dated November 14, 1709 of

Count F. M. Apraksin; an ukaz of September 30, 1788 to Governor Piel of Pskov; a letter to Baron Grimm, September 30, 1785; and a letter to the elector of Trier announcing the birth of the Grand Duchess Ekaterina Pavlovna, May 23, 1788.

The archives hold materials divided into 20 sections. The first 7 are office/business files of the association, and the last comprises correspondence and papers relating to the library and archives. Sections 8 and 9 hold letters, manuscripts, and illustrations from *Morskiia zapiski*, the association's own journal, and from *S beregov Ameriki* (New York, 1939), a commemorative publication. Section 10, with personal and family papers, is arranged alphabetically by donors' names. It fills several file drawers currently. Among these letters and documents are data on the education of Russian naval officers and sailors, the Russo–Japanese War, the First World War, the Revolution and the Civil War, and emigre life. Further items in section 11 (originals and copies) concern the Romanovs, naval voyages, Russian naval history (arranged chronologically), the history of military-educational institutions, ships' histories, naval and other military biographies, history of the army and air force, classified official publications, and other topics. Sections 12–15 contain items about the Russian naval emigration. Newspaper and journal clippings are in section 16. The Naval Bibliography section (17) has indexes, catalogs, and other bibliographic aids for naval research. Finally, there are graphic materials (portraits, paintings, photographs, albums) in sections 18 and 19.

CATALOGS   No catalogs or finding aids reported, but there is a card file on the premises.

BIBLIOGRAPHY   John W. Long "The Russian Naval Museum, Lakewood, New Jersey." *Slavic Review* (June 1971). See Grant & Brown, pp. 271–272.

H3
HOFFMAN, CHARLES J.
PRIVATE COLLECTION

540 Fulton Street
Elizabeth, NJ 07206

TELEPHONE   201 353–3177

SCHEDULE   Mon–Fri 9:00 a.m.–9:00 p.m.

ACCESS   By permission.

FACILITIES   No reading room, but accommodation to use collection can be made. Permission can be obtained to photograph or photocopy items.

HOLDINGS   Mr. Hoffman reports that he now has about 200 items. In Grant & Brown he listed 150 magic lantern slides, mostly taken by L.D. Woodridge, ca. 1895–1914, that pertain to the Russian Empire. These include 88 slides of Moscow, 62 slides of St. Petersburg, 7 slides of Warsaw, and 1 slide of a police permit to photograph Moscow, August 15, 1913. There is also a T.L.S., December 19, 1917, from W.S. Crosley, U.S. Naval Attache in Petrograd, to Mrs. Marion McAllister-Smith, 3 pp., and a 14 x 18 in. oil painting of half-clad women, signed verso "W. Borisoff, Moskau, 18–7–1919." In addition, he now includes the following items:

22 x 32 in. oil, "Retreat from Moscow," signed Jan V. Chieminski. It depicts a French officer on horseback, in full gallop, and with drawn pistol aimed at three pursuing Russian cavalry horsemen with sabers drawn.

12 x 9 in. charcoal portrait, "Freedom Fighters," signed Ted. J. Witonski, ca. 1917. On back of drawing rubber stamp statement, "Conservatory Lodz City."

20 x 18 in. oil, "Gen. J. Pilsudski," by E. Boldanski, 1919.

"Tygodnik Illustrowany," 1911. 1,052 pages of illustrations of cities, maps, paintings, personalities, etc. 11 x 15 in. in bookform.

Several articles from the *National Geographic Magazine* ca. 1924–1937, on Manchuria and Siberia, including one on his exile, under the tsarist regime, above the Arctic Circle.

CATALOGS   No catalogs reported.

BIBLIOGRAPHY   See Grant & Brown, p. 271.

H4
HOLY TRINITY SEMINARY LIBRARY

See also SYNOD OF RUSSIAN BISHOPS OUTSIDE RUSSIA
CATHEDRAL OF THE SIGN

Jordanville, NY 13361–0036

Larissa Litwinowicz
Librarian

TELEPHONE   Monastery office: 315 858–0940

SCHEDULE   Mon–Fri 1:00 p.m.–6:45 p.m.; Sat 9:00 a.m.–11:50 p.m.

ACCESS   Open to scholars. Researchers are advised to write ahead to insure availability of materials and facilities.

FACILITIES   Reading room. Photocopying machine, as a rule limited to the use of Seminary students and staff, but available by special permission and arrangement.

HISTORY   The Library principally serves students and faculty of the Seminary as well as the entire community of the Holy Trinity Monastery, which is under the jurisdiction of the SYNOD OF RUSSIAN BISHOPS OUT-SIDE RUSSIA. The collections in this Library, however, are more extensive than academic needs and acquisition policies would suggest. Its scope extends beyond the usual interests of the community and many items were acquired before the Seminary was established. Bequests of private collections constitute the Library's most valuable accessions. Thus the character of its holdings has been determined not only by the needs of the Seminary, but also by the special interests of those book lovers who have bequeathed their private collections to the Synod and the Monastery.

HOLDINGS   Of the 35,000 volumes of total holdings, about 15,000 are in Cyrillic. In addition to current periodicals, religious and secular, there is an extensive collection of emigre periodicals mainly of the twenties and thirties. Certain strengths of the collection one would expect—church history, doctrinal theology, liturgical works, sacred music. These naturally include religious thinkers of the emigration, particularly of the twenties and thirties. The fields of monarchical and military history are relatively strongly represented. The Russian holdings in other areas are remarkable not so much for their breadth as for their rarity—historical treatises published in Berlin and Sofia in the twenties and thirties, studies in political science from Berlin and Paris of the twenties through the later forties, and especially philosophical works published in Moscow, St. Petersburg, Riga, Berlin, Paris, and Caracas from the thirties through the fifties. (There are nine different translations of Nietzsche.) Although the Library's holdings are not broad or deep enough to be considered a research collection, they contain unique material for research on Russian emigre thought and culture. The Library itself is worthy of research as a major fund of rare twentieth-century Russian publications abroad.

SPECIAL   The collection of nearly 100 titles of Russian emigre pe-
FEATURES   riodical publications (including eleven U.S. publica-
tions) represents complete and partial runs of titles unavailable elsewhere. Over half the titles are unlisted in the *Union List of Serials* (3rd edition), including eight of the American titles. The geographical representation is remarkable: journals published in Belgrade, Berlin, Chicago, Constantinople,

Czechoslovakia, Harbin, Helsinki, Lausanne, New York, Paris, Prague, Peking, Putnam (Connecticut), Riga, San Francisco, Sevastopol, Shanghai, Sofia, Stratford (Connecticut), Vilna, Uzhgorod, and Warsaw over the period 1914 to 1951, with the greatest number published in the twenties and thirties. Less easily identifiable, but no less remarkable, are copies of rare monographs, particularly on contemporary spiritual and cultural concerns of the early Russian emigration. The Library also has a collection of religious and ecclesiastical brochures published in small runs, usually for local use, on such subjects as biographies and *vita sanctae*, apologetics, music, prayers, liturgical materials, local holidays and celebrations. The Library keeps valuable collections in locked cases, of which most notable are works on the Civil War and the Russian Imperial family and a thirty-four volume photographic archive of dioceses and churches in the jurisdiction of the SYNOD OF RUSSIAN BISHOPS OUTSIDE RUSSIA.

Sharing similar strengths with the book and periodical collections are a Museum and Archive, both also located at the Monastery. The Museum contains valuable historical artifacts and a wealth of memorabilia, also acquired much as the Library received its most valuable accessions. The Archive, at present in the early stages of cataloging, also contains valuable personal papers bequeathed to the Monastery and the Synod.

CATALOGS   A dictionary catalog is available in the Library, which is being expanded to include the entire collection. There is a listing of the periodical collection. However, the bibliographical and cataloging materials are limited at present to serving mainly the needs of the Seminary students and the Monastery community. There is a catalog and description of displays available in the Museum. No aids are available for the Archive (which is not open to the public).

BIBLIOGRAPHY   Edward Kasinec. "Holy Trinity Monastery and Seminary Libraries." *Newsletter of the Slavic Bibliographic and Documentation Center* 3 (March 1971); *The Museum of Russian History at the Holy Trinity Russian Orthodox Monastery, Jordanville, New York* [catalog. Jordanville, NY: The Museum, 1984. 61 p.].

HUGUENOT–PAINE HISTORICAL ASSOCIATION

See NEW ROCHELLE HISTORICAL ASSOCIATION

H5
HUTTENBACH, HENRY R.
PRIVATE COLLECTION

321 Sackett Street
Brooklyn, NY 11231

TELEPHONE   718 624–2301

SCHEDULE   To be arranged.

ACCESS   Open to scholars, following publication of *A History of the Jews of the Riga Ghetto: 1941–1945.*

FACILITIES   Reading room can be arranged. No photography or photocopying.

HOLDINGS   In addition to the microfilms of documents described in Grant & Brown, Mr. Huttenbach reports that he has 100 taped, original interviews (about 2–3 hours each); and around 7,000 pages of documents covering the history of Jews in the Riga ghetto in Latvia 1941–1944. The interviews are in Russian, German, Yiddish and English; the documents cover government material, memoirs, testimonies, etc.

Grant & Brown list the following holdings (which have been corrected and supplemented by Mr. Huttenbach):
Collection of microfilms of documents pertaining to 16th century Muscovy. Includes numerous reels from such archives/libraries as the Swedish State Archive, the Vatican Library, the Lenin Public Library in Moscow, the British Library, the Cambridge University Library, the Bodleian Library (Oxford), and the Public Records Office in London. Also, microfilms from Vienna, Brussels, Copenhagen, Paris, and Venice. Among the many subjects covered are border negotiations between Sweden and Muscovy, the Heresy of the Judaizers, Anglo–Muscovite relations, the Ivan–Elizabeth correspondence, European travel reports about Muscovy, and the Schlitte expedition.

CATALOGS   Henry R. Huttenbach. *An Introduction and Guide to the Riga Ghetto Archive Catalogue.* New York: Waldon Press, 1984. 117 p.

BIBLIOGRAPHY See Grant & Brown, p. 279.

I1
INTERNATIONAL FILM FOUNDATION, INC.

155 West 72 Street
New York, NY 10023

Sam Bryan
Executive Director

TELEPHONE   212 580–1111

SCHEDULE   Mon–Fri 9:00 a.m.–5:00 p.m.

ACCESS   Open by appointment.

FACILITIES   Reading room not available; photocopying and photography not available.

HOLDINGS   The National Center for Film and Video Preservation through the American Film Institute and the National Endowment for the Arts and the International Film Foundation have copied, preserved and printed some 110 minutes of 35 mm black and white film. This footage from the 1930s was shot in the Soviet Union by Julien Bryan and his cameramen, initially for Bryan's travel lectures. (Later some of the footage was incorporated into a few short educational films.) It was decided to select material from only the Soviet Union and from as early as possible (early 1930s). Material chosen was further selected as being from a variety of locations in the Soviet Union (Siberia to Moscow) and to portray a variety of activities (road building to schools). There is a timed 16 mm print at IFF, available for screening by appointment.

CATALOGS   Copies are available of the four pages of descriptions of all the 110 minutes, plus many other written records.

BIBLIOGRAPHY   No bibliography reported.

I2
INTERNATIONAL LADIES' GARMENT WORKERS' UNION ARCHIVES*

Labor-Management
Documentation Center
Cornell University
144 Ives Hall
Ithaca, NY 14853

Richard Strassberg
Director and Archivist

TELEPHONE   607 255–3183

SCHEDULE   Mon–Fri 8:00 a.m.–4.00 p.m.

ACCESS   Open to the public.

FACILITIES   Reading room, photocopying and photography permitted. Oral history tapes and manuscript volumes of the tapes are available by permission.

HISTORY   Established in 1974 to preserve the origins and traditions of the ILGWU, to educate and inspire new generations of workers and Union officers, and as a resource for scholars of labor history in America. The ILGWU's immigrant, ethnic and ideological roots set it apart from other leading American unions.

HOLDINGS   The Archives contain 65 collections consisting of almost 2 million items, including written, oral and photographic material. Materials from the President's Office constitute the most extensive and important collections. These include the correspondence of Benjamin Schlesinger, 1914–1923; Morris Sigman, 1923–28; Benjamin Schlesinger, 1928–32; David Dubinsky, 1932–66; and Louis Stulberg, 1966–75. Material is now being collected on the President Emeritus, 1975–86, Sol C. Chaikin. The David Dubinsky Collection contains more than 450,000 items in addition to material for 1966–80, when he was the Administrator of the Retiree Service Department of the ILGWU. Material on Communism can be found in his collection as well as in the Morris Sigman Correspondence, when the Communists tried to take over the ILGWU. There are also collections that cover reports of the ILGWU conventions, the minutes of its General Executive Board, and a broadside collection. Separate collections have to be checked for individuals or relationships which may be of particular interest to the researcher.

SPECIAL   The Charles S. Zimmerman collection contains cor-
FEATURES   respondence, broadsides, leaflets and publications of the Communist Party and the Lovestone group, 1918–39. In 1929, Zimmerman was expelled from the Communist Party and became involved with the Lovestone group which opposed the Communist Party.

CATALOGS   There is a subject card catalog which is linked to some 25 descriptive guides which index separate collections. The guides include the collections from the President's Office; the Charles S. Zimmerman Records, 1919–1958; Oral History interviews (with 44 persons, including Charles S. Zimmerman), some with manuscript volumes of the tapes; the New York Cloak Joint Board Records, 1926–[1947–1973]; the Joint Board Dress and Waistmakers' Union of Greater New York, Managers' Correspondence, 1928–1972; the Union Health Center Records, 1911–1977;

Records for the Southeast Region, 1937–1970; the Northeast Department Collection, 1935–1972; the Joint Board Records for Boston (1930–1976), Chicago (1914–1975), and Cleveland (1934–56); Collected Documents of the Research Department, 1907–1948; and records for Locals 9, 10, 62, 155. A few of these guides are listed in the *Manuscript and Archives Collection* of the *National Union Catalog*.

BIBLIOGRAPHY   Robert E. Lazar. "The International Ladies' Garment Workers' Union Archives." *Labor History* 23 (Fall 1982): 528–533.

*The ILGWU Archives were sent to Ithaca after this entry was completed. It is not known if the whole collection was transferred, or if the finding aids listed here will continue to be available.

I3
INTERNATIONAL RESEARCH &
EXCHANGES BOARD (IREX)

126 Alexander Street
Princeton, NJ 08540–7102
Jennifer Wilson

Program Officer

TELEPHONE	609 683–9500
TELEX	233508 IRE UR
SCHEDULE	Mon–Fri 9:00 a.m.–5:00 p.m.

ACCESS   Open to the public for information on exchanges. Anyone interested in doing research on the history of IREX itself should contact Ms. Wilson.

FACILITIES   IREX is neither designed nor equipped for research on the premises.

HOLDINGS   At the request of universities in the United States, IREX was established in 1968 by the American Council of Learned Societies (ACLS) and the Social Science Research Council (SSRC) to administer academic exchanges with the Soviet Union and the socialist countries of Eastern Europe. IREX is a private "umbrella" organization: it serves as the "broker" for both governmental and private exchange programs and receives financial support from public and private sources. While it has no in-house collection of Soviet archival material, IREX does have a large number of alumni who have conducted research in a broad range of academic fields in archives and libraries throughout the Soviet Union. The research materials collected during these visits remain in the hands of individual scholars. However, in an attempt to disseminate information about current research, IREX began in 1985 to publish a yearly "Register" which includes a listing of IREX scholars who conducted on-site research, topics and short summaries of the work done. In addition to the "Register," IREX is now conducting yearly surveys on archival access in the Soviet Union. The results of these surveys will be available in early 1989. IREX also publishes a quarterly "Update" which reports on current IREX activities and scholar traffic.

CATALOGS   No catalogs reported.

BIBLIOGRAPHY   *Register of American Field Research on Eastern Europe and the USSR*. Princeton, NJ: International Research & Exchanges Board, 1985–, annual; *IREX Update*. Volume 1, No. 1–, Princeton, NJ: International Research & Exchanges Board, Fall 1986–, quarterly. See Grant & Brown, p. 355 (not reproduced here).

I4
ISDEBSKY–PRITCHARD, ALINE
PRIVATE COLLECTION

31–58 35th Street
Astoria, NY 11106

TELEPHONE   718 932–8067

SCHEDULE   By appointment.

ACCESS   Permission may be obtained to study collection upon proof of scholarly interest.

FACILITIES   No photocopying or photography permitted.

HOLDINGS   Personal documents and photographs of her father, the Russian sculptor Vladimir Isdebsky. Also art works: paintings, drawings, sculpture. Papers of his Polish-born wife, the poet and writer Halina (Huzarska) Izdebska. Works of other Russian artists: Michel Andreenko, Alexandra Exter, Josef Levin, Aizik Feder, Ilya Ehrenburg, Jean Lebedeff, David Dubinsky, and Edouard Wuralt (Estonian).

CATALOGS   No catalogs.

BIBLIOGRAPHY No bibliography reported.

J1
JANET LEHR, INC.

891 Park Avenue
New York, NY 10021

Janet Lehr

TELEPHONE   212 288–6234

SCHEDULE   By appointment.

ACCESS   Not open to the public. Researchers are advised to telephone for an appointment, indicating the nature of the research project.

FACILITIES   No report on reading room. Permission can be obtained
to photograph or photocopy items.

HOLDINGS   Ms. Lehr reports that her collection remains as described in Grant & Brown: some 200 photographs pertaining to Russia.
They include about 100 photos of a Russian military road in the Caucasus by
D. Ermakov, Tiflis, ca. 1870; some 100 photos of people, towns, and
landscapes in Russia, including St. Petersburg and Moscow 1870–80; and
other photographs, some of which relate to the Crimean War.

CATALOGS   No catalogs reported.

BIBLIOGRAPHY   See Grant & Brown, p. 357.

JEWISH DAILY FORWARD

See YIVO INSTITUTE FOR JEWISH RESEARCH,
YIVO ARCHIVES

JEWISH LABOR BUND ARCHIVE

See BUND ARCHIVES OF THE JEWISH LABOR MOVEMENT

J2
JEWISH THEOLOGICAL SEMINARY OF AMERICA
LIBRARY

3080 Broadway
New York, NY 10027

Yael Penkower
Reference Librarian

TELEPHONE	212 678–8982
SCHEDULE	Mon–Thur 8:00 a.m.–10:00 p.m.; Fri 8:00 a.m.–seminary closing time
ACCESS	Open to the public.
FACILITIES	Reading room; photocopying and photography permitted.

HOLDINGS   The library has books that deal with Jews and the Russian Empire/Soviet Union. About 600–700 volumes. Many of these are about persecutions, some under specific massacres. There are 14 periodicals, some of them on microfilm. A large part of the collection is in Hebrew or Yiddish. The collection also includes about 200 books of general interest. Size of collection, 1,000 units. Early Hebrew and Yiddish printings from Russia are included in the collection.

CATALOGS	There are subject and author–title catalogs.
BIBLIOGRAPHY	"The Library." *Academic Bulletin* 5748 (1987–1988): 154.

K1
VICTOR KAMKIN BOOKSTORE, INC.

149 Fifth Avenue
New York, NY 10010

Victor Zabavsky
Manager

TELEPHONE	212 673–0776

SCHEDULE   Mon–Wed, Fri 9:30 a.m.–5:30 p.m.; Thur 9:30 a.m.–6:00
p.m.; Sat 10:00 a.m.–5:00 p.m.

ACCESS   Open to the public.

FACILITIES   No reading room. No photography or photocopying of
                  items.

HOLDINGS   Soviet books, records, gifts, periodicals, maps, newspapers. Collection of over one million titles.

CATALOGS   Monthly catalogs of the latest arrivals of books. Also, a
yearly periodical catalog.

BIBLIOGRAPHY   No bibliography reported.

K2
KERDIMUN, BORIS
PRIVATE COLLECTION

98–05 67th Avenue, Apt. 6–K
Rego Park, NY 11374

TELEPHONE   718 897–0439

SCHEDULE   Call for an appointment.

ACCESS   Not open to the public, but permission may be obtained
                  to study collection.

FACILITIES   No reading room; photocopying and photography per-
                  mitted.

HOLDINGS   Avant-garde books, masonic manuscripts, drawings,
watercolors and paintings of Russian and Ukrainian artists of the beginning
of the 20th century; periodicals and books of different types, 1900–1940.
Size: approx. 5,000 items.

SPECIAL   Masonic manuscripts; children's books (1910–30),
FEATURES   watercolors and drawings of I.I. Ivanov, Kovenatsky,
Koulakov. Collection of catalogs of art exhibitions, 1905–1950.

CATALOGS   None.

BIBLIOGRAPHY   No bibliography reported.

K3
KOMAR AND MELAMID ART STUDIO

181 Canal Street
New York, NY 10013

Vitaly Komar
Artist

TELEPHONE   212 966–6180

SCHEDULE   By appointment only.

ACCESS   Not open to the public, but permission may be obtained
                 to study collection.

FACILITIES   No reading room; permission may be obtained to
photocopy or photograph some items.

HOLDINGS   The collection is devoted to art history. Books, periodicals, art magazines, reproductions, filmstrips, slides of Russian and Soviet
art and culture. 5,000 slides, filmstrips and reproductions.

CATALOGS   None.

BIBLIOGRAPHY   Vitaly Komar and Alexander Melamid. "The Barren
Flowers of Evil." *Art Forum* (March 1980); idem, "In Search of Religion."
Art Forum (May 1980); "On the Experiment of Artistic Associations in
Soviet Russia." *The Journal of Arts Management and Law* 13: 1 (Spring
1983).

K4
KOSCIUSZKO FOUNDATION

15 East 65 Street
New York, NY 10021

Dr. M. Budka
Archivist

TELEPHONE   212 734–2130

SCHEDULE   Mon–Fri 9:00 a.m.–5:00 p.m.

ACCESS Not open to the public. On rare occasions permission can be obtained to use the collection.

FACILITIES There is no reading room. Permission can be obtained to photocopy or photograph items.

HOLDINGS The collection is eclectic, derived from gifts. Size of collection is some 2,500 items, nothing rare, some material pertaining to Polish–Russian/Soviet Union relations. There are a few early editions of encyclopedias, geographical dictionaries of old Polish and Lithuanian lands.

CATALOGS No catalogs reported.

BIBLIOGRAPHY No bibliography reported.

L1
LAMPARD, MARIE TURBOW
PRIVATE COLLECTION

TELEPHONE 212 362–3866; 516 632–7492, 928–2260

SCHEDULE Call for an appointment.

ACCESS Not open to the public, but permission may be obtained to study collection.

FACILITIES No reading room; photocopying and photography not permitted.

HOLDINGS Family purchased and was given works of Russian sculptor Sergei Timofeevich Konenkov, forming a small collection of sculpture, periodicals, newspapers, pictures, tapes, arts and crafts, and letters, some of which have been assembled for research purposes. Ten pieces by Konenkov, and assorted works by other artists of his era.

CATALOGS No catalogs available.

BIBLIOGRAPHY Marie Turbow Lampard. "Sergei Konenkov and the 'Russian Art Exhibition' of 1924." *Soviet Union/Union Sovietique* 7: Pts. 1–2 (1980): 70–88. See Grant & Brown, pp. 356–357 (not reproduced here).

LEO BAECK INSTITUTE

See under BAECK

L2
LONG, ROSE-CAROL W.
PRIVATE COLLECTION

City University of New York
33 West 42 Street
New York, NY 10036

TELEPHONE	212 790–4451; 642–2865, 2866
SCHEDULE	Call for an appointment.
ACCESS	Collection may be researched by doctoral students in art history.
FACILITIES	No facilities reported.

HOLDINGS   Professor Long owns a rare Kandinsky print; membership card for Neue Kunstlervereinigung, linoleum cut, 1909; and has a fine library for research on Kandinsky.

CATALOGS	No catalogs reported.
BIBLIOGRAPHY	No bibliography reported.

M1
MANHATTAN SCHOOL OF MUSIC

120 Claremont Avenue
New York, NY 10027

Joseph Seiger
Professor of Music (Piano)

TELEPHONE	212 749–2802
SCHEDULE	Mon–Fri 9:00 a.m.–5:00 p.m.
ACCESS	Not open to the public. Permission may be obtained to study the collection.

FACILITIES   No reading room. No photography or photocopying.

HOLDINGS   Collection is a gift made by Mrs. Mischa Elman to the Manhattan School of Music. Consists of violin music, pictures, a piano, furniture and books. There are also some manuscripts of music dedicated to Mischa Elman (1891–1967). Grant & Brown report the following:
    The studio holds photographs of Elman and his associates, a scrapbook of clippings, and musical scores once owned by Elman. Most of the music is printed but a few items are in manuscript (not Elman's hand). It is possible that some of the printed music has Elman's notations and fingering marks.

CATALOGS   No catalogs reported.

BIBLIOGRAPHY   See Grant & Brown, p. 358.

NIKOLAI MARTIANOFF COLLECTION

See UNIVERSITY OF ROCHESTER
    RUSH RHEES LIBRARY

M2
METROPOLITAN MUSEUM OF ART

Fifth Avenue and 82nd Street
New York, NY 10028

Various curatorial departments

TELEPHONE   212 879–5500

SCHEDULE   Wed–Sun 9:30 a.m.–5:15 p.m.; Tue 9:30 a.m.–8:45 p.m.

ACCESS   Schedule is for regular museum hours. For information on the Thomas J. Watson Library, the Photograph and Slide Library, and the study rooms for prints, drawings, and textiles, call telephone number given above.

FACILITIES   The Museum is divided into departments and curatorships. Each must be consulted separately in order to determine the possibility to view or study items not currently on display.

HOLDINGS   Concerning Russian and Soviet artists, holdings in the Museum in drawings and watercolors include: Ivan K. Aivazovskii (1817–1900); Leon Bakst (1868–1924); Natalia Goncharova (1886–1962); Boris Grigoriev (1886–1939); Eugene A. Katzman (1890–1969); Klavdy V. Lebedev (1852–1916); S. Lednev-Schukin; Vladimir Serov (1910–1968); Boris Solotareff (1889–1966);

Paintings: Ivan K. Aivazovskii (1817–1900); Abram E. Arkhipov (1862–1930); Leon Bakst (1868–1924); Viktor Brodzki (1825–1904); Marc Chagall (1898–1985)); Vasilii Dmitrievich (1844–1927); Boris Grigoriev (1886–1939); Moise Kisling (1891–1953); Arkhip I. Kuindzhi (1841–1910); Boris M. Kustodiev (1878–1927); Konstantin E. Makovsky (1839–1915); Vladimir E. Makovsky (1846–1920); Il'ia Ivanovich Mashkov (1881–1944); Mikhail V. Nesterov (1862–1942); Vasilii G. Perov (1834–1882); Alexei K. Savrasov (1830–1897); Wassily Schuchaef (b. 1887–); Charles Westchiloff; a number of paintings and icons by unknown painters dating from the 15th–19th centuries.

Sculpture: Jules Leon Butensky (1871–1947); Mika Mikoun (b. 1886–); Antoine Pevsner (1886–1962); Leo L. Tolstoi; Prince Paul Troubetskoi (1866–1938);

Painted Enamels, Textiles, and Tapestries: Jean Baptiste Ronde (fl. 1759–1764). There are also examples of porcelain ceramics; glass from the Bakhmeteff glassworks; woven textiles of the 18th century; silver and metalwork in combination of the 19th century; metalwork and silversmiths' work of the 18th and 19th centuries (Johann Bernhard Hentz, 1834–1855; Nicols & Plinke, 1829–1900; Anders Lang, 1843–1851); embroidered textiles of the 19th century; gold metalwork of the 19th century; a silver chess set from the 19th century; brass chandeliers from the 17th century.

In the department for Arms and Armour there are some pre–20th-century materials from Poland as well as a hunting sword (ca. 1785) and a flintlock pistol (1749), both from Tula; a pair of ivory-stocked flintlock pistols (1786) made for Empress Catherine the Great by Johan Adolph Grecke in Saint Petersburg.

CATALOGS   Consult separate departments.

BIBLIOGRAPHY   The Metropolitan Museum of Art. *Recent Acquisitions: A Selection 1986–1987.* "Johan Adolph Grecke; Pair of Ivory-Stocked Flintlock Pistols of Empress Catherine the Great." New York: The Metropolitan Museum of Art, 1987. Pp. 20–21.

M3
PIERPONT MORGAN LIBRARY

29 East 36th Street
New York, NY 10016

Inge Dupont
Head of Reader Services

TELEPHONE   212 685–0008, Ext. 376

SCHEDULE   Mon–Fri 9:30 a.m.–4:45 p.m. Closed legal holidays and the last two weeks in August.

ACCESS   Application for use of the Reading Room and use of any materials of the Library must be made in writing. Such application should be made, insofar as possible, at least one week in advance. The application shall specify the name, address, profession or occupation of the applicant, and state as specifically as possible the subject upon which the applicant is engaged and the purpose for which specific Library materials must be examined. The primary function of the Reading Room is to serve the readers needing to consult the Library's rare materials. All applications should be accompanied by satisfactory written credentials from a scholar or educational institution of recognized standing, testifying to the applicant's fitness to make use of the Library's material. Applicants complying with these restrictions will be given a reader's card good for a specified period, unless revoked or forfeited. This card is not transferable and must be produced when the reader enters the Library. In cases where microfilm or other forms of photographic reproductions are on file in the Library, readers will be requested to use these for all preliminary study. The Print Room is open by appointment in advance on Tuesday through Friday afternoons only, and rules and precautions as prescribed by the Curators of Prints and Drawings must be followed.

FACILITIES   Reading Room, Print Room. No photographs may be taken by any person other than the Library photographer. Requests for photographic reproductions must be made in writing on the Library's form. These reproductions will be billed according to a published schedule.

HISTORY   The Library's basic holdings reflect the collecting talents of its founder Pierpont Morgan (1837–1913). His concern with literature and history on the one hand, and with art on the other, has resulted in the Library's being partly a museum, and partly a research library. It is a treasury of the cultures from which our civilization has developed. The holdings were enhanced by J.P. Morgan, Jr. (1867–1943), with the aid of the first librarian, Belle da Costa Greene (1883–1950). In 1949, a national association of "Fellows of The Pierpont Morgan Library" was formed. With the aid of the Fellows, with income from generous legacies, and with contributions from many individuals and foundations, the Library has been able to add steadily to its collection, while adhering quite strictly to the pattern set by the founders. The present landmark building, designed by McKim, Mead & White, was completed in 1906. Since then, there have been building additions, in 1928 and 1960, and interior remodeling and expansion.

HOLDINGS   The Pierpont Morgan Library is an independent research library whose materials are available for study by accredited students and scholars. Its holdings of mainly Western Medieval and Renaissance manuscripts, autograph literary and music letters and manuscripts, old master drawings, incunables, and early printed books are particularly important.

Materials relating to the Russian Empire and Soviet Union are primarily in non-Russian languages and are limited in number. These fall into certain broad categories, such as travel narratives and illustrated descriptions of people and places; autograph letters and papers of rulers, travelers, or literary figures; and 19th- and 20th-century composers' letters and scores. What follows is a detailed list of such holdings.

Medieval and Renaissance Manuscripts

Slavonic Manuscripts

Among other Slavonic manuscripts, the Library has the following relating to Russia:

Hymnal in Greek. 17th century. Services for the principal feasts of the church as sung in Constantinople. With musical notation; possibly written in the Balkans or in Russia. (M350)

Six sermons in Russian. Written and illuminated in Russia in the mid-19th century. (M704)

The Four Gospels in Church Slavonic, in Cyrillic script. Written and illuminated in Russia, date 1608. (M794)

Apocalypse in Church Slavonic and in Cyrillic script. Russia, 18th century. (M1064)

Armenian Manuscripts

The Library owns the following thirteen items:

The Four Gospels: Incomplete 13th century (M620); 17th century (M621); Completed in 1659 (M623); 1588 (M624); 1274, written by Kostandin for the Great Marshal Awsin (M740); 1461, illuminated by Minas (M749); Three leaves from a Gospel, probably 10th century. Two Canon tables and one Evangelist portrait. (M789)

Sermons, 16th century. (M437)

Menologium, 1348. Lives of Armenian, Greek, and Latin saints from the calendar period March–August. Illuminated by Sargis Picak. (M622)

Scholium and Epistles of St. Cyril of Alexandria, 1688. (M625)

Fragment, eight leaves, from a Commentary on the Epistle of St. James by Sargis Vardapet. Probably 13th century (M802)

Lectionary, 1334. (M803)

Lives of the Saints and Christ, 17th century. (M949)

Autograph Manuscripts and Letters

Alexander I, Emperor of Russia, ALS to Lieut. Gen. Betancourt, 1813. (Koch Fdt. Deposit)

Alexander II, Emperor of Russia. Large collection of love letters exchanged (1868–1872) between Alexander II and Catherine, his mistress and future wife. (Koch Fdt. Deposit 554)

Dominique Jean Larrey, Baron. *Field Diary in Russia*. In French, signed 4 February 1812–1 October 1813. (MA 2583)

Reminiscences of ten years' chaos in Russia. By X (1916–1928). Typewritten manuscript marked "Confidential. For private circulation only." Piedmont, Northern Italy, 1928. 289 leaves. (MA 3550)

Russia. Navy. Manuscript list, "The Empress of Russia's Navy." October 14, 1764. (MA Rulers of Russia)

Leo Tolstoi. Autograph ms. in Russian. (n.p., n.d.) being a section of his essay, *What is art*, and two printed items relating to the manuscript. (Koch PD 41)

Ivan Turgenev. AMS of a scenario for an opera libretto submitted to Johannes Brahms (ca. 1869). 6 p. (Koch Fdt. Deposit)

Ninety-one letters from members of the Russian Imperial family to the mother of Professor Gregory P. Tschebotarioff, 1915–1918. (MA 2585)

Autograph letters by Russian authors, for example: Maksim Gorkii, Boris Pasternak, Leo Tolstoi, and Ivan Turgenev.

Music Manuscripts and Letters

Scores

Vladimir Dukelsky. *Vocalise*. Autograph ms. of his orchestration of the Rachmaninoff work. 1922. (Cary 344)

Alexandr Konstantinovich Glazunov. (*Liszt, Totentanz. Einlage*) For piano, 1931. (Koch Fdt. Deposit)

Alexandr Tikhonovich Grechaninov. (*Gimn Pushkinu*) For four-part chorus and tenor solo. (Cary 385)

Ignace Jan Paderewski. (*Sonata*, violin & piano. Op. 13) (Lehman)

Sergei Prokofiev. (*Chout*. Op. 21) 1915. Short score of ballet; and (*Pas d'acier*. Op. 41) 1925. Piano score of the ballet. (Both Lehman Deposit)

Sergei Rachmaninoff. (*Kolokola*) (Koch Fdt. Dep. 361)

Maurice Ravel. (*Musorgsky. Khovanshchina*) Full score, for orchestra. Two sections of Ravel's version of Musorgsky's unfinished opera. (Koch Fdt. Dep. 3)

Ottorini Respighi. Various instrumentations of works by Borodin, Glinka, Rimsky-Korsakov, and Tchaikovsky. (Koch Fdt. Dep.)

Anton Rubinstein. (*Quartet*, strings. Op. 106 no. 1 A flat major) (Koch Fdt. Dep. 12)

Igor Stravinsky. (*Le baiser de la fee*) Ballet in four tableaux, arrangement for piano. (Lehman Dep.); (*Etude*. Pianola) 1917. (Koch Fdt. Dep. 144); (*Petrushka*) Full score, 1946. (Lehman Dep.); (*Cinq pieces faciles*) Piano four-hands, 1917. (Koch Fdt. Dep. 143); (*Ragtime*) For piano, 1918 (Lehman Dep.); (*Renard*) Piano-vocal score, 1916 (Koch Fdt. Dep. 142); (*Four Russian Peasant Songs*) 1917. (Cary 393); (*Persephone*) Short score, incomplete, 1936 and 1960. (Cary)

Autograph letters by composers such as: Ignace Jan Paderewski, Sergei Rachmaninoff, Igor Stravinsky, and Pyotr Il'yich Tchaikovsky.

Printed music is also in the Library's collections.

Printed Books

Travel Narratives

Cornelis de Bryun. *Reizen over Moskovie, door Persie en Indie: verrykt met driehondert konstplaten*. Amsterdam: Goeree, 1711. (PML 76291)

Ambrotio Contarini. *Viaggio al re di Persia*. Venice: Foxius, 1487. 1st ed. One of the earliest accounts on the Russian people. (ChL 945A)

Idem. *Viaggi fatti da Vinetia, alla Tana, in Persia, in India et in Constantinopoli*. . . . Venice: Paulus Manutius, 1543. (PML 28278)

Sigismund Herberstein. *Rerum Moscoviticarum commentarii*. Basel: Oporinus, 1556. 3rd enl. ed. (PML 31299)

Idem. *Picturae variae quae . . . varias legationes obeuntem exprimunt*. Vienna: Hofhalter, 1560. Only edition, privately printed. (PML 31299)

Olaus Magnus. *Historia de gentibus Septentrionalibus*. . . . Rome: 1555. 1st ed. (PML 38676)

Thomas Smith. *Sir Thomas Smithes voiage and entertainment in Rushia.* . . . London: Butter, 1605. (PML 54306)

Edward Webbe. *Rare and most wonderful things which Edw. Webbe . . . has seene . . . in the landes of . . . Russia, and Prester John.* . . . London: 1590. 1st ed. (PML 17517)

Illustrated Descriptions

Auguste Ricard de Montferrand. *Église cathédrale de Saint-Isaac.* St. Petersburg: Bellizard, 1845. 99 lithographed plates and 2 chromo-lithographed plates. (PML 76282)

Idem. *Plans et details du monument consacré a la memoire de l'empereur Alexandre.* Paris: Thierry, 1836. 41 hand-collored lith. plates. (PML 76281)

Novelle collection de quarante-deux vues de Saint-Petersbourg et de ses environs. St. Petersburg: 1826. 42 lith. plates. (PML 76279)

Fedor Khristianovich Pauli. *Description ethnographique des peuples de la Russie.* St. Petersburg: Bellizard, 1862. 63 lith. plates. (PML 76283)

Novelles extraordinaires de divers endroits. . . . Leiden: Luzac, 1766. 104 nos. in 1 vol. Commonly known as Gazette de Leyde. (no acc.)

CATALOGS   The Library's cataloging is part of the RLIN system.

BIBLIOGRAPHY   The Library has published a *Report to the Fellows* every three years since its summary *Review of Acquisitions, 1949–1968* (1969). These books, containing detailed listings of the acquisitions in all departments for the period covered, are available in many university libraries; *The Mary Flagler Cary Music Collection. Printed books, and music manuscripts, autograph letters, documents, portraits.* New York: Pierpont Morgan Library, 1970; Avedis K. Sanjian. *A catalogue of Medieval Armenian manuscripts in the United States.* Berkeley: University of California Press, 1976; Rigbie Turner. *Nineteenth century autograph music manuscripts in the Pierpont Morgan Library. A checklist.* New York, 1982; *Music manuscripts in the Pierpont Morgan Library. A catalogue.* January 1988 (typewritten); *Music letters in the Pierpont Morgan Library. A catalogue.* January 1988 (typewritten) (Copies of the latter two catalogs are available at the Music Divison of the New York Public Library at Lincoln Center, Princeton University, the Eastman School of Music in Rochester, and the University of Chicago); *The collection of the Frederick R. Koch Foundation. A checklist.* n.d. (typewritten); *A brief history; The Pierpont Morgan Library.* Undated, unpaginated brochure; *Visitor Information; The Pierpont Morgan Library.* Undated, unpaginated folder; "The Pierpont Morgan Library; The Reading Room." Two-page information sheet.

M4
MORRISTOWN NATIONAL HISTORICAL PARK

Washington Place
Morristown, NJ 07960

Alan Stein
Library Technician

TELEPHONE	201 539–2016
SCHEDULE	Wed–Sat 9:00 a.m.–5:00 p.m.
ACCESS	Open to the public, by appointment only.

FACILITIES   Reading room. Photography and photocopying permitted but not of original materials.

HOLDINGS   The research library contains a rich treasure of original books, manuscripts, and other material on the Colonial and Revolutionary War periods of American history. Total holdings in the library consist of nearly 14,000 books and 40,000 manuscripts. Included are the Park Collection; the Lloyd W. Smith Collection; the Hessian Transcripts; Ford Papers; Diary of Sylvanus Seeley; as well as a large collection of 17th and 18th century newspapers, maps, atlases, almanacs, and pamphlets. The Lloyd W. Smith and Park Collections, Ford Papers, and the Sylvanus Seeley Diary have been indexed and are available in transcript, in photocopy, and on microfilm.

Some material relating to Russia is included in the library. Grant & Brown list 8 items relating to Russia (letters, writings, accounts, newspaper citations) and a 9th item listing 23 pieces (1719–1835), including documents, letters, portraits, clippings, and a biographical sketch of Nicholas I in English, in one folder, all from the Lloyd W. Smith Collection. They are as follows:

John Quincy Adams. ALS, St. Petersburg, December 18, 1810, to Hon. Samuel L. Mitchell with a detailed account of the English and French blockades to shipping, plus an ALS of his wife Louisa. 4 pp. An ADS, St. Petersburg, March 31, 1812, containing an itemized account for his diplomatic services to the U.S., 1811 and first quarter of 1812. 2 pp. (Nos. 3342 and 3343)

Madame de Campan. Author of *Memoires*, reader to Marie Antoinette, and sister of "Citizen" Genet. Autograph manuscript, Paris, October 27, 1801, describing her brother's experiences at the court of Catherine II of

Russia and early events of the French Revolution. 16 pp. plus an unsigned note in her hand. (No. 695)

Charles Carroll. Carroll, of Carrollton, signed the Constitution for Maryland. An ALS of May 9, 1829, discusses tobacco and flour shipments and a Russo–Turkish War. 3 pp. (No. 99)

Ulysses S. Grant. ALS of president from Rome to "Dear Fred," March 22, 1878, concerning Greece, Turkey, Turkish and Russian affairs, and his family. 4 pp. (No. 42)

Andrew Johnson. Signed letter to General U.S. Grant, Secretary of War ad interim, asking him to be present that day when questions about the newly acquired Russian territory will be considered, August 12, 1867. 1 p. (No. 44)

James Madison. Broadside: "National Intelligencer . . . Extra," May 25, 1813; Madison's message to Congress about the St. Petersburg Conference, Tsar Alexander in his role of mediator, and other affairs of state. (No. 842; shelved with Rare Books); also, in papers from members of his cabinet ("The 6th Administration"), an item of Albert Gallatin on his acceptance of a mission to Russia, 1813. (No. 2987)

Maria Feodorovna. Signed letter of the tsarina of Russia, St. Petersburg, October 27, 1789, to the playwright August von Kotzebue, in French; with a fine portrait. 1 p. (No. 750)

Maria Paulovna. The tsarina's signed letter, dated Belvedere, July 17/29, 1831, in Russian. 1 p. (No. 749)

Russian. 1719–1835. Includes documents, letters, portraits, clippings, a biographical sketch of Nicholas I in English, and an unsigned letter concerning autograph collecting. This extraordinary folder contains: a signed letter, October 1, 1719, and an ALS to Count Golovkin(?), October 12[?], 1719, of Peter I; a DS by Catherine II, February 20, 1770, promoting one Grigorii Geikin, her LS to the governor of Pskov, General-Colonel Pil', April 19, 17--, and a fragment of an ALS of Catherine in French; a DS of Paul I, July 21, 1797, promoting Aleksandr Ivanchikov, translator in the Ministry of Foreign Affairs, with his LS to Prince Maintsskii, October 21, 1799; a DS by Alexander I, August 17, 1805, concerning Prince Avgust de Broglio-Revel; an ALS of Marie, wife of Alexander I, to her daughter Anette, May 21, 1810, with addressed envelope; a DS by Nicholas I, June 17, 1835, in Russian and Polish, conferring the order of St. Stanislav second class on Humbert, adviser to the Prussian embassy (also signed by Prince Aleksandr); a DS by Alexander II conferring the order of the White Eagle on Lieutenant General Baron Edwin von Manteuffel; an ALS of Princess Eudosee Galitzin to the historical painter Henry Fuseli, in French, with addressed envelope; and an account by Mr. Balmann(?) of how he came into possession of the Galitzin letter and others. 23 pieces. (No. 2851)

CATALOGS   Card catalog to books and manuscript collection.

BIBLIOGRAPHY   Bruce W. Stewart and Hans Mayer. *A Guide to the Manuscript Collection. Morristown National History Park.* Morristown, NJ: n.p., n.d. See Grant & Brown, pp. 272–273.

M5
MUSEUM OF MODERN ART
FILM STILLS ARCHIVE

11 West 53rd Street
New York, NY 10019

Mary Corliss
Assistant Curator

TELEPHONE	212 708–9830
TELEX	62370 MODART

SCHEDULE   Mon–Fri 1:30 p.m.–5:00 p.m.

ACCESS   Permission may be obtained to study collection.

FACILITIES   Reading room; no photocopying or photography permitted. Black and white, glossy, 8″ x 10″ duplicates of original stills are sold. It usually takes one week upon receipt of order for stills to be processed. Copyright, however, is not inclusive, and should be obtained from the film studios if a still is to be reproduced in a book. Clearance is generally granted for stills reproduced in magazines and newspapers. Mail orders are accepted and phone orders may be placed. 35mm slides are unavailable. Inquire about costs.

HOLDINGS   Approximately 10,000 film stills from Russian films, circa 1920–1985.

CATALOGS   There is no subject classification. All stills must be requested by film title.

BIBLIOGRAPHY   No bibliography reported.

M6
MUSEUM OF MODERN ART
FILM STUDY CENTER

11 West 53 Street
New York, NY 10019

Charles Silver
Supervisor

TELEPHONE   212 708–9613

SCHEDULE   Mon–Fri 1:00 p.m.–5:00 p.m. By appointment.

ACCESS   The collection is open by appointment to qualified
scholars, writers, researchers and filmmakers. Students who wish to view
films must submit a letter from their instructor on university letterhead at
least two weeks in advance. This letter should specify the film(s) being requested and state the nature and validity of the project. Writers who submit
a similar letter from their editor or publisher on letterhead may also obtain
permission to view films. Others with a serious purpose may submit a written request two weeks in advance, but the Department of Film retains the
right of approving all requests. Due to limited facilities, projects requiring
extensively detailed analysis are generally not permitted.

FACILITIES   Reading room; photocopying and photography permitted. A 16mm projector is available and several 16mm viewing tables on
which films from the collection may be viewed (not all films are available).
Unpublished documents may not be photocopied. Inquire about fees for
single reel archive prints, multiple reel archive prints, circulating library
prints, private and group screening of films.

HOLDINGS   Over 100 Russian films (1912–1970s). Clipping files,
scripts, stills, periodicals and books.

CATALOGS   *The Film Catalog: A List of Film Holdings in the Museum of Modern Art.* Boston: G.K. Hall, 1986.

BIBLIOGRAPHY   See Grant & Brown, p. 359 (not reproduced here).

M7
MUSEUM OF MODERN ART
LIBRARY

11 West 53rd Street
New York, NY 10019

Reference Librarian

TELEPHONE   212 708–9433

SCHEDULE   Mon–Fri 11:00 a.m.–5:00 p.m.

ACCESS   Open to the public by appointment.

FACILITIES   Reading room; photocopying and photography permitted depending on the material.

HISTORY   Begun in 1929, the scope of the Library collection largely mirrors the scope of the Museum collections. Since the Museum collection begins in 1880 with Post-Impressionism, the Library documents art since 1880 as intensely as resources will allow; however, it is also necessary to provide some coverage of the period immediately prior to this date. Thus, the Library has developed into one of the most comprehensive research collections of material documenting the international art, architecture, design, film and photography of the modern period (c. 1860 to present). Within this context, material is acquired regardless of language.

HOLDINGS   At present the Library contains approximately 100,000 cataloged items; about 40,000 of these publications are fully cataloged books and substantial exhibition catalogs, and the remaining 60,000 are briefly cataloged slighter exhibition catalogs. The Library also currently subscribes to about 350 modern art periodicals from all over the world, supplemented by periodical titles received as gifts or exchanges. (Photography, film, architecture and design magazines are subscribed to by, and displayed in, the appropriate curatorial study centers.) The total number of periodical titles in the Library including those now defunct is 3,000 and includes over 8,000 bound volumes.

The Library makes a special feature of collecting slight fugitive published or semi-published materials documenting modern and contemporary art on an international scale. These documents are mostly housed in artist or subject files. There are over 20,000 artist files in the Library, containing 200,000 separate items, including exhibition announcements, press-releases, occasional photographs or reproductions, and clippings from newspapers and magazines. In addition there are also subject files documenting groups, themes or movements.

The following description of material on the Russian Empire and Soviet Union has been updated from Grant & Brown by the Library:

The Library contains published material on Russian-Empire–born artists such as Alexander Archipenko, Saul Baizerman, Peter Blume, Ilya Bolotowsky, David Burliuk, Marc Chagall, Nathalie Goncharova, John D. Graham, Wassily Kandinsky, Velemir Khlebnikov, Aleksei Kruchenykh, Mikhail Larionov, El Lissitzky, Kasimir Malevich, Vladimir Mayakovsky, Elie Nadelman, Alexander Rodchenko, Nicholas Roerich, Mark Rothko, Moses Soyer, Raphael Soyer, Vladimir Tatlin, Pavel Tchelitchew, Max Weber, Adja Yunkers. In addition, the Library has extensive holdings documenting Russian art movements of the early 20th century, especially Russian Futurism and Suprematism.

The Library contains the only original copy in the United States reported in RLIN of *Oslinyi Khvost i Mishen.* Moscow: Izd. Ts.A. Miunster, 1913. 153 leaves. (A manifesto of the members of two art groups; signatories include Nathalie Goncharova and Mikhail Larionov and work of both artists is reproduced in the book.)

Specific collections of unpublished material are:

American National Exhibition in Moscow Scrapbooks, 1959. Scrapbooks documenting the first government-organized exhibition to be held in the Soviet Union presenting American science, technology, and culture. "Culture" was represented by a selection of works from the Museum of Modern Art. 3 volumes.

Ballet russe de Monte-Carlo, programs, 1938–45. 1 volume.

Ballets russes Diaghilev, programs, 1911–29. 2 volumes.

Alfred H. Barr, Jr., Papers, 1918–1975, 1929–1970 (bulk). Correspondence, general files, documents, articles, photographs, manuscripts, clippings and printed material from the office of the founding director of the Museum of Modern Art. One series "Soviet Cultural Matters, 1948–1974" is among the papers which are available on microfilm through the *Archives of American Art.* Unfilmed series includes "Russian Culture, 1924–1944" (6 linear ft.). 95 linear ft.

Sergei Mikhailovich Eisenstein Collection, ca. 1900–1949. Material, collected by Jay Leyda, includes filmmaker's own scrapbook of photographs, manuscripts, correspondence, and synopses and drawings for various film projects. Correspondence with Leyda and publications also included. 1 cubic ft., 2 volumes.

"Filmographie russe, 1907–1932" compiled by the Federation Internationale des Archives du Film (Paris), ca. 1950. 37 page unpublished(?) manuscript.

Naum Gabo Research Collection, 1936–1954. Collection of material, including articles and announcements documenting Gabo's long career. 0.4 cubic ft.

Vladimir Isdebsky Papers, 1900–1960. Personal documents, photographs, and clippings recording the involvement of Isdebsky (1882–1965) with artistic activities in Russia and Paris, especially during the 1920s, and in the United States after 1941. 1 cubic ft.

Wassily Kandinsky Letters and "Hauskataloge," 1910–1944. Photocopies of letters from Kandinsky to Dr. and Mrs. Will Grohmann, 1923–1943. Microfilm of Kandinsky's "Hauskatalog," a detailed inventory of his artwork. 5 volumes and 1 microfilm reel.

J.B. (Jsrael Bar) Neumann Papers, 1921–1960. Papers of a prominent German-American art dealer, lecturer, critic and publisher. Includes correspondence and unpublished manuscripts on the work of Wassily Kandinsky among others. 3.3 linear ft.

"The Soviet Attitude to Art." Consists of transcripts of statement delivered in London by Vladimir Kemenov, Director of the Tretiakov Gallery, and an analysis of the statement by Joseph Paul Hodin. 34-page unpublished (?) manuscript.

CATALOGS   *Catalog of the Library of the Museum of Modern Art.* Boston: G. K. Hall, 1976. 14v. Member of RLIN since 1980, all the Library's cataloging records since this time are entered there. Library is presently seeking to convert all its records into machine-readable form.

BIBLIOGRAPHY   Clive Phillpot. "The Library of the Museum of Modern Art New York." *Art Libraries Journal* (Spring 1985): 29–36. See Grant & Brown, pp. 359–360 (not reproduced here).

N1
NATIONAL ARCHIVES–NEW YORK BRANCH

Building 22, Military Ocean Terminal
Bayonne, NJ 07002-5388

Anthony J. Fantozzi
Assistant Director

TELEPHONE   201 823–7561

SCHEDULE   Mon–Fri 8:00 a.m.–4:30 p.m. (except federal holidays)

ACCESS   Open to the public. Individuals wishing to use original records in the National Archives–New York Branch should first write or call the Branch and describe the proposed research and the records desired. By contacting the Branch in advance the researcher will be assured that the pertinent records are present and will be available and ready for use upon the researcher's arrival. Upon arrival at the Field Branch, visitors will be asked to complete an application form. A research identification card, valid for two years, will then be issued to the applicant.

FACILITIES   Reading room. Provision can be made for electrostatic or microfilm copies of original records and paper copies from microfilm publications. The charge for copies will depend on the size and method of reproduction.

HISTORY   The National Archives of the United States includes the permanently valuable records of the three branches of the federal government. It now maintains more than one million cubic feet of records in a nationwide system of depositories that includes the National Archives Building in Washington, DC, 11 Field Branches, and 9 presidential libraries. The National Archives Field Branches were established in 1969 to preserve and make available for research those records created by federal courts and offices of federal agencies located outside the Washington, DC metropolitan area. The National Archives–New York Branch is the despository for records created in New York, New Jersey, Puerto Rico, and the United States Virgin Islands. The branches have also acquired copies of some of the many National Archives microfilm publications, which reproduce records deposited in the National Archives Building in Washington, DC.

HOLDINGS   The National Archives–New York Branch has custody of more than 61,000 cubic feet of records created by 41 federal agencies and courts. Records are available for U.S. Courts of Appeals; Immigration and Naturalization Service; U.S. Information Agency (including producers' copies of Voice of America scripts with notes and deletions, additions, and revisions, cover sheets and other background material); district courts of the United States (1685–1973) (including records over actions involving aliens or citizens of different states and laws where the matter in the dispute exceeded $500); U.S. attorneys and marshals (1821–1983) (including Communist activities for New York, Southern District), as well as some 60 other agencies and governmental organizations.

Material has to be gleaned for subjects relevant to a researcher's needs. Some records have draft inventories and some of them are on microfilm. It is impossible for the staff to undertake extensive research for individuals but the Branch will provide information about the records in its custody in response to written or telephone inquiries.

CATALOGS   Various finding records on site.

BIBLIOGRAPHY National Archives–New York Branch. *Guide to the National Archives–New York Branch.* Bayonne, NJ: National Archives and Records Administration, National Archives–New York Branch, August 1987 (Draft). 32 p.; Charles South. *List of National Archives Microfilm Publications in the Regional Archives Branches.* Washington, DC: National Archives and Records Service, 1975. 50 p. See Grant & Brown, p. 270 (not reproduced here).

NATIONAL BOARD OF YOUNG MEN'S CHRISTIAN ASSOCIATION HISTORICAL LIBRARY

See YMCA OF GREATER NEW YORK

N2
NATIONAL COUNCIL OF AMERICAN–SOVIET FRIENDSHIP LIBRARY

85 East 4th Street
New York, NY 10003

Alan Thomson
Executive Director

TELEPHONE   212 254–6606

SCHEDULE   Mon–Fri 9:00 a.m.–5:00 p.m.

ACCESS   Open to the public. Lending library only. Copying and photography of items permitted.

HOLDINGS   Founded in 1943 to increase understanding, peace and disarmament. Collections include 600 16 mm Soviet-produced, documentary films for rent; all current publications of the following Soviet publishers: Progress, Raduga, and Novosti. There is also a selection of current Soviet periodicals and newspapers.

CATALOGS   Catalog of available films, revised 1988. A topical title list is available upon request for English-language material.

BIBLIOGRAPHY A brochure lists local societies in the United States, the Advisory Council and its activities.

N3
NEIZVESTNY, ERNST

81 Grand Street
New York, NY 10013

TELEPHONE	212 226-2677
SCHEDULE	Mon–Fri 12:00 p.m.–8:00 p.m.
ACCESS	Permission may be obtained to study collection.
FACILITIES	Reading room; photocopying and photography permitted.
HISTORY	Soviet emigre sculptor.

HOLDINGS   Largest part of collection consists of working drawings and sculptures for his monumental project, "The Tree of Life," and also for his personal museum in Sweden. Over 1,000 units.

CATALOGS   No catalogs reported.

BIBLIOGRAPHY   John Berger. *Art and Revolution: Ernst Neizvestny and the Role of the Artist in the USSR*. New York: Pantheon, 1969. 191 p.; Boris Leonidovich Ogibenin. *Ernst Neizvestny, Createur d'une Archaique Novelle*. Lisse, Netherlands: Peter de Ridder Press, 1975. 15 p.; Mario De Micheli. *Ernst Neizvestny*. Milan: Feltrinelli, 1978. 134 p.; Erik Eegland. *Ernst Neizvestny, Life and Work*. New York: Flatiron Books, 1984. 197 p.

N4
NEW JERSEY HISTORICAL SOCIETY

230 Broadway
Newark, NJ 07104

Sandor B. Cohen
Curator of Manuscripts

TELEPHONE	201 483-3939
SCHEDULE	Tues–Sat 10:00 a.m.–4:00 p.m.
ACCESS	Open to the public.

FACILITIES   Reading room; photocopying and photography permitted only when permission is obtained from the Library Director.

HOLDINGS   The manuscripts collection of the Library includes more than one million items organized into approximately 1,300 distinct manuscript groups. Manuscript materials pertaining to Russia as reported in Grant & Brown are:

Chew Family. Papers, 1735–96. Includes the autobiography of Beverly Chew (1794–1844), Vice-Consul in Russia under President James Madison. The original title of this item, transcribed and edited by Morris R. Chew in 1890, is "Notes and Memorandums for Reference 1794–1844," 71 p. 26 items. (MG 596)

Reeve Schley, Sr. (1881–1960). Papers, 1904–44. Banker, lawyer, and President of the American–Russian Chamber of Commerce (1923–40). Ca. 5 ft. of the collection pertains to the organization he headed. 25 ft. (MG 870)

Stevens Family. Papers, 1663–1959. In the business correspondence of Colonel John Stevens (roll 19) for 1817 there are documents from his contacts with Tsar Alexander I concerning the possible use of steam frigates and elongated shells in naval warfare with the Turks in the Black Sea. Count Andrew Dashkoff, Russian Minister of the Court of St. James (London), served as intermediary in these discussions. On roll 20 is a reference to "railroads (including the experimental Montagnes Russes)"—which may refer to roller coasters, an amusement item introduced into Russia during Alexander's reign. 60 ft. (microfilmed in 46 reels). (MG 409)

William Turk. Papers, 1824–33. Naval surgeon. His journal pertains in part to a voyage aboard the U.S.S. Concord (under Matthew Perry's command), taking John Randolph (1773–1833) to St. Petersburg to take up his duties as Minister Extraordinary to the Imperial Russian Court. The ship departed Portsmouth, New Hampshire, in 1830. 61 items. (MG 182)

Edward H. Wright. Correspondence, 1850–51. U.S. Secretary of Legation at St. Petersburg. Several letters in typescript copies, written to his family in Newark when he was serving in Russia. (MG 637)

CATALOGS   Card catalog.

BIBLIOGRAPHY *Calendars of Manuscript Collections in New Jersey* [Variant title: "Calendar of the Stevens Family Papers . . ."]. Newark: The Historical Records Survey, 1940–. 2 v.; Fred Shelley. *A Guide to the Manuscripts Collection of the New Jersey Historical Society.* Newark: [New Jersey Historical Society], 1957. [84] p.; The Edward H. Wright letters were published in *Proceedings of the New Jersey Historical Society* 82 (1964): 75–100, 153–79, 241–71; Miriam V. Studley, Charles F. Cummings, and Thaddeus J. Krom, ed. *Microfilm Edition of the Stevens Family Papers in the New Jersey Historical Society—Guide.* Newark: [New Jersey Historical Society], 1968. 32 p. See Grant & Brown, p. 274.

N5
THE NEW ROCHELLE HISTORICAL ASSOCIATION

983 North Avenue
New Rochelle, NY 10804

Mrs. M. A. Richardson
Curator

TELEPHONE   914 632–5376

SCHEDULE   No schedule reported.

ACCESS   Permission may be obtained to use the collection, by
                 appointment only.

FACILITIES   Reading room; photocopying and photography permit-
                 ted.

HOLDINGS   The purpose of the collection is to document the history of Westchester County, the work and life of Thomas Paine, and the
Huguenot origins of New Rochelle. There is only one item pertaining to
Russia: the diary of Peter Alexander Allaire, which is part of a collection of
documents relating to the Allaire family of New Rochelle. The diary includes a description of his visit to Russia in 1774.

CATALOGS   No catalogs reported.

BIBLIOGRAPHY   See Grant & Brown, p. 288 (not reproduced here).

N6
NEW YORK ACADEMY OF MEDICINE
LIBRARY

2 East 103rd Street
New York, NY 10029

Ms. Anne Pascarelli
Associate Librarian

TELEPHONE   212 876–8200

SCHEDULE   Mon–Sat 9:00 a.m.–5:00 p.m. (Services cease at 4:00

p.m.) Rare Book and History of Medicine Collections closed on Saturdays. Library is closed Saturdays June through August.

ACCESS   Open to public for reading and reference only. Appointment needed for Rare Book and History of Medicine Collections. Reading room; reproduction performed in-house in accordance with copyright regulations.

HISTORY   Established 1847 as private association of physicians. Since 1967, has served as a referral center for medicine and certain allied health fields in the New York State interlibrary loan network. Headquarters for the Greater Northeastern Regional Medical Library Program.

HOLDINGS   Monograph and serial publications pertaining to Russian medicine in Russian and English language. Original Russian materials date from early 19th century to the present. Size: unable to determine for this survey.

SPECIAL   Original and early translations of works by Pavlov and
FEATURES   his contemporaries.

CATALOGS   New York Academy of Medicine. Library. *Author Catalog*. Boston: G.K. Hall, 1969. 43v.; idem. *Subject Catalog*. Boston: G.K. Hall, 1969. 34v. (also supplements through 1974); idem. *Illustration Catalog*. 2d ed., enl. Boston: G.K. Hall, 1965. 237 p. [1st. ed. 1960]; idem. *Portrait Catalog*. Boston: G.K. Hall, 1960. 5v. (also supplements 1–3, through 1975); idem. *Catalog of Biographies*. Boston: G.K. Hall, 1960. 165 p. LS/2000 on-line catalog available to the public.

BIBLIOGRAPHY   No bibliography reported.

N7
NEW YORK CITY MUNICIPAL ARCHIVES
DEPARTMENT OF RECORDS AND INFORMATION SERVICES

31 Chambers Street, Room 103
New York, NY 10007

Kenneth R. Cobb
Reference Archivist

TELEPHONE   212 566–5292

SCHEDULE   Mon–Fri 9:00 a.m.–4:30 p.m.

ACCESS   Open to the public.

FACILITIES   Reading room; photocopying and photography permitted.

HOLDINGS   Historic records of government of the City of New York. There are no collections directly pertaining to the Russian Empire/USSR; however, correspondence may be found within the archives to and from individuals and organizations relating to Russia and the USSR. Collections are under the following headings: Almshouse, 1758–1953; Assessed Valuation of Real Estate, 1789–1975; Brooklyn Bridge, 1867–1938; Department of Buildings, 1866–1975; City Council, 1647–1977; Coroner, 1823–1918; Courts, 1808–1935; District Attorneys, ca. 1800–1951; Genealogy, 1795–1956; Mayors, 1849–present; "Old Towns," 1663–1898; Department of Parks, 1850–1960; Photographs, 1889–1956; WNYC, 1936–1981; W.P.A. Federal Writers' Project (NYC Unit), 1936–1943.

CATALOGS   There are "finding aids" for individual collections. Users work with a staff archivist in using the "finding aids."

BIBLIOGRAPHY   Barbara Kronman. *NYPIRG'S Guide to N.Y.C. Public Records*. New York: New York Public Interest Research Group, Inc., 1975.

N8
NEW-YORK HISTORICAL SOCIETY
LIBRARY

170 Central Park West
New York, NY 10024

Jean Ashton
Assistant Librarian for Public Services

TELEPHONE   212 873–3400 Ext. 265

Thomas J. Dunnings, Jr.
Curator of Manuscripts

TELEPHONE   212 873–3400 Ext. 224

Wendy J. Shadwell
Curator of the Print Room

TELEPHONE   212 873–3400, Ext. 257

SCHEDULE　　　　Tues–Sat 10:00 a.m.–5:00 p.m.; Summer: Mon–Fri
10:00 a.m.–5:00 p.m.

ACCESS　　　　Open to the public; non-members pay a fee of $1.00
daily for use of the Library. Graduate students and other scholars are admitted to the Manuscript Department upon approval of its curators.

FACILITIES　　　Reading rooms; photography, photocopying and microfilming are done at cost; fee for these services must be paid at the time the order is placed. The Library will refuse to photoduplicate any item likely to be damaged in the process. There is a room available for those using typewriters.

HOLDINGS　　　The library contains over half a million books and pamphlets. Its great strength is in the field of American history, broadly defined. An extensive pamphlet collection begins with the Colonial and Revolutionary periods and continues through the Civil War. The history of 20th-century New York—the City, the State as a whole, and the local communities within the State—is collected as comprehensively as possible. Thousands of items are preserved in addition to formal histories of all kinds, official documents, directories, guide books, and the publications of patriotic, political, religious and cultural organizations. The Library has the fourth largest collection of original issues of newspapers published in the United States before 1820; a specialty is New York City newspapers. There is also a strong collection of periodicals designed for research in most phases of American history up to the 20th century; the library has complete files of publications of most historical societies and currently receives the journals of virtually all of the regional and state historical societies in the United States.

　　While the Library does not have much in Cyrillic, it does have monographs on Russia spanning the 16th to 20th centuries. Some examples are:

　　J.B. Scherer. *Histoire Raisoneé du Commerce de la Russie.* Paris, 1788;

　　John Bell. *Travels from St. Petersburgh in Russia, to Various Parts of Asia.* London, 1788;

　　R. Eden. *The History of Trauayle in the West and East Indies, and Other Countries Lying eyther way . . . as Moscouia. . . .* London, 1577, &c.;

　　Joseph Florimond, duc de Loubat. *Narrative of the Mission to Russia, 1866, of the Hon. Gustavus Vasa Fox, Assistant-Secretary of the Navy. From the Journal and notes of J.F. Loubat.* New York, 1873.

　　Other works include a 19th-century *sluzhebnaia kniga* in Old Church Slavonic given by Bishop Nicholas of Alaska and the Aleutians to Isabelle Hapgood in 1896, who was preparing a translation into liturgical English for the Russian church (see also her ALS for receipt of the book; she donated it to the Society after she was finished with it); a 16th-century edition of Baron Sigismund Herberstein's travels to Muscovy; an account of Andrei Ia. Dashkov's reception at Georgetown for a celebration of Alexander I's victory over Napoleon, arranged by the president of the United States; an account of Nicholas I's death, officially translated and sanctioned for the English-speaking world; *Struggling Russia*, a weekly magazine put out by the Russian Information Bureau in New York, 1919–1920. There are also subject entries for: The Russian Fleet—Navy history; Foreign Relations—with Great Britain and other countries; The Revolution of 1917; Russian America; Russia's Hawaiian adventure; Russian Mennonites; and at least one entry on Russian wood engraving.

Items in the manuscript collection, including those listed in Grant & Brown are:

William Bainbridge (1774–1833). Papers, 1800–33, Naval officer. Includes material relating to his stay in Russia in 1811. Ca. 100 items.

George Bliss (1830–1897). Lawyer. His autobiography, typed, describes his 1846 trip to Russia and Western Europe. 3 volumes.

The Bradish Papers. A letter from Luther Bradish to Washington Irving, October 1825(?), in which Bradish promises to smuggle Irving's "new book" in to the Russian Empress.

Neill S. Brown. U.S. minister to Russia. ALS, October 25, 1850, from him to A.O.P. Nicholson, describing St. Petersburg and Moscow, the weather, and their people.

George Washington Campbell (1769–1848). Correspondence, 1808–20. U.S. secretary of the treasury, minister to Russia in the reign of Alexander I. Letters to Albert Gallatin discuss Russian affairs. 14 items.

Luigi Palmer di Cesnola (1832–1904). Correspondence, 1870–73. Archeologist. Typewritten copies of letters exchanged between Cesnola, the Imperial Hermitage Museum, and the Museum's agents, all concerning archeological matters, primarily Cesnola's excavations on Cyprus. A proposed sale of a Cypriot collection and some other Mediterranean art objects to the Hermitage did not materialize. 50 items.

George Coggleshall (1784–1861). Life and voyages, 1799–1846. Includes account of his stay in Riga during the winter of 1810–11. 2 volumes.

Francis Dana (1743–1811). Correspondence, 1778–87. 21 items. Diplomat and jurist, U.S. minister to Russia. Drafts of 11 letters he wrote to Robert R. Livingston while in Russia, 1781–83, some quite lengthy. Livingston was secretary for foreign affairs. 10 other letters, 1778–87.

William Darlington (1782–1863). Papers, ca. 1800–63. Physician and botanist. Among his correspondents was Professor Fischer of St. Petersburg, with whom he exchanged 5 letters, 1800–63. Ca. 3,300 items.

Admiral D.G. Farragut (1801–1870). A facsimile letter signed by Simon Stevens et al., Committee regarding a proposition that 250 gentlemen present to the Emperor of Russia the painting by William Page representing Admiral Farragut . . . in token of American appreciation of sympathy manifested by the Russian government and the people during the Civil War. Dated, New York 1869.

Gustavus Vasa Fox (1821–1883). Papers, 1841–83. Assistant Secretary of the Navy. Traveled to Europe and Russia in 1866. Includes his diary for the time he was in the Russian Empire, plus related documents. 8 ft. (NUCMC 60–2751)

Robert Fulton (1765–1815). A portfolio of pen-and-ink drawings executed and signed by Fulton and presented to Augustin de Betancourt, an officer in the corps of engineers in Russia.

Albert Gallatin (1761–1849). Papers. Statesman and diplomat. In 1813 he served as U.S. envoy to St. Petersburg to negotiate peace with England under Russian mediation. Includes letters from George W. Campbell, minister to Russia, November 6, 1818 and October 26, 1819. Other correspondents, primarily 1780–1849, were: John Quincy Adams, John Jacob Astor, Andre de Dashkoff, Comte N.P. de Romanzoff, and Madam de Stael (at one time an exile in Russia). The materials discuss European affairs, Polish relief in 1834, and an American–Russian commercial treaty, 1813–14. 28 ft. and 17 volumes.

Maltby Gelston. Collection, 1806–10. New York notary public. Book of protests (37 in all) made by ships' masters arriving in New York. Protests record details of voyages and damage to ship and cargo. Some relate to Cronstadt (Marine Protests). 1 volume.

Levett Harris. Correspondence, 1804–19. U.S. consular official in St. Petersburg. Primarily letters to or from Albert Gallatin, secretary of the treasury in 1802–14. Most date from 1813–14. 12 items.

Charles Heartmann. Collection, 1770s–1870s. Includes 3 letters exchanged between Karl Robert Nesselrode, Russian foreign minister, and William Pinkney, U.S. minister to Russia, ca. January 1817, concerning a crime of theft. Ca. 4,000 items.

Hendricks Family. Papers, ca. 1790–1938. Includes papers of Harmon Hendricks (1771–1838), a New York merchant and copper entrepreneur. His business correspondence, office files, and account books, late 1790s–early 1800s, reveal aspects of his trade in Russian linen and sheeting. Ca. 12 ft. and 30 volumes.

Isaac Hicks (1767–1820). Papers, 1791–1808. Quaker merchant. Correspondence and other items relate to his trade dealings with Russia in 1799 and 1803–1806. Ca. 30 ft. and ca. 40 volumes.

Wickham Hoffman (1821–1900). Papers, 1863–66. Army officer and diplomat. Contains a translation of the memoirs of the Countess Choiseul-

Gouffier, which have been published in English, 1900, about Alexander I and the Russian court. Ca. 40 items.

Christopher Hughes (1786–1849). Correspondence, 1815–27. Diplomat. Letters from Stockholm and Brussels, mostly to Albert Gallatin. References to Russia. 21 items.

Rufus King (1755–1827). Papers, 1785–1826. American statesman and diplomat, minister to Great Britain in 1796–1803 and 1825–26. Includes correspondence concerning the 1799 commercial treaty negotiations (abortive) and letters to him from Joseph A. Smith in Russia. 12 ft. and ca. 66 volumes.

Randall J. LeBoeuf, Jr. (1897–1975). Robert Fulton Collection, 1764–1857. Includes letter, February 24, 1810, from Fulton to Andre de Dashkoff; letter, July 26, 1812, from Fulton to Chevalier Svinin about the development of Fulton's steamboats in Russia; and letter, July 28, 1815, from John Q. Adams to Levett Harris in St. Petersburg enclosing a letter from William Cutting, Fulton's executor, asking that Fulton's grant for constructing steamboats in Russia be confirmed for the benefit of his family. Ca. 215 items.

John Ledyard (1751–1789). Papers, 1772–91. Explorer, traveler in Siberia. Includes 6 letters to Thomas Jefferson concerning his explorations. 22 items.

Robert R. Livingston Family. Papers, ca. 1685–1885. Primarily papers of Robert R. Livingston (1746–1818), member of the Continental Congress and secretary of the Department of Foreign Affairs. Includes instructions to Francis Dana as minister to Russia, 1781–83, and related items. Ca. 65 ft. and 100+ volumes.

Henry C. McLean (1887–1955). Diaries, 1940–45. U.S. army intelligence officer. First volume, February–June 1940, includes comments on the attitude of Asians toward the U.S., Britain, Russia, etc. 4 volumes.

John Stevenson Maxwell (1817–1870). Correspondence and miscellaneous papers covering the period 1830–1863. Includes 70 letters to his parents, Mr. and Mrs. Hugh Maxwell, 1842–1846, mostly while serving as Secretary of the U.S. Legation in St. Petersburg, Russia.

Hoyt and Meacham Families. Correspondence, 1830–70. Includes some correspondence, 1860s, from Timothy Smith in Odessa, Russia. Ca. 700 items.

Miscellaneous Manuscripts: Vibbard, Chauncy. A letter from Vibbard to W.H. Seward concerning financial difficulties with Russia (1868?).

Naval History Society. Generic, not integral, collection. Includes an ALS, October 12, 1839, to James Barnes from George Washington Whistler, introducing a Colonel Melnikov of the Russian engineers.

George Newbold (d. 1858). Papers, 1801–58. Merchant and banker. Includes some letters from Charles S. Todd in St. Petersburg. Ca. 2,900 items and 19 volumes.

Jonathan Ogden. Business records, 1800–1824. Merchant. Letterbook for

September 1811–April 1817 includes frequent correspondence with Vincent Lassalette in St. Petersburg. Ca. 9 volumes. Available on microfilm.

David Parish (d. 1826). Letterbooks, 1802–16. Merchant. Among his correspondents were the Brothers Cramer in St. Petersburg. 7 volumes.

Joel Root (b. 1770). Seaman. An account of his sealing voyage to St. Petersburg, etc. and return, 1802–1806. 1 volume.

Russian Fleet in New York. Collection, 1863. Letters from public officials, military officers and leading citizens, responding to invitations issued by a reception committee to accompany an admiral and officers of the Russian fleet on a trip from New York City to Niagara Falls. Addressed to Watts Sherman, Daniel Drew, and J.C. Bancroft Davis, members of the committee. 50 items.

T.P. Shaffner (1818–1881). A letter from Shaffner who secured the Fulton portfolio from the estate of a nephew of Betancourt and presented it to the New-York Historical Society. Other letters from Shaffner are in the Naval History Society and James Barnes collection and written to James Barnes in 1858, regarding an arrangement to deliver railroad iron (rails) to the Russian government.

Gulian Crommelin Verplanck (1786–1870). Correspondence received, ca. 1805–57, and other papers, early-18th–mid-19th centuries. Author, politician, lawyer, and reformer. Includes 9 letters, 1829–31, from Secretary of State Martin Van Buren to the U.S. Minister to Russia. Correspondence, ca. 2,000 items; other papers, ca. 900 items.

Edward Wyer. Letterbook, 1813–16 and correspondence, 1825–38. American consul in the port of Riga, September 1813–March 1816. Contains copies of letters he wrote during this period. They touch on such questions as debt settlements, difficulties in obtaining passage to the U.S., his low opinion of Russians (and of Levett Harris, U.S. Charge d'Affaires in St. Petersburg), his brief partnership with a St. Petersburg merchant named John Venning, and other personal matters, especially his complaints and animosities. Correspondents include Harris, James Monroe, John Graham, John D. Lewis, Henry Clay, various naval officers, friends at home, and people in Europe.

The Print Room reports the following holdings of photographs: Exterior photograph of the Russian–American Line, Broadway, ca. 1916; photographs of Russian gypsies, part of the Alland Photography Collection; an album relating to the Russian Ball at the New York Academy of Music, 1863; lithograph of Russian baths, New York City, ca. 1878–79; wood engravings of Russian Mennonite settlement in Kansas, 1875; Russian Orthodox Church, East 93rd Street, designed 1917–28.

CATALOGS   The Library has a dictionary card catalog, which includes periodicals. Special collections—music, broadsides, rare imprints, anti-slavery, naval history, Seventh Regiment, etc.—are catalogued separately. Newspapers are also catalogued separately, alphabetically by state, by town within the state, and by title. The Society is a member of RLIN (AMC subsystem since its inception in 1984; only about 500–600 records are on line). The Manuscript Room has a pre-1984 catalog of typed cards arranged by names, collections, and subjects. There is also a new catalog for cards generated by AMC, beginning May 1984.

BIBLIOGRAPHY *Collections of the New-York Historical Society,* 1869–1973, a Publication Fund Series, describes many of the manuscript collections in detail; *New-York Historical Society Quarterly.* New York, 1917–1980; Arthur J. Breton. *A Guide to the Manuscript Collections of the New York Historical Society.* Westport, CT: Greenwood Press, 1972. 2v.; *The United States and Russia: The Beginning of Relations, 1765–1815.* Editors Nina N. Bashkina . . . [et al.; prepared under the direction of a joint Soviet–American editorial board, David F. Trask . . . et al.]. Washington, DC: U.S. Govt. Print. Off., 1980. 1,184 p.; The New-York Historical Society. *Welcome to the Library.* Undated, unpaged brochure. See Grant & Brown, pp. 361–363.

N9
NEW YORK LIFE INSURANCE COMPANY
RESEARCH CENTER/ARCHIVES

51 Madison Avenue
New York, NY 10010

David S. Sanders
Senior Research Associate

TELEPHONE   212 576–6738

SCHEDULE   Mon–Fri 9:00 a.m.–5:00 p.m.

ACCESS   Open by appointment only to qualified researchers with advance permission.

FACILITIES   Reading room; photocopying available. Permission required to photograph.

HOLDINGS   The collection was described as follows in Grant & Brown:

Company Archives total ca. 500 ft. of material, of which about 34 ft. are Russian-related. Records of the company's business in Russia, 1883–ca. 1935, include correspondence, policy forms, premium history cards, accounts for Russian branch office, Russian account books, claims and policy settlements, claims against the USSR and other litigation. Also, records relating to the Russian government's regulation and taxation of insurance.

The Archives reports that there has been no material relating to the Russian empire or Soviet Union added since the Grant & Brown report.

CATALOGS   Limited access.

BIBLIOGRAPHY   See Grant & Brown, p. 363.

N10
NEW YORK PUBLIC LIBRARY
BERG COLLECTION

Fifth Avenue and 42nd Street
New York, NY 10018

Lola L. Szladits
Chief

TELEPHONE   212 930–0802

SCHEDULE   Mon–Wed, Fri–Sat 10:00 a.m.–5:45 p.m.

ACCESS   Open by card of admission from the Office of Special Collections (Room 316) to those engaged in scholarly research.

FACILITIES   Reading room.

HOLDINGS   While the collection is concerned solely with English and American literature, there are a few items of interest to users of this guide. One consists of the manuscripts of Parts I, III, and IV of Joseph Conrad's *Poland Revisited*. Grant & Brown list the others:

Russia. Foreign Office. Diplomatic passport issued at St. Petersburg 24 October 1896, to Norman Douglas, secretary of the British embassy, 2 pp.

Ivan Sergeevich Turgenev (1818–1883). Russian author. ALS to George Eliot, Paris, 25 February 1874, 1 l.; and ALS, Spasskoie (Orel province, Uzensk village), 20/8 May 1880, also to George Eliot, 1 p. Both have been published.

CATALOGS   Author catalog in alphabetical order. *Dictionary Cata-*

log of the Henry W. and Albert A. Berg Collection of English and American Literature. Boston: G.K. Hall, 1969. 5v.

BIBLIOGRAPHY   Lola Szladits. *Brothers: The Origins of the Henry W. and Albert A. Berg Collection of English and American Literature, The New York Public Library*. New York: New York Public Library, 1985. 76 p. See Grant & Brown, p. 363.

N11
NEW YORK PUBLIC LIBRARY
JEWISH DIVISION

Fifth Avenue and 42nd Street
New York, NY 10018–2788

Leonard Gold
Chief

TELEPHONE   212 930–0601

SCHEDULE   Mon, Wed, Fri, Sat 10:00 a.m.–6:00 p.m.; Tues 10:00 a.m.–9:00 p.m.

ACCESS   Open to the public.

FACILITIES   Reading Room. Photocopying and photographing based on condition of material.

HISTORY   The Jewish Division was established as a distinct collection with funding contributed by Jacob Schiff in 1897, just two years after the formation of The New York Public Library. The Library's foundation for collections on Jewish subjects in Hebrew and other languages was provided by holdings from the Astor and Lenox libraries. This existing nucleus was quickly expanded by the acquisition of the private libraries of Leon Mandelstamm, scholar and educator, who served as secretary to the Russian government commission established to draw up an educational system for Jews, Meyer Lehren, and Isaac Meyer, as well as some holdings of the Aguilar Free Library, a small public library system operated by a group of philanthropic Jews in the 19th century that merged with The New York Public Library in 1903. By the early 1900s the Jewish Division already rivaled the oldest and best Jewish libraries in Europe. In subsequent years the Division continued to grow by purchases, gifts of books, and contributions of funds. Today the Jewish Division contains a comprehensive and balanced chronicle of the religious and secular history of the Jewish people in over a quarter of a million books, microforms, manuscripts, newspapers, periodicals, and ephemera from all over the world.

HOLDINGS   The Jewish Division is uniquely constituted as both a subject and a language division. While the collection offers commentary on all aspects of Jewish life, it also includes Hebrew- and Yiddish-language texts on general subjects. Thus, the Division's mandate carries it far beyond the bounds of the Russian Empire and Soviet Union. About forty percent of the Division's holdings are in Hebrew characters (Hebrew, Yiddish, Ladino, etc.) and the remainder are in other languages, primarily English, German, Russian, and French. The Division is especially strong in bibliographies and reference works, Jewish Americana, history and social studies, Kabbalistic and Hasidic works, texts by Christian hebraists, rabbinic responsa, Hebrew and Yiddish literature, and periodicals and newspapers.

In addition to early, rare monograph material published in Poland in the 17th and 18th centuries, covering commentaries, essays, and histories in Hebrew, there are also Hebrew and Yiddish titles for the 19th and 20th centuries, including Yiddish literature published in Soviet Russia in the 1920s and 1930s. Works by Simon Dubnow, *History of the Jews in Russia and Poland* (Philadelphia, 1916–20); Bernard D. Weinryb, *The Jews of Poland: A Social and Economic History ... from 1100 to 1800* (Philadelphia, 1973); *Historja i literatura zydowska*, 3 v. (Lwow, 1924–25); *Zabytki historyczne zydow w Polsce* (Warsaw, 1929) are examples. Unusual is a journal published under the monarchy called *Evrei na Voinie*, and a rare work against the Whites published in Moscow in 1926 by Zalman Solomonovich Ostrovskii, *Evreiskie pogromy, 1918–1921*. Virtually the whole of the Division's pamphlet collection has been filmed, as well as hundreds of popular Yiddish novels published in Vilna, Warsaw, and New York at the turn of the century.

There are about 3 drawers in the shelf list covering the history of Jews in Russia, Jews in Poland, and listing such topics as agriculture, anti-semitism, concentration camps, economics, histories of Jews in various regions (Bessarabia, Byelorussia, Latvia, Poland, Ukraine, etc.), Jewish Khazars, legal status in Russia, pogroms, schools, and Zionism, among others. There is also coverage for Jews in North and South America. This is in addition to periodicals and microforms, literary works, rabbinics, etc.

The Library received 300 Yiddish manuscripts from Harry Thomashevsky in 1940 representing the collection of Boris Thomashevsky, a leading actor and producer of Yiddish plays in New York City. The collection includes works by Thomashevsky, Leon Kobrin, Joseph Lateiner, Osip Dymov and others, and includes some 150 plays, and scenarios performed primarily in the New York Yiddish theatre. Also included were classic Yiddish authors, such as Shalom Jacob Abramowitsch, Isaac Loeb Perez and Sholom

Aleichem. Some of this material, as is the case with other collections, has been dispersed throughout the Library.

Perhaps the most important resource for insight into the turbulent history of the Jews in 19th and 20th centuries is the extensive collection of newspapers and periodicals printed in Europe and America in the last two centuries. Publications printed in Central and Eastern Europe, many in German, Polish, Russian, Hungarian, and Czech, describe the day-to-day cultural, religious, and social events in the lives of the once-flourishing Jewish communities. Rare publications printed for the communities of Jewish immigrants within America's cities document the conditions facing the newly arrived. In many cases, the Library's issues are the only extant copies. Periodicals on microfilm include titles in Hebrew, Yiddish and Russian from Russia and Poland, such as *Ha-Meliz* (Odessa, 1860–1904); *Jutrzenka. Tygodnik dla izraelitów polskich* (Warsaw, 1861–1863); *Izraelita. Pismo tygodniowe* (Warsaw, 1866–1913); *Razsviet* (St. Petersburg, 1879–1881); *Russkii Yevrei* (St. Petersburg, 1879–1884); *Voskhod* (St. Petersburg, 1886–1906); *Yevreiskaya biblioteka* (St. Petersburg, 1871–1903); *Di Yidishe Folksbibliotek* (Kiev, 1888–1889); *Ahiasaf* (Warsaw, 1893–1923); *Ha-Goren* (Berdychev, 1898–1928); *Budushchnost'* (St. Petersburg, 1900–1904); *Der Fraind* (St. Petersburg, 1903–1913); *Ha-zman* (St. Petersburg, 1903–1914); *Perezhitoye* (St. Petersburg, 1909–1913); *Razsviet* (St. Petersburg, 1907–1913); *Sefer ha-shanah* (Warsaw, 1900–1906); *Yevreiskii mir* (St. Petersburg, 1909–1911); *Haynt* (Warsaw, 1914–19, 1923–39); *He-'avar* (Petrograd, 1917–1918); *Jedność. Organ żydów polskich* (Lwow, 1910–1911); *Yevreiskaya zhizn'* (Moscow, 1915–1917); *Emes* (Moscow, 1921–1935); *Af di Vegn zu der neier Shul* (Moscow 1924–28); *Oktiabr* (Minsk, 1926–1935); *Ratnbildung* (Kharkov, 1928–1936); *Yevreiskaya letopis'* (Petrograd, 1923–1926). There is also a hard copy and film of *Hamagid* (Lyck, Berlin, Cracow, 1856–1903), the first Hebrew newspaper.

SPECIAL FEATURES   The Division possesses an excellent collection of memorial or *Yizkor* books, works which deal with a specific locality in Eastern Europe. These volumes, assembled by survivors and emigres of communities liquidated by the Nazis, give a full account of the employment, customs, and lifestyles of people in a world that is no more. The maps, illustrations, and commentary contained in the *Yizkor* book are often the only trace remaining of entire communities and have wide historical value.

CATALOGS   *Dictionary Catalog of the Jewish Collection*. Boston: G.K. Hall, 1960. 14v. Also, Supplement 1. Boston, G.K. Hall, 1975. 8v. *Hebrew-Character Title Catalog of the Jewish Collection*. Boston: G.K. Hall, 1981, 4 v. Finding aids include extensive cross index by subject, geographical origins, etc. Material cataloged after 1971 is listed in the *Dictionary Catalog* *of The Research Libraries*, an automated book catalog, and its supplements, and records are available on- line through the RLIN and CATNYP bibliographic facilities. There are also finding aids for the periodicals on microfilm and the *Yizkor* collection.

BIBLIOGRAPHY   Leonard Gold. "New York Public Library. Judaica." In *East Central and Southeast Europe: A Handbook of Library and Archival Resources in North America*, pp. 337–346. Edited by Paul L. Horecky and David H. Kraus. Santa Barbara, CA: Clio Press, [1976]; The New York Public Library. "Jewish Division," [1988]. Unpaginated brochure.

N12
NEW YORK PUBLIC LIBRARY
MIRIAM AND IRA D. WALLACH DIVISION OF
ART, PRINTS AND PHOTOGRAPHS

ART AND ARCHITECTURE COLLECTION

Room 313
Fifth Avenue and 42nd Street
New York, NY 10018

Paul A. Baxter
Chief

TELEPHONE   212 930–0834

SCHEDULE   Mon, Wed, Fri–Sat 10:00 a.m.–5:45 p.m.; Tues 10:00 a.m.–8:45 p.m.

ACCESS   Open to the public. Restrictions apply to access of rare, unique, or fragile materials.

FACILITIES   Reading room, open-shelf reference section. Materials paged from closed stacks at reader's request.

HOLDINGS   Book and periodical collection of over 200,000 volumes. Materials on fine and visual arts from prehistoric to contemporary periods. Russian material in English and Western European languages held in the collection number about 400 items. Material in Cyrillic is held in the SLAVIC AND BALTIC DIVISION. Materials on Russian art include monographs, exhibition catalogs and books on individual artists. Strong holdings in Russian paintings, decorative and folk arts.

CATALOGS   Book catalog of Art and Architecture Collection holdings. On-line access to post-1972 published materials via CATNYP (on-line
catalog of New York Public Library).

BIBLIOGRAPHY   *Bibliographic Guide to Art and Architecture*. 1975–. Boston: G.K. Hall, 1976–, annual.

N13
NEW YORK PUBLIC LIBRARY
MIRIAM AND IRA D. WALLACH DIVISION
OF ART, PRINTS AND PHOTOGRAPHS

PHOTOGRAPHIC COLLECTION

Room 308
Fifth Avenue and 42nd Street
New York, NY 10018

Julia Van Haaften
Curator

TELEPHONE   212 930–0837

SCHEDULE   Mon–Wed, Fri, Sat 1:00 p.m.–5:45 p.m.

ACCESS   Open by card of admission from the Office of Special
               Collections (Room 316).

FACILITIES   Reading room; photocopying and photography not
               permitted.

HOLDINGS   Consists of 19th-century books and albums of photos.
One item relating to Russia: *European Russia: Portraits, Cities and Villages,
Street Scenes and Country Views, Ethnic and Occupational Types*. Album of
pictures collected by George Kennan. [St. Petersburg, etc. 188–]. Photos. 33
cm. (Mounted and bound by NYPL, 1936.)

CATALOGS   There is a photographers' file available.

BIBLIOGRAPHY   No bibliography reported.

N14
NEW YORK PUBLIC LIBRARY
MIRIAM AND IRA D. WALLACH DIVISION OF
ART, PRINTS AND PHOTOGRAPHS

PRINTS

Room 308
Fifth Avenue and 42nd Street
New York, NY 10018

Roberta Waddell
Curator

TELEPHONE   212 930–0817

SCHEDULE   Mon–Wed, Fri–Sat 1:00 p.m.–6:00 p.m.

ACCESS   Open by card of admission from the Office of Special
                Collections (Room 316).

FACILITIES   Reading Room. No photocopying allowed except for
clipping files; photography permitted depending on condition of print or
book. No flashes can be used.

HOLDINGS   Collection of 180,000 original prints and, selectively, illustrated books, which survey the history of printmaking. Reference books
on the graphic arts include the history of printmaking, monographs on
printmakers, books on technique, on illustrated books, cartoons and caricature. Russian material includes a small collection of late 19th- and 20th-
century prints including some Russian material in reproductive prints; Imagerie Populaire (reproduction of some cards in catalog); Russian material,
approximately 100 prints. Political lithographs by Kasimir Malevich, from
1914–15.
    Grant & Brown list the following "Original graphic material":
    Alexander Archipenko (1887–1964). Lithographs: portfolio entitled
Dreizehn Steinzeichnungen (Berlin, 1921), no. 59 of 60 printed, with artist's
autograph (1 l., 12 plates); and "Figuerliche Komposition."
    Nick Bervinchak (20th c.; Ukrainian). 2 etchings: "Employed" (1940) and
"Reflections" (1940).
    Caricatures. Russian cartoons from the Napoleonic era; a few items.
(Caricatures arranged chronologically by country.)
    Mykola Butovych (1895–1961; Ukrainian). 2 woodcuts(?): cover for the

women's magazine *Nova Khata* (1932, no. 5) and bookplate for M. Khomyn, M.D.

Eugene I. Charushin (b. 1901). Lithograph: "Crow" (1938), in color.

Mstislav Dobuzhinski (1875–1957). Lithuanian extraction. Original drawings: 2 illustrations for "The Steel Flea . . ." of Nikolai Leskov, in pencil, unsigned (1943); and 2 illustrations to the *Wonder Book* by Nathaniel Hawthorne, in pencil, not signed (1949).

Nataliya Sergeyevna Goncharova (1881–1962). Portfolio of 14 lithographs—*Misticheskiye obrazy voiny* (V. N. Kasin, Moscow, 1914), with yellow board cover and title page. Subjects include Saints George the Victorious and Alexander Nevskii, The White Eagle, The English Lion, The French Rooster, Angels and Airplanes, The Condemned City, Archangel Michael, Christian Soldiers, The Pale Horse, and Mass Grave.

Yakiv (Jacques) Hnizdovsky (b. 1915). Ukrainian. 16 woodcuts, including 10 bookplates (for Jean Thiebault, W. E. Holiyan, I. W. Manastyrsky, Ihor Kostetzky, N. and I. Ivakhniuk, Bohdan Kravtsiv, and the Ukrainian Free Academy), a book cover with scribe, 3 items from 1944 (a study of trees, an old man, and "Youth and old age"), "The Cat" (1968), and "Great Horned Owl" (1973).

George Sviatoslav Hordynsky (b. 1906). Ukrainian. 2 woodcut covers for the women's magazine *Nova Khata*, 1935–37, and a bookplate for R. G. Berezovsky.

Vytautas Kazys Jonynas (b. 1907). Lithuanian. 1 lithograph, "Bacharach on the Rhine" (1951), in color; and 4 woodcuts: "L'Étoile de l'Amour" (1951), a Christmas scene; "The Shepherds in the Field" (1949); "Saint Antoine" (1950), artist's proof; and "Fifth Avenue, N.Y." (1957).

Anatoli Lvovich Kaplan (b. 1902). 2 lithographs: "The Village of Anatovka" (1961) and "Man of Air (1957/61).

K. A. Klenenteva (b. 1897). A lithograph entitled "Funeral Procession of S. M. Kirov, December 3, 1934" (1934).

Moissey Kogan. 5 linoleum cuts: "Tanzende in langem Gewand" (1922); 2 kneeling figures, "Thais," Greek deity with deer, and 2 standing nudes, all 192–?

Myron Levytsky (b. 1913). Ukrainian. 5 bookplates (woodcuts): for M. Denysiuk, Tetyana Mohylnytska, M. K. Levytska, Ilse Fumanelli, and O. Mokh.

Karin Luts-Arumaa. Lithographs: Portrait of Gustav Suits, Estonian poet and literary historian (1943), and 3 illustrations for the poems of Betti Alver, "Art and Life," 1944.

Antin Maliutsa (1908–1970). Ukrainian. 2 etchings: of a steeple in the Carpathian Mountains and of a wooden church, same locale, both 1946.

Halyna Mazepa (20th c.). Ukrainian. Cover for the women's magazine *Nova Khata*, 1934 (woodcut?).

Nikolai Semionovich Mosolov (1846–1914). Etching.

N. N. Nagorsky. Wood engravings: "Ex libris Eremina" (1923), and 2 theatrical designs (1924).

Alexander (Aleksandr Ossipowitsch) Orlowski (1777–1832). 12 lithographs: battle between Asiatic horsemen and fighters on foot (1829), "Un Voyageur en Quibitka, ou Traineau a trois Chevaux" (1819), 2-horse sleigh with driver and officer passing a sentinel (1820), and 6 pieces from *Collection de dessins lithographies* (1819) in original printed wrapper with Orlowski's signature in ink.

Ivan Padalka (1895–1961). Ukrainian. Woodcut (photostat?) of Cossacks.

Peter Simon Pallas (1741–1811). *Flora Rossica*, n.p., 18th c. 104 original drawings in pencil, ink, and wash, 74 colored, by Karl Friedrich Knappe, and 3 related items.

Eduard Ruega. 2 linoleum cuts, both in color: "Woman with the mirror" (1952); and "Tuedruk lindudega" (Girl with the birds; 1953).

Russkii narodnii lubok 1860-kh–1870-kh gg.; al'bom. Collection of 200 lithographed picture sheets, 33 printed by A. A. Abramov, 21 by I. G. Gavrilov, 31 by I. A. Golyshev of Mstera, 32 by P. A. Glushkov, 26 by A. V. Morozov, and 52 by Ye. Ya. Yakovlev.

Russkii narodnii lubok 1870-ky[sic]–1880-kh gg.; al'bom (Binder's title: Les images nationales de Sitin et Co.). Collection of 62 lithographed picture sheets colored by hand: 41 printed by V. A. Vasil'yev, 12 by A. V. Morozov, and 9 by V. V. Ponomariov.

Gabriel Skorodumov (1748?–1792). Stipple.

Yurii Solovii (Jurij Solovij). 8 linocuts: "Pantocrator," "Princess Yaroslavna," and "Cymbal" from 1950; and "Crucifixion" (2), "Madonna and Child," "Horned Fish," and "Nude" from 1958.

Peter (Piotr) N. Staronosov (b. 1893). Wood engraving (linoleum block print) entitled "Airplane over the Taiga forest, Siberia" (1938), in color.

Vasilieff. Stipple engraving—"Susanna at the bath"—printed in sanguine.

Georgi Vereysky (Georgii Semionovich Vereiski). 2 lithographs, both 1922: "Portrait of the painter Constantin Somoff" and "Constantin Somoff at work before easel."

Arno Vihalemm (b. 1911). Estonian. 2 woodcuts: "Homage to Rilke" (1955) and "Keerub" (Cherub; 1954); 1 lithograph: "Lilith" (1955); and 4 serigraphs in black: illustrations to the short stories of Jaan Oks (1956).

Eduard Wiiralt (1898–1954). Estonian. "Arkeia," a 1938 drypoint; "Berber Girl and Dromedary," etching from 1940; and 2 wood engravings: "Head of a Negro" and "The Absinthe Drinkers" from 1933.

Ossip Zadkine (1890–1967). Woodcut figures; and 3 lithographs: "Le Rêve" (1955), "Trois Personnages" (195–?), and "Les Rois Mages" (1952 or 1953), all in color.

Sergei Zalshupin. 10 linoleum cuts: portraits of Aleksandr Blok and

Andrei Belyi (both 1922); street scene (192–?), signed "Salschupin"; and illustrations for Belyi's *St. Petersburg* (192–?).

Many of the preceding items are signed by the artists. In addition, for individual artists, the division holds clipping files (in envelopes) with such materials as exhibition announcements, dealers' catalogues, reviews, reproductions, and some letters (from or about the artists). Among those for whom there are such files are: A. Archipenko, Ya. Hnizdovsky, V. Jonynas, A. Kaplan, M. Kogan, N. Mosolov, N. Nagorsky, A. Orlowski, Yu. Solovii, G. Vereysky, A. Vihalemm, E. Wiiralt, and O. Zadkine.

CATALOGS   Card catalog and shelf list. G.K. Hall, 1975. 5v; *Dictionary Catalog of the Prints Division.* Boston: See Grant & Brown, pp. 383–385.

BIBLIOGRAPHY   No bibliography reported.

N15
NEW YORK PUBLIC LIBRARY
ORIENTAL DIVISION

Room 219
Fifth Avenue and 42nd Street
New York, NY 10018

John M. Lundquist
Chief

TELEPHONE   212 930–0721

SCHEDULE   Mon, Wed, Fri–Sat 10:00 a.m.–5:45 p.m.; Thur 10:00 a.m.–8:45 p.m.

ACCESS   Open to the public.

FACILITIES   Reading room; photocopying and photography allowed depending on the materials.

HOLDINGS   Some of the non-Slavic languages of the Soviet Union are the collecting responsibility of the Oriental Division: Turko-Tataric, Tungus-Manchu, Mongolic (collectively known as the Altaic languages), Iranian (Tajik, Ossetian), Paleo-Caucasian, Armenian, and Georgian.

The holdings of the Altaic special collections vary and are of potential interest to a broad range of users, from philologists to sovietologists. For the most part, however, they stand apart from the mainstream of the Oriental Division's selection policy. The Division has a double but related focus: to acquire representative scholarly editions of the principal works in the Altaic languages as well as works about them, and to have the principal scholarly periodicals. Since such works are often integrated in scholarly series and journals, an estimate of the number of volumes would be tentative at best. More feasible, on the other hand, is an estimate of the number of works published since 1945 in the Soviet Union. Most of this group is cataloged for Oriental Division stacks, but basic dictionaries and reference works are given a Reading Room reference classmark; however, Russian–Oriental language dictionaries usually go to the SLAVIC AND BALTIC DIVISION reading room. Moreover, the national encyclopedias of the Turkic and Tajik republics (i.e., Azerbaijani, Kazakh, Kirghiz, Tajik, Turkmen, and Uzbek SSRs) have also been cataloged for the SLAVIC AND BALTIC DIVISION. A special feature of this group is the collection of materials from the Soviet Union which, along with pamphlets in other Soviet "minority" languages, was published before 1940. A recently acquired collection of 200 volumes of Kalmuck literature from the Kalmuck ASSR has been cataloged for the Oriental Division.

Regarding Armenian holdings, a strong commitment to building the collection rests upon a foundation laid by the Astor Library. The Cogswell Catalog lists a number of grammars, dictionaries, and other linguistic works dealing with Armenian and published in the 17th–19th centuries. They include a grammar published in Rome in 1675, one by Johann Schroeder published in Amsterdam in 1711, and a number of editions of Armenian and English lexicographical works of Father Mkrtich Awgerian of the Armenian Academy of St. Lazarus in Venice published in the early 19th century. An important publication of this academy is the complete works of the 10th-century mystic Grigorius Narekatsi, published in 1840. Another extraordinary work from Astor is the *Essai sur la langue arménienne* by Bellaud, published in 1812 (Armenian 1261) in Paris by the Imprimerie Imperiale. The Division holds the exceptionally rare *Thesaurus Linguae Armenicae*, by J.J. Schroder, published in 1711 in Amsterdam, the first work by a Western scholar to give a detailed history of the language. Many Bibles and lectionaries in Armenian are present, as well as literary and historical works. There is an ongoing commitment to excellence in this area. The Armenian literature collection is considered one of the best collections in the United States, containing some 720 volumes. Material is acquired on a representative basis. Periodical holdings are strong: *Gotchnag* (New York, 1910–), *Hayrenik* (Boston, 1901–), and literary and popular journals from Armenia as well as the daily newspaper *Sovetakar Hayasdan* can serve as examples. Some 100 items by Armenians in the United States represent the remarkable literary production of a small ethnic group. Other holdings emphasize Bibles and saints' lives.

The Georgian literature collecting policy is representative and holdings were minimal before 1950. There are now about 300 volumes with particular strength in linguistics and belles-lettres, although scientific material is also collected. Editions of Shot'ha Rusthaveli's epic, "The Knight in the Tiger Skin," both in the original and in translation, are a feature of the resources. Additional materials in Georgian received in the 1920s and 1930s are found in the "n.c." (not cataloged) classmark in the SLAVIC AND BALTIC DIVISION (material preserved but not separately cataloged).

CATALOGS   Some of the materials from the Soviet Union form the above-mentioned retrospective collection of pamphlets and books published in the 1920s and 1930s. They were bound in pamphlet volumes and given a SLAVIC AND BALTIC DIVISION classmark. Their status is currently being reviewed in terms of cataloging and preservation. The bulk of the Azerbaijani collection has been cataloged and filmed for the Oriental Division, a procedure likely for the rest of this collection (except for the Finno-Ugrian, German, and other non-oriental languages whose status remains undetermined).

BIBLIOGRAPHY   Edward Allworth. *Central Asian Publishing and the Rise of Nationalism: An Essay and a List of Publications in The New York Public Library.* New York: New York Public Library, 1965; Edward Allworth. *Nationalities of the Soviet East: Publications and Writing Systems. A Bibliographical Directory and Transliteration Tables for Iranian- and Turkic-language Publications, 1818–1945, Located in U.S. Libraries.* New York: Columbia University Press, 1971.

N16
NEW YORK PUBLIC LIBRARY
RARE BOOKS AND MANUSCRIPTS DIVISION

Room 324
Fifth Avenue and 42nd Street
New York, NY 10018

Bernard McTigue
Curator of the Arents Collection and Keeper of Rare Books

TELEPHONE   212 930–0801

SCHEDULE   Mon–Wed, Fri–Sat 10:00 a.m.–5:45 p.m.

ACCESS   Open by card of admission from the Office of Special

Collections (Room 316) to those engaged in scholarly research.

FACILITIES   Reading room. Photocopying or photography depending on material.

HOLDINGS   Of more than one hundred thousand items in the Rare Book Room, only about two hundred are of "Russian" interest. The majority of these would fall into the general subject category of "Description and Travel," e.g., works by Allison, Giovio, Krusenstern, Olearius, Smith, Svinin, etc.

While most examples of Church Slavonic printing are in the SLAVIC AND BALTIC DIVISION, some of the earliest examples are in the Rare Book Room: the New Testament in Church Slavonic, printed in L'viv in 1574; also one from Vilno, 1575; most notable is the "Ostrog" Bible, the first complete Bible printed in Church Slavonic by Ivan Fedorov in 1581.

There are perhaps a dozen works concerned with Russian America, the most interesting of which is Khlebnikov's *Zhizneopisanie . . . Baranova*, printed in 1835. Among broadsides and ephemera there is the occasional Mayakovsky poster or Bolshevik pamphlet. Another unusual item is *Les Solennités du saint couronnement . . . 1899*, a large, lavish souvenir book which, besides illustrating ceremonies and crowned heads, reproduces all the menus from the coronation banquets.

Grant & Brown list the following works:

Ivan Belogonov. [Original water color paintings of Russia, n.p., 1848–56]. 30 mounted colored plates, 29 with manuscript Russian titles, signed by the artist, 23 dated in manuscript. (Call no. *KW)

Decorations of Honor. Includes [charters for] the Russian orders of St. Stanislaus (3), St. Vladimir, Ste. Anne, and the White Eagle.

Fiodor Grigor'yevich Solntsev (1801–1892). 326 water-color illustrations of *Odezhdy russkago gosudarstva* [St. Petersburg?], 1869, which bears the bookplate of Nicholas II. These original drawings show folk costumes, military and ecclesiastical costumes, apparel of the nobles and tsars, etc., ca. 1820–79. Signed, with manuscript captions. "List of drawings" and "Names of governments, cities and villages to which these drawings relate," 2 ll., in Russian manuscript, laid in. (Call no. *KW)

CATALOGS   *Dictionary Catalog of the Rare Book Division of the New York Public Library*. Boston: G.K. Hall, 1971. 21 v.; Supplementary volume, 1973.

BIBLIOGRAPHY   See Grant & Brown, p. 385.

N17
NEW YORK PUBLIC LIBRARY
RARE BOOKS AND MANUSCRIPTS DIVISION

ARENTS COLLECTION

Room 324
Fifth Avenue and 42nd Street
New York, NY 10018

Bernard McTigue
Curator of the Arents Collection and Keeper of Rare Books

TELEPHONE   212 930–0801

SCHEDULE   Mon–Wed, Fri–Sat 10:00 a.m.–6:00 p.m.

ACCESS   Open by card of admission from the Office of Special
Collections (Room 316) to those engaged in advanced scholarly research,
and to undergraduates only by special permission.

FACILITIES   Reading room. Photocopying and photography permit-
                 ted.

HOLDINGS   The collection holds 11,000 volumes, devoted to works
in which tobacco is mentioned, and a Books in Parts Collection. There is
only one work reported pertaining to Russia and the Soviet Union:
   Oktiabr' 1917–1918. Geroi i zhertvy revoliutsii. Risunki: Boguslavskoi,
Kozlinskogo, Makletsova i Puni. Text: Vladimira Maiakovskogo.
[Moscow?]: Izdanie Otdela Izobrazitel'nykh Iskusstv Komissariata Narod-
nogo Prosveshcheniia, n.d. 19 sheets.

CATALOGS   *Tobacco: Its History Illustrated by the Books, Manuscripts
and Engravings in the Library of George Arents, Jr.* New York: n.p.,
1937–1969. 7v.; a card catalog exists for materials added to the collections
after the book catalogs were published. See also the Research Libraries general catalog/data base (CATNYP). There is also a divisional computerized
listing of the most recent additions to the collection which are awaiting
cataloging.

BIBLIOGRAPHY   No bibliography reported.

N18
NEW YORK PUBLIC LIBRARY
RARE BOOKS AND MANUSCRIPTS DIVISION

MANUSCRIPTS AND ARCHIVES SECTION

Room 324
Fifth Avenue and 42nd Street
New York, NY 10018

Mary Bowling
Curator

TELEPHONE   212 930–0801

SCHEDULE   Mon–Wed, Fri–Sat 10:00 a.m.–5:45 p.m.

ACCESS   Open by card of admission from the Office of Special
Collections (Room 316) to those engaged in advanced scholarly research,
and to undergraduates only by special permission.

FACILITIES   Reading room. Photocopying, photography and microfilming services available with strict limitations; inquire of the section. All
collections are in storage in an off-site facility, therefore 48 hours notice is
required to have material delivered to the reading room.

HOLDINGS   The Section contains numerous collections and individual items of interest to scholars of Russian and Soviet history and culture. In
general, materials document the 19th and 20th centuries, but several are
representative of the medieval and early modern periods. The oldest volume
is an Old Church Slavonic lectionary (de Ricci 119) from the 14th century
containing lessons from Acts and Epistles. The 16th century is documented
by the diplomatic correspondence of Cardinal Giovanni Francesco Commendone, Papal envoy to Poland.
    Several collections contain the papers of those involved in radical move-
ments of the 19th and 20th centuries. Foremost among these are the George
Kennan Papers, 1866–1919. There is a collection of the letters of Catherine
Breshkovsky covering 1923–34, written from Czechoslovakia to her American supporter, Irene Dietrich. The papers of William Frey (Vladimir
Konstantinovich Heins), 1860–1888, contain letters, diaries, manuscripts

and other papers of the Russian positivist relating in part to his founding of an agrarian commune in Cedar Vale, Kansas.

The most extensive collection of Russian emigre manuscripts is the Michael P. Riabouchinsky Papers, 1917–1960. Riabouchinsky was a member of the prominent family of Moscow merchants, industrialists, and financiers. Emigre organizations are represented by the records of the Federation of Russian Organizations in America, 1918–24, and the Russian Lawyers Association in the U.S.A., 1922–47. The papers of other emigres include those of Russian Jews who settled in the United States, for instance, the Miriam Shomer Zunser Papers, 1900–1907, and the Gershoy Family Papers, 1923–30.

There is a small collection of family papers of the writer and diplomat Alexei Grigorevich Yevstafiev covering the years 1829–1916. Yevstafiev served as Russian consul to the United States during the first half of the 19th century. The records of the Russian Artillery Commission in the United States, 1917, contain transcripts of an investigation conducted by Commission member Boris Brazol into alleged espionage activities by an official of the Commission. The Nikolai M. Khravrov Papers, 1916–37, contain correspondence and legal papers regarding further allegations of espionage and sabotage by Commission officials made by Edmond A. Walsh in his book *The Fall of the Russian Empire.*

Russian arts and letters are represented by the papers of the translators Isabel Hapgood (covering 1888–1922) and John Jacob Robbins (covering 1893–1953), set designer Mstislav Dobuzhinsky (1914–1952), and the writer Alexei Remizov, which consists of 20 letters to Nicholas Slonimsky, 1924–1934. The Section also holds the papers of three Russian scholars: Vladimir Jochelson, containing notes, writings, photographs, and other papers resulting from his leadership of the Ethnological Division of the Riaboushinsky Expedition to Kamchatka and the Aleutian Islands, 1909–1910; Viktor Adiassewich, a petroleum engineer whose unpublished writings cover the history of the Cossacks, the petroleum industry in Russia, and economic sketches of the Ukraine and the Caucasus, 1917–1922. The David J. Dallin Papers, 1948–1959, contain research notes, card files and typescripts of interviews used when preparing his books, including names and sources kept secret in the footnotes of the books.

There are several collections which contain first-hand accounts of Russia written by visiting Americans. The most extensive of these is the Harold M. Fleming Papers, 1922–1971, which include Civil War era posters, 1918–1922. Fleming served as field inspector in the Russian Unit of the American Relief Administration, 1922–23. The papers of Herma Hoyt Briffault contain her unpublished manuscript relating the story of the Russian–American telegraph expedition to the Arctic regions of Siberia and

Alaska, 1865–67, as well as related source material and letters from Vilhjalmur Stefansson. Other accounts can be found in the diaries of Anna McNeill Whistler, 1843–44; the letters of Bernard Peyton to his wife, 1856–57; the diary of engineer Levi Hayden's travels in Russia in 1878; the pocket diary kept by a member of the Owen family of New Harmony, Indiana, while travelling in southern regions of Russia, 1869; the diary of Mrs. Mary Stoughton, wife of the United States Minister to Russia in 1878–1879; the sketchbooks and diaries of journalist Poultney Bigelow, 1891–92, who travelled to Russia with artist Frederic Remington; and the many notes and letters written by Anthony J. Griffin, Congressman from New York City, and his wife Katherine Byrne Griffin, regarding their experiences during a trip to the Soviet Union in 1931.

There are also many small collections and single items in the Section, which is particularly strong in personal papers and organizational records documenting American radical movements. Included are the Emma Goldman papers, the Norman Thomas Papers, the records of the American Fund for Public Service, and the Rand School of Social Science, all of which contain material of Russian interest.

Recent additions to the collection are the letters of Harry Miller Lydenberg, 1923–1924 (then Chief Reference Librarian, later Director of The New York Public Library), written to his family during a book purchasing trip to Europe, including Latvia and the Soviet Union. He was accompanied by the Chief of the Slavonic Division, Avrahm Yarmolinsky, and his wife Babette Deutsch, the American poet. The Deutsch papers include her snapshots, sketches, and letters commenting on the new Soviet state and on the prominent poets and cultural figures she met during the visit.

CATALOGS   The card catalog contains listings by title and personal names, but the subject approach is the best access. Material is now being processed for RLIN. *Dictionary Catalog of the Manuscript Division*. Boston: G.K. Hall, 1967, 2v.

BIBLIOGRAPHY   Melanie A. Yolles. "Materials for the Study of Russian and Soviet History and Culture in the Manuscript and Archives Section, New York Public Library." Arbeitsgemeinschaft der Bibliotheken und Dokumentaltionsstellen der Osteuropa–, Suedosteuropa– und DDR– Forschung (ABDOSD). *Mitteilungen*. 5:4 (1985): 9–11. Some collections are reported in *National Union Catalog of Manuscript Collections*. Hamden, CT: Shoe String Press, 1962–. Robert A. Karlowich, "Stranger in a Far Land: Report of a Bookbuying Trip by Harry Miller Lydenberg in Eastern Europe and Russia in 1923–24," *Bulletin of Research in the Humanities* 87 (2–3), (1986–87): 182–224. See Grant & Brown, pp. 364–373 (not reproduced here).

N19
NEW YORK PUBLIC LIBRARY
SLAVIC AND BALTIC DIVISION

Rooms 216–217
Fifth Avenue and 42nd Street
New York, NY 10018

Edward Kasinec
Chief

TELEPHONE	212 930–0713, 0714, 0715
SCHEDULE	Mon–Wed, Fri–Sat 10:00 a.m.–6:00 p.m.; Tues 10:00 a.m.–9:00 p.m.
ACCESS	Open to the public.

FACILITIES   Reading room; photocopying and photography allowed depending on the materials.

HISTORY   The Astor Library had a small group of Slavic dictionaries and other material. The few important accessions of the 19th century came principally from the A.M. Bank collection, acquired in 1897. The Slavonic Division of the New York Public Library was founded in 1898 with 1,300 volumes, including 570 volumes of periodicals, proceedings of learned societies, and 281 volumes of literature. In the early years, the collection was overwhelmingly Russian, but later there was a concerted attempt to build up other holdings, especially in Polish, Ukrainian, Czech, and other Slavic and Baltic languages. Chiefs of the division have numbered important, nationally distinguished literary scholars, philologists, and bibliographers: Herman Rosenthal (1899–1917); Woislav Maximus Petrovitch (1917); Avrahm Tsalevich Yarmolinsky (1917–1955); John Leo Mish (1955–1976); and Viktor Koressaar (1976–1984). The name was recently changed to Slavic and Baltic Division.

HOLDINGS   The New York Public Library holds upwards of 200,000 titles of historic and contemporary materials in Western languages for the study of Russia, the Soviet Union, and Eastern Europe, as well as materials in Estonian, Albanian, Romanian, and Hungarian in other divisions. The

Library's holdings in Slavic and Baltic languages, as well as in the Finno-Ugric, Paleo-Siberian (Hyperborean), Uzbek, Yakut and Chuvash languages of the Soviet Union that use Cyrillic script are centered in the Slavic and Baltic Division. Languages represented include twelve Slavic languages— Russian, Polish, Czech, Ukrainian, Serbo-Croatian, Bulgarian, Slovak, Byelorussian, Slovenian, Macedonian, Sorbian (Lusatian), Church Slavonic and Romanian imprints in Cyrillic script, including modern Moldavian; and three Baltic languages— Lithuanian, Latvian, and Wendic (Old Prussian). Broadly, the subject areas include the humanities, social sciences, and (selectively) the physical sciences. As of July 1988, the Division's collections included 281,000 books, serials, pamphlets, and leaflets; 1,390 current periodical titles (a preliminary list is available at the librarian's desk); 13,562 microforms; and thousands of serials and books awaiting processing, under terms of a grant from The Andrew W. Mellon Foundation. The overall collection grows through purchase, exchange, and gift by more than 11,000 cataloged items per year. The collections represent an extraordinary chronological breadth and diversity, ranging from early 14th-century manuscripts to recent *samizdat* publications of the Soviet Union and Eastern Europe: there are, for instance, 2,650 titles from the Russian Imperial and Grand Ducal libraries (acquired between 1926–31); the Jochelson and Bogoraz Paleo-Siberian Collections; rare emigre pamphlets; collections of pre-1860 rare books and precious art and photographic albums; Russian periodicals of the 18th, 19th and 20th centuries; and more than 6,000 volumes in the Division's Reference Room open-stack collections (Room 217). Past gifts have included the George Kennan Collection on the tsarist penal system, which includes over 500 photographs; 636 volumes of Russian pre-revolutionary public and government documents offered by Count Mikhail Mikhailovitch Perovsky (October 1907); 400 volumes given by Anna Toumanova; the John Reed Collection of Russian revolutionary posters; about 100 manuscript letters by eminent Russians donated by Isabel F. Hapgood; the recently acquired Glaser microfilm collection of negatives on 19th-century archival and statistical materials, and Soviet literary publications of the 1920s; rare autographs, and letters transferred in 1988 by the estate of Maria Yorosh; and the Monsignor Basil Shereghy Collection of old Slavonic printed books and manuscripts. Periodically, the division prepares special exhibits based on its collections, concerning topics such as children's books, fine bindings, the works of literary figures, and important recent acquisitions, to name but a few.

Nearly 58 percent of the collection is in Russian, followed by Polish with 13.6 percent, Czech and Slovak with 7.46 percent, and Ukrainian with 5.2 percent. A more detailed analysis of the collection as it relates to the Russian Empire and Soviet Union follows:

Russian Literature

Imaginative literature in all forms is a strong feature of the Division, especially outstanding in the Russian holdings. Important editions of the great classic Russian writers, such as Turgenev, Dostoevsky, Tolstoi, and Pushkin are present—some 21,000 volumes represent collected editions of belles-lettres in the Russian language. All collected editions of Russian authors published by learned institutions are acquired as a matter of policy. In certain cases, where major authors have not been published in collected editions (the Symbolists, for example), an attempt is made by the Division to obtain works in any form, either as separate book publications, in photocopy or on microfilm. Literary criticism and bibliographies of Russian authors are well represented in all languages. The Division also collects a sampling of current science fiction. Translations of literature into Russian are acquired selectively, with the exception of world classics. Translations into Russian of texts in other Balto-Slavic languages are rarely purchased. The Division, however, collects translations of poetry into Russian on the theory that these translations have been made by poets and are themselves works of literary merit. In addition, translations from Russian into other languages are well represented. Also included are a number of first editions of translations into English of Turgenev, Chekhov, and Lermontov. Translations of minor languages into Russian are generally not collected. Russian fiction is only collected representatively, poetry is collected comprehensively. Children's books of the 18th and 19th centuries are well represented; among them are some bibliographical rarities and examples of fine printing. At present, juvenile literature is collected selectively in all languages. The Division has strong holdings in the collected works of dramatists, theatrical biographies, histories of theater and theater groups, as well as stage periodicals. These include the Soviet publications *Teatr'*, *Teatral'naia zhizn'* and a run of *Ezhegodnik imperatorskikh teatrov*, 1890–1919, and 17 plays by Catherine II which appeared in *Rossiiskii teatr'*, 1786–87.

The Division collects works on Russian mystics primarily as examples of literature and only secondarily for their philosophical or religious aspects. A rare title, edited by Johann Amos Comenius, *Lux in Tenebris* (1657), was acquired in 1952, and was described at the time as the only copy in the United States. The book deals with prophesies made by three 17th-century seers.

In Russian literature, periodical and learned society publications form an outstanding feature of the resources. From the 18th century, there are the *Ezhemesiachnya sochineniia*, 1755–64, and the *Drevniaia rossiiskaia vivliofika*, 1783–84. Representative titles include *Sovremennik*, 1848–65 inclusive, *Vestnik Evropy*, 1803–26, 1866–1917, *Biblioteka dlia chteniia*, 1834–65 inclusive, and *Otechestvennyia zapiski*, 1839–84. Twentieth century holdings include *Apollon*, *Vesy*, and *Shipovnik*, as well as the current titles *Oktiabr'*, *Novyi mir*, and *Iunost'*. There are also Russian-language publications from other countries: from the United States, *Novyi zhurnal* and *Vozdushnye puti*; from France, *Sovremennyia zapiski* and *Vozrozhdeniie*; from Germany, *Grani* and *Mosty*. The Division currently receives 25 literary periodicals in Russian.

Ukrainian and Byelorussian Literature

For Ukrainian literature, periodical and learned society publications are collected comprehensively; literature is acquired representatively. Periodicals are perhaps the strongest feature of the 2,000 volumes of holdings. The most important pre-revolutionary *Kievskaia starina* is held in a nearly complete run. A rare group of periodicals published during the turbulent 1920s include *Zhytya i revolutsiya*, *Chervonyi shlyakh*, and *Visti*. Works of individual authors are equally rare, as in the case of Mykola Khyl'ovyi. The library currently receives 7 periodicals in Ukrainian literature, one of the most important being *Zapysky Naukovoho Tovarystva*. Fiction and poetry are a stronger aspect of this literature than drama. The Division has a good selection of the emigre publications from areas in the United States, Canada, and Germany. Shevchenko is the most fully represented Ukrainian author with 90 titles, including collected works and individual editions, the larger part consisting of 20th-century printings. Critical works about Shevchenko are more numerous, over 300 entries. Ivan Franko is represented by 80 original titles, including a 20–volume jubilee edition of 1956, and a similar number of critical works and bibliographies. The Division has the first edition of his work on Ukrainian proverbs, published in 1901–1910.

For Byelorussian literature, literary periodicals and learned society publications are collected comprehensively, fiction selectively (there are about 500 volumes of belles-lettres). The 19th century is represented by several pamphlets printed in Krakow and London in 1870. The Division has either photostatic reproductions or microfilm copies of all of Francis Skaryna's writings, as well as an example of his original work. The holdings from 1905–20 are uneven; when possible, gaps are filled with photocopies. From 1920 to the early 1930s, the holdings are fairly strong in belles-lettres; representation is uneven in all fields for the period 1935–55. After 1960, the collections are good for publications from the Byelorussian Soviet Republic and western Byelorussian publications in Poland. As with the case for most of the national republics in the USSR, the Division holds all publications of the various academies of science in the Byelorussian republic. The Division has a complete set of the national bibliography, *Letapis belaruskaha druku*. The Division receives emigre materials published abroad and in the United

States. The Library currently receives 20 Byelorussian periodicals and newspapers.

Literature of the Baltic Republics

For Latvia, literature represents two-thirds of the total 3,500 total volumes in the Division. The collection holds materials in linguistics, archaeology, history, political science, economics, ethnography, folklore, and especially folksongs. The collection is essentially complete for items published in Latvia, fair for material published outside the country. The Division tries to develop resources in this category. Bibliographical control exists from 1587 to the present via bibliographies of Karl Napiersky and Janis Misins, the *Latvijas valsts bibliotekas biletens*, and the Latvijas PSR Preses Hronika. Also, the "exile" bibliographies of Benjamin Jegers and Janis Velde give similar coverage. Dictionaries of the language include F.F. Stender's *Let-isches Lexicon*, 1789–91, in a first edition, and a copy of the monumental *Latviesu Valodas Vardnica*, 1923–56, by Karlis Muelenbachs and J. Endzelins. Folksong holdings center on the exhaustive *Latwju Dainas*, 1915, 2nd ed. 1922, by K. Barons, which lists 35,789 basic songs and 182,000 variations. The collected works of major authors are a feature of the holdings, together with all standard works in literary criticism. Rudolf Blaumanis is repre-sented by about 50 titles and 3 critical works about him. The Division holds first editions of his novels *Andriksons, Naves Ena*, and *Salna Pavasari*, all published in 1899. Janis Plieksans (known as J. Ranis) is represented by about 50 works, with 12 translations into Esperanto, English, Russian, etc. The author himself translated the works of Dumas, Goethe, and Schiller into Latvian, all of which are in the Division. There are also 6 books of criticism on his works. Of exiled writers, there is a good collection of Zenta Maurina in Latvian and German, as well as her translations from English, French, and Swedish. There are complete holdings of the poetry of Veron-ika Sterlete, Zinaida Lazda, and Klara Zale, and fiction and drama of Anslvs Eglitis. Journals include *Karogs*, 1946–, perhaps the most outstanding liter-ary periodical. Among those published outside Latvia are *Akademiska dzive* (Indianapolis), *Jauna gaita* (Ann Arbor), and *Universitas* (Stuttgart). The Division also has a strong Latvian periodical collection published between the two world wars, such as *Daugava* (1929–39), etc.

For Lithuanian literature, monographs, periodicals and learned society publications are representative. The Lithuanian periodical collection is particularly strong for the period between the world wars. Most Soviet Lithuanian academic publications are received on exchange, but little else is received. Only a small proportion of Lithuanian books published outside the USSR comes to the Division, and they remain difficult to obtain. There are a number of pamphlets in the classmark "n.c." (not cataloged). The Library currently receives 3 literary periodical and learned society publications.

Polish Literature

For Polish literature, history, criticism, and bibliography are collected comprehensively, while poetry, fiction, and drama are collected only on a representative basis. Fiction is the genre held most extensively, some 4,700 volumes. Currently the Division receives 10 periodical titles related to the literature of Poland, including *Wiadomosci literaki*, both in the original Polish and the London continuation, and *Kultura*. Translations of works of Polish literature into English are acquired as a matter of policy; other translations are purchased sparingly. More than 25 works of Henryk Sienkiewicz are present in languages other than Polish, including *Quo Vadis*, which is held in 6 English translations, and as a play and a libretto. While first or early editions are not a strong feature of the collection, a notable exception is Adam Mickiewicz's epic "Pan Tadeusz," 1834. Mickiewicz is represented by 150 entries in the Public Catalog, and 290 entries for works about him, including the *Mickiewicz-Blatter*, 1956–. When possible, the Division obtains collected editions of major authors if available; individual works are only acquired if they contain new critical material. The Division adds to its holdings of Polish imprints before 1600 and other rare materials as funds become available.

Social Sciences

The social sciences, in the broadest sense, are well covered. The library attempts to obtain any original contribution in the exact sciences, especially mathematics, chemistry, and physics. The applied sciences are less well covered. There is almost no material relating to medicine, a field in which the library does not specialize, though it does subscribe to a large and increasing number of scientific and technical periodicals. Until 1964, periodicals in the Balto-Slavic languages were held in the Slavic and Baltic Division. Some of the more significant titles have been transferred to the Science and Technology Research Center. A contemplated policy change will probably place all scientific titles in that subject division of the library, regardless of the language in which they are written.

Exceptional strength is represented by a group of documents from the Russian pre-revolutionary period. There are imperial, standard and popular histories and travel accounts that form an important group, as well as many royal biographies. Important collections relate to Peter I (including collected editions of his letters and documents: *Pis'ma i Bumagi Imperatora*

Petra Velikogo), and to Catherine II. The collection of Grand Duke Vladimir Aleksandrovich consists of 2,200 volumes and is most valuable for dynastic, administrative and military history of the Russian Empire, containing many important government publications, including confidential reports. Court life for 1695–1815 is chronicled in 143 volumes of *Kamer fur'erski tzeremonial'nyi zhurnal*. In addition, there are over 250 manifestos issued in the 19th century to mark occasions (births, etc.) in the imperial family. The *Svod Vysochaishikh Otmetok* is an annual publication of Tsar Alexander II. Nicholas II's notations on reports of provincial governors are included, as well as annual reports of various government departments, some of them secret. A large portion of the collection deals with military affairs, costumes, regimental histories, etc. There is a wealth of geographical, topographical and statistical material on Asiatic possessions found in General Staff publications entitled *Sbornik geograficheskikh, topograficheskikh i statisticheskikh materialov po Azii (1883–1914)* and the *"Materialy" of the Imperial Commission for the Study of Land Ownership in the Trans-Baikal Region (1898)*. As the result of a buying trip to Europe (including the Soviet Union) in 1923–24, Avrahm Yarmolinsky and Harry Miller Lydenberg bought some 9,000 pieces of 19th- and 20th-century material dealing with the Slavic world. One thousand volumes of history formed a prominent part of the purchase, including sources like the *Polnoe sobranie russikikh letopisei* (1853–1922), published by the Russian Archeographic Commission. There are also family records of Prince Kurakin's archives (1890–1912) and those of Count Mordvinov (1901–03), Skrebitzki's *Documents Relating to the Emancipation of the Serfs (1867–68)*, special studies, local and municipal histories, and substantial additions to holdings of Peter I and Napoleon's invasion of Russia. Important periodical and society publications, such as *Beiträge zur Kenntnis der russischen Reiches (1839–1900)* and *Archiv fur wissenschaftliche Kunde von Russland*, which, while essentially scientific, contain some papers on history, topography, and geography. There is also the *Sbornik istoricheskago obshchestva* for 1867–1916 as well as the "Trudy" and other publications of the Akademiia Nauk, Institut Istorii.

There is an extensive collection on various rebellions in Russia, e.g., 1825, 1833, 1863, 1905. The revolutionary movements of 1917 are exceptionally well covered, and the rise and progress of the USSR is thoroughly covered in Cyrillic and Roman. Every effort has been made to secure important emigre works and representative periodicals: documentation books, pamphlets, periodicals, clippings, and other ephemera. Such "non-cataloged" material is represented only by subject cards in the public and division catalogs. Hundreds of uncataloged titles, such as leaflets, pamphlets in various languages, volumes of newspapers clippings, an extensive but inclusive file of Rosta, the mimeographed bulletin of the Ryska Socialistika Federativa Sovjket-republikens Telegramyra of Stockholm are of interest to the specialist. Political theory concerning the USSR has very rich holdings. The complete *Krasnyi Arkhiv: Istoricheskii Zhurnal* (1922–41) exemplifies the periodical and society materials available in the collection.

Public Documents

Regarding public documents, the Division has the complete set of the 13 Duma sessions, the *Stenograficheskie otchety* (1906–17), the three series of the *Polnoe Sobranie Zakonov*, and the *Svod zakonov rossiiskoi imperii* (1857–1916 and 1906–14). There is a substantial file of the official gazette *Pravitel'stvennyi Vestnik* (1869–1917), and official journals of the Ministries of Education and Interior. Other public documents are in the Grand Duke Vladimir Alexandrovich's collection (see above). For the Soviet period, the Library receives the *Stenograficheskii otchet* (1939–) of the Supreme Soviet and its official *Vedomosti* (1938–), among other materials. Statutes form a considerable, if scattered, group, consisting mostly of bound volumes of law in specific fields, such as labor accidents or criminal law.

Publications of the member republics parallel those of the central government. Proceedings of the Verkhovna Rada of the Ukraine is one example, as well as a large number of individual statutes ranging from those published by the Ukrainian Revolutionary Committee in 1919–20 through laws of the German-occupied Ukraine in World War II, to the present. Armenia, Georgia, and Altaic-speaking areas of the USSR also represent particular collecting interest. The Library receives official Communist Party and local government publications of most republics of the USSR. Except for vernacular publications of Belorussia, Ukraine, and the Baltic republics, these publications are received in Russian-language versions. Some particular strengths are: For Estonia, the Estonian official gazette *Riigi Teataja* complete for 1918–40; the party and government publication *Rahva Haal* since 1959; proceedings of the Constitutional Assembly, 1919–20 complete; parliamentary proceedings begin with the 2nd, 1923, and run through 1940. For Latvia, public documents are very extensive until 1940, including parliamentary proceedings from 1918; the legislative journal *Likumu un Ministru Kabineta Notukumu* from the beginning, July 1919–; and the official gazette *Vladibas Vestnesis*, 1922–40, complete. The Library has received the Latvian Communist Party and Council of Ministers publication *Cina* since 1957. For Lithuania, the Library has the official gazette *Vyriausybes Zinios*, 1918–40, complete; parliamentary proceedings (meeting as the Constitutional Assembly 1920/22) are complete until 1927, when the body was dissolved. Currently the Communist Party publication *Tiesa* is received.

For Poland, the Division has the *Sprawozdania Stenograficzne* of the Sejm, 1919–, and the *Senat*, 1922–38. Currently the official gazette *Monitor Polski* is received. Statutes include the early 17th century and later examples, continuing with the *Dziennik Ustaw*, 1939–; a separate set of publications for the goverment in London, 1939–45, is also in the collection. Other documentary material is mostly statistical in nature, although there is much from the Instytut Geologiczny. There are a few muncipal documents, again mostly statistical, from Warsaw, Lodz, etc.

History

The resources for the history of Russia, Poland, and other Slavic countries are substantial, both in native tongues and in Western languages. The holdings include histories, books of travel, and descriptions of social life, with particular emphasis on Russia. Biographies of Russian royalty include important material on Peter and Catherine II. There are also significant items documenting the dynastic, administrative, and political history of the Russian Empire during the last three centuries of its existence. The purchase of some 450 books from the libraries of Czar Nicholas II and other members of the Imperial family began about 1926. In 1931, the library of the Grand Duke Vladimir Alexandrovich was acquired; the 2,200 volumes contain valuable documentation on various phases of the history of the Empire and include an outstanding group of regimental histories (see above).

There are over 3,000 volumes concerned with the history of Poland. Outstanding authors of the 19th century include Lelewel, Kalinka, Szajnocha, Szujski, and modern writers include Korzon, Askenazy, Halecki, Knonopczynski, Limanowski, Kutrzeba and Haiman. There is also a large number of memoirs, works on genealogy, and works of political leaders. The Division has specimens of litcrature that appeared during the German occupation, and selections of books and pamphlets produced by emigres and displaced persons. In 1952, the Division received from the Polish Research and Information Service in New York City a collection of over 2,000 post–World War II books, pamphlets, and periodicals which document recent trends in life in Poland.

Religion

The Division holds about 1,200 entries for the Eastern Orthodox Church. There are extensive holdings of works in Old Church Slavonic which are notable for their linguistic value, but the resources contain numerous liturgical works. In 1914, Isabel Hapgood was instrumental in obtaining for the Library over 500 theological works, presented by the Holy Synod of the Russian Church through the courtesy of the Most Reverend Platon. There are rare Gospel translations into Mordvinian and Mari made by the Russian Bible Society in 1821. There are New Testament translations into Livonian from the early 19th century, and a first edition of the Bible in Lettish (Latvian) published in Riga, 1685–89.

Slavonic Reserve Section

The Slavonic Reserve Section contains approximately 1,500 items, the large majority of them Russian, including some Petrine editions (the first books printed in the new Russian script introduced by Peter the Great). Other rare and valuable Slavonic publications are housed in the Rare Book Division; manuscripts are preserved in the MANUSCRIPTS AND ARCHIVES SECTION.

Serials and Newspapers

The Division has over 2,000 bound volumes of learned society publications of a general nature. The largest single group is made up of various publications of the Akademiia Nauk of Leningrad and Moscow, of which the Division has a complete set, which has passed through many changes of title and subdivisions, including *Memoires*, 1726–1890; Bulletin, 1779–; *Doklady*, 1849–. There are, in addition, the publications of the various academies of science of the Soviet Republics, such as Armenia (in Russian), Georgia, Azerbaidzhan, Byelorussia, Kirgiz, Kazakh, Tajik (in Russian), Ukraine, etc. The Division also has a complete file of the Naukove Tovarystvo Imeny Shevchenka *Zapysky*, 1892–.

Current newspapers collected include a large group of American Slavic publications, such as *Ameryka* (Philadelphia), *Bat'kivshchyna* (Toronto), *Nasha strana* (Buenos Aires), *New Yorkse Listy* (New York), *Novoye russkoye slovo* (New York), *Svoboda* (Jersey City), and *Ukrains'ki visti* (Detroit); from Europe: *Literaturen front* (Sofia), *Nedelya* (Moscow), *Niva* (Bialystok), *Ukrains'ke slova* (Paris), *Zvyazda* (Minsk), and many others. Total currently collected is 79 of which 41 are in Cyrillic, 38 in Latin script.

Photographs and Postcards

A collection of 40 albums contain photographs from the 1880s through the 1930s. Photo subjects include (1) religious subjects, churches, monasteries; (2) geographic, cities and towns; and, (3) political subjects, tsars, February and October 1917 Revolutions, May Day celebrations (sizes range to 10 x 14 inches). The collection of postcards numbers in the thousands.

Unpublished Materials

The Slavic and Baltic Division reports that the statement on its unpublished material in Grant & Brown remains in force. The following information is taken from that source:

Like nearly all the major divisions of the Research Libraries of the New

York Public Library, the Slavic and Baltic Division holds a large amount of unpublished or archival materials relating to the Russian Empire/Soviet Union. It is impossible to estimate how much and what kind of archival material is deposited in the Slavic and Baltic Division, since no distinction is made between archival or manuscript materials and published titles. Even the suject heading "Manuscripts" is of limited usefulness. All manuscripts, unpublished typescripts, albums of photographs in bound form, and other archival materials in original form or in photoreproduction are treated the same way as published monographs, i.e., they are cataloged by author, title, subject, bound and classed according to the subject with published books.

There is also a large quantity of unpublished short articles, personal biographies, and memoirs, bound, in the Division's pamphlet volume collections. These pamphlet volumes are all physically located in one area (though again cataloged separately). Below are listed some examples of specific holdings of archival materials found in the collection of the Slavic and Baltic Division:

Anna Akhmatova (1888–1966). Poetess. "Amedeo Modil'iani," 15 ll. typescript with manuscript corrections, at end: Bolshevo 1958–Moskva 1964; accompanied by a typewritten copy of N. I. Khardzhiev's "O risunke A. Modil'iano."

Alexander II (1818–1881). Emperor of Russia. "Pis'ma Imperatora Aleksandra II, pisannyia Im v bytnost' Ego Naslednikom Tsesarevichem k S. A. Iur'evichu, v 1847 g." ([St. Petersburg?] 1847), 3 ll.

Avtografy. Autographs of Andrei Belyi, Valerii Briusov, Riurik Ivnev, Pimen Karpov, A. Lunacharskii, Ivan Novikov, Matvei Roizman, Semen Rubanovich, Ivan Tukavishnikov, Fedor Sologub, Marina Tsvetaeva, and Ilya Erenburg (Moscow, 1921), 15 ll.; also, a microfiche (negative) of this item.

Cracow Union of Help for Political Prisoners in Russia. Tsirkuliarnoe pis'mo, no. 6 (Krakow? 1914), manuscript.

Saint Demetrius (1651–1709). Letopis' keleinyi preosviashchennago Dimitriia, mitropolita rostovskago i iaroslavskago, ot nachala Mirozdaniia do Rozhdestva Khristova, ego zhe arkhiereiskimi trudami sochinennaia [n.p., n.d.], 7 pp., 369ff. + 21 ll., with 2 miniatures; film reproduction (negative) of an 18th(?)-century cursive manuscript, text written in red and black by various hands, compiled by Saint Demetrius.

[Yelizaveta Alekseyevna (Ashanina) Drashusova] (d. 1884). Al'bom Elizavety Alekseevny Karlgof. Petersburg, Moskva, Kiev, Parizh, Vena, Rim, Praga, Drezden, 1832–44 (n.p., n.d.), 83 ll. Photostatic reproduction on 97 ll. of an autograph album with 55 inscriptions, mainly in Russian and in verse, by Russian and non-Russian notables. An indication of the contents can be gleaned from her "Zhizn' prozhit' ne pole pereiti" in *Russkii vestnik*, 1881, vol. 5, pp. 133ff.

Grigorii, a monk of the Spaso-Yevfimiyev monastery (16th c.?). Zhitie i zhizn' blagovernykh velikiia kniazhny Evfrosinii Suzdal'skiia (St. Petersburg, 1888), 148 pp., with hand-colored plates.

Georg de Hennin (fl. 1730s). Manuscript dated 1735, 2 vols., on mines and metallurgical plants in Siberia. A Yarmolinsky article describes the manuscript in detail, NYPL *Bulletin*, vol. 40 (1936).

Ivan IV Groznyi (1530–1584). [Otvet tsaria Ioanna Vasil'evicha Groznogo, dannyi protestantu Ianu Rokite v 1570 godu iiunia 18 dnia], 83 ll. Photostatic reproduction of the original now found in the Harvard University Houghton Library. Jan Rokyta (or John of Rokycan) was archbishop of Prague and a leader of the Moravian Brethren, ca. 1440.

George Kennan (1845–1924). Collection of clippings from different publications, mostly American and English, on contemporary Russian history, most for the period of World War I and the Russian revolutions, 1914–1918; manuscript documents; and letters to Kennan. These materials are in envelopes, arranged alphabetically by subject, New York?, 1923. In addition there is a bound volume of portraits of Russian political exiles and convicts, with some photos depicting the life of both political and common criminals in Siberia, collected by Kennan and given to the library in 1920, 2 pp., 60ff., photos mounted.

Pomorskiye otvety. Copy of a work completed in 1723 by Andrei Denisov (with Semion Denisov and Trifon Petrov), leader(s) of the Vyg community of Old Believers (Priestless) near the White Sea. The full title of the manuscript is "Otvety pustynnozhitelei na voprosy ieronomakha Neofita," n.p., 176–?. The work is ca. 400 ff., with colored illustrations.

Pravda. Biulleten' "Pravdy," nos. 1–4 (Vienna, 1912), typescript.

Yevgenii Mikhailovich Prilezhayev (b. 1851). "Kratkaia istoricheskaia zapiska ob Olontse" [Olonets, 1887], 16 ll., in honor of the visit to Olonets of their Imperial Highnesses Grand Prince Vladimir Aleksandrovich and Grand Princess Mariia Pavlovna, 29 June 1887.

[Rodoslovetz]. "Nachalo i koren' velikikh kniazei rossiiskikh" [n.p., n.d.], 14 ll. The text begins: "Iz variag priide Riurik. . ." Photostatic reproduction (negative) of a cursive Russian manuscript, probably executed in the first third of the 17th c.

Russia. Armiya. Gvardeiskaya strelkovaya brigada. Prikazy otdannye po Gvardeiskoi strelkovoi brigade. . . (Tsarskoe Selo, 1872–73). Orders issued by His Imperial Highness the Grand Duke Vladimir Aleksandrovich, 21 April 1872; some orders issued at Krasnoe Selo; in manuscript.

Russia. Armiya. Opisanie deistvii otriadov sostoiavshikh pod nachal'stvom Ego Imperatorskago Vysochestva Velikago kniazia Vladimira Aleksandrovicha na bol'shikh manevrakh 1871 goda v sostave sil iuzhnago korpusa, n.p., 1871, 77 pp., chart, 9 colored mounted plans, a colored mounted plate, in manuscript, bound in black grained morocco.

Russia. Armiya . . . Prikazanie po Uchebnomu pekhotnomu batalionu. S 1go iiulia po 8^e avgusta 1864 goda, n.p., 1864, 39 ll., manuscript, at head of title: Kopiia; bound with: Russia. Armiya. Prikaz po Uchebnomu pekhotnomu batalionu (n.p., 1864); with bookplate of Grand Duke Vladimir Aleksandrovich.

Russia. Ministerstvo vnutrennykh del. Departament obshchikh del. Tret'-ye otdeleniye. "Zapiska o sovremennom sostianii raskola, sostavlennaia po delam III otdeleniia Departamenta obshchikh del," n.p., 1862, 417 pp., including tables. The manuscript is signed by Aleksandr Vishniakov.

Russia. Ministerstvo vnutrennykh del. Departament politzii. [Sbornik sekretnykh tsirkuliarov obrashchennykh k Nachal'nikam gubernskikh zhandarmskikh upravlenii, gubernatoram i pr. v techenie 1902–1907 g.g.], n.p., n.d. [New York, 1929], 266 ll., photostat copy by the New York Public Library, December 1929; most of the circulars are typewritten, some are printed; folder containing this collection reads: Delo 191 goda po opisi No. Nizhegorodskago gubernskago zhandarmskago upravleniia . . . Concerns the Russian secret police, revolutionary movement, and criminology.

Mykyta Iukhymovych Shapoval (1882–1932). Sociologist and author. Contains his published and unpublished works; correspondence with family members, political and literary associates; and books, pamphlets, magazines, and newspapers edited by him. A large part consists of minutes and reports of institutions he founded, such as The Ukrainian Technical Institute (Ukrains'kyi tekhnichno-hospodar'skyi instytut) and the Ukrainian Sociological Institute in Czecholsovakia. Also, some material unrelated to Shapoval (published and unpublished) found in his library after his death by Sava Zerkal, who donated the collection to the library. Ca. 200 titles have been catalogued.

[Ivan Kornil'yevich Shusherin] (ca. 1630–1690). "Izvestie o rozhdenii i o vospitanii, i o zhitii, sv. Nikona patriarkha," n.p., 171–224 ll. The manuscript has caption-title and initials in red. Composed about 1687, the first printed edition of the work appeared in 1784. Biographical data on Nikon appears on leaf 224 in a different hand.

Ivan Dmitrievich Sytin (1851–1934). Autographed copy of his own book *Polveka dlia knigi* (Moscow, 1916).

Leo Nikolaevich Tolstoi (1828–1910). Autograph on the title-page of the translation of Henry George's works into Russian: *Izbrannyia rechi i stat'i Genri Dzhordzhe* (Moscow, 1906).

[Triod tsvetnaia]. Photostatic reproduction of a manuscript on vellum, written probably in the 14th c.; uncial, with headpiece and ornamental initials. This Triodion relates to the liturgy and ritual of the Russian Orthodox

Church, 108 ll., n.p., n.d.

Leon Trotzky (Trotskii) (1879–1940). The first 6 items are all electrostatic reproductions of typescripts: "Pis'mo frantsuzskim rabochim; izmena Stalina i mezhdunarodnaia revoliutsiia," 10 June 1935, 6 ll.; "Pered vtorym etapom," 9 July 1936, 6 ll., concerning French politics; "Novaia moskovskaia amal'gama," 22 January 1937, 11 o'clock, 17 ll., written in Mexico, about the show trials; "Terror biurokraticheskogo samosokhraneniia," 6 September 1935, 7 ll., on Russian internal politics; "Iaponiia dvizhetsia k katastrofe," Prinkipo, 12 July 1933, 9 ll., with manuscript corrections, concerning social conditions in Japan; and "Zaiavleniia i otkroveniia Stalina," 18 March 1936, 8 ll., on international relations; an anonymous bibliography of Trotskii's writings published in English in the press and in bulletins, n.p., 1959, 61 ll.; and a photostatic reproduction, on 19 ll., of a published pamphlet: *Sowjetrussland und Polen* (speeches of Kamenev, Lenin, Trotskii, Marchlevski, Sokolnikov, Radek, and Martov, 5 May 1920), n.p., 1920, 38 pp.

[Andrei G. Ukhtomskii]. "Sobranie fasadov," 2 vols. of plates, 100 aquatints, printed from copper (or steel?) plates.

Vidy. "Vidy Valaamskago monastyria," n.p., n.d., 40 photos on 21 ll., letterpress in manuscript, with bookplate of Emperor Nicholas II. Views of the Valaam, Finland, monastery.

Semion Alekseyevich Yur'yevich (1798–1865). Tutor to the children of Alexander II. "Pis'ma ab Avgusteishikh synov'iakh Imperatora Aleksandra II, pisannyia S. A. Iur'evichem v 1847 g. k Ego Velichestvu v bytnost' Ego Naslednikom Tsesarevichem" [St. Petersburg? 1847], 138 pp., reproduced from typewritten copy.

Vladimir Mikhailovich Zenzinov (b. 1880). 17 letters to Red Army soldiers gathered by Zenzinov in Finland during the Russo–Finnish War, n.p., 1939, 43 ll. Illustrated, photostatic reproduction, includes envelopes; 9 letters are in the languages of the minorities of the USSR, 8 are in Russian. The letters became part of Zenzinov's book *Vstrecha s Rossiei* (New York, 1945).

Note: Many of the preceding items are on Reserve; for conditions of access, please inquire at the Slavic and Baltic Division.

CATALOGS   *Dictionary Catalog of the Slavonic Collection.* 2nd revised, enlarged edition. Boston: G.K. Hall, 1974. 44v; "The New York Public Library: Slavonic Division." *Guide to the Research Collections of the New York Public Library.* Compiled by Sam P. Williams. Chicago: ALA, 1975; *Bibliographic Guide to Soviet and East European Studies.* Boston: G.K. Hall, 1979–. (In part, an annual supplement of the *Dictionary Catalog of the Slavonic Collection.* 2nd ed., 44 vols.). There is a two-drawer card file for current periodicals and newspapers which lists, by language, then in alphabetical order, the newspapers and magazines published in the Balto-Slavic area and available in the Division. Information includes the name of the journal or newspaper, its dates and place of publication. The Library's holdings are listed in the Division's Cardex file. All information relative to exhibits prepared by the Division has been retained since 1955. Material consists of labels, notes, and other items. Exhibits are often mounted in commemoration of an anniversary of an important author, e.g., Dostoevsky and Mickiewicz in 1956, Turgenev in 1958, Chekhov in 1960, and Shevchenko in 1961. In 1964, an alphabetical listing was established by name of author or issuing institution of all Division materials which have been filmed and for which there is a master negative.

BIBLIOGRAPHY Avrahm Yarmolinsky, Chief of the Division 1917–55, wrote a number of articles describing the holdings in the Library. Examples are: "The Slavonic Division: Recent Growth." *Bulletin of The New York Public Library* 30 (February 1926): 71–79; "The Library of Grand Duke Vladimir Alexandrovich (1847–1909)." Ibid. 35 (1935): 779–782; also *The Kennan Collection.* New York: New York Public Library, 1921. Other works describing holdings in the Division are: "A Bibliography of Slavonic Bibliography." *Bulletin of the New York Public Library* 51 (1947): 200–208; Edward Allworth. *Central Asian Publishing and the Rise of Nationalism; An Essay and a List of Publications in The New York Public Library.* New York: New York Public Library, 1965; Edward Kasinec. "Eighteenth-Century Russian Publications in the New York Public Library: A Preliminary Catalog." *Bulletin of the New York Public Library* 73 (1969): 599–614; Roman Malanchuk. "New York Public Library. Poland." In *East Central and Southeast Europe; A Handbook of Library and Archival Resources in North America,* pp. 346–355. Edited by Paul L. Horecky and David H. Kraus. Santa Barbara, CA: Clio Press, [1976]; John W. Long and Elliot S. Isaac, "Red Versus White: The Russian Civil War in the Slavic and Baltic Division's Pamphlet Collection." *Bulletin of Research in the Humanities* 87 (2–3, 1986–87): 158–179; Edward Kasinec. "A Brief Survey of Materials for the Study of Communism, Socialism, and Labor History in the Slavonic Collections of The New York Public Library." *Socialism and Democracy* 6 (1988): 157–164; Robert H. Davis, Jr. "The Imperial Russian Periodicals Project at the Slavonic Division, The New York Public Library." *Microform Review* 3 (1988): 150–154; Robert H. Davis, Jr. "Early Soviet Periodicals Collection in the Slavic and Baltic Division, The New York Public Library: A Note." *ACRL SEES Newsletter* 5 (1989): 41–45. See Grant & Brown, pp. 385–387.

N20
NEW YORK PUBLIC LIBRARY
SPENCER COLLECTION

Room 308
Fifth Avenue and 42nd Street
New York, NY 10018

Robert Rainwater
Curator

TELEPHONE   212 930–0817

SCHEDULE   Mon–Wed, Fri–Sat 1:00–6:00 p.m.

ACCESS   Open by card of admission from the Office of Special Collections (Room 316).

FACILITIES   Reading Room. No photocopying allowed except for clipping files; photography permitted depending on condition of print or book. No flashes can be used.

HISTORY   Created by bequest of William Augustus Spencer, who died in 1912, for a collection "of the finest illustrated books and manuscripts ... of any country and in any language and of any period, and that the books be in handsome bindings representative of the arts of illustration and book-binding throughout the centuries."

HOLDINGS   Illuminated manuscripts and illustrated books of the Byzantine and Slavic world. Dictionary catalog contains 22 listings of Russian illustrated books from 1606 through the 1920s; Russian Futurist items include works by El Lissitsky, Malevich, and Iliazd (I. Zdanevich). Ten listings of Slavonic Manuscripts from 15th century (religious books) through 1797 (a Grant from Emperor Paul I).
    The following entries are listed in Grant & Brown:

Armenian Manuscripts

Four Gospels, A.D. 1301; hymnal, 14 century; four Gospels, A.D. 1623; four Gospels, A.D. 1661; "The Jewish Bride," 18th–19th century; and four Gospels, 17th century.

Japanese Manuscripts

Includes: Roshia Zokkoku Jimbutsu Zu (Picture book of People in the Territories of Russia). Sketches of people in Siberia and Kamchatka, made during the later years of the Edo Period (Edo, ca. 1845). 1 volume.

Slavonic Manuscripts

In order, Slavonic Manuscripts 1–10:

Gospel according to Saint Luke, n.p., n.d., but Russia, 15th century. Contemporary binding. Paper, 98 leaves, 1 miniature. In Church Slavonic.

Four Gospels, n.p., n.d., Russia, 15th century. Contemporary binding. Paper, 320 leaves. 4 full-page miniatures of the four Evangelists, other illustrations. In Church Slavonic.

The Ladder by Saint John Climachus (ca. 525–600), n.p., n.d., Russia, 16th century. 18th-century(?) binding. Paper, 210 leaves, 1 full-page miniature, and other illustrations.

Johannes Damascenus: Philosophia (Fountain of Knowledge), n.p., n.d., Russia, 17th century. Contemporary binding. Paper, 308 leaves.

The Life of St. Basil the Younger, written by Gregorius, the monk, 10th century, bound with selections from the Synod, n,p., n.d., Russia, 18th century. Contemporary binding. Paper, 377 folios. 238 full-page colored drawings, headpieces, initial letters. In Church Slavonic.

Canticles of the Eastern Orthodox Church, Liturgy and Ritual "for the sweet singing and the solemn hymns for the good holidays of Our Lord," n.p., n.d., Russia, 18th century. Contemporary binding. Paper, 287 leaves. 1 full-page decoration and other illustrations. In Church Slavonic.

Canticles and Chants of the Eastern Orthodox Church, n.p., n.d., Russian, 18th century. Contemporary binding. Paper, 2 volumes. In Church Slavonic.

Kniga-Tzvetnik (Garden of Flowers; the Passion of Christ; the Last Judgment), n.p., n.d., Russia, 18th century. Contemporary binding. Paper, 354 leaves. 133 full-page watercolor drawings, initial letters. In Church Slavonic.

Apocalypse, n.p., n.d. Russia, 19th century. Contemporary binding. Paper, 212 leaves, preceded by 6 and followed by 5 leaves with notes in a contemporary hand, in Russia [sic]. 63 full-page watercolor drawings. In Church Slavonic.

Paul I's gramota (grant), signed and dated: Gatchina, 24 October 1797. Vellum, 3 leaves. Border decorations, many signatures at end, bound in silk. In Russian.

CATALOGS *Dictionary Catalog and Shelflist of the Spencer Collection of Illustrated Books and Manuscripts and Fine Bindings*. Boston: G.K. Hall, 1971. 2v.

BIBLIOGRAPHY See Grant & Brown, p. 388.

N21
NEW YORK PUBLIC LIBRARY
DONNELL LIBRARY CENTER
CENTRAL CHILDREN'S ROOM

20 West 53rd Street
New York, NY 10019

Angeline Moscatt
Supervising Librarian

TELEPHONE   212 621–0639

SCHEDULE   Mon 12:30 p.m.–8:00 p.m.; Tues–Fri 12:30 p.m.–5:30 p.m.; Sat 10:00 a.m.–5:30 p.m.; Sun 1:00 p.m.–5:00 p.m. (mid-September–May)

ACCESS   Open to the public.

FACILITIES   Reading room, photocopying and photography permitted depending on the condition of the materials.

HOLDINGS   One of the richest and most extensive holdings of juvenile literature in the United States. The room opened in 1911 and in the course of its 75-year history the bookstock has grown to its present size of over 100,000 books. The room serves adults, professionals in publishing, authors, artists, illustrators, editors and collectors of children's books as well as children. The reference holdings of both current and retrospective titles are of unique importance for research. Foreign language books constitute a small (approximately 12,000 volumes) part of the collection but have been considered an integral part of the selection policy, reflecting the international world of children's literature.

There are Russian/Soviet books in the collection from 1910 to the present. The emphasis is on children's classics, folklore and poetry. There are some translations of children's classics from other languages. Size of collection: over 450 titles catalogued; 800 uncatalogued titles (part of a gift from the Soviet Government).

SPECIAL   Illustrated books from the 1920s by noted authors and
FEATURES   artists. Collection of books illustrated by Ivan Yakovlevich Bilibin.

CATALOGS   Dictionary card catalog.

BIBLIOGRAPHY   No bibliography reported.

N22
NEW YORK PUBLIC LIBRARY
DONNELL LIBRARY CENTER
FOREIGN LANGUAGE LIBRARY

20 West 53rd Street
New York, NY 10019

Bosiljka Stefanovic
Chief Librarian

TELEPHONE   212 621–0641

SCHEDULE   Mon, Tues, Thur 9:30 a.m.–8:00 p.m.; Wed, Fri 9:30 a.m.–5:30 p.m.; Sat 12:30 p.m.–5:30 p.m.

ACCESS   Open to the public.

FACILITIES   There is a reading room. Photocopying and photography permitted depending on materials.

HOLDINGS   Materials are chosen to serve all three "waves" of Russian immigrants in the 20th century, so a variety of subjects and approaches is covered. Some materials circulate, some are for reference only. There are approximately 10,000 volumes in the Russian language (much more in other Slavic languages, including Ukrainian, Polish (2,000), Czech (500), Slovak, Byelorussian). Holdings are strong in fiction, plays, collected works, poetry, literary criticism, biography, and periodicals (about 20 titles). There is a good collection in non-fiction, including some philosophy, human rights, philology (and dictionaries), some sciences, cooking, art books, theater, history. Collections of the circulating material form what is called a "circuit collection" of internal loans to branch libraries throughout New York City, specially designed to fill special needs of patrons not able to come into Donnell. Materials also circulate to libraries within the state of New York.

CATALOGS   The New York Public Library Book catalog, 1972–, is available to the public, as it is for other divisions of the library.

BIBLIOGRAPHY   No bibliography reported.

N23
NEW YORK PUBLIC LIBRARY
DONNELL LIBRARY CENTER
MEDIA CENTER

20 West 53rd Street
New York, NY 10019

Marie Nesthus
Librarian

TELEPHONE (Call after 12:30) Film, Video, Record Information: 212 621–0609; Film or Video Circulation: 212 621–0610; Study Center Appointments: 212 621–0611

SCHEDULE Mon 12:30 p.m.–8:00 p.m.; Tues–Sat 12:30 p.m.–5:30 p.m.; Fri 9:30 a.m.–5:30 p.m.

ACCESS Individuals or non-profit organizations may borrow films and videotapes on a permanent New York Public Library borrower's card, without charge. The card must first be presented at the Media Center for authorization, with two additional items of traceable identification. Films and tapes may be borrowed for free showings only. No admission fee may be charged, nor may films be used for fundraising or other commercial purposes. Films are not available for classroom use nor for school assemblies. Film reservations may be made in person or by mail on appropriate forms three to eight weeks in advance.

FACILITIES Reading room. There is also a Film/Video Study Center for private viewing of films and tapes.

HOLDINGS The Media Center is one of the largest of its kind in the nation, holding 7,000 16mm films and 250 features films with an emphasis on independently produced films: documentary, fiction, animated, avant-garde and experimental; 1,200 videotapes ranging from video art to independently produced documentaries and special "exemplary" television programs. Most tapes are available for circulation in half-inch and three-quarter-inch format; a collection of nearly 31,000 music and non-music recordings and audio cassettes, including foreign language instruction, literature, and musical recordings ranging from classical to jazz.

The following extensive list of 16 mm films is concerned with topics relating to this guide and gives some idea of the range of material. Other films that might be of interest cover the labor movement in America (such as the

Passaic strike and the Industrial Workers of the World), Ellis Island, and broader ethnic studies. This list includes items in Grant & Brown:

An Afternoon with Gregor Piatigorsky (15 min.), 1977. Dir. Steve Grumette. A portrait of the master cellist at 73, filmed shortly before his death.

Alexander Nevsky (107 min.), 1938. Dir. Sergei Eisenstein.

The Battle of Russia (80 min.), 1944. Sixth in Frank Capra's series "Why We Fight," with coverage of the Nazi attack on the USSR, Russian music, footage from feature films, ending with the Siege of Leningrad. The editing of the film resembles Eisenstein.

The Battleship Potemkin (60 min.), 1925. Dir. Sergei Eisenstein. There is also an 8 minute film of the Odessa steps sequence.

Bed and Sofa (112 min.), 1926. Dir. Abram Room. The setting for this comedy is Moscow's housing shortage. The film was not widely seen outside the Soviet Union due to its treatment of forbidden subjects, adultery and abortion.

The Birth of Soviet Cinema (49 min.), 1972. Examines the golden age of cinema in the 1920s in Russia by presenting excerpts from the masterworks of Eisenstein, Pudovkin, and Dovzhenko.

Blind Bird (45 min.), 1963. Dirs. Doris Doline, Anatoli Jedan. A young Russian boy takes his pet pelican to an eye specialist in Moscow who restores the bird's sight.

By the Law (90 min.), 1926. Dir. Lev Kuleshov. Based on "The Unexpected" by Jack London. Three people in Alaska undergo inner turmoil as a result of their complicity in a murder.

Chaim Soutine (28 min.), 1970. Dir. Jack Lieberman. Examines the life and work of Chaim Soutine, who was born in Lithuania and spent his early productive years in Paris.

Chess Fever (20 min.), 1925. Dir. Vsevolod I. Pudovkin. A witty, satirical comedy made during the International Chess Tournament in 1925.

Children of Labor (55 min.), 1976. Dirs. Richard Broadman, Noel Buckner, Mary Dore, Al Gedicks. Portrays successive generations of Finnish-Americans in the Upper Midwest. Emphasizes how they came into conflict with industrial America and established their own churches, temperance halls, and socialist farm movement.

Committee on Un-American Activities (45 min.), 1962. Documentary history of the origins, purposes and practices of the House Committee on Un-American Activities (HUAC). Combines newsreel footage, interviews, still photos, recorded testimony and live footage.

Counterpoint: The U2 Story (55 min.), 1974. Follows the career of Francis Gary Powers during and after his high-altitude spy plane was brought down over the Soviet Union. Examines this embarrassing international incident in terms of the Cold War.

Earth (54 min.), 1930. Dir. Alexander Dovzhenko. The fourth and last silent film by the Ukrainian director. The young peasants of a Ukrainian village want to set up collective farms. The Kulaks (wealthy landowners) try to protect their land.

Eisenstein's Mexican Study Film (pt. 1, 126 min.; pt. 2, 129 min.), 1930–31. Dir. Sergei Eisenstein. The aim of this film is to summarize Eisenstein's plan and to restore a few fragmentary sequences from the unfinished "Que Viva Mexico!" without attempting to convey the final form the footage would have taken.

Eternal Glory (30 min.), 1972. Dir. James Khlevner. Deals with the present day search for the many Russian World War II soldiers whose bodies were never found or identified. Some of the relatives of these missing soldiers received no compensation, suffered from oppression, and were looked upon with suspicion.

First Encounter: A Russian Journal (20 min.), 1978. A documentary of uncensored glimpses of Russian life rarely seen in the West, filmed in provincial cities and villages.

Free Voice of Labor—The Jewish Anarchists (60 min.), 1980. Dirs. Steve Fischler, Joel Sucher. Focuses on the Jewish anarchists as disillusioned immigrants in American sweatshops. Historian Paul Avrich articulates the group's history and philosophy and shows how the spirit of the anarchists remains alive as they reminisce about the group's experiences.

Frogland (5 min.), 1925. Frogs demand a king and get a stork who eats them. A fable of democracy by Polish puppet animator Ladislas Starevitch.

Galina Ulanova (37 min.), 1964. Dirs. Leonid Kristi, Maria Slavinskaia. Traces the life of the celebrated Russian dancer.

Hollywood on Trial (100 min.), 1976. Dir. David Helpern. Details the hysteria of the blacklist era through the presentation of key events leading up to the cold war, actual news footage of the Hollywood Ten and the 1947 House Un-American Activities Committee hearings on alleged Communist infiltration into the movie industry, and present-day interviews.

Ivan the Terrible (pt. 1, 96 min.; pt. 2, 90 min.), 1944. Dir. Sergei Eisenstein.

Jaraslawa (10 min.), 1975. Dir. Dee Dee Halleck. Shows Jaraslawa Tkach, an old Ukrainian woman, as she bakes bread and talks about her life as an immigrant.

The Kremlin (54 min.), 1963. An overview and brief tour through the Kremlin in Moscow with General Andrei Iakovlevich Vedenin as guide.

The Last Journey (25 min.), 1981. Dir. Philip Gittelman. Before emigrating from the Soviet Union, Nodar Djindjihashvili took a hazardous journey across his native land documenting the eroding state of remaining Jewish life and culture. Includes views of the Moscow Synagogue, a remote congregation outside Minsk, and Babi Yar, the infamous Jewish burial grounds.

Last Year of the Tsars (19 min.), 1971. Dir. Norman Swallow. Newsreel footage and sequences from Sergei Eisenstein's *October* and *Strike* are used to dramatize events in early 20th-century tsarist Russia.

Man With a Movie Camera (55 min.), 1928. Dir. Dziga Vertov. A Russian film, historically important because of its advances in cinematography. Filmed in Moscow and Odessa, it belongs to the "city symphony" genre.

Marc Chagall (25 min.), 1965. Examines the style and content of Marc Chagall's work.

March–April: The Coming of Spring (9 min.), 1967. A film essay showing the coming of spring in Russia, photographed mostly in rural forested areas.

Marx for Beginners (7 min.), 1978. Dir. Bob Godfrey. Adapted from the book by Mexican cartoonist Tius, this film highlights, in an amusing manner, the major economic and philosophical theories of Karl Marx.

Meet Comrade Student (54 min.), 1963. Dir. Nicholas Webster. A report on the Soviet educational system, its curriculum, and the emphasis placed on competition, discipline, physical fitness, and common ideology.

The Mirror (106 min.), 1974. Dir. Andrei Tarkovsky. In Tarkovsky's looking glass, images of the director's childhood are mixed with fragments of his adult life.

The Moiseyev Dancers in The Strollers (6 min.), 1959.

Molly's Pilgrim (24 min.), 1985. Dir. Jeff Brown. Based on the book by Barbara Cohen. The story of a nine-year-old Russian Jewish immigrant girl who overcomes the insensitivity of her classmates and adapts to her new American environment.

Mother (80 min.), 1936. Dir. Vsevolod I. Pudovkin. Based on the novel by Maxim Gorky.

Navigator (10 min.), 1934. Dirs. Irene and Ladislas Starevitch. A humorous puppet animation about animals aboard a passenger ship with a bulldog as navigator.

The Nose (11 min.), 1963. Dirs. Alexander Alexeieff, Clair Parker. Animated version of Gogol's surrealistic fantasy about a man who loses his nose and makes frantic efforts to get it back.

October (161 min.), 1927. Dir. Sergei Eisenstein.

Olga: a Film Portrait (47 min.), 1974. Dir. John Sheppard. Presents a biographical study of the Russian gymnast Olga Korbut.

One Day in the Life of Ivan Denisovich (100 min.), 1971. Dir. Casper Wrede. Based on the novel by Solzhenitsyn.

Point of Order (97 min.), 1964. Dir. Emile de Antonio. A political documentary without narration of the Army–McCarthy Hearings of 1954.

Poland (27 min.), 1965. Dir. Julien Bryan. The story of the Polish people from the founding of the nation a thousand years ago to life today under the Communist regime.

Polka Graph (6 min.), 1953. Dir. Mary Ellen Bute in collaboration with

Norman McLaren. A pioneering abstract animation that visually interprets Shostakovich's Polka from "The Age of Gold."

Prince Igor (105 min.), 1969. Dir. Roman Tikhomirov. Borodin's epic opera is brought to the screen in a lavish production by the Kirov Opera.

Pysanka—The Ukrainian Easter Egg (14 min.), 1975. Dir. Slavko Nowytski. One of the pre-Christian celebrations of spring in the Ukraine was the painting of prayer designs on eggs by means of sealing designs onto the eggs with wax drawings and dipping the eggs in successively darker dyes. This art is demonstrated and the symbolic meanings explained by Luba Per-chyshyn, a master of egg decoration.

Raoul Wallenberg—Buried Alive (78 min.), 1983. Dir. David Harel. Inter-cut with period footage and still photos are interviews with survivors, Wal-lenberg's family, colleagues, and witnesses to Wallenberg's whereabouts in Russia.

Red Pomegranate (75 min.), 1972. Dir. Sergei Parajanov. The words of the 17th-century Armenian poet Arutuin Sayadian, also known as "Sayat Nova" (the King of Song) are captured in this visual pastiche which is both a styl-ized biography of the writer and a tribute to his work.

Reds in Hollywood (10 min.), 1948. Adolph Menjou and other stars testify in Washington about Communist infiltration of the film industry.

Reflections of a Dancer: Alexandra Danilova (52 min.), 1981. Dir. Anne Belle. A portrait of Alexandra Danilova, the great Russian-American prima ballerina assoluta, who was one of America's favorite ballerinas in the 1930s, 40s, and 50s with the Ballet Russe of Monte Carlo.

Religion in Russia (20 min.), 1968. Prod. Julien Bryan. Traces the history of five of the major religions of Russia, and discusses the restrictions sur-rounding worship in the Soviet Union as of 1968.

Reminiscences of a Journey to Lithuania (82 min.), 1971. Dir. Jonas Mekas. Early years of Mekas as an immigrant in Brooklyn, NY, 1950–1953; August 1971 in Lithuania in the village where Mekas was born.

Revenge of the Kinematograph Cameraman (9 min.), 1912. Dir. Ladislas Starevitch. This stop-frame puppet animation by Polish artist Ladislas Starevitch is a fable about an insect couple's marital infidelity.

Russia (24 min.), 1958. Prod. Julien Bryan. An examination of Russia, and the impact of the Soviet system on various phases of Russian life.

The Russian Peasant (20 min.), 1968. Prod. Julien Bryan. Studies the Rus-sian peasant in historical perspective through the use of photographs and paintings and examines his role in modern Russia against a background of authentic peasant music.

Russian Rooster (6 min.), 1975. Dir. Steve Segal. Combines the music of Rimsky-Korsakov's "Coq d'Or" with a simply animated story about a group of hunters frantically chasing a rooster.

Shadows of Forgotten Ancestors (99 min.), 1964. Dir. Sergei Parajanov. Set in the early 1900s in a small Carpathian village, this impressionistic film tells of the tragic love of Ivan and Marichka.

Siberia: A Day in Irkutsk (51 min.), 1967. Portrays life in Irkutsk and the surrounding area as it was in the mid-sixties. Visits homes, schools, and places of recreation.

The Soviet Union: A New Look (26 min.), 1978. Prod. Sam Bryan. Made during several trips to the Soviet Union in the late 1970s, the film opens with an animated sequence which sets the stage for rare newsreel footage of life under the tsars followed by historical material shot by Julian Bryan in the 1930s.

Stalker (161 min.), 1979. Dir. Andrei Tarkovsky. Based on the novel *Picnic By the Roadside*, by Arkady and Boris Strugatzky. The story concerns two disenchanted intellectuals, a physicist and a writer, who want to explore a mysterious region called the Zone.

Stanislavsky: Maker of the Modern Theater (28 min.), 1972. Explores the life, times and ideas of theatrical innovator Konstantine Stanislavsky who created method acting and founded the Moscow Art Theater.

Steppe in Winter (13 min.), 1965. A poetic evocation of winter life on a collective farm in the Russian steppes.

Stravinsky (49 min.), 1976. Dirs. Roman Kroitor, Wolf Koenig. Follows composer Igor Stravinsky as he records his Symphony of Psalms with the CBC Symphony Orchestra.

Tanya the Puppeteer (25 min.), 1981. Dir. Don Owen. Tanya Nicolev, age 12, lives with her family in Moscow. . . . She is accepted into the beginners' class in puppetry by Sergei Obratsov, one of Russia's greatest puppeteers.

Ten Days that Shook the World (60 min.), 1927. Dir. Sergei Eisenstein. Details the events which culminated in the Russian Revolution of October, 1917, using actual locations and many of the real participants in the events. Based on the novel by John Reed.

The Train Rolls On (33 min.), 1974. Dir. Chris Marker. A film about the famous Cine-Trains organized by Alexander Medvedkin in 1932 which left Moscow to cross the Soviet Union and made films on the problems of production. The film-train was a self-contained studio that could pull in anywhere, shoot its films, edit them on the spot and show them to the people who had been filmed.

Uncle Vanya (110 min.), 1972. Dir. Andrei Mikalkov-Konchalovsky. An adaptation of Chekhov's play.

War Without Winners (28 min.), 1978. Dir. Haskell Wexler. Explores the danger of nuclear war and examines such issues as the power of the nuclear arms race, the spread of nuclear weapons, and the consequences of SALT treaties. Average American and Russian citizens express their fears and hopes for a future in an age of nuclear weapons.

Women of Russia (12 min.), 1968. Prod. Julien Bryan. Shows the role of the Russian woman in Soviet life.

Video material on Russia is on three-quarter inch tape and cannot be used on home sets. Items will have to be viewed at the Media Center. The following 3 items on Russian/Soviet topics are available at the Center:

Media Shuttle: New York–Moscow (30 min.), 1978. Dirs. Nam June Paik, Dimitri Devyatkin. "What would happen if the people of New York and Moscow had a kind of citizen's band talk show and could see and talk to each other via satellite? The idea of a media shuttle provoked this science fiction fantasy by two artists." In Paik's "Selling of New York" (1972), Russell Connor describes New York's rapid development in the later years of the 20th century as the information capital and multinational headquarters of the world. This is followed by scenes recorded in the Soviet Union by Dimitri Devyatkin during trips in 1974 and 1977. Other New York scenes including some from Paik's Suite 212 are intercut with the Russian footage.

Russian Soul (29 min.), 1978. Dir. Dimitri Devyatkin. A personal tour by video artist Devyatkin shot in 1977. Interviews include a Bulgarian psychotherapist and proponent of Suggestopedia, an innovative form of hypnosis; a Moscow pediatrician who teaches parents to "swim" their infants; and Ivanov, a village patriarch and healer who "teaches people to take cold showers and walk barefoot." There are scenes of Palace Square, Middle School No. 45, a historic church, and a veterans' gathering at Gorky Park, where Devyatkin asks people, "Do the Russians want war?" The tape also includes an excerpt from a Soviet science film about psychotherapy and hypnosis.

Soviet Dissidents in Exile (30 min.), 1981. Dir. Alan Goldberg. The narrator introduces five prominent Soviet dissidents now living in exile in the United States. He describes who they are, their activities in the Soviet Union, and the circumstances under which they left their country. In separate interviews, poet Joseph Brodsky, physicist Pavel Litvinov, Boris Shragin, Vladimir Bukovsky, and Alexander Ginzburg respond to a series of questions about adjustment to American society. Photographs of other dissidents imprisoned or living in internal exile in the Soviet Union end the tape.

CATALOGS   The book catalog serving the New York Public Library and the Brooklyn Public Library contains listings for the Media Center's record and audio cassette holdings. For their film and video holdings the following two catalogs must be used: *Films 87, The New York Public Library.* New York: The New York Public Library, 1987. 466 p.; *Video. Donnell Media Center. New York Public Library, The Branch Libraries.* New York: New York Public Library, n.d. 60 p. (The Media Center is in the process of updating the video catalog.)

BIBLIOGRAPHY   *A Guide to the Three Units of: The Central Library of the Branch Library System, The Mid-Manhattan Library, The Donnell Library Center, The New York Public Library at Lincoln Center.* The New York Public Library, [1986?]. Unpaged brochure. See Grant & Brown, pp. 363–364.

N24
NEW YORK PUBLIC LIBRARY
LIBRARY AND MUSEUM OF THE PERFORMING ARTS
AT LINCOLN CENTER
BILLY ROSE THEATRE COLLECTION,
PERFORMING ARTS RESEARCH CENTER

111 Amsterdam Avenue
New York, NY 10023

Dorothy L. Swerdlove
Curator

TELEPHONE   212 870–1639 (Reference)

SCHEDULE   Mon and Thur 10:00 a.m.–7:45 p.m.; Tues, Wed, Fri–Sat 10:00 a.m.–5:45 p.m.; summer hours: Mon–Sat 10:00 a.m.–5:45 p.m.

ACCESS   Open to the public.

FACILITIES   Reading room. Photocopying and photography permitted depending on copyright/donor restrictions and on physical condition of material.

HISTORY   1929 gift of the David Belasco Collection of typescripts, photographs, original designs, and scrapbooks prompted the establishment within the New York Public Library of a special Theatre Collection in 1931.

HOLDINGS   Newspaper/periodical clippings, promptbooks, programs, playbills, letters, legal papers, manuscripts, costume and stage designs, photographs, posters, correspondence, books, periodicals, scrapbooks, prints, lithographs, slides, motion picture and television stills, pen and pencil portraits (including theatrical caricatures), pamphlets devoted to performing arts, including stage, film, radio, television, circus, carnivals, amusement parks, industrial shows, vaudeville, burlesque, night clubs, magic, minstrels, and marionettes.

SPECIAL Oliver Sayler collection of photographs, scrapbooks, **FEATURES** clippings, etc., on the Moscow Art Theatre. A collection of photographs, programs, clippings and memorabilia on Nikita Balieff and the Chauve-Souris Company. Elizabeth Reynolds Hapgood papers, documenting her long association with Stanislavski as friend and translator of his works into English; the collection includes a 715–page typescript in Russian of *An Actor Prepares* (with each page initialed by Stanislavski), as well as correspondence between Stanislavski and Gordon Craig concerning Stanislavski's autobiography, *My Life in Art*.

Grant & Brown list entries from the "Catalog" (see below, CATALOGS) citing an "impressive amount of Russian/Soviet-related material under a variety of headings, such as "Drama, Russian";

"Drama, Ukrainian—Translations into Carpatho-Russian." Under "Drama, Russian—Translations into English" and "Drama—Promptbooks and typescripts" there is a listing of working scripts for plays by Leonid N. Andreyev, Mikhail P. Artzybashev, Blok, Bulgakov, Chekhov, Jacques Deval, Dostoevskii, Osip Dymov, Aleksei M. Faiko, Gogol', Gorkii, Valentin P. Katayev, Konstantin Ya. Khal'fin, Piotr Korvin-Krukovski (pseud.: Pierre Newsky), A. J. Kosorotow, August Friedrich Ferdinand von Kotzebue, Albert Lortzing, Lev Natanovich Lunz, Princess Alexandra Melikoff, A. Nabatov, Attila Orbok, Mendel Osherowitch, Aleksandr N. Ostrovski, Yevgenii Petrovich Petrov, Pushkin, S. Semionov-Polonski, George Shdanoff, Konstantin M. Simonov, Vladimir S. Solov'iov, Aleksandr V. Sukhovo-Kobylin, Il'ya D. Surguchev, Aleksei K. Tolstoi, Sergei M. Tret'yakov, Boris Tumarin, L. Tur, Ivan S. Turgenev, Lev N. Urvantzov, Nikolai N. Yevreinov, and Gerald Zoffer.

Under the heading "Non-Book Collection" and "Cage File," Grant & Brown give a *"selected"* list of individuals, subjects, and works . . ., stating that the "collections include such material as photographs, clippings, programs, reviews, and articles."

Actors and Acting—Russia;

Chingiz Aitmatov;

Aleksei Arbuzov;

Brooks Atkinson—Correspondence from the 1950s about the Russian theater, A. Chekhov, etc.;

A. Chekhov;

"The Cherry Orchard"—Correspondence, business papers, graphics, etc., concerning U.S. productions of this play, actors and actresses in it, etc.;

Cinema—Russia/Russian;

Cinema—Stars—Russian;

Circus—Russia;

Sergei Mikhailovich Eisenstein—Original caricatures;

Alexandra Exter—Original design (curtain) for Moscow's Kamerny Theatre (1914);

Hallie Flanagan—Scrapbook with programs, clippings, manuscript notes, and letters relating to her trip to visit Russian theaters (1926);

N. Gogol;

Maksim Gorkii;

Boris Goudounov—Color costume sketch by Leon Bakst; and wash drawings of costumes for Boris (Kate Friedheim Collection);

Vassily Ivanovitch Katchaloff (also, Katshalow)—Autographed photographs, one of him as Vershinin in "The Three Sisters";

Vsevolod Meyerhold;

Sonia Moore—Typescript of "Eugene B. Bakhtangov. Director, Actor, Teacher, Man" (n.d.); signed letter concerning a 1970 U.S. production of "The Cherry Orchard"; and signed letter, 1961, with reviews of her *The Stanislavksi Method*;

Moscow Art Theatre—Painting by George A. de Pogedas from June 1926 (Morris Gest originals); material relating to a 1900 MAT production of "Uncle Vanya"; original poster; filmstrips of MAT productions in 1965; and autographed photos of Olga Knipper-Chekhova and V. Kachalov;

Alla Nazimova—Autographed photo; undated caricature (in Alfred Frueh originals); caricature of her in "The Cherry Orchard" (1928); ALS to Nila Mack ca. 1917; and a program;

V. Nemirovich-Danchenko;

Vera Mentchinova;

Puppets for Proletarian Revolution;

Radio—Russia;

John Reed—Leaflets and periodicals with play casts from Moscow in 1917;

Nikolai Vladimirovich Remizov—Photographs of original drawings by N. V. Remizov for a photoplay, "The Gambler," after Dostoevskii . . . [n.p., 193?], 8 leaves and 16 plates, with a typewritten description of the drawings by the owner, Mr. Remizov (catalog listing under "Cinema: Stills");

Soviet Circus;

Stage—Russia;

Konstantin Sergeyevich Stanislavski (real name Constantin Sergeivich Alexiev)—Photographs of him, his productions, and later Moscow Art Theater productions; scrapbooks; clippings; articles from around the world; text of "Stanislavsky and America," a broadcast by N. Solntsev, 7 August 1958; pencil sketch for "The Mistress of the Inn"; tape recording (7″) of a series of 12 talks given in Hollywood (1955) by Michael Chekhov (actor, director, and teacher at the MAT for 16 years and head of the Second Moscow Art Theatre); medals; and stamps;

V. Stanitsin (Stanitzyn);

Aleksandr Tairov (Tairoff);

Theatrical Postage Stamps—Honoring the Soviet film industry, 1969, for the second international Tchaikovsky competition, 1962, and others;

Yevgenii Bogratinovich Vakhtangov—See also under Sonia Moore.

Also from Grant & Brown: The collections include a number of phonodisc recordings of plays by Russian/Soviet authors (e.g., Anton Chekhov). (See listings under "Theatre—Recordings.")

CATALOGS   *Catalog of the Theatre and Drama Collections.* Boston: G.K. Hall, 1967–76. 51v. Material is filed under (transliterated) names of personalities, titles of productions, performance groups (e.g., Moscow Art Theatre), general subjects (e.g., Theatres: Russia: Moscow).

BIBLIOGRAPHY   *The Billy Rose Theatre Collection.* The New York Public Library, undated, unpaginated brochure. See Grant & Brown, pp. 381–383 (partially reproduced here).

N25
NEW YORK PUBLIC LIBRARY
LIBRARY AND MUSEUM OF THE PERFORMING ARTS
AT LINCOLN CENTER
DANCE COLLECTION

111 Amsterdam Avenue
New York, NY 10023

Dorothy Lourdou
Acting Curator

TELEPHONE   212 870–1655

SCHEDULE   Mon, Thur 10:00 a.m.–7:45 p.m.; Tues, Wed, Fri, Sat 10:00 a.m.–5:45 p.m.

ACCESS   Open to the public.

FACILITIES   Reading room; photocopying and photography permitted with some limitations.

HOLDINGS   Extensive holdings in the history and present state of Russian dance. Includes books, periodicals, clipping files (reviews in all major languages, but collection consists mostly of U.S. press), programs, libretti, photographs (approx. 5,000), manuscript collections, art works, motion pictures (less than 100 films of ballet and folk dance in many areas of Russian Empire and Soviet Union); materials on Russian ballet abroad and opera ballet companies, vidcotapes. Size of collection, well over 5,000 items.

SPECIAL   Several manuscript collections of the Diaghilev Ballets
FEATURES   Russes; Diaghilev correspondence and notebooks; rare
ballet caricatures by Nikolai Legat. Libretti by Golizowski; 1-hour film of Pavlova, Pavlova letters; materials of Ballet Russe de Monte Carlo; materials of Sol Hurok, Marius Petipa, George Balanchine, Lincoln Kirstein.

The following entries are excerpted from Grant & Brown, which are themselves a partial listing from the Dance Collection's published catalog and 1973 monograph (see BIBLIOGRAPHY below):

Gabriel Astruc (1864–1938). Papers, 1904–25, 123 folders, ca. 1,300 items. French impressario, journalist, publisher, and director of the Théâtre des Champs-Elysées (Paris) in 1913. Includes correspondence, financial papers, inventories, notes and plans, programs, contract drafts, reports, and clippings. Much relates to the early activities of Sergei Diaghilev, who brought Russian ballet and opera to Western Europe. Most items are from 1907–14, none from 1915–24. Astruc and Diaghilev became close collaborators. The collection has detailed information about the first Saison Russe of Diaghilev at the Théâtre du Châtelet in Paris, 1909, including inventories of costumes and scenery and even Astruc's report to Baron Frederiks, minister of the Russian court. Among correspondents and others mentioned in the papers are Ida Rubinstein, Natasha Trouhanova, Baron Dmitri Guenzburg, Vaslav Nijinsky, Anna Pavlova, Fedor Shaliapin, and Boris Shidlovskii. Requires special handling. Published register: *Bulletin of the NYPL* 75 (October 1971).

Leon Bakst (Lev Samoilovich Rosenberg) (1866–1924). Manuscripts include several autograph letters, signed, 1917–21, some to George Wague in Paris, which discuss costumes, S. Diaghilev, his designs for the ballet *Sleeping Beauty*, and his designs for the ballet *Firebird*. There are also his pencil and watercolor sketch, signed in pencil, of a "Man in Spanish costume," St. Petersburg, 1902–1903, and his Cretan Sketch Book, Greece, ca. 1907. The latter, in pencil and watercolor, is annotated. Bakst sketched the palace of Knossos on Crete, the site of major archeological discoveries just at this time. Hellenic inspiration showed in 3 of his ballet collaborations in 1912: M. Fokine's "Narcisse" and "Daphnis et Chloe" and V. Nijinsky's "Faune."

George Balanchine (Georgii Melitonovich Balanchivadze) (b. 1896). A rare ALS to S. Diaghilev, Paris, 1925, discusses recruitment of dancers in Latvia and Germany among Russian exiles, in Russian, but signed in

French; a telegram from Igor Stravinsky to Balanchine, 1957, concerns the first performance of "Agon" by the New York City Ballet; photo by Gjon Mili of the Stravinsky–Balanchine "Movements for Ballet and Orchestra" (New York, 1963); and the complete working correspondence between the painter Eugene Berman in Rome and Balanchine in New York during their collaboration on "Pulcinella," 1971–72. (Collections such as that of José Limón hold letters and other items to, from, and about Balanchine.)

Alexandre Nicolaievich Benois (1870–1960). Painter and writer. Watercolor, signed twice in ink, of a set design for scene II of "Le Pavilion d'Armide" (St. Petersburg, 1908); the ballet's libretto was also by Benois.

Jean Cocteau (1889–1963). 2 posters (colored lithograph by Verneau and Cochoin) of V. Nijinsky and T. Karsavina, designed by the poet and draftsman to advertise the third Diaghilev season in Paris (Paris, 1911); and a signed holograph article by Cocteau on the third season of the Ballets Russes (Paris, 1911)—in the Lincoln Kirstein Collection.

Edward Gordon Craig (1872–1966). Craig–Duncan Collection, 1901–57, 360 folders. Theater artist and author. Material relating to the dancer Isadora Duncan includes correspondence, 1904–1905, from Duncan when she appeared in St. Petersburg and Moscow. Special handling. Published register: *Bulletin of the NYPL* 76 (1972), pp. 180–98.

Aleksandra Dionisievna Danilova (b. 1904). Russian-born ballerina. Miscellaneous manuscripts; scrapbooks, 15 vols., of clippings, programs, and photos from 1937–56; scrapbook of clippings from U.S. tours, 1954–56; and photo scrapbook from a 1957 tour of Japan. Plus microfilm copies of the scrapbooks.

Agnes De Mille (b. 1918). 5 notebooks and 3 folders of material. American dancer, choreographer, and writer. Correspondence, scenarios, choreographic notes, and other writings. "Russian journals" kept by De Mille in 1966 and 1969, the latter diary from her trip to Moscow by invitation to judge an international ballet competition, handwritten and typed. The finished 1969 diary appeared as "Judgment in Moscow" in *Dance Perspectives* (New York, 1970, no. 44, Winter). Permission required.

Irvin Deakin (1894–1958). Correspondence, 1934–55, 83 folders, ca. 1,245 items. In holograph, manuscript, and typescript, primarily relating to Deakin's work in association with Hurok Attractions and as general manager of the San Francisco Civic Ballet, 1947–48. Arranged chronologically, the letters concern Deakin's relations with the Original Ballet Russe, the Ballet Russe de Monte Carlo, Tamara Toumanova, and Adol'f Bolm. Unpublished register.

Sergei Pavlovich Diaghilev (Dyagilev) (1872–1929). Papers, ca. 1909–29, 600 items. Impresario. Correspondence, 1918?–29, 195 items.... The letters are in French, English, and Russian, holographs and typescripts, business and personal. They concern his ballets, dancers (e.g., V. Nijinsky), and social life. The Black exercise book, in Diaghilev's holograph, was written in St. Petersburg, Paris, and elsewhere, 1909–11. In great detail it reveals his business and artistic negotiations, casts and programs for planned ballets and operas, financial records, budgets and plans for the 1920–21 season, lists of members of the Ballets Russes de Diaghilev, projected schedules through 1913, salaries, matters of decor and costume, etc.—with his doodles on many pages, 177 pp. Mostly in Russian, it is written in pencil and ink. (The contents are described by Brian Blackwood in the *NYPL Bulletin*, vol. 75, no. 8 [October 1971]. A microfilm of this book is also available.) Diaghilev's small brown notebook, London–Paris, 1921–23/24, also in his autograph, contains notes on programs, schedules, finances, and many names. Some 400 letters and documents accompany these 2 notebooks, bearing the signatures of Leon Bakst, George Balanchine, Vaslav Nijinsky, Igor Stravinsky, and others. In addition, there are photos of Diaghilev's ballet companies, various productions, the 1916/17 American tour, and individual dancers. Finally, the collection has 2 autograph schedules for ballets and rehearsals, for London in 1921 ("La Belle au Bois Dormant") and for Paris, 1924. Special handling. Unpublished register. (Lincoln Kirstein Collection)

Mstislav Valerianovich Dobuzhinskii (Dobujinsky) (1875–1957). Stage designer. Miscellaneous manuscripts, including letters to Sol Hurok and David Lichine concerning Graduation Ball, a list of Russian stage artists, a list of stage designers before 1900 and in later years, before and after the Revolution in Russia and abroad, and stage decoration sketches.

Irma Duncan Collection of Isadora Duncan Materials. 183 folders, ca. 300 items. Manuscripts, photographs, programs, correspondence, memorabilia, and clippings relating to the lives and careers of Isadora and Irma Duncan. 1 group of manuscripts relates primarily to the years Isadora Duncan spent in Russia, 1921–24. Among the correspondents are Gordon Craig, Sergei Esenin (Isadora Duncan's husband), Eleanora Duse, Ellen Terry, Ivy Low Litvinova (Moscow, 1921), and Anatolii Lunacharskii. Permission required. Unpublished register.

Isadora Duncan (1877–1927). Miscellaneous manuscripts, including a letter to Augustin Duncan in which she discusses the Duncan School in Moscow. Note: There is much Isadora Duncan material in other collections such as the Edward Gordon Craig papers.

Mikhail Mikhailovich Fokin (Fokine) (1880–1942). Papers, 1914–41, 52 items in 14 folders. Choreographer, dancer, and teacher. Includes letters from Arnold L. Haskell, Cyril W. Beaumont, Sara Yancey Belknap, Alexander Levitoff, and others; essays and articles by Fokin and others; bookplates; calling cards; hotel bills; an invitation from Ruth St. Denis; and miscellaneous items, holograph and typescript, in English, French, and Russian. Subjects covered in the papers: Mary Wigman, Isadora Duncan, the evolution of modern dance, Fokin's ideals when creating, Sergei Diaghilev, Les Ballets Russes, and Les Ballets Russes at Teatro Colon (Buenos Aires). Special handling. Unpublished register and folder list.

Serge Grigoriev (Grigorieff). Régisseur of the Diaghilev (Ballets Russes), De Basil, and other ballet companies. Eight exercise books, ca. 1,100 pp., in Russian, contain journals of all performances of the companies. Included are statistics on all performers, production notes, and information about more than 50 Diaghilev shows (49 ballets) from 1916–29. Grigoriev used these basic sources for his book on the *Diaghilev Ballet, 1909–29* (London, 1953).

Sergei Ismailoff (b. 1912). Papers, 1929–47, ca. 50 items. Dancer and teacher. Includes letters from Bronislava Nijinska, N. Singaevsky, S.J. Denham, and the Marquis de Cuevas; contracts; biographical notes; identity cards; and memorabilia, in English and Russian. Unpublished register and folder list.

Lincoln Kirstein (b. 1907). Besides important Diaghilev materials, this collection also contains such additional items as the autograph manuscript, 42 pp., bound, of Kirstein's biography *Fokine* (New York, 1932), requested by the British critic Arnold Haskell. Although Fokin dictated much of the material in a series of interviews, he did not care much for the end product, which was published in London in 1934. (Kirstein had studied under Fokin briefly in 1931–32 in order to write the book.) There is also a bronze portrait head of Fokin rendered by Emanuelle Ordono Rosales (New York, 1929?).

David Lichine (1910–1972). Papers, in French and Russian. Includes photocopy of his holograph notebook on Graduation Ball, with his description of the choreography, illustrated by small drawings throughout. This was the first ballet choreography accepted for copyright in the U.S.

Allan Ross Macdougall (1893–1957). 65 folders, ca. 250 items. Collection of holographs, typescripts, and photographs, especially notes and drafts for his biography of Isadora Duncan entitled *Isadora: A Revolutionary in Art and Love* (New York, 1960). Also correspondence about the work, including letters to him from Irma Duncan concerning the Isadora Duncan School in Moscow, 1928, from Sergei Essenine, typed copy, and copies of original Isadora Duncan letters in the Irma Duncan Collection (q.v.).

Leonide Massine (1896–1979). Choreographer. Miscellaneous manuscripts; photographs; motion pictures; oral history interviews; and a typescript ballet scenario—the prompt-book (with manuscript notes) for *La boutique fantastique* [New York, 192–?], 16 ll., performed at the Alhambra Theatre, London, 5 June 1919. Permission required for some items.

Jean Miró (b. 1893). Painter. Miscellaneous manuscripts, including 2 ALS to Serge Grigorieff, régisseur of Le Ballet Russe de Monte Carlo, concerning the company's productions, Barcelona, 1933–34.

Lillian Moore (1911–1967). Papers, ca. 1936–67, 20 drawers. Dance historian and critic. Includes correspondence between Moore and 2 Soviet colleagues, Natalia Roslavleva (pseud.) and Vera Krasovskaia.

Bronislava Nijinska (1891–1970). Sister of Vaslav Nijinsky, dancer, and choreographer. An ALS to Richard Pleasant about working again with his Ballet Theatre (Hollywood, 1940). (Isadora Bennett Collection)

Vaslav Nijinsky (1890–1950). Dancer. Assorted manuscripts, in French, including a signed receipt, 22 September 1917, for payment from S. Diaghilev and sheets of jottings from 1948; Nijinsky's red and blue wax crayon design (ca. 1922, Switzerland) entitled "A Mask of God"; documents relating to his assiciation with Les Ballets Russes; photographs, including 1 from 1908 supposedly taken on the day of his graduation from the Imperial Dancing Academy in St. Petersburg; and a bronze portrait head of him by Una, Lady Troubridge, London, 1913, in the Lincoln Kirstein Collection.

Rudolf Nureyev (b. 1938). Dancer. Charcoal and conté crayon drawing of him by Lisa Rhana (New York, 1966?).

Oral Interviews with Dancers. Tape recorded interviews with such figures as Alicia Markova ("The Art of Ballet," 80 min.), Natalia Dudinskaia (with Marian Horosko, 25 min., about the Kirov Ballet and the training of dancers), Olga Spessivtzeva and Tamara Karsavina (M. Horoska, 12 min.), I. Youskevitch and L. Danielian (M. Horosko, 23 min.), and Leonide Massine (M. Horosko, 23 min., about S. Diaghilev, E. Cecchetti's system of teaching, American modern dance, and Isadora Duncan). (Oral History Archives)

Pavley-Oukrainsky Ballet Russe. Records, 1915–50, 5 folders, 73 items. Holographs, typescripts, business records, itineraries, and correspondence of Serge Oukrainsky and Adolf Schmidt among others. Includes a small notebook with income and expense records for 3 tours of the company between December 1927 and January 1929.

Anna Pavlova (1882–1931). Dancer. 2 scrapbooks, 1917–24, of the ballerina with photos and clippings (in French, Russian, Italian, and German), articles, programs, and postcards; extensive collection of photographs; a drypoint etching, signed, of Pavlova by Troy Kinney (New York, ca. 1930), also bearing the dancer's autograph; charcoal drawing with gouache highlights, signed, by Francis A. Haviland (London, 1910)—in the Cia Fornaroli Collection; and Pavlova's bronze death-mask (The Hague, 1931), from the original plaster now in London.

Marius Ivanovich Petipa (1819–1910). Choreographer. Miscellaneous manuscripts, in French, including a photostat of a letter, signed, to an unknown correspondent, 31 March 1870, mentioning a Léon (probably Léon Espinosa).

Pablo Picasso (1881–1973). Painter. 2 ALS to Jean Cocteau, Paris, 1917, about the Ballets Russes, S. Diaghilev, and his own work on the ballet "Parade."

Maia Mikhailovna Plisetskaia (b. 1925). Dancer. Programs; photos; 2 interviews, 1966, one with M. Horosko (15 min.) and the other with W. Terry (20 min.), the second concerning the Bolshoi Ballet.

Natalia Roslavleva, pseud. Isadora Duncan Collection, mainly 1904–1905. 322 items in 22 folders. Soviet dance historian. Reviews and material relating primarily to Duncan's performances in St. Petersburg and Moscow. Typescript and holograph copies of Russian newspaper and periodical articles, most with English translation, obtained from Russian archives and sent to Francis Steegmuller for his book *"Your Isadora": The Love Story of Isadora Duncan and Edward Gordon Craig* (1974). Unpublished register.

Joseph Schillinger (1895–1943). Composer and author. Holograph and typescript of his "Graph method of dance notation" [ca. 1934 and 1942], ca. 17 ll. plus diagrams.

Francis Steegmuller (b. 1906). Author. Correspondence, 1974–present, including some from Irma Duncan and Natalia Roslavleva relating to Isadora Duncan, especially her times in Russia. Also, papers relating to his book *"Your Isadora,"* 1972–75, 94 folders. Includes correspondence with Irma Duncan and the Soviet dance historians Vera Krasovskaia and Natalia Roslavleva (pseud.). Permission required for the second collection.

Pavel Tchelitchev (1898–1957). Artist. Signed costume designs, Paris, 1933, in gouache and pen and gouache for the Balanchine–Schubert–Koechlin ballet "L'Errante": Hero and child, and Hero companions.

Galina Ulanova (b. 1910). Dancer. Photos of her teaching, in "Romeo and Juliet" (ca. 1960), and as "Giselle" (Moscow, 1960–61), taken by Albert E. Kahn. Kahn took hundreds of photos of her professional and private life for his 1962 monograph. Permission required. (Robert W. Dowling Collection)

Igor Youskevitch (b. 1912). Miscellaneous manuscripts.

Furthermore, under such headings as "Russian Ballet," "Ballet—Russia to 1917," "Ballet—U.S.S.R.," and "Ballet Russe," the catalog often has scores of entries, including photographs, motion pictures, scrapbooks, clippings, programs, and oral interviews. For virtually every Russian/Soviet ballet (i.e., with music, choreography, or libretto by Russian/Soviet artists) there are again materials. Thus, not only does the library hold large quantities of items for such standards as "Swan Lake" and "Nutcracker," but it also has photos and a motion picture for "The Little Humpbacked Horse."

CATALOGS   *Dictionary Catalog of the Dance Collection: A List of Au-*

thors, Titles, and Subjects of Multi-Media Materials in the Dance Collection of the Performing Arts Research Center of the New York Public Library. Boston: New York Public Library and G.K. Hall, 1974. 10 v.; *Bibliographic Guide to Dance.* 1st–, 1975–. Boston: G.K. Hall, 1976–. Annual. See under individual Grant & Brown entries above for references to registers and folder lists.

BIBLIOGRAPHY   *A Decade of Acquisitions: The Dance Collection 1964–1973.* New York: New York Public Library, 1973. See Grant & Brown, pp. 374–378 (some of the entries above refer to published registers or articles in the *NYPL Bulletin* and *Dance Perspectives*).

N26
NEW YORK PUBLIC LIBRARY
LIBRARY AND MUSEUM OF THE PERFORMING ARTS
AT LINCOLN CENTER
MUSIC DIVISION

111 Amsterdam Avenue
New York, NY 10023

TELEPHONE   212 870–1650

SCHEDULE   Mon, Thur 10:00 a.m.–8:00 p.m.; Tues, Wed, Fri, Sat
               10:00 a.m.–6:00 p.m.

ACCESS   Open to the public.

FACILITIES   Reading room. Photocopying and photography depending on the nature of materials.

HOLDINGS   Books, scores, fine prints, microfilms and fiches, photographs, original scene designs, manuscripts, documents, clippings, programs, etc., 4 million total; Russian/Soviet materials not separated from rest of collections and are not identifiable as such.
    Grant & Brown presents a "selected listing, taken from published finding aids":
    Joseph Achron (1886–1943). A kapelle Konzertisten [n.p., 1928?], facsimile, 9 pp.

Fiodor Stepanovich Akimenko. Mélodie élégiaque for violoncello and piano, op. 47b, no. 1, in G minor [1912?], score, 7 pp., and part, 4 pp.; and Romance, score, 2 pp., and part, 1 p., 1911.

Ivan Belza. Arsenal [192–?], 52 pp.

Nina Borovka. Autograph on her compilation of Crimean Tatar folk songs and dances (Stockholm, 19—), 8 pp.

Petr Il'ich Chaikovskii. Aveux passionnés, n.p., n.d., 2 ll. (facsimile of autograph manuscript); and a photostat reproduction of 3 measures of his Andante cantabile from the String Quartet, in his hand, signed P. Chaikovskii, 1 p.

Aleksandr Nikolaevich Cherepnin. [Duo for violin and violoncello(?)], copyist's manuscript, 3 ll. [n.d.].

Charles Davidoff (i.e., Carl Iulevich Davidov?). ALS from London, 15 May 1862?, 2 pp.

Karl Dondo. "Marsh dlia fortepiano" dedicated to the Grand Duke Vladimir Aleksandrovich by the bandmaster of the 111th Don Infantry Regiment, Karl Dondo (Kovno, 1888), 2 ll., full score; and "Marsh dlia orkestra" with the same dedication (Kovno, 1888), 3 ll., full score.

Mischa Elman (b. 1891). Approximately 9 letters and postcards to Sam Franko from the Russian-born violinist, 1910–16 and n.d., including 1 ALS from London(?), 4 pp., 10 December, no year. (In the Sam Franko *Collection of programmes of performances.* . . .)

John Field. [Fragment], 13 pp., autograph manuscript(?) for piano, a score partly in another hand; [Nocturne, piano, no. 5, B-flat major; arr.], for piano and orchestra (1815?), a score, 47 ll.; facsimile of the same, Serenade, 3 pp.; facsimile of Nocturne no. 6 in F Major, ca. 1814, 12 pp. on 6 ll.

Michael Fokin. Autographed presentation copy (to P. L. Miller) of his biography of *Feodor Chaliapin*, 23 pp. (New York, 1952).

B. A. Frisek. "Marsh 'Vladimir,' " composed by the bandmaster of the 90th Onega Infantry Regiment, B. A. Frisek, n.p., late 19th c., 2 ll., for piano. Dedicated to the Grand Duke Vladimir Aleksandrovich.

Ossip Gabrilowitsch. ALS of 13 November 1900 and 11 December 1902 (in Mason Collection) and ALS to Mr. W. Weyman, Berlin, of 1 and 29 October 1908.

Aleksandr Konstantinovich Glazunov. [Cortège solonnel] (Torzhestvennoe shestvie), an 1894 score, 47 pp.

Mikhail Ivanovich Glinka. Russische National-Gesaenge (n.d.), 1 l.; and a facsimile of the same or a similar piece (Russian national airs) in his own hand, n.d., 2 pp.

Ludwig Goede. "Vladimir Aleksandrovich, marsh," composed by L. Goede, n.p., 1882, 5 ll., full score, dedicated to the grand duke.

Aleksandr Tikhonovich Grechaninov. "Arise," for soprano and piano,

text by Elizabeth Nathanson, holograph in ink, 3 pp.; "Crépuscule," for low
voice and piano (poetry of Luc Durtain), holograph, 4 pp.; "Dobrinia
Nikititch, suite symphonique" [1944?], 97 pp., orchestral score reproduced
from his autograph manuscript; "Grande fête," overture, op. 178, score,
holograph in ink on transparent paper (New York, 1945), 26 ll.; same, score,
26 pp. [1945?], reproduced from holograph with title page in his own hand;
"Lamentations de Jaroslavna" (text of Denis Roche), from the *Slovo a polku
Igoreve*, holograph in ink with pencil corrections, 4 pp., for voice and piano;
"Zhenit'ba" (Marriage), full score, 486 pp., and vocal score, 155 pp., in
English and Russian, reproduced from holograph; a comic opera in 3 acts
based on N. Gogol's "A bachelor's room" (op. 180, [1946?]), score, 148 pp.,
reproduced from holograph; "Les oeillets roses," for low voice and piano
(poetry of Diana Tichengoltz), holograph in ink, 3 pp.; "Poème lyrique" for
orchestra [op. 185], score, 64 ll., holograph in ink on transparent paper, and
reproduction of same, New York, 27 March 1948; Polka-vocalise for
soprano and piano [1933?], holograph in ink, 4 pp.; Septet, op. 172a [1948?],
score, 34 ll., holograph in ink on transparent paper; "Slavlenie S. A.
Kusevitskago. K 20–ti letiiu dirizhirovaniia Bostonskim orkestrom. Slova i
muzyka A. Grechaninova" (English translation added in pencil: "Glorifica-
tion of S. A. Koussevitzky for his 20th anniversary as conductor of Boston
symph."), for voice and piano, holograph in ink with corrections and additions in pencil, 16 May 1944, 3 pp.; Sonata for balalaika and piano, op. 188,
no. 1 [1948?], 1 vol., reproduced from autograph manuscript; Sonata no. 1
for clarinet and piano, op. 172 [1940?], holograph in ink, 18 and 25 pp.;
Sonata no. 2 for clarinet and piano, op. 172 [1940?], 19 pp., reproduced
from holograph; Symphony no. 5, op. 153, score, holograph in ink (February
1938), 190 pp.; Symphony no. 6 [194–?], holograph in ink plus additional
leaves in pencil, 28 pp.; "Towards victory," full score, "heroic poem" for orchestra and male chorus, in English and Russian, text by A. Pushkin,
holograph in ink, New York, 1943, plus photostatic reproduction of same,
56 pp.; and 5 reels of microfilm with his collected manuscripts and published
works, n.d., 134 items, and the same, ca. 150 items, 3 ft.

Louis Gruenberg. Signor Formica [1910], piano-vocal score in German,
165 pp.; and Volpone, score, various pagings (1948–59).

Aloysius Hauptmann. "1814, 19go Marta 1889. Iubilei marsh; po sluchaiu
semidesiatipiatiletiia polka vsepokorneishe posviashchaet Ego Im-
peratorskomu Vysochestvu velikomu kniaziu Vladimiru Aleksandrovichu,
Avgusteishemu Shefu leib gvardii Dragunskago polka, kapel'meister Aloizii
Gauptman," n.p., 1889, for piano, 5 pp.

Vladimir Heifetz. Babi Yar, score [196–?], 17 pp.

Herbert Reynolds Inch. A bibliography of Glinka [New York, 1935],
typed, 16 ff., with annotations, plus a supplement bound with this item.

J. Karnavicius. "The impostor," a ballet in 1 act (samozvanets), 127 pp., copyist's manuscript in ink, signed on last page: J. Karnavicius, Kaunas, 1940, with superlinear descriptive text in English and Russian and a typed scenario in Russian inserted, 4 pp.

Kogda. "Kogda moia radost' nachnet govorit' vorkuia nezhnee golubki . . ." n.p., late 19th c., 3 ll.; these are the first lines of a song with Russian words, music for 1 voice with piano accompaniment.

Serge Koussevitzky. TLS, Boston, 15 March 1927 (Sam Franko Collection).

W. Labunski (b. 1895). Impromptu [1925?], 2 pp. (facsimile).

Theodore Leschetizky. Visiting card with several words in script; [Arabesque, piano, op. 45 no. 1 in A-flat major] (Deux arabesques), [1899], [2], 4 pp.; and [Souvenirs d'Italie], 10 pp. [ca. 1888].

Anatolii Konstantinovich Liadov. [Morceaux, piano, op. 31] (Deux morceaux pour le piano), [ca. 1893], 16 pp. (5 blank).

Sergei Mikhailovich Liapunov. Reproduction of Concerto for violin (ca. 1915), score, 31 pp.

Alexander Lipsky. Sonata for violin and piano (192–?), score, holograph in ink, 19 ll.

Arthur Louiré (b. 1884?). Song of Mitya Karamazov, ca. 1950, 9 ll., music (sheet); and Toska Vospominaniya [1941], 10 ll.

Samuil Moiseyevich Maikapar. "Prélude in Des dur fur Clavier," Vienna, 13 May 1895, in manuscript (probably Maikapar's hand), with presentation note to Ossip Gabrilowitsch, 2 ll.

Nicolas Nabokov. [Sonata no. 2 for piano], (1940?), 24 pp., reproduced from his manuscript, autographed presentation copy to Andor Foldes.

Karl Nawratil. Autograph musical quotation (Andante from "C moll Konzert"), undated, received in 1919, 1 p. (Miscellaneous Collection)

Vaslav Nijinsky. Autograph (W. Nizhinski) in Roberto Montenegro's biography *Vaslav Nijinsky* (London, 1913?).

Nikolai Platonovich Ogariov. Facsimile of his autograph "Romance," setting of M. Lermontov's poem "Tuchki" (Clouds) for 1 voice with piano accompaniment (original apparently in the Moscow Gosudarstvennyi literaturnyi muzei).

Henryk Pachulski. Meditation, score, 9 pp., for string orchestra, op. 25, n.d., and 2 parts.

Sergei Puchkov. "Marsh 'Razsvet'," dedicated to the Grand Duke Vladimir Aleksandrovich (n.p., 1880), autograph manuscript, for piano; title page design in watercolors, 3 ll.

Max Rabinoff. Signed postcard to Mr. Robinson Locke and TLS to Locke, New York, 14 February 1919.

Sergei Rakhmaninov. Christmas card, visiting card, and his wife's visiting card with a few autographed words (Lambert Collection).

Nikolai Andreevich Rimskii-Korsakov. Act 3 from the opera-ballet Mlada, n.p., 1914, score, 98 pp.

Anton Rubenstein. ALS of 7 June 1892 (Lambert Collection); photostatic reproduction of an ALS, 12 December 1888, 3 pp.; and a reproduction of 3 morceaux de salons [n.d.], 1 part, 2 pp.

Vassily Ilyich Safonoff. ALS, 11 April 1907; APS, 10 October 1906; ALS of 4 August 1908 (Mason Collection); and ALS to Mr. W. Weyman, 15 May 1910.

Lazare Saminsky. Autograph on "Little Sorele's Lamb," op. 2, no. 3 (New York, [ca. 1922]); autograph presentation copies of 3 works: Sabbath evening service (New York, 1930)—to Virgil Thomson, Three Shadows [1935] (London, [ca. 1938])—to Richard Singer, and The Vision of Ariel (New York, [1951, 1950])—to Thomson; and photostat reproduction of his IV Symphonie, op. 33, autograph manuscript score, 93 pp. (Vienna, 1927).

Joseph Schillinger (1895–1943). Papers, divided into 3 broad categories: Joseph Schillinger Collection of Posters and Charts (in the Iconography Collection of the Music Division), including items on his work and posters relating to Russian/Soviet music (e.g., jazz in the late 1920s); in the Musical Manuscript Collection—his holograph musical scores, 35 folders, 24 notebooks for the Schillinger system of composition, 33 notebooks with other writings, some in Russian, and some notebooks of his students; and in the Letter Collection: correspondence, ca. 170 items, documents, ca. 60 items, 7 typescripts of general writings, some on Russian music, and miscellaneous notes and other papers, ca. 700 items.

Kurt Schindler. Autograph presentation copy of The Russians in America, paraphrased by Kurt Schindler [n.p., n.d.], 7 pp., song text in his hand, set to printed score of S. Rachmaninoff's Prelude in C# minor (first line: "Chaliapine! Sergei Rachmaninoff, he heads the roster").

Abel' Abramovich Silberg. "Marsh," composed by the bandmaster of the 96th Omsk Infantry Regiment, n.p., late 19th c., 5 ll., full score, dedicated to the Grand Duke Vladimir Aleksandrovich; title page design in watercolors.

Igor Stravinsky. [Capriccio for piano and orchestra, arranged for 2 pianos], 1929, holograph, 53 pp. Symphony in 3 movements, completed in 1945, 107 pp., signed holograph dedicated to Arthur Sachs, full score; and Symphonie des psaumes [1930], song and piano arrangement by his son Sviatoslav, holograph, 40 pp.

Joseph Strimer. Musical manuscripts, ca. 50 items, in process.

Nikolai Topusov. Reproduction from typed copy of his Berlin dissertation Carl Reinecke [Sofia, 1943], cover printed, with author's autograph (one of 100 copies), ca. 461 pp.

Il'ya Tyumenev. "Sbornik khora uchenikov Imperatorskoi Akademii khudozhestv" [St. Petersburg, 1883], iv + 40 pp., reproduced from manuscript. Tyumenev was a pupil at the Academy.

Elias I. Tziorogh. "Ja rusyn byl; karpato-russkij hymn" for piano, mixed chorus, female voices, and male chorus—words of A. V. Duchnovich, arranged by I. S. Tziorogh [New York?, ca. 1927], 3 pp.; and "Podkarpatskiji rusyny, karpatorusskij humn," a march for mixed chorus, arranged by Tziorogh, words by Duchnovich [New York?, ca. 1927], 5 pp.

Pauline Viardot-Garcia. "Der Gartner. Lied von Morike, Musik von Pauline Viardot," song with piano accompaniment, 3 pp.

Vladimir Rudolfovich Vogel. Losung (Devise), full score, for brass and percussion, Strasbourg, 1934, 23 pp.

Henri Wieniawski. Le carnaval russe, 1873, 2 ll., 11 pp.; and musical quotation with autograph signature (New York, 21 May 18—?).

In addition, the library has the Toscanini Memorial Archives, which contain microfilm reproductions of the following items:

Petr Il'ich Chaikovskii. Aveux passionés for piano; Concerto for piano no. 1 in B-flat minor; concerto for violin, Op. 35; Manfred; The Nutcracker; Overture 1812; Quartet, strings in D major, op. 11; Quartet, strings in F major, op. 22; Quartet, strings in E-flat minor, op. 30; Romeo and Juliet Overture Fantasy; Sextet for strings "Souvenir de Florence" in D minor; Suite no. 1 for orchestra in D minor; Suite no. 2 for orchestra in C; Suite no. 3 for orchestra in G; Swan Lake; symphony no. 3; Symphony no. 4; Symphony no. 5; Symphony no. 6 (first draft and final version); Trio for piano and strings in A minor, op. 50; and Variations on a rococo theme for cello and orchestra.

John Field. Nocturne no. 5 in B-flat (piano alone and arrangement for piano and orchestra).

Modeste Moussorgskii. Kinderscherzo for piano.

Igor Stravinsky. Capriccio for piano and orchestra arranged for 4 hands; Le chant du rossignol (ballet); Danses concertantes; L'oiseau de feu (original version); Symphony of psalms, arrangement for piano and voices; and Symphony in 3 movements.

Note: The Juilliard School in New York at present holds some manuscript material of the composer Arkadii Dubenskii which it intends to give to the New York Public Library in the near future.

CATALOGS   *Dictionary Catalog of the Music Collections.* 2nd ed. Boston: G.K. Hall, 1982. 44v.

BIBLIOGRAPHY   See Grant & Brown, pp. 378–381.

N27
NEW YORK PUBLIC LIBRARY
LIBRARY AND MUSEUM OF THE PERFORMING ARTS
AT LINCOLN CENTER
RODGERS AND HAMMERSTEIN ARCHIVES OF RECORDED SOUND

Don McCormick
Curator

111 Amsterdam Avenue
New York, NY 10023

TELEPHONE   212 870–1663

SCHEDULE   Mon, Thur 10:00 a.m.–8:00 p.m.; Tues, Wed, Fri, Sat
10:00 a.m.–6:00 p.m.

ACCESS   Open to the public. Collection designed primarily for
the specialist and scholar in the performing arts and the communications industry.

FACILITIES   Reading room; photocopying and photography permitted. Specially designed carrels and playback equipment make possible the
hearing of recordings of every type, ranging from turn-of-the-century cy-
linders, through commercial discs of all types and periods, to current television sound tracks and on-the-spot tape interviews.

HOLDINGS   Russian materials are present, but not a specialty in the
collection of 460,000 recordings of all types. Subject matter encompasses
every type of material relevant to sound recordings—all types and styles of
music; complete plays, classic and contemporary; literary readings by major
poets, novelists, and essayists; pronouncements of unique historic sig-
nificance by world statesmen and politicians; as well as speech dialects and
sound effects of special interest to the actor and the theatre, film, or television producer. Reading materials cover the entire field of sound recording
activity—artistic, technological, and commercial—from the 1890s to the
present. Included are extraordinary numbers of discographies, record company catalogs, album program notes, and more than one hundred record
review periodicals, current and defunct, in a half-dozen languages. Materials
on the history and development of the recording industry are available, as

well as an imposing collection of trade journals. These materials are supplemented by constantly growing files of clippings, typescript discographies, and privately printed monographs. Russian materials are primarily sound recordings, mostly in the musical category.

CATALOGS   *Dictionary Catalog of the Rodgers and Hammerstein Archives of Recorded Sound.* Boston: G.K. Hall & Co., 1981. 15 v.

BIBLIOGRAPHY   No bibliography reported.

N28
NEW YORK PUBLIC LIBRARY
MID-MANHATTAN LIBRARY

455 Fifth Avenue
New York, NY 10016

Vladimir Wertsman
Slavic and Rumanian Specialist

TELEPHONE   212 340–0835, 0836

SCHEDULE   Mon–Thur 9:00 a.m.–9:00 p.m.; Fri 10:00 a.m.–6:00 p.m.; Sat. 11:30–5:30 p.m.

ACCESS   Open to the public.

FACILITIES   Reading room; photocopying permitted.

HOLDINGS   The "947" Reference (non-circulating) Section on the fifth floor has several hundred English language books dealing primarily with Russian/Soviet history from the formation of the Soviet state to the present decade. The collection may be subdivided into seven groups:

   (1) a small number of primary sources, i.e., Russian historical sources in translation;

   (2) a significant number of general histories, including works by Pokrovskii, Vernadsky, Miliukov, Kliuchevskii, Soloviev, and the Modern Encyclopedia of Russian and Soviet History;

   (3) several excellent historiographical works including those by Mazour and Auty;

   (4) a strong collection of interpretive histories by, for example, Raeff and Pipes;

   (5) many recent specialized studies, particularly in the Soviet period;

   (6) both "traditional" and "revisionist" political science works, ranging from those by Adam Ulam to Stephen Cohen;

(7) and usually one monograph on each of the Union Republics.

As a whole the collection is very strong for non-specialized research, and complements the Russian- and English-language material in the SLAVIC AND BALTIC DIVISION of the New York Public Library.

CATALOGS   Card catalog.

BIBLIOGRAPHY   No bibliography reported.

N29
NEW YORK PUBLIC LIBRARY
MID-MANHATTAN LIBRARY

PICTURE COLLECTION

8 East 40th Street
New York, NY 10016

Mildred Wright
Chief

TELEPHONE   212 340–0877, 0878 (Circulation Desk)

SCHEDULE   Mon, Wed, Fri–Sat 12:00 p.m.–5:45 p.m.; Tues 12:00 p.m.–7:45 p.m.; Thur 10:00 a.m.–5:45 p.m.

ACCESS   Open to the public. To borrow materials, must have an adult borrower's library card. For use in publicity the library has instructions for courtesy credits.

FACILITIES   No facilities reported.

HOLDINGS   In this collection of 5 million photos and published visual materials, items relating to the Russian Empire and Soviet Union number over 30,000. These are arranged in subject folders, e.g., Russia, A–L; Russia, General; Russia, Armenia; Russia, Yakutsk; Russo–Japanese War. Other subject areas contain Russian/Soviet materials, e.g., Posters, Russian; Church Ceremonies, Eastern Orthodox; Book Illustration, Russian; Russian Ballet; Jewelry, Russian; Satellites, Artificial, Russian. Items are not display size and are not an art collection.

CATALOGS   Card catalog.

BIBLIOGRAPHY   No bibliography reported.

N30
NEW YORK PUBLIC LIBRARY
SCHOMBERG CENTER FOR RESEARCH
IN BLACK CULTURE

515 Lenox Avenue
New York, NY 10037

Howard Dodson
Chief

TELEPHONE   212 862–4000

SCHEDULE   Mon–Wed 12:00 p.m.–8:00 p.m.; Thur–Sat 10:00 a.m.–8:00 p.m. Rare Books, Manuscripts & Archives Section closes daily at 5:30 p.m. Hours change June, July, and August.

ACCESS   Open to the public; must be at least 18 years old.

FACILITIES   There are two reading rooms: one for the General Reference and Research Section and one for the special collections. Admission to use materials in the special collections units requires presentation of identification. Photocopying is done by the staff at a cost of $.30 per page. Photographic copies can also be obtained at cost. The Center reserves the right to refuse permission to reproduce some fragile materials and other materials subject to copyright restrictions.

HOLDINGS   The center collects in the subject fields Afro-Americans–Russia, and Russia–Foreign Relations–Africa. The holdings consist of clipping files and books (General Research and Reference Section), photographs (Photographs and Prints Section), as well as other materials. Included are holdings on Pushkin (a basic collection, no rarities) and Black Americans, such as Ira Aldridge, who have visited Russia or the Soviet Union.

The Paul Robeson Collection (which does not contain many personal papers) deals mainly with materials from 1949–56, which relate to his artistic and political career, including the Robeson Passport Case. Papers from William Patterson, Chairman of the Civil Rights Congress, relate to this case and are in the Robeson Collection. There are also materials related to the Civil Rights Congress records. Only a few items relate directly to Robeson's visits to the USSR; there is some correspondence with Soviet writers (such as Alexander Fadeev) and with those involved with the International Writers' Congress held in the USSR.

The Pettis Perry Papers, 1930s–1960s, also contain some items of interest. Perry was a member of the National Committee of the Communist Party

USA and was a major party leader during the early 1950s. He was imprisoned under the Smith Act in 1955. In 1959 and 1965 he traveled to the Soviet Union. Perry died in Moscow in 1965. The collection contains letters written to his wife during his 1959 trip.

CATALOGS   There is an inventory (or guide) to the Robeson Collection. The books are cataloged through the card catalog and the automated catalogs: Catalog of the New York Public Library (CATNYP) and Research Libraries Information Network (RLIN). Clipping files are located in the Vertical File and are indexed by subject. The Photographs and Prints Section has a local catalog located in the Archives Reading Room.

BIBLIOGRAPHY   See Grant & Brown, p. 385 (not reproduced here).

N31
NEW YORK THEOSOPHICAL SOCIETY

242 East 53rd Street
New York, NY 10022

The only connection between the Society and Russia is the fact that H.P. Blavatsky co-founded the Society with H.S. Olcott in New York in 1875. Blavatsky was the first Russian woman to become a U.S. citizen. The Society referred the guide to its national headquarters in Wheaton, IL. For further information, see OLCOTT LIBRARY AND RESEARCH CENTER in this guide. The bookshop in the New York Society sells all currently available works by Blavatsky.

N32
NEW YORK TIMES
ARCHIVES

130 Fifth Avenue
9th Floor
New York, NY 10011

Dr. John Rothman
Director

TELEPHONE   212 645-3008

SCHEDULE   Mon–Fri 9:30 a.m.–5:00 a.m. (except holidays).

ACCESS   Open to the public, by appointment only.

FACILITIES   Reading room. Photocopying and photography within reasonable limits.

HOLDINGS   Founded in November 1969, the purpose of the archives is to collect and organize documentary and other materials relating to the history and operations of the *New York Times*. The collection consists of letters, memoranda, background reports by *Times* reporters and editors; correspondence of *Times* executives with diverse government officials and others. The Archives does not hold material published in the *Times* itself. The holdings total approximately 1,100 cubic ft. Material about Russia and the USSR is included in several record groups and cannot be separately quantified.

CATALOGS   All record groups that have been processed have guides comprising descriptive catalog cards of their contents. All cards are interfiled in a central, comprehensive card catalog. Photocopies of guides to the several record groups are available but have not been published. They may be consulted at the Archives.

BIBLIOGRAPHY   No bibliography reported.

N33
NEW YORK UNIVERSITY
ELMER HOLMES BOBST LIBRARY
SPECIAL COLLECTIONS

70 Washington Square South
New York, NY 10012

Joan Grant
Director of Collection Management

TELEPHONE   212 998–2566 (Joan Grant); 212 998–2500 (Reference Desk)

SCHEDULE   Mon–Thur 8:30 a.m.–11:00 p.m.; Fri 8:30 a.m.–7:00 p.m.; Sat 10:00 a.m.–6:00 p.m.; Sun 2:00 p.m.–10:00 p.m.

ACCESS   The library honors Metro passes. Scholars who wish to use unique materials may apply to the Access Office (212 998–2550).

FACILITIES   Reading room; photocopying permitted; prior permission required for photography.

HOLDINGS   Collection supports NYU teaching and research in Slavic languages and literatures, history and politics. Collection includes books, periodicals and microforms. Retrospective strengths exist in Russian literature and language from the 19th century to the October Revolution and in Soviet poetry.

CATALOGS   Materials accessible through library's public catalog.

BIBLIOGRAPHY   No bibliography reported.

N34
NEW YORK UNIVERSITY
ELMER HOLMES BOBST LIBRARY
TAMIMENT COLLECTION

70 Washington Square South
New York, NY 10012

Dorothy Swanson
Librarian

TELEPHONE   212 598–3708

SCHEDULE   Mon–Fri 10:00 a.m.–5:45 p.m. Some weekends and evenings (schedule changes with university calendar).

ACCESS   Researchers are advised to write ahead, especially if their time is limited, but service will be provided to anyone who arrives during the hours open.

FACILITIES   Reading room. Copying of archival material may be provided by the library for a fee; limit of 100 pages per collection. Reproduction of photographs for a user's fee.

HISTORY   Originally the Meyer London Library of the Rand

School of Social Sciences, the pioneer workers' school in the United States, founded in 1907. Library was an adjunct to the activities of the school and began with gifts from students, alumni, teachers, and supporters. It became a unique collection of primary source material on the history of American radicalism and working class reform.

HOLDINGS Contains 115 manuscript collections which measure 550 linear feet, holdings of papers and records of individuals associated with the Rand School or those associated with its goals and ideals; also papers of leading communists, radicals, and labor officials. Strong representation of English and American accounts of Soviet Russia, 1918–1940s. Over 500,000 items in vertical files of pamphlets, leaflets, internal documents and other printed items. There is a reference collection numbering approximately 15,000 volumes, as well as some 20,000 periodical volumes (including significant holdings of American socialist and Communist movements), 400 titles currently received.

SPECIAL FEATURES Personal library of Eugene V. Debs; the Edward Falkowski Collection, consisting of 14 boxes of correspondence (incoming and outgoing), journal entries, manuscript and published writings, scrapbooks and union communications of UAW Local 365. The bulk of material from Falkowski's two years at Brookwood Labor College (1926–28) is in the archives at Wayne State University, but a few diary entries, class notes and letters are here as well. (At present only the correspondence [1922–1982] and papers which document Falkowski's residence in the Soviet Union [1930–1937] have been fully processed. The correspondence measures 18 linear inches; the Soviet period papers, 12 inches); papers of Kalmuk Resettlement Committee, 1950–1951; papers of Sergius Ingerman (1868–1943), one of the founders of the Socialist Party of America; records of Russian Artillery Commission in North America, 1915–1917; personal library and papers of Max Shachtman (which include some files on Leon Trotsky).

CATALOGS Dictionary catalog and indexes available in library. Material is listed in AMC system of RLIN. See also: *Guide to the Manuscript Collection of the Tamiment Library*. NY: Garland, 1977, 82 p.; Thomas C. Pardo, ed. *Socialist Collections in the Tamiment Library, 1872–1956: A Guide to the Microfilm Edition*. Sandford, NC: Microfilming Corporation of America, [1979], 181 p.; *Guide to Microfilm Edition of Radical Pamphlet Literature: A Collection from the Tamiment Library 1817 (1900–1945) 1970*. Glen Rock, NJ: Microfilming Corporation of America, [n.d.], 721 p.

BIBLIOGRAPHY Dorothy Swanson. "Tamiment Institute/Ben Josephson

Library and Robert F. Wagner Labor Archives." *Labor History* 23 (Fall 1982); "Tamiment Institute Library and Robert F. Wagner Labor Archives." *Information Bulletin/8.* New York University. Elmer Holmes Bobst Library. See Grant & Brown, pp. 388–389; for Edward Falkowski, p. 354 (entries have not been reproduced here).

O1
OLCOTT LIBRARY AND RESEARCH CENTER

See also NEW YORK THEOSOPHICAL SOCIETY

P.O. Box 270
Wheaton, IL 60189

Lakshmi Narayanswami
Librarian

TELEPHONE   312 668–1571

SCHEDULE   Tues–Fri 9:00 a.m.–12:00 noon; 1:15 p.m.–5:00 p.m.; Sat, Sun 1:00 p.m.–5:00 p.m. (C.S.T.). Closed Mondays.

ACCESS   Open to the public.

FACILITIES   Reading room; photocopying and photography permitted.

HISTORY   Collection contains works by H.P. Blavatsky, the first Russian woman to become an American citizen. She helped to found The Theosophical Society and wrote extensively on the esoteric traditions of the East and West.

HOLDINGS   Approximately 10,000 titles, but only a few hundred by Blavatsky. Includes the Boris de Zirkoff collection; de Zirkoff was the grandnephew of Blavatsky who devoted his life to collecting her writings. The periodical *Lucifer*, edited by Blavatsky, is included. Some of her major titles included are: *The Secret Doctrine, Isis Unveiled, The Voice of the Silence, The Key to Theosophy, H.P. Blavatsky Collected Writings, From the Caves and Jungles of Hindustan.*

CATALOGS   Card catalog.

BIBLIOGRAPHY   Annotated bibliographies on Blavatsky and *The Secret*

Doctrine. H.P. Blavatsky and Her Writings. Wheaton, IL: The Theosophical Society in America; *Introducing You to the Theosophical Society.* Wheaton, IL: The Theosophical Society in America; *The Theosophical Year Book,* 1937 ed. S.v. "H.P. Blavatsky—Co-founder."

O2
ORTHODOX CHURCH IN AMERICA
ARCHIVES

P.O. Box 675, Route 25–A
Syosset, NY 11791

Alexis Liberovsky
Archivist

TELEPHONE   516 922–0550

SCHEDULE   Mon–Fri 9:00 p.m.–5:00 p.m.

ACCESS   Not open to the public, but permission can be obtained to use the collections.

FACILITIES   Reading room; permission can be obtained to photograph or photocopy items.

HISTORY   The origins of the collection are related to the history of the Orthodox Church in America. The Russian Orthodox mission to Alaska was established in 1794 by St. Herman and a group of monks. Major missionary and evangelization work with the Alaskan natives continued under St. Innocent Veniaminov in the 1820s, 1830s, and 1840s. In the 1860s, Orthodoxy began to penetrate the American mainland. Small groups of Greeks, Russians, Serbs and other ethnic groups found themselves in widely scattered parts of the country—San Francisco, New York, New Orleans, Galveston—and in cooperation they established Orthodox parishes. During the administration of Bishop Tikhon (1898–1907), who was later to become Patriarch of Moscow, the diocesan administration was transferred from San Francisco to New York. After the 1917 revolution the American Diocese functioned independently and was known as the Russian Orthodox Greek Catholic Church in North America. In 1970, it was granted canonical autocephaly by the Patriarch of Moscow, and became known as the Orthodox Church in America.
The goals of the Archives of the Orthodox Church in America are:

to preserve and maintain the inactive administrative records of the Chancery of the Orthodox Church in America;

to preserve, maintain and enlarge its holdings in any materials relevant to the history of the Orthodox Church in America;

to make its holdings available for research to competent scholars and other interested individuals or groups;

to promote interest in history and its importance in the life of the Orthodox Church.

HOLDINGS The oldest documents found in the Archives of the Orthodox Church in America date from the 1840s. The administrative archives include Russian imperial government and synodal decrees, decrees on various matters, both secular and ecclesiastical, pre- and post-revolution official and private correspondence with Russia on matters both secular and ecclesiastical, records relating to the bishops, priests, parishes, administrative officers and units of the Orthodox Church in America, records of litigation, ledger books of incoming and outgoing correspondence, correspondence and reports within and outside the church. The Archives also include personal papers of a number of bishops, as well as clergy and lay leaders of the Church. On a broader plane, there is a wealth of information regarding the immigration and settlement patterns of the various ethnic groups which have been a part of the Church during its history, particularly in the period before 1917—Russian, Carpatho-Russian, Galicians, Syrians, Bulgarians, Albanians, Greeks, and Serbs. Also found in the Archives are large collections of photographs, commemorative books, periodicals, church directories and calendars, as well as books dealing mostly, but not exclusively, with church history and theology. In recent years a collection of video and audio tapes as well as academic theses relating to church history has been established.

The Administrative Archives of the Orthodox Church in America comprise 270 linear feet; personal papers and collections, 240 linear feet; publications (books and periodicals), 200 linear feet.

SPECIAL FEATURES The Archives contain materials from or about St. Innocent, Apostle to America and Metropolitan of Moscow; St. Nicholas, apostle to Japan; St. Theophan the Recluse; Patriarch Tikhon (formerly archbishop of North America); Professor Michael M. Karpovich of Harvard; composer Sergei Rachmaninoff; Ambassador Boris Bakhmetev; Colonel S. Obolensky, and many other church leaders. Other noteworthy holdings are:

Correspondence: pre- and post-revolutionary correspondence with the Church in Russia; with the imperial Russian government in tsarist times;

with other ethnic and national Orthodox Churches; with American government agencies (1870–), dealing in part with Russians and other ethnic groups immigrating to the United States.

Church records and resolutions of note dealing with: the establishment of the Church in America; financial records from 1885 on; titles to church properties in Alaska.

Among the rare publications are: church calendars and yearbook directories from 1903; the journal *Tserkovniya Vedomosti*, 1891–1917; the responses by diocesan hierarchs about proposed church reforms in five volumes, 1905–1906; the *Russian-American Orthodox Messenger*, 1896–1973; *Posledniya Novosti*, 1920–1940, published in Paris.

Other rare holdings include: original copies of imperial manifestos including those of Alexander II freeing the serfs, and of Nicholas II establishing the fundamental laws of 1905–1906; autographs of Rachmaninoff and Pasternak; a letter by Rasputin; a collection of letters by St. Theophan the Recluse.

CATALOGS   An unpublished finding aid exists for the administrative chancery records. The rest of the archival materials are partially sorted and available for use, though no catalog exists.

BIBLIOGRAPHY   Edward Kasinec. "New Archival Treasures for the Historian of America and Russia." *The Orthodox Church* 9(7) (1973): 8. See Grant & Brown, pp. 410–411 (not reproduced here).

P1
PILSUDSKI INSTITUTE OF AMERICA FOR RESEARCH IN THE MODERN HISTORY OF POLAND, INC.

381 Park Avenue South
New York, NY 10016

Czeslaw Karkowski
Executive Director

TELEPHONE   212 683–4342

SCHEDULE   Mon–Fri 10:00 a.m.–5:00 p.m.

ACCESS   With few exceptions its collections are accessible to any person without restrictions.

FACILITIES   Reading room; photocopying and photography permitted.

HISTORY   The Institute was founded in New York by a group of political refugees in 1943, and is a continuation of the Jozef Pilsudski Institute established in Warsaw in 1923, later closed by the Nazis. The aim of the Institute is to collect, preserve and make accessible to the public records relating to the history of Poland from 1863 to the present, including the history of the Polish-American community. The Institute maintains an archive, library and art exhibition, and is one of the largest depositories of Polish records outside Poland.

HOLDINGS   The archives are the oldest and largest division of the Institute and make up about 500 linear feet. Included are government records rescued from Poland during World War II, material gathered from pre-1945 Polish embassies and consulates, and collections from organizations and individuals. The Archive is divided into three sections: general, personal, and subject matter. There is material relating to the Soviet Union, the Ukraine, Byelorussia, the Baltic countries and Transcaucasia. Files and records must be consulted to determine relevant material. For instance, the archives of Valerian Platonov pertain to the Polish uprising of 1863 and Poland for the period 1837–1865; the archives of the General Headquarters of the Supreme Command, the "Belvedere Archive," cover the years 1918–1920 and include material on the Polish-Bolshevik War of 1919–1920, as well as reports of the Polish Diplomatic Services from Russia.

The library contains approximately 10,000 volumes dealing primarily with the modern history of Poland, except for the rare-book collection. There are over 3,500 uncatalogued pamphlets arranged topically and primarily published during the two world wars. There is also a newspaper and periodical collection, about 1,500 entries, but not all runs are complete; a photographic collection of approximately 15,000 items; a map collection (about 800); documentary films; sound tapes and recordings; collections of medals, decorations, badges, postage stamps and postcards; and an art collection.

CATALOGS   There are card catalogs for the General, Personal, and Subject-Matter Archives, as well as a register of the General Archives with brief descriptive indexes by folder. There is also a catalog of microfilm reels and a descriptive catalog of their contents. Information on archival holdings has been filed in the *National Union Catalog of Manuscript Collections*. The Library contains a two-part, author and subject catalog; the latter has about 70 subject headings.

BIBLIOGRAPHY   Waclaw Jedrzejewicz. "Jozef Pilsudski Institute." In *East Central and Southeast Europe: A Handbook of Library and Archival Resources in North America*, pp. 387–391. Edited by Paul Horecky & David Kraus. Santa Barbara: ABC CLIO, 1976; Anna M. Mars. "Americana in the Archives of the Jozef Pilsudski Institute in New York." *Political Review*

XXII: 4 (1977): 65–75; J. Golos. "The Platonov Papers in the Jozef Pilsudski Institute of America." *The Polish Review* XXV: 2 (1980): 56–69; Tadeusz Swietochowski. *Guide to the Collections of the Pilsudski Institute of America* . . . New York: Pilsudski Institute of America, 1980. 35 p.; Michael Budny. *The Collections of the Political, Social and Cultural History of the Polish-American Ethnic Community 1890–1980 at the Pilsudski Institute*. New York: Pilsudski Institute of America, 1981. 79 p. See also Grant & Brown, pp. 393–395 (entries have not been reproduced here).

P2
PLESKOW, MARTIN
PRIVATE COLLECTION

21–22 78th Street
East Elmhurst, NY 11370–1310

TELEPHONE	718 932–6759
SCHEDULE	Call for an appointment.
ACCESS	Permission can be obtained to study collection.
FACILITIES	Space available for research. Photocopying and photography permitted.

HISTORY   Begun in the 1930s, the collection has its origins in the fact that the owner was born in Sevastopol, Crimea, and became very interested in the city's history and geography. He also has a comparable interest in the city of Pskov, since its former name was Pleskow.

HOLDINGS   Thousands of individual items, such as books, pamphlets, articles, postcards, stamps, coins, maps, medallions, anything that says Sevastopol, Pskov, or Crimea on it. Also accumulated many interesting facts about the Cantonists, Khazars, Krimchiks, etc. Other materials include owner's 1904 birth certificate, a 1920 Ukrainian passport, coat of arms of Sevastopol (copies of which were presented to the Library of Congress, New York Public Library, and the Historical Museum of Sevastopol). Several hundred photos taken on trip to USSR in 1983 and tape of performance by Ukrainian National Ensemble, Kiev, 1983.

SPECIAL   Coins dating back to the 1600s, from the time of Eliza-
FEATURES   beth and Catherine, up to Nicholas II, including commemorative coins for the Battle of Borodino and Napoleon's defeat. Fairly

extensive except for very expensive items, i.e., over $500.00. Coins of Finland-Russia, Poland-Russia, extensive USSR coinage. Fairly complete collection of postage stamps, including states of Azerbaijan, Georgia, Ukraine—unauthorized issues by Denikin, Wrangel, Kolchak, Shramshenko. Also a 1917 USA shoulder patch from the Allied Expeditionary Force invasion at Archangel and Murmansk.

CATALOGS   Handwritten listing of collection.

BIBLIOGRAPHY   No bibliography reported.

P3
POLCHANINOFF, R. V.
PRIVATE COLLECTION

6 Baxter Avenue
New Hyde Park, NY 11040

TELEPHONE   516 488–3824

SCHEDULE   Call for an appointment.

ACCESS   Not open to the public, but permission may be obtained to study collection.

FACILITIES   No reading room; photocopying and photography permitted.

HOLDINGS   Small collection of books, periodicals and documents pertaining to World War II and displaced persons; Soviet underground postcards, clippings, Russian Boy Scouts and Pioneers. Some rare and unique materials.

CATALOGS   No catalogs.

BIBLIOGRAPHY   Notes on collection are published in Russian in "Collector's Corner." See, for example, *Novoe Russkoe Slovo*, 26 September 1976, p. 6. See Grant & Brown, p. 288 (entries have not been reproduced here).

P4
POLISH INSTITUTE OF ARTS AND SCIENCES OF AMERICA, INC.
ALFRED JURZYKOWSKI MEMORIAL LIBRARY

208 East 30th Street
New York, NY 10016

Feliks Gross
Executive Director

TELEPHONE   212 686–4164

SCHEDULE   Library: Mon–Fri 10:00 a.m.–4:00 p.m. Archives: by appointment.

ACCESS   Open to scholars and researchers.

FACILITIES   Reading room; permission may be obtained to photograph or photocopy items.

HISTORY   The Polish Institute is a non-profit, non-political, educational, academic, cultural organization dedicated to increasing American understanding of Poland's cultural and intellectual heritage. It is also concerned with advancing knowledge about the Polish-American ethnic group and its contributions to America's pluralistic society. The Institute was founded in 1942 in New York City by world-famous Polish scholars Bronislaw Malinowski and Oskar Halecki, who became its first President and Executive Director respectively.

HOLDINGS   The Alfred Jurzykowski Memorial Library is a specialized reference library on Polish studies and contains over 30,000 volumes, 8,000 brochures and 400 titles in the periodical section. From its inception, the Institute has received as gifts and has actively collected documents, papers, and manuscripts relating to Polish and Polish-American history, economics, literature, political science, diplomacy, Polish political parties and their international connections, sociology, and a number of other fields. The Archives of the Polish Institute at present contain about 300 linear feet of processed material in acid-free archival storage containers, and several filing cabinets of oral history recordings and microfilms. A published guide (see below under BIBLIOGRAPHY) provides an index in which individual files can be searched for material relating to the Russian Empire and Soviet Union. Headings such as "Polish-Ukrainian Relations," "Russia" and topics under "Russian . . .," "Ukraine" and topics under "Ukrainian . . .," "White-Russian Minorities" (with a reference to "Byelorussia"), and "Jews—Poland," etc. can be found, as well as entries under individual names.

Grant & Brown provide the following entries:

Waclaw Lednicki (1891–1967). Papers, in process, 6 boxes. Scholar specializing in Slavic literatures. Correspondence, writings, teaching materials, etc., some pertaining to Russia. Also, papers of his father Alexander, a member of the state duma, Kadet Party leader, and lawyer in tsarist Russia. Russian-related materials include correspondence, manuscript books, and miscellaneous other items from 1903–1918. There is photocopy of a memoir written by Alexander Lednicki in 1906 while in prison for his part in issuing the Vyborg manifesto. Among his correspondents were, in 1908, Nikolai Ivanovich Antsyferov, Pavel Pavlovich Korenev, and Petr Andreevich Petrovskii. These letters, and some telegrams from the date are originals. In addition, the senior Lednicki's papers include some copies (photostats) of material in Polish repositories, the British Foreign Office, and, handwritten, the French Foreign Ministry archives. Access requires advance written permission.

Note: The Polish Institute has 2 large collections of materials that include some pertinent holdings: over 300 microfilms relating mostly to Eastern European history and society, in 9 languages; and the oral and sound history collection, ca. 240 cassettes and tapes. Among the microfilms are manuscripts of Kazimierz Baginski on the trial of the 16 Polish Underground leaders in Moscow in 1945 (he was one of the accused), and of I. Nekrasov on Russian labor camps in Dmitrovsk and Samara. In the oral and sound history collection are the taped memoirs of General Michal Tadeusz Karaszewicz-Tokarzewski, commanding officer of the Polish Resistance Movement during World War II. Additions are expected in both these collections. There is also a biographical file which might hold data relating to the Russian Empire and Soviet Union.

CATALOGS   Library has its own card catalog.

BIBLIOGRAPHY   Anna M. Lipski. "Polish Institute of Arts and Sciences in America." In *East Central and Southeast Europe: A Handbook of Library and Archival Resources in North America*, pp. 395–397. Edited by Paul L. Horecky and David H. Kraus. Santa Barbara, CA: Clio Press, [1976]; George Simor. *Guide to the Archives of the Polish Institute of Arts and Sciences of America.* New York: [Polish Institute of Arts and Sciences of America], 1987. 377 p. See Grant & Brown, p. 395.

POSSEV-USA

See EFFECT PUBLISHING

P5
PRELACY OF ARMENIAN APOSTOLIC CHURCH OF AMERICA
ST. NERSES SHNORHALI LIBRARY

138 East 39th Street
New York, NY 10016

TELEPHONE   212 689–7810

TELEX   International 238790; Domestic 968003

SCHEDULE   During Spring 1987 the building of the Prelacy was being expanded and new quarters were being constructed for the library. Until the new building is available the books are stored in New Jersey. During the renovation, inquiries concerning the library should be made at the Prelate's temporary office:

> Archbishop Mesrop Ashjian, Prelate
> St. Illuminator's Armenian Apostolic Cathedral
> 221 East 27th Street
> New York, NY 10016

ACCESS   Open to the public. There is a reading room and photocopying and photography are permitted.

HOLDINGS   Established in 1976, there are 8,000–10,000 titles. The collection is rich in the following subjects: Armenian Church (history, role, interpretation), including the Armenian Church in the United States (books as well as documents); Armenian history (with titles in West European languages), art and architecture; publications of the diaspora (from Lebanon and France) and pre-1915 imprints from Turkey; reference sources and maps. There are also works from Soviet Armenia, mainly art albums, belles-lettres, monographs of Yerevan State University and the Academy of Sciences of the Armenian Republic. The collection also holds publications in Eastern and Western Armenian, as well as in classicial Armenian.

CATALOGS   A dictionary catalog is now in process.

BIBLIOGRAPHY No bibliography reported.

P6
PRINCETON UNIVERSITY LIBRARY
FIRESTONE LIBRARY

Princeton, NJ 08544

Alan P. Pollard
Slavic Bibliographer
Reference and Collection Development

TELEPHONE   609 258–3592, 6668

SCHEDULE   Library hours campus-wide change according to whether or not classes are in session. Hours for Slavic Bibliographer are: Mon–Fri 9:00 a.m.–5:00 p.m.

ACCESS   Persons not associated with the Princeton University Campus can use the library only by obtaining an access card or a borrower's card. Access cards for the academic year 1989/90 are $12.50 per week, $25.00 per month, $105.00 per year. The access card does not provide borrowing privileges. Certain restrictions may apply to patrons holding access-only IDs. Borrowers' cards for the academic year 1989/90 are $280.00 for an individual; $1,460.00 for organizations with fewer than 50 staff and $2,920.00 for larger organizations. Borrowing privileges generally run for four weeks and some restrictions apply. For more detailed information consult the Access Office, 609 258–5737. Hours are: Mon–Fri 8:00 a.m.–5:00 p.m.; Sat 9:00 a.m.–1:00 p.m.

FACILITIES   Open stacks. Reading rooms. Photocopy machines are available in the library.

HISTORY   Before World War II, Princeton acquired some publications, largely scientific, of Soviet academic institutions by exchange. Systematic collecting of Russian materials, including retrospective acquisitions, began in the 1950s. A university program of the 1960s to develop international studies supported the building of a Slavic and Eastern European collection of breadth and depth. The first curator of the Slavic Collection, Zdenek V. David, served from 1966 to 1974. From 1974 to 1985 Orest L. Pelech was the bibliographer for Russia and East Europe. Though budget cuts during the 1970s narrowed the collection's scope and slowed its rate of growth, an excellent research collection has been maintained in selected areas.

HOLDINGS   Traditional fields of strength include archeology, architecture, art, classical studies, demography, East Asian studies, history, history of science, literature, Near Eastern studies, philosophy and religion. (Princeton does not have graduate programs in business, education, law, or medicine.) Under the current collection development policy, the Slavic bibliographer is responsible for Slavic-language monographs and serials in the social sciences and humanities, and for all serials about the Soviet Union and Eastern Europe. Collecting is heaviest in Russian, Ukrainian and Byelorussian; less in Polish and Czech; lightest in Serbo-Croatian and Bulgarian. Materials in the Baltic, Romance and Ural-Altaic languages of the Soviet Union and Eastern Europe are not actively collected, and vernacular publications from Transcaucasia and Central Asia are excluded. Materials about these areas are collected along with Russian and English translations from their literatures. A conservative estimate of the present size of the social sciences and humanities collection in Slavic languages is about 125,000 volumes and 750 current journal and newspaper subscriptions.

CATALOGS   The public catalogs in Firestone Library consist of the Card Catalog, representing items cataloged through 1979, and the Online Catalog, representing items cataloged since 1980. The Card Catalog contains approximately 6 million cards and is both a union and dictionary catalog. The Online Catalog is also a union catalog and terminals are available for its use.

BIBLIOGRAPHY   The following sources were compiled by Zdenek V. David: "Russian Literature/Bibliographic and Other Reference Aids." Princeton University Library, July 1969. 18 leaves [typescript]; "General Bibliographic and Reference Aids in Russian Studies." Princeton University Library, October 1970. 53 leaves [typescript]; "Russian Studies/A Selective Guide to Bibliographies and Reference Aids." Princeton University Library, October 1973. 10 leaves [typescript]; "Soviet and Russian Studies. Collections of Primary Sources in History, Law, Politics and Statistics." Princeton: Princeton University Library, November 1973. 15 leaves [typescript]; also Zdenek V. David. "Princeton University." In *East Central and Southeast Europe: A Handbook of Library and Archival Resources in North America*, pp. 399–402. Edited by Paul L. Horecky and David H. Kraus. Santa Barbara, CA: Clio Press, [1976]. See also, Princeton University Library, Slavic Collections. "Russian Bibliographic Aids (Selected Bibliography)." Undated, 22 leaves [typescript]; "Selected Aids to Research in Soviet and East European studies" [APP (i.e., Alan P. Pollard), 12/89], 6 leaves [typescript]; "Soviet and East European periodicals and newspapers currently received by Princeton University Libraries: A Users' Guide" [12/21/89], 39 leaves [typescript]; Alan P. Pollard. "Princeton University's Slavic Collection." Association of College and Research Libraries. Slavic and East European Section.

Newsletter 4 (1988): 69–79; Princeton University. *Library Handbook, 1988–1989*. [Princeton]: Princeton University Library [1988?]. 39 p.; "Princeton University Library. Access and Borrowing Policy. Firestone Library." Broadsheet. Revised July 1988. There are numerous "Information Sheets" in Firestone that provide more details on policy, services, and libraries.

P7
PRINCETON UNIVERSITY LIBRARY
FIRESTONE LIBRARY
RARE BOOK, MANUSCRIPT, AND SPECIAL COLLECTIONS

Princeton University
Princeton, NJ 08544

William J. Joyce
Associate University Librarian
for Rare Books and Special Collections

Each division is supervised by its own curator. The main office for the department is on the first floor of Firestone Library, 1–16–E.

TELEPHONE   609 258-3184

SCHEDULE   Mon–Fri 9:00 a.m.–5:00 p.m. Schedule for some collections varies. Summer and school holiday schedule varies.

ACCESS   All the Collections are open to scholars from outside the University. Identification and registration are required of all readers. The collections are non-circulating and materials are used only in the reading room serving a particular collection. Because of the unique, rare, valuable, and/or fragile condition of many special collections materials, use of these materials is under strict supervision and access may be limited by the curator or for other reasons.

HOLDINGS   Collections dealing with various aspects of the Russian Empire and Soviet Union are (includes entries in Grant & Brown):
    Louis Adamic (1898–1951). His papers contain some material on Ukrainian Americans. 37 cartons and 8 boxes.
    Armenian. Princeton lists three Armenian manuscripts: No. 1 (Am. 13658). Two leaves from a Menologium, A.D. 1683. Paper; No. 2 (Am.

14399). Four Gospels, A.D. 1730. Paper; 217 folios; No. 3 Bible. O.T. Psalms. Armenian. Ms undated [14th century?] on vellum. One full-page miniature (the Psalmist?). Figures of saints(?) in margins. (Formerly: MS 2491.17.1350). See also under Robert Garrett and William Scheide for other Armenian manuscript holdings.

Ray Stannard Baker (1890–1946). Papers containing materials collected at the meetings of the American Commission to Negotiate Peace in 1919 by Mr. Baker who was then chief of the American Press Bureau. Includes material pertaining to Wilson, Russia, and the Tyrol region (box 18). 18 boxes.

Archibald F. Becke (b. 1871). Typescript with autograph corrections and additions, 281 pp., entitled "Notes on Development of Tactics, 1740–1907." Includes sections on the Crimean War, 1854–55; Turkish War, 1877; and some tactical lessons and deductions from the Russo-Japanese War, 1904–1905; with maps and illustrations.

John Peale Bishop. Among his correspondence (box 23, folder 7) is a prose piece by Gorky, "Mother Kemsky" (8 pages, translation with manuscript corrections) for the *Virginia Quarterly Review*.

Claude Bragdon (1866–1946). Architect and writer. Miscellaneous material in the general manuscripts collections. Includes letter, June 24, 1904, to him from Willard Straight, war correspondent, describing the situation in Korea during the Russo-Japanese War.

Church Slavonic. See under Robert Garrett.

John Foster Dulles (1888–1959). An original set of the personal papers (1888–1961) of Dulles is in the Firestone Library, Rare Book, Manuscript and Special Collections. Includes materials relating to his work on the American Commission to Negotiate Peace, 1919; United Nations General Assembly, 1946–1950; Council of Foreign Ministers, 1945, 1947, 1949; Japanese Peace Treaty, 1951, etc. He had close contact with the Soviet Union while he was Secretary of State, but the papers at Princeton which refer to his tenure as Secretary of State, 1953–1959, do not include the official files of that office, which are under the regulations of the Department of State. 621 boxes. See "A Guide to the Personal Papers of John Foster Dulles" [Princeton: Princeton Library], 1977. 3 vol. (939 p.) Copies of the bulk of the papers are also available in the SEELEY G. MUDD MANUSCRIPT LIBRARY.

John Foster Dulles Oral History Collection. The collection consists of a "series of memoirs concerning John Foster Dulles and his times," 1888–1959, by the "men and women who knew him and worked with him" which was compiled by the Princeton University Library, 1964–1967, and described in a published catalogue. Greatest emphasis is on his colleagues during his tenure as Secretary of State in the Eisenhower administration. Includes Stewart Alsop, Charles E. Bohlen, Willy Brandt, James W. Fulbright,

Averell W. Harriman, Christian A. Herter, Jacob K. Javits, George F. Kennan, Arthur Larson, Henry Luce, Robert D. Murphy and Richard M. Nixon. 275 transcripts of interviews. See *The John Foster Dulles Oral History Collection: A Descriptive Catalogue.* [Princeton]: Princeton University Library, 1967; Revised 1974. 63 p. Also located in the SEELEY G. MUDD MANUSCRIPT LIBRARY.

Father Georges Florovsky. Papers covering his writings; correspondence; notes and bibliographical references regarding his writings and notebooks; bibliographical card files; official documents; manuscripts of translation of St. Teresa of Avila and of St. Catherine of Siena; material on St. Vladimir's seminary, St. Albans, St. Sergius and the Ecumenical Institute in Edinburgh; financial affairs, medical records, address books and cards, desk calendar, immigration papers, programs for conferences, invitations, bibliography of his writings, clippings and notices about Florovsky; material on World Council of Churches; photographs, official papers and documents, notes on various Russian historic figures, correspondence regarding *Put Russkogo Bogoslaviia*, 3 tape recordings . . . as well as material unidentified and miscellaneous. 26 cartons.

Robert Garrett. Collection of medieval and renaissance manuscripts donated by him includes a number of Armenian items: No. 17. Four Gospels, late 17th century. Paper, 297 folios; No. 18. Four Gospels, A.D. 1449. Paper, 244 folios; No. 19. Psalter and Breviary, 16th century. Vellum, 100 folios; No. 20. Breviary, 17th century. Paper, 267 folios; No. 21. Hymnal, 17th century. Paper, 267 folios; No. 22. Psalter, 16th century. Vellum, 236 folios; No. 23. Six leaves from the Alexander Romance, A.D. 1526. Paper, contains miniatures. "The major part of the manuscript, to which these folios belonged, is now in the H. Kurdian Collection (No. 82), Wichita, Kansas." Also in the Garrett Collection but numbered in a different sequence are the following Armenian manuscripts: No. 1. Discourse by St. Gregory the Illuminator, 10th–11th centuries. Vellum, 180 folios; No. 2 (Dep. 1466). Four Gospels, early 11th century. Heavy vellum, 208 folios; No. 3. Astronomy, A.D. 1774–1775. Paper, 58 pages; No. 4. Eleven miniatures from a phylactery, 18th century. On paper; No. 5. One leaf, with miniature, from a Gospel, A.D. 1311. Thick paper; full-page portrait of the Evangelist Matthew. There are also four Church Slavonic manuscripts in the Garrett Collection: Music Book, 17th–18th century. Musical notation throughout. Slavonic neumes ("Kriuki"). Written in Cyrillic script; Service Book, 17th–18th century. Cyrillic script; Music Book, 17th–18th century. Musical notation throughout. Slavonic neumes ("Kriuki") with "Cinnabar letters." Written in Cyrillic script; Tetraevangelion (Four Gospels), 17th–18th century. Preceded by Kanon Tables. Supplementary Liturgical calendric tables. Illuminated. Cyrillic script; And one "Slavonic" manuscript: Missal, ca. 1480. Vellum, 1 folio. (No. 25 in De Ricci catalog). In the same De Ricci catalog, No. 24 is a Georgian palimpsest: Hymns, 11th century. Vellum, 99 folios. Mostly palimpsest, the underwriting mainly a Greek theological text.

Maxim Gorky. See below under Leo Tolstoi.

Richard Halliburton: Box 7 of his collection contains photographs of Russia; some are official (from Soiuzfoto), others were taken by Halliburton or with him in the photograph.

Osip Emil'evich Mandel'shtam (1891–1938). Collection of poems; correspondence; typescripts of his work; a publisher's contract (Sovetskii Pisatel') for "Staryi i Novyi Voronezh," January 5, 1935; a 1932 ID listing O.E.M. as a pensioner receiving 200 rubles a month, with a photograph. Includes letters, postcards, notes, and telegrams from Akhmatova to Nadezhda Mandel'shtam in the late 1950s. (Owing to the poor condition of the originals, researchers will be expected to use copies of the original documents.) 4 boxes.

Aleksei Mikhailovich Remizov (1877–1957). A manuscript, ca. 1930, includes prose and preface to "Turgeniev Snovidetz," AMS (in Russian); 22 letters by Remizov, 1930–1935; 1 document, 1930: permission to publish George Reavey's translation of the author's "Along the Cornices" in *European Caravan*. Ca. 25 items.

Russia. Foreign Office. Passport issued at St. Petersburg, July 2, 1846, to Edward E. Rankin, an American citizen; Russo-Chinese preliminary agreement of May 10, 1909, in regard to the administration of the lands of the Chinese Eastern Railway Co., copy of text given informally by Mr. Kozakoff of the Russian foreign office, 7 pp.

Russia, 1793. Permit to an officer to stay in Warsaw from April 3, 1792 to January 1, 1794. Signed by General Dolgorukij, Commander-in-Chief of the Russian army, April 10, 1793.

William Scheide Library. Contains two Armenian manuscripts: M74. Gospels, preceded by the letter of Eusebius to Carpianus and Canon Tables. Paper, 251+2 folios. Written in 1219 (Armenian era 668) in the church of Holy Sion and the Life-giving Cross in Cilicia, Armenia, by Kostandin (Constantine). Six full-page miniatures of the Four Evangelists, the Annunciation, and the Nativity are on lighter paper and are of crude 17th-century execution. M80. Gospels in Armenian, dated 1633. Vellum, 332 folios. Canon Tables. Misbound at the end. Written from 1627–1633 with great care, at the Monastery of Tathev (old form Statheus) in the northeastern part of greater Armenia by the monk Luke, by whom it is signed and dated 1076 (Armenian era) and who copied it from a manuscript by Gregory of Tathev (14th or 15th century). Three full-page miniatures, 1 small miniature and 25 pen-and-ink drawings, by the artist Khatchatur of Julfa.

Frederick G. Sikes, Jr. (1893–1957). Princeton class of 1915. TLS, April

12, 1918, to L. Fredericks, written while Sikes was stationed at Vologda, Russia, in the U.S. Army.

Irina Skariatina (Mrs. Victor F. Blakeslee). Papers of a Russian noblewoman, writer and journalist. Corrected typescripts, and correspondence relating to her writings; *First to Go Back* (1933), *Skyroad to Russia* (1942), "Doctors, Stalin and Important People and Views," "The Red Navy," and "First to go Home." Also, other articles and papers relating to her childhood in Russia and work as a war correspondent for Collier's during World War II. 2 boxes.

Slavonic manuscript. See under Robert Garrett.

Igor Stravinsky (1882–1971). An autograph by Igor Stravinsky, "Requiem Canticles," to the memory of Helen Buchanan Seeger, 1966 (40 leaves). Two AMS of Igor Stravinsky in the Mixsell Collection of Autographs of Musicians.

Leo Tolstoi (1828–1910). The Scribner publishing archive contains publishing correspondence about Russian as well as other authors. There are at least 23 letters about Tolstoi editions, 1898–1934, in box 152, and 40 letters about Gorky editions, 1901–1903, in box 66. In MSS Misc there is a single letter from Tolstoi, in English, 1907 (to Benedict Prieth); a portrait of Lev Tolstoi by his son, Lev L'vovich, done from memory in Paris on January 2, 1922 (crayon 11¾ x 9¼); a handcopy of *Kreutser Sonata* by N. Simonov in 1890.

The miscellaneous papers of Charlemagne Tower (1848–1923), including his Diary of a European Trip, 1872–1873 (1 volume, AMS).

Evgenii Ivanovich Zamiatin (1884–1937). Manuscripts, correspondence, and related items, 1927–1934. Includes correspondence with George Reavey, Paris, 1932; 4-page typescript of synopsis of film scenario of *We*; 18-page typescript scenario of *Master of Asia*; 9-page manuscript of article "Budushchee Teatra"; 20-page typescript of article "The Modern Russian Theater"; 3-page manuscript of short story *Drakon* (1918); 4-page typescript synopsis of *In Siberia* (novel); 4-page typescript synopsis of *The Flea* (play). Ca. 17 pieces.

Mikhail Zoshchenko (1895–1958). Documents and letters relating to Zoshchenko in the Archives of *Story* magazine and Story Press. Ca. 8 boxes.

There is a rare book collection of Russian history and literature, approximately 200 volumes, including translations: observations of Russian life written by German, French, English and American travelers between 16th–20th centuries (first edition of Giles Fletcher *Of the Russe Commonwealth*, London, 1591, by Giles Fletcher); a collection of works by the Symbolist poets and novelists: Balmont, Bely, Briusov, Nekrasov, Remizov, Soloviev and others.

In the Western Americana Collection: two Russian manuscripts from the 18th century: the Vologodskaia Fabrika Soderzhatelia Toruntaevskogo

(1765–1776); and a history of the Kazan Khanate; also a metal and enamel triptych of uncertain date.

CATALOGS   Printed books in the graphic arts, theater, general rare books . . . are catalogued and may be located through the main card catalogue on the main floor of Firestone Library. For manuscripts and other special materials one should consult the curator of the respective collection. Each collection has special files covering unique material . . . which should not be overlooked. In addition, some collections have uncatalogued but organized material . . . available for public use. There is a local data base of 48,000 records covering manuscripts and other special materials in the Princeton University Library and administered by the Manuscripts Division of the Department of Rare Books and Special Collections. A ten-volume author index to the data base is available, as well as a volume of collection descriptions and indexes (subject, title, form) and a two-volume summary of holdings for the 13,000 individuals that have been indexed to date. There is a 12-page handout entitled "Information about the Rare Book, Manuscript, and Special Collections in the Princeton University Library." August 1986. It provides a general description of the collections and the names and telephone numbers of the curators.

BIBLIOGRAPHY   The major sources for accounts of the library's history and collections are *The Princeton University Library Chronicle* (1939–) and *Biblia* (1930–1938). See Grant & Brown, pp. 275–276.

P8
PRINCETON UNIVERSITY LIBRARY
SEELEY G. MUDD MANUSCRIPT LIBRARY

Olden Street
Princeton, NJ 08544

Nancy Bressler
Curator of Public Affairs Papers

TELEPHONE   609 258–3242

SCHEDULE   Mon–Fri 8:45 a.m.–5:00 p.m.

ACCESS   Nearly all of the papers in the Seeley G. Mudd Manuscript Library may be read on site by any qualified scholars upon presentation of appropriate identification; occasionally all or part of a holding is closed by the donor for a specified term in order to protect the privacy of persons mentioned in the files and for other reasons; and in a very few instances written permission is required as a condition of use. The Library may also be compelled temporarily to deny access to a set of papers that is not yet adequately organized and processed.

FACILITIES   Reading room. Unless prohibited by the donor, the Library will furnish a single copy of a limited number of items to visitors at specified rates; otherwise, no reproduction of any portion of the papers either in whole or in part may be made by photocopy or any other device. Under special circumstances, persons unable to visit the Library may also receive a limited number of photocopies by requesting clearly specified and easily identifiable materials.

HOLDINGS   The collection of 20th-century papers in public affairs ... in the Seeley G. Mudd Manuscript Library ... consists of major archives in American statecraft and public policy which include materials pertaining to (1) elected or appointed government officials and members of the armed services whose actions shaped decisions and events; (2) organizations with a primary interest in influencing the conduct of public affairs; and (3) persons in finance, the professions and the private sector who had a special interest in the origins and consequences of various aspects of national and international policy. The collection also includes relatively smaller cognate holdings containing such materials as reports on specialized topics and projects, observations by and about political leaders of other nations, and descriptions of foreign and domestic events that, taken collectively, constitute a valuable adjunct to the historical record of the recent American past.

The following entries contain materials relevant to this guide:
   American Civil Liberties Union. Archives, 1912–present, refer to the activities and cases of the ACLU, which was founded in 1920, and include earlier materials bearing on civil liberties. The files pertain to the organization's main areas of concern, which are freedom of belief, expression, and association, equality before the law, and within these categories to such issues as academic freedom, censorship, international civil liberties, police practices, etc. Records include only a few relevant items, such as: an immigration case in 1950 involving a "Russian war bride"; correspondence in 1951 about American correspondents with Russian wives; 1959 cases involving the prohibition of demonstrations during the visit of Soviet Premier Nikita Khrushchev in Ames, Iowa, and Washington, DC. 1861 albums, 975 cartons (as of 1988, the Library receives annual installments of papers).
   Norman Armour (1887–1982). The files, 1913–1983, of a career diplomat

include the "Recollections of Norman Armour of the Russian Revolution," 1916–1917, based on his observations as Third Secretary of the United States Embassy in Petrograd, as well as some of his correspondence as United States Minister to Haiti, 1932–1935. 2 boxes.

Bernard M. Baruch (1870–1965). The papers, 1905–1965, mainly relate to Mr. Baruch's government services on the Council of National Defense, 1917–1918; War Industries Board, 1917–1918; American Commission to Negotiate Peace, 1919; and United Nations Atomic Energy Commission, 1946. The section of his papers pertaining to his UN post includes a few items concerning the attitude and position of the Soviet Union toward international control of atomic energy. 521 volumes, 169 boxes, 121 cartons.

Arthur Bullard (1879–1929). Papers, 1905–1929, of a foreign correspondent and editor of *Our World* which refer to his services as a member of the Committee on Public Information in Russia, 1917–1918, in the Russian Division of the Department of State, 1919–1921, and as a member of the Secretariat of the League of Nations, 1926–1927. 20 boxes.

John Foster Dulles (1888–1959). Personal papers, 1888– 1961. Original set of the personal papers of Dulles is in Firestone Library [for description see under PRINCETON UNIVERSITY LIBRARY/FIRESTONE LIBRARY/RARE BOOK, MANUSCRIPT AND SPECIAL COLLECTIONS]. Copies of the bulk of the papers are also available in the Seeley G. Mudd Library.

John Foster Dulles Oral History Collection [for description see under PRINCETON UNIVERSITY LIBRARY/FIRESTONE LIBRARY/RARE BOOK, MANUSCRIPT AND SPECIAL COLLECTIONS].

Louis Fischer (1896–1970). The papers of a journalist, author, and lecturer who specialized in Soviet affairs and was in the USSR during the 1920s and 1930s, was a correspondent during the Spanish Civil War, 1936–1939, a house guest of Mohandas K. Gandhi during 1942–1945, a visiting lecturer at Princeton University, 1961–1970, etc., include notes on his interviews with world leaders. 101 boxes. Fifteen boxes of personal correspondence are not available for any use until the year 2000.

George Frost Kennan. Papers, 1925–1973, of George F. Kennan, the Ambassador to the Soviet Union in 1952 and to Yugoslavia, 1961–1963, mainly include his early official and semi-official files, 1934–1949, as an officer in the Foreign Service of the United States concerning German, United States relations with the Soviet Union, etc. The papers also contain works of his authorship, selected exchanges of correspondence, 1939–1964, as well as some of his outgoing letters, 1955–1967. At present, there are almost no papers in the file relating to Kennan's brief ambassadorship in the USSR in 1952. 38 boxes. Reproduction of the papers is not permitted by Professor Kennan. A section of the files will not be available during the lifetimes of Mr. and Mrs. Kennan and in no case before the year 2000.

Germany, Federal Republic of—Anti-Communist Collection. A collection of files, 1951–1953, consists of anti-Communist propaganda materials from West Germany, including pamphlets, newspapers, stickers, etc. One box.

Robert Lansing (1864–1928). The selected papers, 1881–1929, of the Secretary of State during World War I include correspondence with President Woodrow Wilson and materials concerning the American Commission to Negotiate Peace. The files also contain his diaries, 1908–1910, 1917–1928, and his drafts of the *War Memoirs of Robert Lansing*, Indianapolis: Bobbs [ca. 1935]. Correspondence, manuscript memoirs, and reports refer to the Soviet Union. 16 boxes.

Ivy Ledbetter Lee (1877–1934). Selected files of clippings on Russia, 1924–1933, were compiled by Ivy Lee, a publicist in the firms of Ivy L. Lee and Associates and T.J. Ross, 1912–1934. The materials consist mainly of newspaper columns and printed reports. 15 boxes.

"Paix et Liberté." A collection of files, 1950–52, of "Paix et Liberté," a French anti-Communist organization in Paris, includes some circular letters, posters, radio scripts, tracts, etc. 1 box.

Hugh Lenox Scott (1853–1934). The Hugh L. Scott papers on Russia, 1910–1923, refer primarily to General Scott's mission as a military member of the Special Diplomatic Commission which was sent to Russia by President Woodrow Wilson from June to July 1917 to encourage the Russian people to continue to participate in World War I. 1 box; 7 scrapbooks.

Howard Alexander Smith (1880–1966). The papers, 1902–1966, of the Senator from New Jersey, 1944–1959, mainly refer to his work on the Foreign Relations Committee, 1946–1959. The records also include a handwritten diary, 1927–1954, 1958–1959. He traveled to Europe in 1947; memoranda and daily reports concern his visits to Eastern European nations. 286 cartons.

Harry Dexter White (1892–1948). The selected papers, 1930–1948, in the field of international finance are mainly studies and reports by Mr. White while he was in the Treasury Department from 1934–1948, serving as the Assistant Secretary of the Treasury beginning in 1945. The files pertain to fiscal policies and proposals for foreign assistance involving China, Great Britain, etc., refer to postwar policy toward Germany, and include materials on the United Nations Stabilization Fund, 1942–1944, and the International Monetary Fund, 1945–1948. Includes 4 items on the Russian loan question, 1944–1945, and some references to the Cold War. 13 boxes; 2 ring binders.

CATALOGS   For each important set of papers there is a guide or checklist.

BIBLIOGRAPHY   Nancy Bressler. *A Descriptive Catalogue of Twentieth-Century Papers in Public Affairs in the Seeley G. Mudd Manuscript Library.*

Princeton: Princeton University, revised 1988. 52 p. See also Grant & Brown, pp. 276–277. (The entries for this guide have been taken from the Bressler catalog and do not necessarily agree with or repeat those in Grant & Brown.)

R1
RABINOVICH, ALEX
PRIVATE COLLECTION

85–11 34th Avenue, #2–M
Flushing, NY 11372

TELEPHONE   718 424–6534

SCHEDULE   Call for an appointment.

ACCESS   Open to the public by appointment.

FACILITIES   No reading room; photocopying and photography may be allowed depending on the material.

HISTORY   Began working as antiquarian book dealer in Leningrad in 1955 in a store near the Kirov Theater, then on Liteiny Prospekt.

HOLDINGS   Paintings, drawings, prints (a few *lubki*), rare books, autograph books, e.g., Chekhov, illustrated editions (many hand colored, e.g., Atkinson on Russian manners and customs). Materials deal exclusively with Russia and the Soviet Union, and in a variety of languages (French, Russian, primarily). Approximately 100 fine arts, though altogether thousands of visual materials can be found throughout the collection; approximately 10,000 books from 16th century to current.

SPECIAL   First editions. Literary classics and a section on the his
FEATURES   tory of Russian books, and history of St. Petersburg. Russian views and customs. Imperial presentation copies, 17th-century maps. Third edition (1591) of the first published Russian book, *Apostol*. Historical photography (including album of Franz Josef, 1890s), some of which were brought from Russia (the Leningrad Public Library permitted export in exchange for rare materials given to the Library; policy was 45 books to each of three family members). Russian futurist materials. A few hundred postcards, 1900–1920s, artists and views, military insignias, 18th–19th centuries.

CATALOGS   No catalogs.

BIBLIOGRAPHY   No bibliography reported.

R2
RADIO FREE EUROPE/RADIO LIBERTY
NEW YORK PROGRAMMING CENTER

1775 Broadway
New York, NY 10019

Irene Dutikow
Reference Librarian

TELEPHONE   212 397–5343
TELEX   427123

SCHEDULE   Mon–Fri 8:30 a.m.–4:30 p.m.

ACCESS   Open to the public. Reading room, copying and pho-
                   tographing permitted.

HISTORY   Radio Free Europe and Radio Liberty were founded in
1950 and 1951, respectively, as independent broadcasting stations. They
originally received the bulk of their financing from the United States
government, channeled through the CIA. In 1971 all connections with the
CIA were severed, and the stations were temporarily financed through the
United States State Department, pending their reorganization by the Congress.
    The Board of International Broadcasting (BIB) Act of 1973 established
the present structure, which is designed to ensure RFE/RL's editorial inde-
pendence within the broad guidelines authorized in the basic legislation.
The BIB is a bipartisan board. Its members are nominated by the President
of the United States and are subject to Senate confirmation.
    In pursuit of its basic purpose of promoting freedom of opinion and ex-
pression, RFE/RL broadcasts uncensored news and information on
domestic and relevant world affairs to East Europe, the Baltic States, and
the USSR.

HOLDINGS   The RFE/RL Reference Library in New York City was
consolidated in 1975 from the collections of the Radio Liberty and Radio
Free Europe libraries. As a broadcasting library, it strives for in-depth
coverage of the countries of Eastern Europe and the Soviet Union, and for
coverage of all aspects of important world affairs from 1950. Though there is
ever-increasing emphasis on non-book materials, the library also has a good
collection of some retrospective materials, such as encyclopedias, histories,

and classics of literature, which serves as a basis to define and characterize each country, its history, peoples and traditions.

Clipping files cover Western and Soviet press and various other materials, such as budget items and research reports. Size: 98 drawers holding about 550,000 items and 8 Samizdat drawers holding about 400 files (5,000 items). This archive is one of the most useful assets of the library collections.

Size of collections: 17,800 books (11,094 in English; 6,706 in Russian and other languages); 3,284 microfilm reels; 74 newspapers (6 English; 13 Russian; 55 other languages); 260 periodicals (149 English; 58 Russian; 53 other languages).

Geographical Distribution of Periodicals and Newspapers

Language	Periodicals	Newspapers
Russian	58	13
Byelorussian	12	6
Ukrainian	8	11
Estonian	9	8
Latvian	4	9
Lithuanian	10	6
Bulgarian	—	1
Czechoslovak	1	1
Hungarian	4	1
Polish	7	7
Rumanian	1	5
English	146	6
Total	*260*	*74*

CATALOGS   Card catalog available for collection.

BIBLIOGRAPHY   Publications: *Library Notes*; *Week Ahead*; *Current Books* (quarterly); *Book Reviews* (monthly). *RFE: Research Papers*, 1973–; *Week in Eastern Europe*, 1974–; *Institute for the Study of the U.S.S.R. Bulletin*, 1954–71; *Studies in the Soviet Union*, 1957–71; *RL: Research Bulletin*, 1964–; *Arkhiv Samizdat*, No. 1–; all subject and biographical files for *Arkhiv Samizdat*.

R3
REFERENCE CENTER FOR MARXIST STUDIES, INC.

235 West 23rd Street
New York, NY 10011

Alfred J. Kutzik
Director

TELEPHONE   212 924–2338

SCHEDULE   Mon–Wed, Fri 10:00 a.m.–3:00 p.m.; Thur 10:00 a.m. –
8:00 p.m. Other times by appointment.

ACCESS   Open to interested public, particularly scholars, journalists, writers, students, trade unionists, political and minority activists. Researchers with specific projects should call in advance to expedite assistance.

FACILITIES   Reading room. Photocopying permitted.

HOLDINGS   This is the only reference center in the United States
devoted entirely to the study of Marxist literature and commentary. Collec-
tion composed of the private libraries of outstanding American Marxist and
labor leaders. Many of the books and pamphlets have long been out of print.
In the collection are books once belonging to Max Bedacht, Ben Bordofsky,
Benjamin J. Davis, Jr., Elizabeth Gurley Flynn, William Z. Foster, Ben
Gold, David Gordon, Hyman Lumer, Robert Minor, Gibby Needleman,
Joseph North, William Patterson, Helen Rueben, Charles E. Ruthenberg,
Jessica Smith, Rose Wortis and others. Many of the volumes have handwritten annotations and commentary by their original owners. The collection of books, periodicals and pamphlets is also enriched by material from
the library of the Jefferson School of Social Research and from its 1930s'
predecessor, the Workers' School and its Ruthenberg Library. In addition,
newly published works are regularly added by gift or purchase. Over ten
thousand books have already been classified. The pamphlet collection is invaluable, ranging from out-of-print "penny pamphlets" of bygone activist
days which have come out of closets onto the Center's shelves, to current issues relating to working class struggles. Bound volumes of historically significant periodicals include INPRECORR (International Press Correspondence), *The Liberator*, *New Masses*, *Mainstream*, *Masses and
Mainstream* and others.

Over 500 books on the Soviet Union categorized from "Agriculture" to "Youth," two to three thousand pamphlets on the Soviet Union by United States and Soviet authors; some English-language Soviet journals, such as *Social Sciences*.

CATALOGS   Author-title card catalog.

BIBLIOGRAPHY   Brochure on the Center is available.

R4
UNIVERSITY OF ROCHESTER
RUSH RHEES LIBRARY
NIKOLAI MARTIANOFF COLLECTION

Rochester, NY 14627

Laura Janda   Claude Noyes
Assistant Professor of Russian   Director of Collection
                                     Development

TELEPHONE   Laura Janda, 716 275–4251
                Claude Noyes, 716 275–4474

SCHEDULE   Mon–Thur 8:00 a.m.–midnight; Fri 8:00 a.m.–9:00 p.m.;
Sat 10:00 a.m.–6:00 p.m.; Sun 12:00 p.m.–midnight.

ACCESS   Open to the public.

FACILITIES   Reading room; photocopying and photography permitted.

HISTORY   Nikolai Martianoff, born in 1893, was a publisher/editor in the New York City Russian colony. At the time of his death, his collection was distributed among the University of Rochester, the Synod of Russian Bishops Outside Russia, and Alex Rabinovich.
    The Nikolai Martianoff Collection is the inventory of a Russian bookshop which was donated to the University of Rochester when the owner passed away.

HOLDINGS   The collection contains largely emigre publications, plus some items published in the USSR. Includes monographs, some of which are in poor condition and are being transferred to microfilm. Approximately 2,000 titles in the collection, many in multiple copies. Many emigre publications (mostly printed in Germany), 1910s–1920s; Gorky's emigre publications; Russian Orthodox emigre publications, 1930s–1950s.

CATALOGS As of September 1987 the collection had not been fully cataloged. When it is, it will become part of the library's permanent collection and will be logged into the on-line catalog. It will not constitute a separate collection and individual titles will not be tagged as originating in this collection.

BIBLIOGRAPHY No bibliography reported.

R5
ROCKEFELLER ARCHIVE CENTER

Pocantico Hills
North Tarrytown, NY 10591–1598

Dr. Darwin H. Stapleton
Director

TELEPHONE 914 631–4505

SCHEDULE Mon–Fri 9:00 a.m.–5:00 p.m.

ACCESS Open to the public.

FACILITIES Reading room (closes at 4:45 p.m.). Photocopying services available and photographing permitted.

HISTORY Between 1965 and 1973, representatives of The Rockefeller University, The Rockefeller Foundation, the Rockefeller Brothers Fund, and the Rockefeller family explored the possibility of creating a single scholarly research center based on their combined record collections. Three of these organizations had, by 1970, active archival programs. The family archives were organized in 1954 as part of the Office of the Messrs. Rockefeller, the Foundation archives were established in 1967, and the University's in 1969.

By 1973, all three archives were open for limited scholarly research, although their principal function was reference service to their parent organizations. In 1974, the Foundation published a guide to the open collections in its custody that included the records of the General Education Board, the Laura Spelman Rockefeller Memorial, the China Medical Board, and other smaller philanthropic organizations founded by the Rockefeller family. The Foundation's holdings were transferred to the Rockefeller Archive Center when it opened in 1975.

The Archive Center is a joint project of the four founding organizations and is a division of The Rockefeller University.

HOLDINGS   Material relating to the activities of organizations founded and supported by the philanthropies of the Rockefeller family, plus the personal papers of family members and other individuals associated with their endeavors, total some 40 million documents to date and comprise an invaluable and irreplaceable reference source for historians and other scholars. The Archive Center is a permanent repository and as more material becomes available from the Rockefeller family and from organizations that they have supported, it is added to the archives. In 1986 the Center's scope was expanded by the additions of The Commonwealth Fund and the Russell Sage Foundation archives.

There is a large collection of photographs created by several organizations.

Material dealing with Russia and the Soviet Union is located in various collections housed at the RAC. Given the large size of the Center's holdings and the comparatively small amount of material pertaining to Russia, it is impossible to present a comprehensive description or listing of all relevant documents. What follows is just a brief summary of some of the more noteworthy documents at the RAC.

Rockefeller Foundation

Record Group 1.1 Series 708 Baltic States: a report by H.O. Eversole, "Medical Education in the Baltic States" (1925), 0.4 cubic feet. Series 785 Russia/Soviet Union: 1.2 cubic feet of material. Topics include health programs, agriculture, the humanities, natural and social sciences, relief operations, and nursing. Mainly correspondence and reports dated from 1919 into the 1970s. Some material is cross-listed Rockefeller Foundation Health Commission—Russia. Series 786 Latvia: mostly concerning emergency aid to the University of Latvia 1924–1938, 0.4 cubic feet.

Record Group 2 General Correspondence. Arranged by year and then by country. Reference to Russia is scattered throughout these files, therefore an exact determination of size cannot be given, but the amount is nominal.

Record Group 3 Series 900 Program and Policy: Reports and program development material/correspondence, 1920s to 1940s. Several folders.

Laura Spelman Rockefeller Memorial

Documents on the Student Friendship Fund, Russian Refugee Relief Association—London, Russian Zemstvos Committee, Russian Student Fund. This material covers mainly 1921–1929, and generally deals with Russian relief operations. About 0.8 cubic feet.

International Health Board

Again, cursory mention of Russia, contains some material on the Pan-Russian Malaria Conference and reports by Doctors Kandelaki, Dobreitzer, Rothermel; all material is circa 1924/1925. About one folder.

Commonwealth Fund

This collection is currently unprocessed, therefore an accurate description of size and contents cannot be provided, but not more than 1.2 cubic feet of material is located in the records. Mainly it consists of appeals by various Russian emigres after World War I and also Russian relief in 1944.

Rockefeller University

Correspondence between Ivan Pavlov and Boris Babkin, Simon Flexner, Ernest H. Starling, and correspondence between Vladimir Pavlov and Simon Flexner; about 200 items dated between 1921–1925. The RU material is indexed by individual, hence more correspondence or material involving the Soviet Union is no doubt in the files.

Researchers interested in specific individuals or organizations are encouraged to write to the Center to inquire about the scope and availability of relevant materials.

Grant & Brown have the following entry:

Duncan Arthur MacInnes (1885–1965). Papers, 1926–65. Chemist. A diary, photocopies of newspaper reports, and a mimeographed copy of "Trip to Moscow" by A.L. Nadai all concern his 1945 trip to Moscow to attend the 220th anniversary of the founding of the Russian Academy of Sciences (box 3). Scattered throughout the papers is correspondence that reflects MacInnes's continuing interest in the American Soviet Science Society. Unpublished description and container list. 8 feet.

CATALOGS   The holdings of the Archive Center are divided into two parts—archives and manuscript collections. The archival materials are the records of the founding organizations. The manuscript collections are the records of individuals and organizations that have participated in the Rockefeller experience. The Center preserves the integrity of each archive or collection as a discrete unit. Large collections of archives are divided into record groups, series, and items as necessary for descriptive and control purposes, but the original order is preserved. Both subject and name in-house card files and registers are available to researchers. Registers of processed collections contain folder descriptions. The Rockefeller Archive Center is a member of RLIN.

BIBLIOGRAPHY *Archives and Manuscripts in the Rockefeller Archive Center.* North Tarrytown: Rockefeller Archive Center, 1984 [Third Printing January 1987]. 70 p. There are also guides to the photograph collection, and surveys of sources on the history of nursing, on labor and industrial relations, psychiatry, and child studies, all of which can be obtained by writing to the Center. See Grant & Brown, p. 407.

R6
NICHOLAS ROERICH MUSEUM

319 West 107th Street
New York, NY 10025

Mr. Daniel Entin
Executive Director

TELEPHONE   212 864–7752

SCHEDULE   Tues–Sun 2:00 p.m.–5:00 p.m.

ACCESS   Painting collection open to the public; access to other holdings will be considered on an individual basis. Permission must be requested in advance in writing.

FACILITIES   No reading room; permission might be granted for photocopying and photography.

HISTORY   The principal purpose of the Nicholas Roerich Museum is to exhibit the paintings of Nicholas Roerich, to publish and distribute his writings, and to promote his ideals of art and culture: "Art will unify humanity. . . where culture is, there is peace."

HOLDINGS   Permanent collection of 200 paintings by Nicholas Roerich, and his published works. Archival materials (unorganized) relating to Nicholas Roerich's life and work; some materials (also unorganized) of ARCA (American Russian Cultural Association) of the 1940s.

CATALOGS   A catalog of the collection is in preparation.

BIBLIOGRAPHY   Irina H. Corten. *Nicholas Roerich: An Annotated Bibliography.* A list of publications by Nicholas Roerich and prints of his work will be sent out on request.

R7
RONALD FELDMAN FINE ARTS, INC.

31 Mercer Street
New York, NY 10013

Susan Yung
Publicity Coordinator

TELEPHONE   212 226–3232

SCHEDULE   Tues–Sat 10:00 a.m.–6:00 p.m.

ACCESS   Open to the public.

FACILITIES   Reading room; photocopying and photography permitted.

HOLDINGS   Represent two artists who collaborate: Vitaly Komar and Alexander Melamid, who average one exhibition of their new artwork every two years in this gallery. Have archives documenting the artwork of Komar & Melamid (photographs, press releases). See entry for KOMAR AND MELAMID ART STUDIO.

CATALOGS   No catalogs.

BIBLIOGRAPHY   Current biography/bibliography of the artists available upon request.

R8
RUSSIAN BOY AND GIRL SCOUT ARCHIVE

86 Durand Road
Maplewood, NJ 07040

John L. Bates
Curator

TELEPHONE   201 763–4189

SCHEDULE   Hours by appointment. Closed February, July, and August.

ACCESS   The archive is not open to the public, but permission may be obtained to study the collection. Thorough knowledge of Russian is essential.

FACILITIES   Reading room; permission may be obtained to photograph or copy a limited number of items.

HISTORY   Russian scouting was founded in 1909 by Colonel Oleg Pantuhoff, Sr. (1882–1973), who, in 1919, became Chief Scout. Colonel Pantuhoff continued Russian scouting after 1920 from abroad in exile. Russian scouting is little known to non-Russians but it was an important factor in the pre-revolutionary social and educational fabric of Russia. After 1920, and then again after World War II, Russian scouting became a strong link among Russian emigre groups and displaced persons in some fourteen countries of their exile and continues today. Scouting was prohibited in the Soviet Union after 1923.

HOLDINGS   The collection is essentially the accumulation of some seventy years of correspondence and Russian scout material by Colonel Pantuhoff and occupies 25 feet of shelf space. There are thousands of letters addressed to the founder from scoutmasters and leading Russians, including a number from the late Lord Robert Baden-Powell, the founder of world scouting in 1908; photographs of Russian scouting, some as early as 1911; and pamphlets, books, manuals, newspapers, scout magazines and many clippings, all pertaining to Russian scouting and all in Russian.

There is a small collection of Pantuhoff family letters, ca. 1890–1905, photographs and manuscripts relating to Colonel Pantuhoff's book *O dniakh bylykh*. There is also a small collection of Colonel Pantuhoff's library: rare, old books on Russian history, Russian arts and crafts, and old engravings—10 engravings by Mikheev (1753) and old maps of St. Petersburg (1750–1820).

There are also two separate collections:

One consists of paintings and photographs of portraits done by Colonel Pantuhoff's Russian-born younger son, Igor Pantuhoff. A graduate of the National Academy in New York, he painted such personalities as Princess Grace of Monaco, Secretary and Mrs. James V. Forrestal, Laurence Rockefeller, Benson Ford, Madame T.V. Soong and others;

The other contains the biographical notes of Colonel John L. Bates, who was U.S. Liaison Officer with the Soviets in the U.S. Army Persian Gulf Command (1943–45), and at the sites of all three Big Three conferences—Teheran, Yalta, and Potsdam—and was liaison officer and interpreter for Generals Eisenhower and Clay in Berlin (1945–1947).

CATALOGS   No catalogs reported.

BIBLIOGRAPHY   See Grant & Brown, p. 272 (not reproduced here).

RUSSIAN NAVAL MUSEUM

See HISTORICAL MUSEUM RODINA

R9
(RUSSIAN) ORTHODOX CATHEDRAL OF
THE PROTECTION OF THE HOLY VIRGIN

See also ORTHODOX CHURCH IN AMERICA

59 East 2nd Street
New York, NY 10003

Christopher Calin
Parish Council

TELEPHONE   212 677–4664

SCHEDULE   Office: Mon–Fri 10:00 a.m.–5:00 p.m. (by appointment only). Church: Wed 6:30 p.m.; Sat 6:00 p.m.; Sun 9:00 a.m.

ACCESS   Open to the public.

FACILITIES   Now in the process of setting up a reading room; permission can be obtained to photograph or photocopy items. There is a bookstore on the premises for materials on Russian and English language and art.

HOLDINGS   This was the procathedral of the Russian Orthodox Church in America, 1926–1982, and the administrative center of the Church until 1982, when the Episcopal See was transferred to Washington, DC.
    Collection consists of parish registries and related information, letters, photographs (including letters and photographs from pre-revolutionary Russia), and artwork. Periodicals include *The Anglican Digest* (St. Louis, MO), *The Journal of the Moscow Patriarchate* (Moscow), *Orthodox Life* (Jordanville, NY), *The Orthodox Church* (Syosset, NY), *Orthodox Observer* (n.p.), *Orthodox News* (Great Britain), *Religion in Communist Dominated*

Areas (R.C.D.A.) (n.p.), *The Russian Orthodox Messenger* (n.p.), *Solia* (n.p.), *St. Vladimir's Seminary Theological Quarterly* (Crestwood, NY), *The Word* (n.p.). Size of the collection is unknown at present.

CATALOGS   No catalogs are available at this time.

BIBLIOGRAPHY   Bibliography provided upon request. There is a monthly newsletter of educational, historical, and current events.

R10
RUSSIAN ORTHODOX ST. NICHOLAS CATHEDRAL

15 East 97th Street
New York, NY 10029

Father Gennadi Dzitchkovski
Archpriest

TELEPHONE   212 289–1915, 876–2190

SCHEDULE   The church is open for services Sunday mornings. There is also a schedule available of liturgies, vespers, etc. Call for admission at other times. For information about the church or a tour, Father Dzitchkovski should be contacted.

ACCESS   Permission to study the building and icons, etc., must be obtained in advance from Father Dzitchkovski.

FACILITIES   No reading room. May photograph, but not photocopy.

HOLDINGS   The church was built in 1902. In the 1950s, a legal battle for possession of church was finally won by the Moscow Patriarch. Many original furnishings were apparently scattered during the legal battle. There are murals from 1907 by S.V. Sokoloff, and 19th- and 20th-century icons. Altar cross from Russian ship Retzvitan. There is no treasury.

BIBLIOGRAPHY   M. Pokrovsky, ed. *St. Nicholas Cathedral of New York: History and Legacy.* New York: n.p., 1968. (Contains brief information on icons.)

R11
RUSSICA BOOK AND ART SHOP

799 Broadway
New York, NY 10003

David Daskal   Irene Kuharets
Director   General Manager

TELEPHONE   212 473-7480

SCHEDULE   Mon–Fri 9:00 a.m.–6:00 p.m.; Sat 12:00 p.m.–6:00 p.m.

ACCESS   Open to the public.

FACILITIES   No reading room; no photocopying or photography.

HOLDINGS   Russica specializes in art (paintings, prints, engravings, etc.) and art books, as well as emigre publications. It also offers antiquarian books, rare and out-of-print material.

CATALOGS   At least once a year catalogs in Cyrillic and Latin scripts are mailed to subscribers.

BIBLIOGRAPHY   No bibliography reported.

S1
SAINT VLADIMIR'S ORTHODOX THEOLOGICAL SEMINARY
THE FATHER GEORGES FLOROVSKY LIBRARY

575 Scarsdale Road
Crestwood, NY 10707

Eleana Silk
Assistant to the Librarian for Circulation

TELEPHONE   914 961-8313

SCHEDULE   Mon–Fri 9:00 a.m.–5:00 p.m.; Mon, Tues, Thur 6:30 p.m.–9:30 p.m. (Schedule is for regular academic sessions; call at other times.)

ACCESS   Permission may be obtained to use collection.

FACILITIES   There is a reading room; photocopying and photography are permitted.

HOLDINGS   The Library contains over 50,000 volumes and currently receives over 360 periodicals. The collection is especially strong in areas of Orthodox history, theology, philosophy and culture (its policy is to collect all materials published on the Orthodox Eastern Church, as much as possible on patristics, church fathers, and cultures of countries where Orthodoxy is strong today or in history). Through the acquisition of Archimandrite Anthony Repella's library in 1956, the collection is unique in the field of Russian theological literature. The Library acquired the Kolchin collection of Russian liturgical music in 1973. Other collection gifts have come from Father Michael Czap, Father Georges Florovsky, Father John Kivko, and Walter Scarloss. Gifts now awaiting cataloging are from Father Adamov, Paul Anderson, Georges Barrois, Father Paul Lutov, and Bogdan Miskhovich. About 25 percent of the collection is in Russian and other Slavic languages; 25 percent in English; 15 percent each in French and Greek; 10 percent in German; and another 10 percent in other languages, e.g., Aleutian, Japanese, Latin, Italian, and Spanish.

SPECIAL   Among the most important journals at St. Vladimir's
FEATURES   Seminary are those published in Russian before 1917.
From the four major theological academies, the library holds nearly complete sets of the following: *Khristianskoe chtenie* (St. Petersburg); *Bogoslovskii vestnik* (Moscow); *Trudy* (Kiev); *Pravoslavnyi sobesednik* (Kazan). There are less substantial holdings of the following journals: *Voskresenoe chtenie* (Kiev); *Pravoslavnoe obozrenie* (Moscow). There are, in addition, some holdings in numerous smaller literary and philosophical journals, such as: *Vera i razum* (Kharkov); *Strannik* (St. Petersburg). The library also has an Ostrog Bible, rare old prayer books and liturgical texts, the complete collection of the minutes and reports of the Holy Synod in Russia, and the records of the Alaskan Russian Church from the Library of Congress on microfilm (375 roles).

CATALOGS   The card catalog was closed in 1985. At present, over 23 percent of the book collection, 75 percent of periodicals, and all microfilm, fiche, cassettes, and videos are in the computer.

BIBLIOGRAPHY   Meinrad Dindorf, O.S.B., and Edward Kasinec. "Bibliographical Note: Russian Pre-Revolutionary Religious-Theological Serials in the St. Vladimir's Seminary Library." *St. Vladimir's Theological Quarterly* 14: 1–2 (1970); Edward Kasinec. "Bibliographical Census: Russian Emigre Theologians and Philosophers in the Seminary Library Collection." *St. Vladimir's Theological Quarterly* 16: 1 (1972): 40–44.

S2
JOSEPH SCHILLINGER COLLECTION

340 East 57th Street
New York, NY 10022

Mrs. Joseph Schillinger
Archivist

TELEPHONE 212 355–3596

ACCESS Original materials in Mrs. Schillinger's private collection consist of literary manuscripts (in Russian and English), notebooks, art works, music manuscripts (some published in the USSR), and are not available to the public.

FACILITIES No facilities available.

HOLDINGS Since the publication of Grant & Brown, most of the items listed there have been transferred to the Lincoln Center Music Library (*see entry for* NEW YORK PUBLIC LIBRARY, LIBRARY AND MUSEUM OF THE PERFORMING ARTS AT LINCOLN CENTER, MUSIC DIVISION), which has had a large Schillinger Collection for a long time. The two Theremin letters to Mrs. Schillinger were sold at auction, but the buyer wishes to remain anonymous. Other institutions within the New York metropolitan area that contain materials on or by Joseph Schillinger are: MUSEUM OF MODERN ART: Schillinger Archive of Art; COLUMBIA UNIVERSITY LIBRARIES, RARE BOOK AND MANUSCRIPT LIBRARY: Joseph Schillinger Papers; for paintings, drawings, and photographs (series developed from the system presented in *The Mathematical Basis of the Arts* around 1934): METROPOLITAN MUSEUM OF ART; Smithsonian Institution: National collection of fine arts, Cooper-Hewitt Museum; BROOKLYN MUSEUM; SOLOMON R. GUGGENHEIM MUSEUM; the Whitney Museum of American Art; and the Newark Museum.

CATALOGS For catalogs, see individual institutions.

BIBLIOGRAPHY Frances Schillinger. *Joseph Schillinger: Memoir*. New York: Da Capo Press, 1976, ca. 1949. 224 p.; Nicolas Slonimsky. "Schillinger of Russia and of the World." *Music News* 39 (March 1947). See Grant & Brown, p. 396 (entry has not been reproduced here).

S3
SCHWAB, GEORGE
PRIVATE COLLECTION

Director
CUNY Graduate Center
Conference on History and Politics
33 West 42nd Street
New York, NY 10036

TELEPHONE   212 790–4579

SCHEDULE   By appointment.

ACCESS   Private collection. Researchers should write for an appointment.

FACILITIES   No reading room, but permission may be given for photocopying and photography.

HISTORY   The collection is a family inheritance. The family originally lived in Riga and Libau, Latvia, and began collection in the 19th century. This entire collection was lost during World War II. Family emigrated to United States in 1947, and started a new collection of Russian and Slavic arts in 1949. George Schwab's wife, nee Eleonora Storch, lived in Sweden during World War II, 1940–41, where her family collected some relevant artifacts, but the couple's collection grew substantially in New York City after 1965.

HOLDINGS   Approximately 50 items: fine arts, crafts, antique silver, and furnishings. There are also 15–20 oils on glass and canvas by Yugoslav primitive artists, collected between 1962 and 1970. A small library of about 50 books and auction catalogs supports the collection.

SPECIAL   Three watercolors of Sudeikin; about 20 theatrical
FEATURES   sketches, costume designs (1900s to 1950s) of Alexandre Benois, plus landscapes. A watercolor theater curtain sketch by M. Dobuzhinsky; 10 pastel scenes of old wooden synagogues (which were destroyed in World War II) in the Russian Empire by George Loukomski, critic and draftsman (these were bought by Professor Schwab's father-in-law, Gilel Storch); drawing by Ilya Repin. Antique silver, 18th or 19th century,

from tsarist collections. Huge cobalt and 24k gold chandelier (125 lbs.) from tsarist palace, has Cyrillic inscription inside.

CATALOGS   No catalogs.

BIBLIOGRAPHY   No bibliography reported.

S4
SHEVCHENKO SCIENTIFIC SOCIETY
LIBRARY AND ARCHIVES

63 Fourth Avenue
New York, NY 10003

Ms. Svitlana Andrushkiw
Librarian

TELEPHONE   212 254–5130

SCHEDULE   Thur 9:00 a.m.–4:30 p.m.

ACCESS   By appointment only.

FACILITIES   Reading room, photography and photocopying permitted.

HISTORY   The Shevchenko Scientific Society, which has devoted itself to promoting a free and independent scholarship, was founded in Lviv (present-day L'vov), Western Ukraine, in 1873 and honors the great Ukrainian poet, Taras Shevchenko (1814–1861). Before World War I, the Society became the unofficial Ukrainian Academy of Arts and Sciences and possessed a large library, museum, and its own printing plant. After the outbreak of World War II and the annexation of Western Ukraine to Soviet Ukraine, the Soviet government disbanded the Shevchenko Scientific Society. In the course of the war, a majority of the Society's members escaped to the West and re-established the Society in Western Europe, the United States, Canada, and Australia. The present library of the Society was organized in the early 1950s.

HOLDINGS   The purpose of the Library is to collect materials which relate directly or indirectly to the Ukraine with a particular interest in Ukrainian history, literature, art, language, Ukrainians in the United States and in foreign countries. Holdings include Ukrainian periodicals, some newspapers; Shevchenko Society publications; Ukrainian history, art, literature—approximately 40,000 volumes. There is a rare-book section and an archives area consisting of approximately 50 cataloged archives.

The Society also reports the following materials:

In the rare book collection the Library has:

Piramyz Albo Stolp' . . . *Innokentiia Gizeliia Arkhimandryty Sviatoi Velychno Chudotvornoi Lavry Pechens'koi Kyivs'koi* . . . Kiev, 1685. 18 ll. manuscript.

Letopis' Samovidtsa. Kiev, Izd. Kievskoiu Vremennoiu Kommissieiu dlia Razbora Drevnikh Aktov, 1878.

Letopis' Hryhoriia Hrabanki. Kiev, Izd. Kievskoiu Vremenoiu Kommissieiu dlia Razbora Drevnikh Aktov, 1854.

Ivan Franko. *Z Vershyn i nyzyn: Zbirnyk Poezii.* [1st Ed.] Lviv, 1887. *M. Mykhailo Drahomanov Pavlyk (1841–1895): Eho Iubilei, Smert', Avtobiografiia i Spys Tvoriv.* Lviv, 1895.

In the archives section the Library has the papers of Aitol Vitoshynskyi, a member of the Ukrainian diplomatic mission of the Ukrainian National Republic, 1919–23; documents of the collectivization drive of the Krynychanska Silska Rada, Dnipropetrovskyi raion, 1929–33; documents from the Displaced Persons Camp, Ashaffenber, Germany, 1946; documents from the Displaced Persons Camp, Bertesgaden, Germany, 1946–48; a World War II photo-archive; and archives dealing with Ukrainian immigration to Paraguay (the O. Paduchak papers), 1945–50.

Grant & Brown make the following statement:

The archives include minutes of meetings and other records of the organization itself as well as papers of members, photographs, and other documents. Holdings include papers of Professor Nicholas Chubaty, Prince Ivan Tokarzhevsky-Karasevych, and Professor Andriy Jakowliv; correspondence of Myhaylo Hrushevsky and S. Faryniak; documents of Bohdan Lepky; papers of Dr. Sophia Parfanovych; and some archives of the Voliansky family.

CATALOGS   The catalog of the Library is arranged alphabetically by author, first in Cyrillic, then in English, German, and Polish. There are also separate catalogs of rare books and periodicals/microfilm; archives; commemorative almanacs; music; and periodicals.

BIBLIOGRAPHY   *Publications of the Shevchenko Scientific Society, 1945–1980.* New York: Shevchenko Scientific Society, 1980. 47 p.; Y. Bozhyk, R. Waschuk, and A. Wynnyckyj. "The Archival and Manuscript Collection of the Shevchenko Scientific Society, New York City." *Journal of Ukrainian Studies* [Toronto, Canadian Institute of Ukrainian Studies] 9:2 (1984): 93–104. See Grant & Brown, p. 396.

S5
SOVART
c/o LIVET REICHARD COMPANY, INC.

11 Harrison Street
New York, NY 10013

Todd Bludeau
Curator

TELEPHONE	212 431–6850
SCHEDULE	Mon–Fri 10:00 a.m.–6:00 p.m.
ACCESS	Not open to the public, but permission may be obtained to study collection.
FACILITIES	No reading room. Photocopying and photography permitted.

HISTORY   A private collector and Livet Reichard Co., Inc., have formed SOVART, a company conceived to promote the sale and exhibition of contemporary Soviet art in the United States. Goals are to discover new Soviet artists and promote existing artists by placing them with appropriate galleries in the United States which will exhibit their work on a regular basis. Services provided by SOVART in order to facilitate representation of artists in the Soviet Union include organizing trips to meet with the artists and visit their studios in order for American dealers to develop direct links to the artists they represent; arranging the purchases of the artworks on a regular basis; coordinating shipment and delivery of the artworks in the United States; reporting on general artistic developments in the Soviet Union.

HOLDINGS   Contemporary paintings, prints from USSR with catalogs, artists' biographies, art journals, etc. The size of the collection varies; as of Fall 1987, 300 works of art. Noteworthy are works by Eric Bulatov and Ilya Kabakov.

CATALOGS	No catalogs.
BIBLIOGRAPHY	Many on Soviet artists.

S6
SOVFOTO/EASTFOTO

25 West 43 Street, Room 1008
New York, NY 10036

Leah Siegel
Ownership/Management

TELEPHONE   212 921–1922

SCHEDULE   No schedule reported.

ACCESS   Sell one-time reproduction rights only. All material is sent out on approval and must be returned after use by the date specified. Do *not* sell individual prints. There is a small postage and handling charge if an appropriate selection is sent but none of the photos is used. A research fee may be charged on large, complex orders. Price list available for standard publication rates; all other rates are given out on request.

FACILITIES   No facilities reported.

HOLDINGS   The following statement incorporates Grant & Brown material: Commercial stock photo agency, specializing in photo-graphs from the Soviet Union, Eastern Europe (Albania, Bulgaria, Czechoslovakia, East Germany, Hungary, Poland, Rumania, Yugoslavia), and the People's Republic of China. Photographs, current and historic, cover international trade, economic and political life, agriculture, industry, science, geography, sports, culture, and the arts. Over 800,000 photos on file. Current selections include the Soyuz–Apollo joint space program, SALT talks, cultural exchange, international trade, summit meetings, etc. Some other categories are: prominent personalities, workers, farmers, families, students, medicine and public health, weaponry, army, navy, space exploration, architecture, atomic power.

CATALOGS   No catalogs reported.

BIBLIOGRAPHY   See Grant & Brown, p. 397.

S7
STRAVINSKY-DIAGHILEV FOUNDATION

STRAVINSKY-DIAGHILEV FOUNDATION COLLECTION
PARMENIA MIGEL EKSTROM COLLECTION

525 East 85th Street
New York, NY 10028

Parmenia Migel Ekstrom
President

SCHEDULE   Tues–Sat 10:00 a.m.–1:00 p.m./3:00–5:00 p.m.

ACCESS   Not open to the public. Visitors are welcome if they write and state exactly what their project is so the material they wish to study can be assembled. When writing, persons should indicate where they can be reached by telephone.

HOLDINGS   The Foundation is a research center for both Stravinsky and Diaghilev, and all their associates. There is a vast collection of documents, photographs, books, original art works, music scores, etc., for the use of students and authors. The Foundation also assists with documentation for television, films and publishing houses. Loan exhibitions are also sent to museums and universities in the United States and Europe.

Grant & Brown have the following entry:

The combined collections of the Foundation and the Parmenia Migel Ekstrom are too large to detail fully in these pages. They contain the following materials concerning Russian dance and music: original stage designs by such artists as B. Anisfeld, L. Bakst, A. Benois, B. Bilinsky, N. Goncharova, M. Larionov, N. Roerich, and others; correspondence of Igor Stravinsky and Serge Diaghilev (including approximately 800 telegrams to and from Diaghilev); some 15,000 business documents, bills, and records relating to Diaghilev and his Ballets Russes (among them, the contracts signed by his dancers, singers, and artists); a great quantity of original music scores; and a large number of photographs.

CATALOGS   Lists and card files only. Useful finding aids might be the published catalogues for exhibitions of holdings of Roerich, Bakst, Bilinsky, and Stravinsky/Diaghilev.

BIBLIOGRAPHY   Some illustrated catalogs of loan exhibitions are available. See Grant & Brown, pp. 397–398.

S8
ST. BASIL'S COLLEGE
LIBRARY

195 Glenbrook Road
Stamford, CT 06902

Reverend John Terlecky
Librarian

TELEPHONE   203 327–7899 Ext. 6

SCHEDULE   Mon–Fri 9:00 a.m.–4:00 p.m.

ACCESS   Not open to the public, but permission may be obtained to study the collection.

FACILITIES   Reading room; photocopying and photography permitted.

HOLDINGS   Collection has a special interest in the Ukraine and especially the Ukrainian Catholic Church. It is made up primarily of books and periodicals on the Ukraine. Church books published by the Assumption Brotherhood of Lviv (present day L'vov) in the 17th century are included as well as some archival materials. The museum on campus contains Ukrainian arts and crafts for ethnographical studies. Between the library and the museum there are 8,000 books and 53 periodical titles.

CATALOGS   No catalogs reported.

BIBLIOGRAPHY   No bibliography reported.

S9
ST. NICHOLAS UKRAINIAN CATHOLIC CHURCH

216 President Street
Passaic, NJ 07055

Reverend R. Turkoniak
Pastor

TELEPHONE   201 777–0230

SCHEDULE   Sundays

ACCESS   Open to the public.

FACILITIES   No reading room, but permission may be obtained to photocopy or photograph items.

HOLDINGS   Collection consists of church records: church baptismal documents, death registries, and the like. Records are in Ukrainian and date from 1910.

CATALOGS   Records are maintained by year.

BIBLIOGRAPHY   No bibliography reported.

S10
SYNOD OF RUSSIAN BISHOPS OUTSIDE RUSSIA
CATHEDRAL OF THE SIGN

See also HOLY TRINITY SEMINARY LIBRARY

75 East 93rd Street
New York, NY 10128

Bishop Hilarion

TELEPHONE   212 534–1601, 397–5343 (Irene Dutikow)

SCHEDULE   By appointment only.

ACCESS   Holdings are divided into two parts: archives and library. To use the archives a letter should be written to Bishop Hilarion at the Synod stating the purpose of the visit and background; to use the library, Irene Dutikow should be consulted.

FACILITIES   A table is available in the library. Permission might be obtained to photograph or photocopy items.

HOLDINGS   The library is primarily for use of the clergy or the Synod. The collection has titles on Orthodox theology, liturgy, and church history as well as philosophy, art and architecture, history of Russia, biographies, and some reference books, including dictionaries. There are about 1,000 books, 100 periodicals, and a file of approximately 1,000 newspaper clippings pertaining to church matters. There are also 10,000 uncataloged books.

The archives contain material from the 1920s, 1930s, and from World War II. There is material on parish life and the Dioceses, archives of priests, and biographies of clergymen, as well as archives on the church choir, and material on churches not only in North America but also in Europe, Australia, and South America.

CATALOGS   There is no card catalog.

BIBLIOGRAPHY   No bibliography reported.

T1
TARASSUK, LEONID
PRIVATE COLLECTION

50 East 96 Street, Apt. 5-A
New York, NY 10128

TELEPHONE   212 722-7954

SCHEDULE   Call for an appointment.

ACCESS   Permission may be obtained to study collection after it is systematized.

FACILITIES   No reading room; photocopying and photography permitted.

HISTORY   Dr. Tarassuk worked as a specialist in arms and armor, medieval period to modern times, at the Hermitage Museum in Leningrad. Collection assembled between 1940 and 1980 as memorabilia related to collector's life, imprisonment (1959–61), and emigration process (1970–73).

HOLDINGS   Correspondence, documents, photographs, newspaper clippings; approximately 1,200 items.

SPECIAL   Large archives of photographs and official documents
FEATURES   relating to Dr. Tarassuk's life in the USSR and his specialization (arms and armor).

CATALOGS   No catalogs, but papers are systematized.

BIBLIOGRAPHY   No bibliography reported.

T2
TATYANA GALLERY

145 East 27th Street, 6th Floor
New York, NY 10016

Tatyana B. Gribanova
Director

TELEPHONE   212 683–2387, 691–7947

SCHEDULE   Tues–Sat 12:00 p.m.–5:00 p.m.

ACCESS   Open to the public.

FACILITIES   No reading room, but, if necessary, the Gallery may be used. Photocopying and photography permitted.

HOLDINGS   Russian realistic paintings, 18th century–beginning of 20th century. Oils, watercolors, pastels, drawings, and, recently, sculpture. Russian Art Library. About 500 items of art, about 1,500 volumes of art books. Artists included are: I. Aivazovsky, K. Briullov, I. Levitan, C. Makovsky, I. Repin, D. Levitzky. Books: *Starye gody*, 1906–1917 (art magazine).

CATALOGS   Inventory catalog available upon request as well as photos from the paintings.

BIBLIOGRAPHY   Exhibition Isaac Levitan, 1860–1900. Oil, Watercolor, Pastel, Drawing. February 10, 1988; Seventh Anniversary Exhibition, Ivan Konstantinovich Aivazovsky, 1817–1900. Oils, Watercolors, Pastels, Drawings. May 19, 1988.

T3
TCHEREPNIN SOCIETY, INC.

170 West 73rd Street, Apt. 8-B
New York, NY 10023

Mrs. Ming Tcherepnin
President

TELEPHONE   212 724–6763

SCHEDULE   By appointment only.

ACCESS   Not open to the public. Permission can be obtained to study the collection by recommendation and appointment only.

FACILITIES   There is no reading room, but space can be made available to serve that purpose. Permission can be obtained to photograph or photocopy selected items.

HOLDINGS   The Tcherepnin Society was formed to perpetuate the music and ideals of Alexander Tcherepnin (1899–1977), pianist-composer and internationalist. As part of its goals and philosophy the Society encourages originality and individuality of expression in gifted young composers, musicians, and scholars of all nationalities, and helps them broaden their experience through personal contact with cultures other than their own. Activities of the Society include commissions to young composers, scholarships to student musicians, and an exchange program, providing fellowships and financial assistance to musicians and scholars. The Tcherepnin Archive consists of hundreds of musical scores and manuscripts, concert programs, and recordings, as well as articles written by Alexander Tcherepnin or about him, and reviews.

CATALOGS   The inquirer will be assisted by the curator.

BIBLIOGRAPHY   Enrique Alberto Arias, comp. *Alexander Tcherepnin: A Bio-Bibliography*. Westport, CT: Greenwood Press, 1988. 280 p.; "The Tcherepnin Society," a six-panel leaflet published by the Society; Other lists which can be obtained from the Society are "Alexander Tcherepnin on Records (Selections)" and "Alexander Tcherepnin; A Selective Bibliography," "Compositions of Alexander Tcherepnin; Complete List." See Grant & Brown, p. 297 (not reproduced here).

T4
TOLSTOY FOUNDATION, INC.

200 Park Avenue South, Suite 1612
New York, NY 10003

Leon O. Marion
Executive Director

TELEPHONE   212 677–7770

SCHEDULE   Not open to the public.

ACCESS   Permission is not obtainable to study collection at this
time, as the library must be put in order.

FACILITIES   No report on reading room. Photocopying and photog-
                raphy permitted.

HOLDINGS   The Tolstoy Foundation library and archives started
with donations in 1941, with selections of Russian, English, and other languages on Russian subjects. Books are still received from donors. Among
noteworthy collections are those from Professor Arseniev, and 18th-century
Slavonic church books. Size of collection, 30,000. Mr. Marion reported in
1987 that a very active library committee had been working on the holdings
for the purpose of culling out texts which do not meet the criteria for the
collection and integrating a new category system with holdings in Munich
and Vienna. He had expected to be able to present a more comprehensive
listing of the holdings and hoped to open their doors a little wider for
serious Russian classical scholars by June 1988. The collection is located at
the Tolstoy Foundation Center, Valley Cottage, New York, 10989. Telephone there is 914 268–6140, although it appears best to inquire through
the director's office.

Grant & Brown make the following statement concerning the Tolstoy
Foundation holdings and location:

Researchers might be interested in both the records of the Foundation itself and the various manuscripts which scholars and literary figures have
deposited with the Center over the years. Some years ago Professor I.
Shumilin prepared a preliminary list of holdings in the Foundation Archives. His headings were the following: Manuscripts (concerning T.F.),
Manuscripts "B" (other) Tolstoy Farm. Correspondence with wel-
fare/church organizations. Correspondence with various minor organizations. Confidential. Personal—Alexandra Tolstoi and Tatiana Schaufuss.
Psychological warfare (psychological strategy in Cold War). Budget and
financial reports. Statistical reports. Reports of T.F. Working plan of T.F.
T.F. meetings—Tolstoy Foundation board of directors. Correspondence of
T.F. with branches. Refugees relief. Laws and immigration documents—
legislation testimonies for hearings. Search—tracing department. Immigration: cases, sponsors, assurances (alphabetized and unalphabetized). Escape
and USEP, IRO. American Council of Voluntary Agencies for Foreign Service (Foreign Operations Administration—F.O.A.). Material help, medical
help, CARE CRALOG, etc. Lists of DPs—arrival and departure (Tolstoy
Foundation and others) (alphabetized and individual items listed). Jobs,
employments, recommendations. Resettlements of DPs (on farm, immigrat.,
etc.). Reports of new addresses. Miscellaneous materials about DPs and

immigration in general (outside U.S.A.). DP camps (outside U.S.A.). Exerptions [sic] from general DP-file: (a) Nationality, (b) Territory, (c) Students. Personal and general correspondence of: (a) A. L. Tolstoi, (b) T. A. Schaufuss, (c) E. I. Tomaschewskaja. Repatriation. Clippings of newspapers in 7 divisions (DP—varia; T.F.—activities; articles, notes, speeches of A.L. Tolstoi; laws, notes about a new immigration law; about Leo Tolstoi; "Berezoffs illness"; Varia). The news—Tolstoy Foundation (with general correspondence). Russian Language Program. Unclassified material. Information, books, newspapers, concerning refugees' problems. Contributions.

The Foundation's archival material at present is located at the Center in Valley Cottage, New York. Access to these materials require the written permission of the Foundation's management, which will reply to inquiries directed to the above address in New York City.

CATALOGS   No catalogs reported.

BIBLIOGRAPHY   See Grant & Brown, p. 398.

U1
UKRAINIAN MUSEUM

203 Second Avenue
New York, NY 10003

Ms. Maria Shust
Director

TELEPHONE   212 228–0110

SCHEDULE   Office: Mon–Fri 9:00 a.m.–5:00 p.m.; Sat–Sun 1:00 p.m.–5:00 p.m. Closed Mondays during summer. Visitor hours: Wed–Sun 1:00 p.m.–5:00 p.m.

ACCESS   Study collection by appointment only.

FACILITIES   No reading room; library is not catalogued and is for in-house use only, though appointment may be made to study a particular publication. Photocopying and photography permitted.

HISTORY   Museum was founded in 1976 by the Ukrainian National Women's League of America from its sizable folk art collection, gathered since the 1930s. The Museum is incorporated in order to collect, preserve, interpret and exhibit objects of artistic and historic value relating to Ukrainian life and culture. Through a program of exhibitions, publications, workshops and lectures, the Museum strives to familiarize the general public with the many aspects of the Ukrainian art, history and culture.

HOLDINGS　　Ukrainian folk art, photographic archives (largest section covers the Ukrainian immigration to the United States), numismatics, beginnings of fine arts, and library relating to Ukrainian folk art, fine art, and architecture. Artists represented include the naif (primitive) Nikifor, Vasyl Krychevsky, Nicholas Bervinchak, Mychajlo Andreenko, Ivan Trush, and Oleksa Novakivsky. Approximately 3,000 items in folk art; 500 in fine art; 1,000 in numismatics; 6,000 volumes in the library; approximately 4,000 in the archive.

SPECIAL　　Strongest in area of textiles, including costumes, *kilims*
FEATURES　　(flat woven rugs), ritual cloths, the majority dating from the first quarter of the 20th century.

CATALOGS　　No catalogs reported.

BIBLIOGRAPHY　Exhibition catalogs: *Traditional Designs in Ukrainian Textiles*; *Ukrainian Embroidery Craft*; *Pysanky and Their Symbols*; *Rushnyky: Ukrainian Ritual Cloths*; *The Lost Architecture of Kiev*; *Ukrainian Kilims*; *Ukrainian Folk Art*; *To Preserve a Heritage: The Story of Ukrainian Immigration in the United States*; Stefania Hnatenko. *Treasures of Early Ukrainian Art*; *Religious Art of the 16th–18th Centuries*. New York: Ukrainian Museum, 1989. 44 p. (Bibliographies are included in all major exhibition catalogs.)

U2
UKRAINIAN ORTHODOX CHURCH
THE SEMINARY LIBRARY

P.O. Box 240
Corner of Easton and Davidson Avenues
South Bound Brook, NJ 08880

Reverend Wasyl Iwashchuk
Librarian

TELEPHONE 201 356–5556
SCHEDULE Mon 4:00 p.m.–7:00 p.m.; Tues 8:00 a.m.–7:00 p.m.;
Wed–Sat 9:00 a.m.–1:00 p.m.

ACCESS Open to the public. Permission can be obtained to
photocopy or photograph items.

HOLDINGS Founded in 1975, the library is national in scope, providing resources for both undergraduate and graduate level research, and
collects material and manuscripts, holding 20,000 books, 10,000 pamphlets,
and 165 journals. Collection includes works of art, 68 boxes of sheet music,
records, and 50 audiovisual materials. There are books, pamphlets, periodicals, newspapers, government documents, maps, arts, music, and crafts
pertaining to the Russian Empire and USSR, including about 300 books,
1,000 pamphlets, and 25 periodicals and newspapers. Periodical publications
arranged alphabetically include odd issues of *Kievskaia starina*, *Literaturno-
Naukovyi Visnyk*, and interwar publications of the Ukrainian Catholic University of Lviv. The library contains first editions of Galician authors, Vol-
hynian authors of the interwar period, and scholarly and literary journals of
the interwar period, as well as archeographic publications of the Shevchenko Scientific Society. Noteworthy: holdings of late 19th–early 20th-
century Galician-Ukrainian publications dealing with church history, as well
as art publications from the Soviet Ukraine of the 1920s. Among the old
printed books held are a *Trebnik* (1713); an unidentified *Molitoslov*; an 18th-
century musical manuscript; an *Apostol*, an *Apocalypse*, and *Molitoslov*
(1787), as well as manuscript documents of the early 17th and 18th centuries.

Grant & Brown cite the Archives-Library of The Ukrainian Orthodox
Church, U.S.A. under the above address and make the following statement
about the collection:

Organized in 1966 by the Most Reverend Archbishop Mstyslav Skrypnyk,
the Archives-Library contains both published and manuscript materials
dealing primarily with Ukrainian history, culture, religion, language, and
politics. Approximately 57 percent of the material is in Ukrainian, 15 percent in Russian, and 10 percent in English. Items include correspondence,
office files, literary manuscripts, miscellaneous documents, photographs,
orthodox ritual books, and maps. There are some rare religious and political
manuscripts concerning the Ukraine during the Middle Ages and dating
from the 15th to the 18th centuries. Much of the material relates to the
UAPTsA (Ukrainian Autocephalic Orthodox Church in America). There is
also documentation on the Ukrainian Liberation Movement of 1918–1922
and the dissident movement in the Ukraine, 1960s–1970s. A card catalog is
in preparation. For lengthy research projects it is advisable to make advance
arrangements with the Archives-Library.

CATALOGS   There are catalogs for books, periodicals and pamphlets. Material is available for ILL.

BIBLIOGRAPHY   See Grant & Brown, p. 277.

U3
UKRAINIAN RESEARCH AND DOCUMENTATION CENTER
UKRAINIAN INSTITUTE OF AMERICA

2 East 79th Street
New York, NY 10021

Taras Hunczak	Luba Gawur and Olena Nessin
Director	Archivists

TELEPHONE   212 288–2917

SCHEDULE   Mon–Fri 10:00 a.m.–5:00 p.m.

ACCESS   Not yet open to the public, but access to the collection is available by appointment.

HOLDINGS   Established in 1986 as a center for collecting and storing archives, archival materials, and documents on Ukrainians in the 20th century, The Ukrainian Research and Documentation Center (URDC) focuses especially on topics for which documents are scarce or difficult to find. For example: Ukrainians in World War I; the Ukrainian Famine of 1932–33; the history of the national liberation movement; Ukrainians in World War II, including the Ukrainian National Army, which fought against the Soviets; the history of the dissident movement in the Ukraine since 1960; and the history of Ukrainian organizations and institutions of the diaspora. There are now about 60,000 individual items.

An oral history collection is being created and there is at present testimony from persons who were witnesses to the famine and terror of the 1930s.

The URDC also provides information on archives and libraries worldwide where documents pertaining to Ukrainians may be found.

CATALOGS   The collection is now in the process of being cataloged.

BIBLIOGRAPHY   *Ukrainian Research and Documentation Center.* Unpaginated, undated brochure.

U4
UNITED NATIONS
ARCHIVES

345 Park Avenue South, 12th Floor
New York, NY 10010

Reference Desk

TELEPHONE   212 963–8681

SCHEDULE   Mon–Fri 9:00 a.m.–5:00 p.m.

ACCESS   Open to the public by appointment. The following
policy concerning accessibility of records is in effect: Records classified as
strictly confidential shall be reviewed by the Archives for possible declassification when twenty years old. At the expiration of this time limit, records
so classified shall be declassified only upon explicit ad hoc, item-by-item approval by the Secretary General or by such officials as the Secretary General
so authorizes. Strictly confidential records not approved for declassification
when twenty years old shall be reviewed by the Archives for possible declassification every five years thereafter. Records classified as confidential shall
be declassified automatically by the Archives upon the expiration of twenty
years.

FACILITIES   Reading room; photography and photocopying allowed
by special arrangement for open records.

HOLDINGS   There are at present some 40,000 linear feet of material
in the Archives comprising non-current records of the UN Secretariat and
some pre–United Nations agencies (such as the War Crimes Commission).
The Archives do not contain material on the United Nations Children's
Fund (UNICEF) or the United Nations Development Programs (UNDP),
which have their own archival holdings.
    The bulk of the records concern the Office of the Secretary General and
are divided by the Executive Office, Special Political Affairs Office, General
Assembly Affairs Section, the Protocol and Liaison Office, and the Executive Assistant and Chef de Cabinet. There are also records for Missions and
Commissions. Material of relevance to Soviet students in any of these
records would have to be sought by perusing the finding aids and locating

records would have to be sought by perusing the finding aids and locating references to Soviet attitudes or reponses to any actions under-taken by the Office of the Secretary General or its various offices and sections.

Among the pre–United Nations agencies for which records are held are those of the United Nations Relief and Rehabilitation Administration (UNRRA), 1943–49. There are several sets of records concerned with data on the Soviet Union: The records of the UNRRA headquarters contain 1,089 feet of reports, office files, account books, correspondence, and miscellaneous documents with material interspersed throughout on the Ukraine and Byelorussia; records of the European Regional Office, which contain material on Ukrainian and Byelorussian affairs; the Byelorussian Mission, 1946–47, 10 feet, established in Minsk in April 1946, and concerned exclusively with the receipt and distribution of relief supplies; Ukraine Mission, 1946–47, 5 feet, established in Kiev on March 20, 1946.

CATALOGS   Various finding aids, accessions lists and inventories are available.

BIBLIOGRAPHY   Guide to the Archives of International Organizations. *I. The United Nations System.* [Paris]: UNESCO, 1984. pp. 187–232. See Grant & Brown, pp. 399–400 (entries have been cited only briefly above).

U5
UNITED NATIONS
DAG HAMMERSKJOLD LIBRARY

UN Plaza
New York, NY 10017

Mrs. Fenote-Selam
General Reference Collection

TELEPHONE   212 963–7394

Miss Moreen Ritynski
United Nations Reference

TELEPHONE   212 963–7412

SCHEDULE   Mon–Fri 9:00 a.m.–5:30 p.m. (the hours of the Secretariat).

ACCESS   Use is restricted to diplomats, Secretariat staff, journalists accredited to the UN, and exceptionally to some scholars and students. Generally, it is difficult to accommodate outsiders. Usually, it is recommended that applicants use one of the United Nations depository collections, for instance, at the New York Public Library, New York University, or Columbia University. To inquire about permission to use the library call the Senior Reference Librarian, 212 963–7416.

FACILITIES   There are reading rooms for each reference collection and one for the periodical reading room. Photocopy machines are available in three locations in the Library. Services provided are loans within agency; compilation of reference lists; periodicals circulation within agency; letters and phone calls answering requests; searching external and internal data bases; and document delivery.

HOLDINGS   The building, dedicated in 1961, is a gift of the Ford Foundation. The General Assembly defined the library's basic function as service to the delegations, and to the Secretariat in its international work. There are 400,000 volumes, including 80,000 maps, gazetteers, etc. Subject coverage includes political problems; international relations; international law; legislation; economic development; social development; statistics; human rights; population; and public administration. The collection contains material in Russian from the Soviet Union. This material falls within the acquisition policy of the library, and is generally obtained on exchange from partners in the USSR.

SPECIAL   The UN/SA Reference Library contains the personal
FEATURES   collection of Woodrow Wilson (which has been filmed), documents of the League of Nations, and documents relating to the founding of the United Nations.

CATALOGS   There are dictionary public-card catalogs for each reading room. Since 1979, the UNBIS (United Nations Bibliographic Information System) on-line system has been available. It contains bibliographic files which act as a guide to the documentation published by and about the United Nations, as well as data about the proceedings of the deliberative organs of the United Nations, the votes taken in the General Assembly and Security Council, and the full text of UN resolutions.

BIBLIOGRAPHY *The Dag Hammarskjold Library: Services and Collections.* New York: United Nations, 1986. 13 p.; *UNBIS: An Overview of the Databases.* New York: United Nations: Dag Hammarskjold Library, 1987. 8 p.; *Current Bibliographical Information.* v. 1–, New York: United Nations, 1971–, monthly.

U6
UNITED STATES MILITARY ACADEMY
LIBRARY

West Point, NY 10996–1799

Alan Aimone
Head, Special Collections

TELEPHONE   914 938–2954

SCHEDULE   Mon–Fri 8:00 a.m.–4:30 p.m.

ACCESS   Not open to the public. Permission can be obtained to
               study the collection.

FACILITIES   Reading room available; photocopying and photographing at the discretion of the manuscript librarian.

HOLDINGS   The library reports that since the publication of Grant
& Brown, the following entries have been added to the collection:
    Donald Frederic Carroll (1899–1948). Papers, 50 items. U.S. Army Of-
ficer, 27th Infantry. Included 30 letters, 6 June–20 March 1920, describing
his journey to Vladivostok and events during his tour of duty with the
American Expeditionary Forces, Siberia.
    Siberian Expedition Photographs. 29 photographs taken of a member of
the American Expeditionary Forces, Siberia from the collection of Major
Emile Cutrer, Commanding Officer, Kskotous District.
    Grant & Brown list the following entries:
    Arthur Pendleton Bagby (1794–1858). Governor of Alabama and diplo-
mat. Letter, April 2, 1849, to his son, Cadet Arthur P. Bagby, Jr., written
while Bagby, Sr. was U.S. minister to Russia.
    Benjamin Abbot Dickson (1897–1975). Papers, 1919–75. U.S. Army of-
ficer. Includes diary, August 20–November 7, 1919, 54 letters, and 138 photographs pertaining to the colonel's experience as an officer with the North
Russian expedition. Ca. 192 items.
    William Sidney Graves (1865–1940). Papers, 1919–20. Commander of
American Expeditionary Forces in Siberia, 1918–20. Photograph of the 27th
Infantry officers seated beneath the Siberian Expedition insignia, an insignia
lapel pin, and some Russian currency. 10 items.
    Ernest Kuhn (1864–1935). Papers, 1885–1935. U.S. Army general. In-
cludes 8 diaries and over 300 photographs covering the period he was mili-

tary attache to the U.S. legation in Tokyo for the purpose of observing the Japanese army during the war with Russian in 1904. Over 300 items.

Amos Blanchard Shattuck (1896–1934). Son of an army officer stationed in the Philippines. Copy of the journal "From Manila to New York via Trans-Siberian," July 26–September 9, 1913, 110 pp., accompanied by copies of a time table, map, and brochure from the International Sleeping Car Co. Young Shattuck was en route to Exeter via Manchuria, Siberia, Germany, and England.

George Evans Stewart (1872–1946). Papers, 1918–40. U.S. Army Officer. Participated in the North Russian expedition during the American intervention in the Russian Civil War. Ca. 205 items 1918–1919, including official correspondence, documents, reports, and maps, pertain to his career and the North Russian expedition in particular. 1 box.

CATALOGS   No catalogs reported. *Preliminary Guide to the Manuscript Collection of the U.S. Military Academy Library.* J. Thomas Russell, comp. New York: West Point, 1968.

BIBLIOGRAPHY   See Grant & Brown, pp. 412–413.

V1
VON LOEWE, KARL
PRIVATE COLLECTION

38 Van Doren Avenue
Somerset, NJ 08873

TELEPHONE   201 873–0267

SCHEDULE   No schedule reported.

ACCESS   Not open to the public. Permission can be obtained to study the collection.

FACILITIES   No reading room; permission can be obtained to photograph or photocopy items.

HOLDINGS   Professor von Loewe reports no change in his collection since publication of Grant & Brown, which makes the following statement:

Professor Von Loewe is in possession of a substantial collection of microfilmed materials on 15th–17th c. Lithuanian history from archives in Warsaw, Krakow, Vilnius, Leningrad, and Kiev. Some of these films are duplications (negative and positive) of microfilms in the Oswald Backus Collection

The originals are in the following repositories: Mokslu Akademija Centrine Biblioteka (Vilnius), Leningradskoe Otdelenie, Institut Istorii Akademii Nauk SSSR, Archiwum Glowne Akt Dawnych (Warsaw), TsDIAK (Kiev), and Archiwum Panstwowe Miasta Krakowa i Wojewodztwa Krakowskiego. (Vilnius microfilm is not a copy of the Backus Collection holdings.)

CATALOGS   Grant & Brown states there is an unpublished list of the *fondy* materials duplicated (from Soviet and Polish repositories).

BIBLIOGRAPHY   See Grant & Brown, p. 273.

Y1
YESHIVA UNIVERSITY
MENDEL GOTTESMAN LIBRARY OF HEBRAICA/JUDAICA

500 West 185th Street
New York, NY 10033

Leah Adler
Head Librarian

TELEPHONE   212 960–5382

SCHEDULE   Call for information.

ACCESS   Permission granted to researchers with proper credentials.

FACILITIES   Reading room; photocopying and photography permitted with restrictions.

HOLDINGS   Research library collecting Judaica/Hebraica, i.e., Jewish literature, history, philosophy, Hebrew language and literature, etc. Books and periodicals by and about Russian Jewry, Russian imprints in the Hebrew alphabet dating back to the 18th century. Total collection, 182,000 volumes. Figures for Russian-USSR materials not available.

CATALOGS   Card catalog.

BIBLIOGRAPHY   No bibliography reported.

**Y2
YESHIVA UNIVERSITY
ARCHIVES**

500 West 185th Street
New York, NY 10033

Roger Kohn
Archivist

TELEPHONE	212 960–5451
SCHEDULE	Call for information.
ACCESS	Permission granted to researchers with proper credentials.
FACILITIES	Reading room; photocopying and photography permitted with restrictions.

HOLDINGS   Louis Levine Collection (approx. 33 linear feet): Louis Levine was involved in the Jewish Council for Russian War Relief. His papers contain records of the Jewish Council for Russian War Relief (later American Jewish Council to Aid Russian Rehabilitation) 1943–1947. Records include correspondence concerning relations with local committees, Ukrainian and other *landsmanshaften* (brotherhoods), American Society for Russian Relief, Workmen's Circle, and other organizations, as well as fundraising, clothing, book and food drive, relief work in the Soviet Union, annual conferences, and other events; financial records, including paid bills, budgets, bank statements, and donation records; lists of Jewish survivors in certain Soviet cities; press releases; staff reports; personnel records. No published inventory; card catalog available at the Archives.

National Council of Jewish Women—Service for the Foreign Born (approx. 90 linear feet) ca. 1939–1968. Case files of immigrants assisted by the service. An undetermined number of Holocaust survivors immigrating to the United States spent World War II in territories occupied by the Soviet Union. Unprocessed collection.

Vaad Hatzala (27 linear feet) 1940–1963 (bulk, 1942–1949). Founded in 1939 by the Union of Orthodox Rabbis of the United States and Canada as an Emergency Committee for war-torn *Yeshivot* (Jewish academies of higher learning). The records contain some files on work in the USSR. Published inventory ($5.00).

Total collection, 500 linear feet.

CATALOGS   See catalog information included with HOLDINGS (above).

BIBLIOGRAPHY   No bibliography reported.

Y3
YESHIVA UNIVERSITY MUSEUM

2520 Amsterdam Avenue
New York, NY 10033

Bonni-Dara Michaels
Curator

TELEPHONE   212 960–5390

SCHEDULE   Office: Mon–Thur 9:00 a.m.–5:00 p.m.; Fri 9:00 a.m.–12:00 p.m. Museum: Tues–Thur 10:30 a.m.–5:00 p.m.; Sun 12:00 p.m.–6:00 p.m.

ACCESS   Museum is open to the public, but not the files. Admission fee applies for visiting museum galleries.

FACILITIES   No reading room, but permission can be obtained to study the collection. Archival material available for supervised examination by prior arrangement. Photographs can be made but a fee is charged for the service.

HOLDINGS   The Yeshiva University Museum is a teaching museum whose purpose is to preserve, enrich, and interpret Jewish life as it is reflected in art, architecture, anthropology, history, literature, music, and science. The museum collection contains paintings, drawings, sculpture, ceremonial objects, textiles, costumes, ethnographic materials, over 1,500 photographs, and approximately 200 documents relating to Jewish life in Russia, Poland, and Czechoslovakia. It is a growing collection, and unfortunately the photographs and documents are the least well catalogued, and many were never cataloged at all. It is therefore quite difficult to ascertain at this time how many there are, or which might apply to the Russian Empire or the Soviet Union.

CATALOGS   No catalog of archival holdings. Catalogs are produced for each museum exhibition. The Museum is in the process of acquiring a computer and plans to update its inventory and put it on computer during the next year (June 1988). The Museum should be able to provide more precise information by then and be better able to answer scholars' inquiries. However, the inventory will will not be directly available to anyone from outside the Museum. Given a specific request, the Museum will be willing to search a particular topic and to notify scholars of the existence and nature of relevant material in the collection.

BIBLIOGRAPHY   "Yeshiva University Museum, the First Decade; Tishrei 5745/October 1984." New York: Yeshiva University Museum, 1984. Unpaged. Contains a listing at end of exhibitions held since 1973 and notes which exhibitions have catalogs, e.g., "Life in the Old Jewish Shtetl: Paintings and Silver by Ilya Schor"; "The Changing Face of New York Synagogues 1750–1974." Copies of current and past museum catalogs are available for purchase through the Museum giftshop, or for consultation at the Museum offices.

Y4
YIVO INSTITUTE FOR JEWISH RESEARCH
LIBRARY

1048 Fifth Avenue
New York, NY 10028

Zachary Baker
Head Librarian

TELEPHONE   212 535–6700 Ext. 25

SCHEDULE   Mon–Tues, Thur–Fri 9:30 a.m.–5:30 p.m.

ACCESS   Open to the public.

FACILITIES   Reading room; photocopying, microform reader printer available, as well as microfiche and microfilm readers. Photography allowed depending on purpose.

HISTORY   The Yiddish Scientific Institute—YIVO was founded in 1925 in Vilna as a home for Yiddish scholarship. Libraries and archives formed an integral part of it from the beginning. By 1927, with donations from friends all over Poland, the library had amassed material to the point where older items outnumbered current publications, some 1,200 periodical titles and 4,000 volumes. The library was also collecting popular editions of folk literature, publications of various societies and organizations celebrating anniversaries, or submitting reports, bulletins of schools, and works of other local organizations. By 1938, the library had 40,000 volumes, including rare editions and unique copies. In 1941, many YIVO treasures were lost to the Nazi occupation. Much of this material was later uncovered in the American Zone of Germany and turned over to YIVO headquarters in New York where it was reconstituted as YIVO's Vilna collection. A number of the YIVO Library's rare Yiddish and Hebrew books and pamphlets were hidden in the Vilna ghetto. After World War II they were recovered and returned to YIVO in New York, where they form the Sutzever-Kaczerginski Collection (after the Vilna Yiddish writers Abraham Sutzkever and Shmerke Kaczerginski). The YIVO institution in New York grew out of the Central Jewish Library and Archives founded in New York in 1935 by a group of Jewish cultural leaders. This library, dedicated mainly to the Yiddish press and literature in America, opened in 1938. In October 1939, it was absorbed by the American branch of YIVO. In 1940, the YIVO headquarters were transferred from Vilna to New York. Since 1940, the Library has received many important collections of writers, publishers, and civic leaders who left their books to YIVO. The Vilna collection was supplemented by several thousand volumes of books and periodicals through the Jewish Cultural Reconstruction, and by purchases from a special fund made available to the YIVO for the restoration and replacement of books destroyed by the Germans during World War II. The Institute and Library have been in the present location since 1955; in 1956, the name was changed to the YIVO Institute for Jewish Research.

HOLDINGS   Today the holdings of the Library number about 320,000 volumes, including books, pamphlets, and periodicals. A general estimate of language groupings posits about 35 percent in Yiddish, 25 percent in English, 20 percent in Hebrew, 10 percent in Polish and Russian, with the remainder in German, French, and other languages. A brief resume of some of the collections held by the Library gives some idea of the spread of the holdings:

The Nazi Collection consists of ca. 5,000 volumes of political and anti-Semitic books and periodicals of Nazi-Germany provenance.

The Vilna Collection has some 50,000 books and periodicals in Hebrew, Yiddish, Russian, German, Polish, and other languages and is divided into subcollections:

Rabbinica—the largest portion;
Yiddish—secular material;
Hebrew—secular material (uncataloged);

Press—Russian, Yiddish, and other Judaica newspapers and periodicals from the tsarist empire, the Soviet Union, Poland, Germany, and other countries.

Russica/Sovietica Collection, which includes the Elias Tcherikowker Collection, has ca. 2,000–3,000 volumes. (Tcherikower was a founding member of YIVO; see his listing in the ARCHIVES entry.)

The Max Weinreich Library Collection contains a strong representation of material on Yiddish linguistics.

The Phillip Friedman Collection of ca. 2,000–3,000 volumes emphasizes mainly Holocaust materials, and Eastern European (particularly Polish) Jewish history.

Subject holdings are strong on Holocaust and anti-semitic material, especially for 25 years after World War II. Of the 500–600 volumes of memorial books (*Yizkor*) books published for Eastern Europe, the Library has over 90 percent. Other subject areas are American Jewish history, particularly emphasizing the period from the 1880s on; Eastern European Jewish history; the Jewish labor movement, both in Europe and the United States; Yiddish language and literature, folklore, theater and music books (the sheet music collection has been transferred to the Archives).

Microfilm consists of 1,500–2,000 reels, mainly material in Yiddish. At present, the Library is in the middle of a three-year preservation program to microfilm 6,000 Yiddish books.

YIVO publications are held in separate shelving in the reading room.

CATALOGS   The card catalog is divided into author/title and subject sections. The author/title section is further subdivided by language and/or alphabets: Yiddish, Hebrew, Cyrillic (9 drawers), Roman, and a separate catalog for Vilna Rabbinica. The subject catalog is numerically classified and represents the entire collection. Index cards in the author/title section provide access to the subject numbers in the subject catalog. G.K. Hall is preparing the Yiddish catalog, microfilm catalog (consisting mainly of Yiddish periodicals), and the Yiddish authority file for publication sometime toward the end of 1989.

BIBLIOGRAPHY   Yiddish Scientific Institute—YIVO. *Bibliography of the Publications of the Yiddish Scientific Institute—YIVO, 1924–1941*. New York: YIVO, 1942, 210 p.; idem. *Bibliography of the Publications of the Yiddish Scientific Institute—YIVO, Volume II, 1942–1950*. New York: YIVO, 1955. 158 p.; Dina Abramowicz. "The YIVO Library." *Jewish Book Annual* 25 (1967–68): 87–102; Estelle Gilson. "YIVO—Where Yiddish Scholarship Lives; History and Mission on Fifth Avenue." *Present Tense* (Autumn 1976): 57–65; Dina Abramowicz and Isaiah Trunk. "YIVO Institute for Jewish Research." In *East Central and Southeast Europe: A Handbook of Library and*

Archival Resources in North America, pp. 445–454. Edited by Paul L. Horecky and David H. Kraus. Santa Barbara, CA: Clio Press, [1976]; Joseph Berger. "Broadway to Aid Yiddish Archives." *New York Times* (March 1, 1987): 38. There are many bibliographies published in which the entries are based in whole or part on the holdings of the YIVO Library. Examples are: *Jewish Publications in the Soviet Union, 1917–1960*. Bibliographies compiled and arranged by Y.Y. Cohen with the assistance of M. Piekarz; edited by Kh. Shmeruk. Jerusalem: The Historical Society of Isarel, 1961. 502 p. (Galuyot Series); *Russian Publications on Jews and Judaism in the Soviet Union, 1917–1967*. A bibliography compiled by B. Pinkus and A.A. Greenbaum; edited by Mordechai Altshuler. Jerusalem: Society for Research on Jewish Communities; the Historical Society of Israel, 1970. 273 p., 113 p. in Yiddish; Mordecai Altshuler, ed. *Soviet Jewry in the Mirror of the Yiddish Press in Poland, Bibliography, 1945–1970*. Jerusalem: Hebrew University of Jerusalem, 1975. 213 p.; the following 3 volumes are examples of a 13-volume set on Holocaust literature, with most of the material contained in them located in the YIVO Library: Jacob Robinson and Philip Friedman. *Guide to Jewish history under Nazi impact*. New York: YIVO Institute for Jewish Research, 1960. (Co-published with Yad Vashem Martyrs' and Heroes' Memorial Authority. Joint documents project; bibliographical series 1); Philip Friedman and Joseph Gar. *Bibliography of Yiddish Books on the Catastrophe and Heroism*. New York: YIVO Institute for Jewish Research, 1960. (Co-published with Yad Vashem . . . bibliographical series 3); Joseph Gar. *Bibliography of articles on the Catastrophe and Heroism in Yiddish Periodicals*. New York: YIVO Institute for Jewish Research, 1966–1969. 2 v. (Co-published with Yad Vashem . . . bibliographical series 9–10).

Y5
YIVO INSTITUTE FOR JEWISH RESEARCH
YIVO ARCHIVES

1048 Fifth Avenue
New York, NY 10028

Marek Web
Chief Archivist

TELEPHONE   212 535–6700

SCHEDULE   Mon–Tues, Thur–Fri 9:30 a.m.–5:30 p.m.

ACCESS   Open to the public.

FACILITIES   Reading room available. Photocopying and photography possible depending on material and permission.

HOLDINGS   The Archives hold a variety of materials, including diaries, sheet music, playbills from the Yiddish theater, records of Jewish fraternal and political organizations, family papers, and manuscripts. Subject interests include American Jewish history (from the 1880s); Eastern European Jewish history; Holocaust; Jewish Labor movement; Yiddish language; literature; folklore; and theater. There is a Jewish Music Collection and manuscript collection of sheet music. Specific holdings are:

YIVO Archives has put approximately 17,000 photographs concerning Eastern Europe on video disc. The photographs can be searched geographically by subject or title word.

Records of the Forward Association, which published the *Jewish Daily Forward* and the *Zukunft*. Ca. 8 ft., inclusive dates 1913–72. Includes bookkeeping records, budget and donation records, circulation and advertising records; correspondence and financial records from Chicago and Boston; records for Detroit, Los Angeles, and Philadelphia only for 1968–69. Miscellaneous items from anniversary celebrations. Records relating to the Liberal Party, 1944–51.

Records of *Jewish Daily Forward*. Letters to the Bintel Brief, 1954–56. 10 inches.

The Archives also has the personal papers of many individuals connected with the *Forward* (for instance, Abraham Kahan).

Among recent new acquisitions of importance at YIVO are the Landsmanschaften Archives, consisting of more than 300 linear ft. of records and iconographic material covering the emigre society's existence from the 1880s to the present. Many of the society's members were from the Ukraine and a portion of the collection consists of information about their native towns.

Grant & Brown list the following entries taken from the YIVO Archives Record Group Inventory (unpublished). Some of the entries have been abbreviated here:

American Jewish Joint Distribution Committee. War Orphans Bureau. Records, 1919–23, 7.5. ft. on 14 microfilm rolls. Organized relief work for Jewish orphans mainly in Eastern Europe. . . . Indexes by name of orphan and by foster parents' names.

American Jewish Joint Distribution Committee, New York. Landsmanschaften Department. Records, 1937–40 and 1945–50, 15 ft. Memoranda, correspondence, reports, etc. Landsmanschaften are benevolent associations of emigrants from the same town. . . . Substantial portion relates to Russian Jewish localities. Unpublished inventory.

American Joint Reconstruction Foundation (AJRF). Records, 1920–39, ca. 12 ft. Established as a joint effort of the Joint Distribution Committee and the Jewish Colonization Association in 1924 to aid economic reconstruction of Jewish communities in Eastern Europe after World War I by establishing cooperative credit institutions, commercial banks, and workers' cooperatives and rebuilding destroyed housing. . . . Reports on Russia in the AJRF general records, 1921–28 (series 1); on the Ukraine, 1920 (2); on Lithuania, 1920–25 (4); on Latvia and Estonia, 1922–26 (5); and on Agro-Joint, from the Moscow office, etc., 1925–37 (12). Also clippings, photos, and other material. Inventory.

Leon Baratz (b. 1871). Papers, 1920s–1954, ca. 0.5 ft. Jewish-Russian lawyer, teacher, and publicist (pen name L. German) in Kiev and Western Europe. . . . Also, clippings, letters, autobiography, and materials on his father, Herman Baratz, historian and public figure in Kiev.

Berlin Collection, 1931–45, 24 ft. Records from the Reichsministerium für Volkaufklärung und Propaganda and the Reichskommisariat für das Ostland (i.e., for occupied territories in the East) . . . reports on the morale of the Red Army; materials concerning the church in Latvia, Lithuania, and White Russia; reports and correspondence on the situation of the Jews in Estonia; letters from Ukrainians to Hitler, 1932 and 1941; list of 118 leading personalities of the Ukrainian emigration; and much more material on the Baltic countries, White Russia, Poland, Ukraine, and the USSR as occupied territories. Card catalogue in English and draft of detailed catalogue.

Herman Bernstein (1876–1935). Papers, 1897–1935, 29 ft. Journalist, author, diplomat, and political leader. Includes correspondence, 1908–35, with many prominent cultural figures (e.g., the family of Leo Tolstoi, Leonid Andreyev and his wife) and other family/general correspondence . . . translations of works by Tolstoi, Andreyev, M. Gorkii, and A. Chekhov; interviews (one with Tolstoi); and clippings. Also, news dispatches from Russia and the Paris Peace Conference, filed when he was a correspondent for the *New York Herald*, 1917–20 . . . other items relating to the Russian Revolution, Russian Jews, pogroms, and Jewish journalism. Unpublished finding aid.

Julius Borenstein–Leah Eisenberg Collection on Early Jewish Migration, 1868–1930, ca. 3.5 ft., 5 microfilm reels. Materials on the history of Jewish immigration, mainly 1860s–1914. Includes items on the reaction of European and American Jewish organizations to the persecution of Russian Jews and their efforts to assist emigration of these Jews to America. . . . Unpublished inventory.

Central Archives of the Editorial Committee on Collection and Investigation of the Materials Relating to the Pogroms in the Ukraine. Records, 1802–1924, 61 microfilm rolls. Records relating to the daily operation of the Central Archive as well as documents, correspondence, minutes of meetings, manuscripts, memoranda, reports, etc., pertaining to the pogroms, 1903–21, and to Jewish life. . . . Inventory.

A. Charash. Papers, 1912–18, 2 microfilm rolls. Doctor of sociology, author, and member of the Zionist Socialist Workers' Party and other groups . . . correspondence with Rafael Asch, Z. Gordin, Yitzchak Gorsky, Pinchas Dubinsky, Y. Zakalnik, H. Manilevitsch, Aron Syngalowski, and others. Some material on Russian-Jewish emigre students in the West. Inventory.

Daniel Charney (1888–1959). Papers, ca. 1920s–59, ca. 6.5 ft. Yiddish writer and journalist. Includes his correspondence with such individuals as S. Dubnow, S. Nepomnyashtchy, Barukh Vladeck, and Shmuel Niger (the last two his brothers) . . . correspondence with Eduard Bernstein, Karl Kautsky, S. Asch, Marc Chagall, and others . . . List of correspondents.

Simon Dubnow (1860–1941). Papers, 1632–1938, 8 microfilm rolls. Historian, political writer, and educator. Community records from Mstislavl (his birthplace), 1760–1895, Pinczow, 1632–1740, Piotrowice, 1726–1809, and the Burial Society of Stary Bychow, 1686–1869—all original *pinkeysim* (record books); copies of record books of Tykocin, 1769–77, Zabludow, 1650–1783, Birze, 1755–96, and Dubno, 1670–71; partial records of the Lublin community from the 18th century, and other communities; documents from blood libel trials in Miedzyrzec, 1816, and Bobowno, 1829; documents from Nowa Uszycz, 1839–40; documents concerning restrictions, privileges, and other matters issued by East European rulers and governments for Jews in various localities; minutes of a commission to publish documents relating to blood libel trials in Russia, 1919–20; material on Gzerot Takh-Tat and Jewish massacres of 1648–49 during the Chmielnicki uprising; copies of archival documents of the Russian Ministry of Justice and Senate, 1799–1800; reports and documents pertaining to Russian pogroms of the 1880s, Kishinev pogrom, 1903, Homel pogrom, 1903, and pogroms of October 1905 and in Bialystok, 1906; Dubnow family papers, including material of Rabbi Benzion Dubnow, Simon's grandfather; and correspondence with, among others, Shmuel Alexandrovich, 1896, Yitschak Antonovsky, 1897, Chaim Zhitlovsky, Maxim Vinaver, 1922–23, Shmuel Silberstein, and Chaim Zuskind. Inventory.

Gershon Epstein. Collection, 16th–20th c., ca. 4.5 ft. YIVO's principal collector in France and Germany after World War II. Includes rare manuscript Judaica from Western and Eastern Europe, some relating to Jewish folklore. Unpublished inventory.

Leon Feinberg (1897–1969). Papers, 1920s–1968, ca. 14.5 ft. Yiddish journalist, poet, novelist, editor, and translator. Correspondence; writings; manuscripts of Feinberg, S.N. Feinberg (his father), Mani-Leib, and Moshe Nadir; speeches and lectures; and clippings, some of which relate to Russia, where Feinberg lived for part of his life. Unpublished inventory.

Baron Horace (Naftali Herz) Guenzburg (1833–1909). Papers, 1850–95, 2 microfilm rolls. Banker, philanthropist, head of the Jewish Committee in St. Petersburg, and chairman of the Jewish Colonization Association in

Leader of the Khevra Mefitse Haskoleh (Society for the Propagation of Enlightenment), pertaining to which there is correspondence and minutes of meetings. Other correspondence between Guenzburg and various Russian authorities about unjust conscription of Jews into the Russian army, about the improvement of the political and legal situation of Russian Jews, with Jewish journalists about the Jewish press in Russia, with Jewish personalities in Russia about educational problems, and with others, especially with rabbis of Russia and Poland concerning the creation of a rabbinical seminary in Russia. . . . Inventory.

Gregori Gurevitch (Gershon Badanes) (1852–1929). Papers, 1880–1929, 2 microfilm rolls. Early Russian-Jewish revolutionary, subsequently disillusioned and became a Jewish communal leader. Correspondence with Pavel Axelrod, 1925, Jacob Lestchinsky, 1929, N. Grinberg, 1924–28, N. Meisel, 1922, the Archives of the Russian Revolution, 1924–27, and others. . . . Inventory.

Isaac A. Hourwich (1860–1924). Papers, 1896–1924, ca. 4.5 ft. Yiddish, Russian, and English publicist, economist, lawyer, lecturer, and one of the organizers of the first American Jewish Congress in 1918. Manuscripts, documents, reports, minutes of meetings, memoranda, correspondence, etc., pertaining to Russia and the labor movement, the fifth Congress of the Jewish Labor Bund, 1903, the Russian Social-Revolutionary Party, and American Jewish affairs. Also, microfilm of his unfinished memoirs, published in the weekly *Die Freie Arbeiter Stimme*. Unpublished inventory.

Jewish Community Board in Vilno. Records, 1820s–1940, ca. 11 ft. Minutes of meetings, correspondence, reports, financial records, printed matter, and miscellaneous documents relating to the activities of the Vilno Tsedakah Gedolah, 1844–1918, and to the Naye Kehilla, 1919–40. . . . Unpublished inventory.

Jewish Community Council in Minsk. Records, 1825–1921, ca. 3 ft. Includes registers of births, weddings, and deaths within the Jewish population of Minsk, Byelorussia. . . .

Khevra Mefitzei Haskolo (Society for the Propagation of Enlightenment). Records, 1909–38, ca. 2 ft. Founded in 1863 to unite "enlightened" groups among Russian Jewry to stem criticism of Jewish separatism in education and culture. . . . Includes correspondence with the Russian government, 1909–11, and with towns around Vilno, 1909–18.

Maxim Kovensky Collection, 1906–13, ca. 1 ft. Former member of the Socialist Revolutionary Party in Russia. Contains original flyers and appeals of the Party, clippings from Russian and Yiddish newspapers about the Socialist Revolutionaries, and typescript declarations of the Party.

Lithuanian Consistory of the Russian Orthodox Church. Records, 1807–1900, ca. 4.5 ft. Consists of 196 files for 290 persons, mostly women, residing in the former Pale of Settlement, applying to the Consistory for conversion to the Greek Orthodox faith. . . . Unpublished inventory in Yiddish.

Lithuanian Jewish Communities. Records, 1844–1940, 40 ft. Primarily from the time of the Jewish national Autonomy in Lithuania, 1919–26, and from the Ministry for Jewish Affairs. Also, much material from local communities. A small amount relates to 1844–1918 and 1927–40. . . . Unpublished inventory.

Kalman Marmor (1879–1956). Papers, ca. 1880–1952, ca. 37 ft. Yiddish writer, literary critic, editor, and lecturer. Member at various times of different political movements and parties, including The World Union of Poalei Zion, Communist Party of the U.S.A., and Mishagola (Russia). . . . The unarranged portion of the papers contains material relating to the CPUSA, Friends of Soviet Russia, 1920s–30s, Marmor's stay in Russia, 1931–35, and many other groups and subjects. Unpublished partial inventory in Yiddish.

Mendel Osherowitch (1887–1965). Papers, 1920s–67, 10 ft. Yiddish journalist, poet, novelist, historian, organizer of the Federation of Ukrainian Jews in America (Association to Perpetuate the Memory of Ukrainian Jews), and editor of a book on Jews in the Ukraine. Correspondents include Sholem Asch, Salo Baron, Albert Einstein, Aaron Glantz-Leyeles, Jacob Lestchinsky, Jacob Shatzky, Zalman Reisin, Abraham Sutzkever, Alexander Kerensky, and many organizations . . . manuscripts by Abraham Cahan (Kahan), Dov Sadan, Moshe Starkman, and Hillel Rogoff; and other materials. Unpublished inventory.

Alexander Pomerantz (1901–1965). Papers, 1920s–60s, 2.5 ft. Yiddish writer and bibliographer, member of the faculty of the Institute for Jewish Proletarian Culture at the Ukrainian Academy of Science, Kiev. Comprises correspondence . . . notes . . . Pomerantz's published and unpublished articles in manuscript. . . .

Rabbinical School and Teachers' Seminary, Vilno. Records, 1847–1914, ca. 18 ft. Correspondence, reports, memoranda, financial records, and other documents. Curriculum of the Rabbinical School, established to train teachers for government schools for Jewish children, included secular subjects and Judaic subjects. In 1873 the seminary was converted into a teacher's institute only. Contains correpondence with the Ministry of Education's office for the province of White Russia; materials on courses, administration, and school activities; and much data on candidates for admittance.

Marc Ratner. Papers, 1906–13, 3 microfilm rolls. Co-founder of SERP (Sotsialisticheskaya Yevreyskaya Rabochaya Partiya), the Jewish Socialist Workers' Party, in 1906. . . . Correspondents include Ber Borochov, Z. Goldin, Pinkhas Dubinsky, Shimon Aronson, Virgilia Verdaro, Alexander

Ziskind, Chaim Zhitlovsky, Michel Levitan, Yehuda Novakovsky, and Misha Fabricant. Inventory.

Reichsicherheitshauptamt (RSHA) (Reich Central Security Office). Einsatzgruppen (task forces) in the USSR. Records, 1941–42, 2.25 ft. Task forces or mobile liquidation units of the RSHA that followed the army to carry out special tasks in various countries. . . . Card index.

Joseph A. Rosen (1887–1949). Agro-Joint director files, 1921–28, 16 ft. Agronomist, leader of Jewish agricultural colony projects, and director of the Agro-Joint project for Jewish agricultural colonies in the USSR. . . . Unpublished inventory.

Sholom Schwarzbard (1886–1938). Papers, 1917–38, 4 microfilm rolls. Jewish political activitist and writer who assassinated Simon Petlyura in May 1926 . . . correspondence with groups and individuals such as YIVO, the French ambassador to Moscow, Israel Ostroff, Noah Prilucki, Zalman Kalmanovitch, and Anna Schwarzbard. Inventory.

Isaac N. Steinberg (1888–1957). Papers, 1910s–63, 25 ft. Russian-Jewish political writer, leader of the Left Socialist Revolutionary Party during the 1917 Revolution, minister of Justice in the first Bolshevik government, leader of the Jewish Territorialist Movement and of the Freland League for Jewish Territorial Colonization, and founding member of the YIVO Institute. . . . Unpublished inventory.

Dr. Mendel Sudarski (1885–1951) and Alta Sudarski. Papers, 1938–58, 5 ft. Physician, Jewish communal leader in Kaunas, Lithuania, chairman of the Federation of Lithuanian Jews in New York, and author; and his wife, active in Yiddish cultural organizations and in relief efforts for Jewish refugees in Shangai and for Russian Jews. . . .

Abraham Sutzkever–Shmerke Katcherginski Collection, 1806–1945, 7 ft. Jewish writers from Vilno active in Vilno ghetto life and in anti-Nazi resistance, 1941–45. Correspondence, manuscripts, reports, circulars, posters, and documents relating to Jewish life in Vilno from 1806 to the extermination of the ghetto. . . . Unpublished inventory in Yiddish.

Elias Tcherikower (1881–1943). Papers, 1903–63, 45 microfilm rolls. Historian, secretary and founder of the Eastern Jewish Historical Archive in Kiev and Berlin, founding member of YIVO, chairman of the Historical Section and Research Secretary of YIVO. . . . Correspondents include Alfred de Ginzburg, Simon Dubnow, and Ilya Dijeur. Inventory.

Union of Russian Jews. Records, 1945–60, 14 ft. Fraternal organization based in New York providing relief for relatives in the Soviet Union after World War II. General correspondence and minutes of meetings of the Executive Committee; correspondence with Soviet Jews; index of persons contacted in the USSR; manuscript on Russian Jewry, 1860–1917, and Soviet Jewry, 1918–61; and other correspondence and financial records.

Maxim Vinawer (1862–1926). Papers, 1918–23, 4 microfilm rolls. Lawyer, Kadet Party leader, historian, foreign minister in the Crimean regional government, 1918–19, and editor of the Yevreyskaya Tribuna, Paris, 1920s . . . . correspondence with, inter alia, the Institut d'Études Slaves, Chaim Zhitlovsky, the Conférence Politique Russe, N. Tchaikovsky, M. Rostovstev, and D. Merezhkowsky. Inventory.

Lucien Wolf and David Mowshowitch. Papers, 1890s–1950s, ca. 14 ft. Mowshowitch (1887–1957) was on the Jewish Board of deputies in England, secretary to Lucien Wolf and later secretary of the Foreign Department of the Board of Deputies. Wolf (1857–1930) was a publicist, historian, and secretary of the Joint Foreign Committee formed by the Board of Deputies and the Anglo-Jewish Association. . . . Includes Wolf's lectures on English-Russian relations, his correspondence with Prof. Simon Ashkenasy, 1921, and Maxim Vinaver (Vinawer), 1917; documents and correspondence pertaining to Soviet Jewry; materials relating to the Beilis Trial; Vladimir Jobotinsky's appeal about military service; and Mowshowitch's papers, including items on Russian anti-semitism and translations of Russian poems in Yiddish. Published inventory in Yiddish; unpublished inventory in English.

YIVO Collection of Autobiographies of Jewish Youth, 1932–39, 7.5 ft. YIVO-sponsored contest produced ca. 375 autobiographies of young Jewish men and women, aged 16–22, living mainly in Poland and Lithuania before 1939 (arranged geographically by author's place of origin). . . . Unpublished inventory with name index and Moses Kligsberg's published guide, 1965.

YIVO Vilno Collection on Russia and the Soviet Union, 1845–1930s, ca. 6 ft. Correspondence, reports, clippings, posters, documents, and printed matter relating to Jewish (and non-Jewish) affairs. Materials on Jewish Political activities, 1845–1921; records relating to Birobidjan; government ukases and edicts relating to Jewish life; police reports about Jews and non-Jews under police custody, 1870–1911; materials about Jews in the Russian military, 1885–1915; police documents on Polish revolutionaries, 1863–70; and general records about different localities in Russia, 1902–17.

Chaim Zhitlovsky (1861–1943). Papers, 1886–1943, 30 ft. Russian-born philosopher, radical, and literary figure. He was theoretician of socialism and Jewish nationalism in the Diaspora, one of the founders of the Jewish Socialist Workers' Party (SERP), and a member of the Socialist Revolutionary Party. Emigrated to the U.S. in 1908. . . . Ca. 33 percent of the collection is in Russian. Unpublished finding aid.

CATALOGS   There are inventories of individual collections, as well as other finding aids in the reading room; consult the archivist. A printed guide to the Archives is being produced by YIVO and should be ready in 1990.

BIBLIOGRAPHY   *Yivo News*; *Yivo Annual*; *Yivo Bleter* (Yiddish); Lucjan Dobroszycki and Barbara Kirshenblatt-Gimblett. *Images Before My Eyes: A Photographic History of Jewish Life in Poland, 1864–1939.* New York: Schocken, 1977. 269 p.; Zvi Gitelman. *A Century of Ambivalence: The Jews of Russia and the Soviet Union, 1881 to the Present* [New York: Schocken, 1988]. 336 p.; Marek Web, comp. *The Documents of the Lodz Ghetto: An Inventory of the Nachman Zonabend Collection.* New York: YIVO Institute for Jewish Research, 1988. 163 p. See Grant & Brown, pp. 401–407.

Y6
YMCA OF GREATER NEW YORK
ARCHIVES

422 Ninth Avenue
New York, NY 10001

Ms. Mary Hedge

Director

TELEPHONE   212 564–1300

SCHEDULE   Mon–Fri 9:30 a.m.–5:30 p.m.

ACCESS   Open to the public. No reading room. Permission may be obtained to copy or photograph items.

HISTORY   To document the history of the YMCA from its founding in 1852 to the present.

HOLDINGS   The James Stokes Society Papers contain correspondence (1916–1956) and legal documents in regard to attempts at compensation for property owned by the Society in Petrograd.

Josef Novotny collection on the American YMCA in Siberia, some materials in Czech. Ca. 1 inch; unprocessed at this time.

The material listed below is found in Grant & Brown. However, the address they give—National Board of Young Men's Christian Association (YMCA) Historical Library, 291 Broadway, New York, NY 10007—has been changed. The material is now located in the following institution:

YMCA OF USA ARCHIVES
University of Minnesota
Social Welfare History Archives
2642 University Avenue
St. Paul, MN 55114
Telephone 612 627–4632

Chekhov Press (New York). Collection, 1945–55, ca. 8 ft. Business correspondence with its authors and manuscripts of books, mostly Russian emigre memoirs. In process.

Russian work. Collection, 1900–1920s, 2 ft. Includes correspondence and reports from YMCA secretaries working in Russia and Western Europe, primarily from before the Revolution but also from later years when the YMCA was involved in the Russian emigre communities. Pre-revolutionary holdings deal mainly with the "Mayak" Society in St. Petersburg, founded by James Stokes in 1900, and closely tied to the American YMCA (it was also known as the Society for Cooperating with St. Petersburg Young Men in the Attainment of Moral and Physical Development) and with the "Student Work" of the YMCA in Russia. Some of the subjects covered are physical education and sports, general education (arithmetic, languages, music), and social service. From the start of World War I the YMCA was increasingly involved in humanitarian and relief work. Though headquartered in Petrograd, the YMCA and its War Prisoners' Aid division operated in such other cities as Moscow, Odessa, Kiev, Minsk, Kazan, Orenburg, Tashkent, Perm, Omsk, Tobolsk, Tomsk, Krasnoiarsk, Irkutsk, Chita, and Khabarovsk. It also helped Russian POWs in enemy hands. After the spring of 1917 (and the visit of the Root Mission in the summer), the YMCA worked more and more with the Russian army and engaged in war-related non-combat support. Among the administrators and secretaries of the YMCA Russian operations were Ethan T. Colton, Russell M. Story, Crawford Wheeler, Paul Anderson, Arthur Eugene Jenny, Reverend William L. Tucker, G. Sidney Phelps, Arthur P. Kempa, Raymond J. Reitzel, Franklin Gaylord, Sherwood Eddy, A. M. Craig, A. C. Harte, E. T. Heald, John R. Mott, Jerome Davis, Donald Lowrie, Luis Penningroth, and Herbert Sidney Gott. Correspondents with various YMCA offices and personnel: Maddin Summers, American consul in Moscow; Ernest L. Harris, consul in Omsk; and Boris Bakhmeteff, Russian ambassador in Washington. Toward the end of its work in Russia, the YMCA was particularly active in Siberia. There is much material on the Revolution and Civil War, relations with the Bolsheviks, contacts with Admiral A.V. Kolchak, the Czech troops in Siberia, the Cheka, and the Russian emigres. Preliminary inventory.

YMCA Press in Paris. Archives, 1921–present, ca. 1 ft. of documents plus a complete set of its published Russian-language books. Additions expected.

YMCA Work in Paris for emigre Russians. Collection, 1925–55, ca. 5 ft. Includes correspondence and other materials on the Russian Student Christian Movement (RSCM), Russian Superior Technical Institute, and the Russian Theological Academy.

Restrictions: Most of the above materials are restricted; information is available at the repository.

CATALOGS   Approximately one inch of cards, or 40 items.

BIBLIOGRAPHY   Edward Kasinec. "The Y.M.C.A. National Board Historical Library." *Newsletter of the Slavic Bibliographic Documentation Center* 5: (November 1971). See Grant & Brown, pp. 360–361. (Grant & Brown state that the description of the Russian work collection was taken largely from Donald E. Davis and Eugene P. Trani. "The American YMCA and the Russian Revolution." *Slavic Review* [September 1974].) Articles based on material in the Historical Library have appeared in YMCA journals. See Mary Hedge for details.

Z1
ZIONIST ARCHIVES AND LIBRARY

515 Park Avenue
New York, NY 10022

Esther Togman
Director and Librarian

TELEPHONE   212 753–2167

SCHEDULE   Mon–Fri 10:00 a.m.–5:00 p.m.

ACCESS   Open to the public.

FACILITIES   Reading room.

HOLDINGS   The Zionist Archives and Library reports that there has been no new material added relative to the Russian Empire and Soviet Union since Grant & Brown was published. Grant & Brown lists three items:
   Zionist organizations in Russia. Letters and reports from 1898–1906. This includes correspondence from the first All-Russian Zionist Conference, which was held in Minsk, August 22–28, 1902. In addition there are typed copies of Zionist reports and letters to party members in the Simferopol' and Ekaterinoslav regions 1900–1903. The collection also contains hectographed circular letters to Zionist groups in Moscow, St. Petersburg, Kiev, Lodz, and Vitebsk, Warsaw, Vilna, Kharkov, and Odessa, 1900–1904. 1 box (12 inches).

ZIMRO (Petrogradskii Kamernyi Ansambl', Obshchestvo Evreiskoi Narodnoi Muzyki). In 1918 a chamber music ensemble, ZIMRO, was organized in Petrograd. This group toured Russia, the Urals area, Siberia, China, Japan, America, and Palestine. The collection comprises scrapbooks containing business correspondence, financial accounts, photos, programs, and reviews for the years 1918–19. 12 inches.

Photographs. The Archives has a collection of photographs of the founders of the state of Israel, some of whom came from the Russian Empire.

CATALOGS   Card catalog.

BIBLIOGRAPHY   See Grant & Brown, p. 407.

How to Use the Index

Robert A. Karlowich

Since this guide covers such a range of languages and subjects in varying degrees of accessibility, it is potentially useful to those who are not trained in the field as well as to the expert. The index has thus been compiled with a particular goal in mind: to give the users as much information as possible on the contents of the entries, but without overburdening them with too many instructions and cross references. In most instances I have kept terms in the index as they occur in the entries, making it easier to find them; consequently, it should be seen more as a finding aid than as a strict list of subject headings according to some authority, e.g., the Library of Congress.

The following explanations will be helpful to users of the index.

Generally, where the entries for the holdings of an institution or individual are brief and can be scanned rapidly, there has been no need to do more than refer the user to these entries. However, when an entry has holdings that run on for two or more pages and are subdivided into topics or individuals, I have tried to index the contents of these holdings according to the subdivisions. For instance, the Leo Baeck Institute holds the papers of Sam Echt, who went to Russia in the 1920s. During his visit, he reported on conversations he had with several prominent people and they are mentioned in the description of his material. One person he met was Anastas Mikoyan. To note this fact, an entry for Mikoyan is given in the index which refers back to Sam Echt:

Mikoyan (Mikojan), Anastas Ivanovich (1895–1978)
(Sam Echt), B1

The entry should be read as follows: Mikoyan is the usual spelling in English for this name and the way most users would be expected to look for it; the spelling in parentheses is the spelling as it appears in the Baeck Institute entry; then follow Mikoyan's given name and patronymic, birth and death dates, and finally, in parentheses, the subdivision in the Baeck Institute holdings where Mikoyan appears. B1 is the locational sign for the Leo Baeck Institute entry in the guide. The name Sam Echt also appears in the index, under Echt, Sam.

There are a few extensive entries that do not contain such clear-cut subdivisions, but where they do not, users will still be referred to the entry and then will have to scan through the material to find the reference they need.

Names of individuals are given under their most common form in English, when known, e.g., Alexandre Benois, Catherine Breshkovsky, Maxim Gorky, Nicholas Roerich. In the few instances when entries have differed on the spelling of well-known persons, e.g., Chaliapin/Shaliapin, I have given the variants separate listings with cross references from one to the other. When an East Slavic given name and patronymic were easily obtained, they are included, as well as birth and death dates; if the name of an individual was not immediately familiar to me, the form given in the entry was kept. The index is thus not consistent in this area, but presents a mixture of anglicized, half-anglicized, half-native spellings, and mutations that come by way of France or Germany. At times, only the last name of an individual is given in an entry. I have included such unclear references in the index because it may be the only clue a researcher needs to find what he or she is looking for. In addition, a reference to the division in an entry in which the name occurs may serve as an additional aid in identification. Thus, "Glebov (Mikhail Iur'evich Lermontov)" can take on added meaning for a researcher who finds it in connection with Lermontov. As in many other cases, I have opted to include rather than exclude whenever in doubt.

An entry for a topic, e.g., Folklore, does not imply that material on the subject cannot be found in other sources listed in the guide, but rather that the given source stated particularly that it had such material. In fact, the Columbia University Libraries and the Slavic and Baltic Division of The New York Public Library could be listed for almost any general entry, and in many instances they are. On the opposite side, there are instances when a collection is much richer than the report indicates. However, I did not take the liberty of adding topics that were not reported by the individual owner or institution. The user of the index will only be led to what is included in the descriptions of holdings in the entries.

When an entry lists different kinds of materials—e.g., documents, letters, etc.—then I have just used the term "materials" to indicate the variety. Letters are listed as correspondence, even if only one letter is reported. Otherwise, the terms used in the index are those from the entries.

Definite and indefinite articles have been eliminated from all initial positions. Except when they are part of a title, all dates are in parentheses, including birth and death, chronological coverage of materials held, publication dates, and scope of holdings of journals. Dates for journals have been provided by the institution or individual (it was not always specified if these dates are for holdings or span of publication). Place of publication is not included in the index but is usually found in the entry itself. Films are identified as such under title entry only, where date released is also given. All journal and film titles are also listed under the separate entries "Journals" and "Film." Book titles are listed under both author (when given) and title.

There has been a considerable amount of cross listing, e.g., Georgian language, but also Language(s), Georgian, etc. Under Russia, Soviet Union, and United States, I have tried to include only entries that relate to the state and government. This is a hazy area at times, and one might not agree with all of my decisions. I have not indicated Soviet republics, but historical names, e.g., Armenia, not Armenian SSR; thus they will not be found in the index under the entries for Russia or the Soviet Union.

I have not made consistent use of diacritical marks for foreign words. Where the decision could be mine, I have followed the Library of Congress system for transliterating from the Cyrillic alphabet.

Index

A

Abel, Elie (William Averell Harriman), C7
Academie Impériale des Sciences de St. Petersbourg, *Atlas Russien* . . . (1745), A2
Acheson, Dean (William Averell Harriman), C7
Achron, Joseph (1886–1943), composition, N26
Adamic, Louis (1898–1951), papers, P7
Adamov, Father, collection, S1
Adams, John Quincy, correspondence, M4
    (Albert Gallatin), N8
Adiassewich, Viktor, manuscripts, N18
Adler, Victor (Julie Braun-Vogelstein), B1
Aeronautical Engineering Review, A3
Aerospace, A3
Af di Vegn zu der neier Shul (1924–1928), N11
Africa and Russia, N30
Afro-Americans and Russia, N30
Afternoon with Gregor Piatigorsky (film, 1977), N23
Age of Gold, Shostakovich (*Polka Graph*), N23
Agon (George Balanchine), N25
Agro-Joint Project for Jewish Agricultural Colonies in the USSR, A7
    (American Joint Reconstruction Foundation), Y5
    (Joseph A. Rosen), Y5
Ahiasaf, Warsaw (1893–1923), N11
AIP (American Institute of Physics), A4
Aitmatov, Chingiz (b. 1928), N24
Aivazovskii, Ivan Konstantinovich (1817–1900), M2, T2
Akademiska dzive, Indianapolis, N19
Akhmatova, Anna Andreevna (1889–1966), N19
    (Osip Emil'evich Mandel'shtam), P7
Akimenko, Fiodor Stepanovich, compositions, N26
Alaska, C7
    (Herma Hoyt Briffault), N18
    (Andrew Johnson), M4
Alaskan Russian Church, records, O2, S1
Aleksei Mikhailovich, tsar (John Milton), C7
Aleutian Islands (Vladimir Jochelson), N18
Alexander I, tsar, collection, M3, M4, N4,
    (George Washington Campbell), N8
    (Andrei Ia. Dashkov), N8
    (Wickham Hoffman), N8
    (Stevens Family), N4
Alexander II, tsar, collection, M3, M4, N19, O2
Alexander III, tsar, correspondence, A12
Alexander Nevsky (film, 1938), N23
Alexander Romance (Robert Garret Collection), P7
Alexandrovich, Shmuel (Simon Dubnow), Y5

Allaire, Peter Alexander, travels (1774), N5
Allied Expeditionary Force, P2
All-Russian Zionist Conference (1902), Z1
Alsop, Stewart (John Foster Dulles), P7, P8
Altaic languages, N15
Amalgamated Clothing and Textile Workers of America, B6
American accounts of Soviet Russia (1918–1940s), N34
American Bible Society, A1
American Civil Liberties Union, archives, P8
American Commission to Negotiate Peace (1919)
    (Ray Stannard Baker), P7
    (Bernard M. Baruch), P8
    (John Foster Dulles), P7, P8
    (Robert Lansing), P8
American communism. *See* Communism and communist parties
American correspondents and Russian wives (American Civil Liberties Union), P8
American Expeditionary Forces, P2, U6
American Fund for Public Service, records, N18
American Geographical Society Collection of the University of Wisconsin Library, A2
American Institute of Aeronautics and Astronautics Library, A3
American Institute of Pacific Relations (192?–1962), office files, C7
American Institute of Physics, Center of History of Physics, Niels Bohr Library, A4
American Jewish Committee
    Blaustein Library, A5
    William E. Wiener Oral History Library, A6
American Jewish Congress (1918) (Isaac A. Hourwich), Y5
American Jewish Council to Aid Russian Rehabilitation (Louis Levine), Y2
American Jewish Joint Distribution Committee
   Landsmanschaften Department, records (1937–1940, 1945–1950), Y5
   War Orphans Bureau, records (1919–1923), Y5
American Joint Reconstruction Foundation (AJRF), records (1920–1939), Y5
American Marxists and labor leaders, book collections, R3
American merchants in Russia, correspondence, A1
American modern dance (Oral Interviews with Dancers), N25
American Museum of Natural History, A8, A9
American National Exhibition in Moscow (1959), scrapbooks, M7
American Numismatic Society, A10
American radicalism, N34
American Red Cross in Siberia (1919–1920) (Frederick Lee Barnum), C8
American Relief Administration, A7
    (Harold M. Fleming), N18
American-Russian Chamber of Commerce (Reeve Schley, Sr.), N4
American Russian Cultural Association (ARCA), R6
American-Russian Welfare Society "Rodina," H2
American socialist movements, N34
American Society for Russian Relief (Louis Levine), Y2
American-Soviet economic relations (Frank A. Vanderlip), C7
American Soviet Science Society (Duncan Arthur MacInnes), R5
American working class reform, N34
American YMCA in the Soviet Union (Alexander W. Grenier), C8
Amur River, A9
An Actor Prepares (Elizabeth Reynolds Hapgood), N24
Anarchists, B6
    (*Free Voice of Labor*), N23
Anderson, Paul, collection, S1
Andreenko, Michel (Mychajlo), I4, U1
Andreev (Andreyev), Leonid Nikolaevich (1871–1919), working scripts, N24
    (Herman Bernstein), Y5
Anisfeld, B., collection, S7

Anna, empress, decrees, H2
Annenkova-Vereshchagina, Elizaveta Arkadievna (Mikhail Iur'evich Lermontov), C7
Anthropology, Jewish, Y3
Anti-communism. *See* Communism and communist parties
Antimensia (portable altar cloths), B9
Anti-Semitism, A5, C4
Antonovsky, Yitschak (Simon Dubnow), Y5
Apocalypse, M3, U2
Apollon, N19
Apostol, U2
    (1591), R1
Apt Art Group, C14
Arbuzon, Aleksei, N24
ARCA (American Russian Cultural Association), R6
Archipenko, Alexander (1887–1964), G1, M7, N14
Archeology, Russian, P6
Architecture
    Armenian, P5
    Jewish, Y3
    Russian, C5, E4, N19, P6, S10
    Ukrainian, U1
Archiv fur wissenschaftliche Kunde von Russland, N19
Archive of the Russian Imperial Army, H2
Archives of the Russian Revolution (Gregori Gurevitch), Y5
Archives of *Story* magazine and Story Press (Mikhail Mikhailovich Zoshchenko), P7
Arents Collection, Rare Books and Manuscripts Division, New York Public Library, N17
Arkhipov, Abram E. (1862–1930), M2
Armenia, A11, N29, P5
Armenia, ethnography, A8
Armenian Academy of St. Lazarus, Venice, N15
Armenian Church, P5
Armenian history, A11, P5
Armenian language, C5, N15, P5
Armenian literature, N15
Armenian manuscripts
    Alexander Romance (Robert Garrett Collection), P7
    Astronomy (Robert Garrett Collection), P7
    Bible. O.T. Psalms, P7
    Church ritural, C7
    Gospels, A1, C7, M3, N20, P7
    Hymnal, C7, M3, N20, P7
    "The Jewish Bride" (18th–19th c.), N20
    Lectionary, M3
    Lives of the Saints and Christ, M3
    Menologium, M3, P7
    Phylactery, C7
    Miniatures (Robert Garrett Collection), P7
    Psalters and breviaries (Robert Garrett Collection), P7
    St. Gregory the Illuminator, Discourse (Robert Garrett Collection), P7
    Sargis Vardapet, commentary, M3
    Scholium and Epistles, St. Cyril, M3
    Sermons, M3
    Theological lectures, C7
Armenian Missionary Association of America, A11
Armour, Norman (1887–1982), collection, P8
Arms and armor, M2
    (Leonid Tarassuk), T1
Army–McCarthy Hearings (*Point of Order*), N23
Army Museum and Archive of the Russian Imperial Army, H2

Aronson, Shimon (Marc Ratner), Y5
Art. *See also* under individual artists and movements
    Apt Art Group, C14
    Armenian, P5
    Avant-garde, C1, C2, G1, K2
    Caricatures, N14
    Chandeliers, M2, S3
    Constructivism, E4
    Costumes, N16, N19
        (Leon Bakst), N25
        (Aleksandr Nikolaevich Benois), N25
        Byelorussian, B8
        Jewish, Y3
        Russian peasant, B5
        Russian uniforms, H2
        (Pavel Tchelitchev), N25
        Ukrainian, U1
        Vestments, B9
    Decorative, N12
    Drawings, C14, M2, N3, R1, T2, Y3
        (Mikhail Iur'evich Lermontov), C7
        (Manuel Rosenberg), C7
    Eastern Christianity, carvings, B9
    Embroidery, B8, M2
    Engravings, R8
    Fine art, M2, T2, U1
    Folk art, B8, N12, N14, U1
    Glass, Bakhmeteff glassworks, M2
    Graphic arts, C9, E4
    Icons, B9, R10
    Jewish, Y3
    Lithographs and etchings, C2, H2, N14, N8
    Lubki (Russkii narodnii lubok), N14
    Maria Feodorovna, tsarina, (1789), portrait, M4
    Metalwork, M2
    Murals, R10
    Paintings, B9, C14, M2, N12, R1, R6, T2, Y3
    Pastels, S3, T2
    Polish collection, P1
    Porcelain ceramics, M2
    Russian, C5, F3, G1, K2, K3, N12, P6, R11, S10
    Russian baths, lithograph, N8
    Russian cartoons (Caricatures), N14
    Russian Mennonite settlement, wood engraving, N8
    Russian monarchs, portraits, H2
    Russian naval history, portraits, H2
    (Russian) Orthodox Cathedral of the Protection of the Holy Virgin (Orthodox Church in
        America), artwork, R9
    Russian Orthodox Church, New York, wood engraving, N8
    Russian painters and the stage, G1, S7
    Sculpture, C14, L1, M2, N3, T2, Y3
    Silver, M2, S3
    Soviet art, C13, C14, K3, S5
    Textiles, B5, B9, M2, U1, Y2
    Tolstoi, Leo, portrait (Lev Nikolaevich Tolstoi), P7
    Ukrainian, K2, S4, S8, U1, U2
    Watercolors, M2, N16, T2
        (Mikhail Iur'evich Lermontov), C7
    Weaving, B8

Art exhibitions, catalogs, K2, M7
Artzybashev, Mikhail P., working scripts, N24
Asch, Rafael (A. Charash), Y5
Asch, Sholem
    (Daniel Charney), Y5
    (Mendel Osherowitch), Y5
Ashaffenber, Camp, Germany, S4
Ashkenasy, Simon (Lucien Wolf), Y5
Askania Nova, photographs, A12
Association of Russian Imperial Naval Officers in America, H2
Association to Perpetuate the Memory of Ukrainian Jews (Mendel Osherowitch), Y5
Assumption Brotherhood, Lviv, church books, S8
Astronomy (Robert Garrett Collection), P7
Astruc, Gabriel (1864–1938), papers, N25
Atkinson, Brooks, correspondence, N24
Atlases, A2
Atlas Climatologique de l'Empire de Russie (1900), A2
Atlas Mira (1954), A2
Autograph collections, H2, M3, N19
Avrich, Paul (*Free Voice of Labor. . .*), N23
Awgerian, Mkrtich, works, N15
Axelrod, Pavel (Gregori Gurevitch), Y5
Azerbaijan, N15, N19, P2
  (Max Rabinoff), C7

B

Babi Yar (*Last Journey*), N23
Babkin, Boris (Rockefeller University), R5
Bacherac, Alexander, papers, C8
Badanes, Gershon (Gregori Gurevitch), Y5
Baden-Powell, Lord Robert, R8
Badges. *See* Numismatics
Baeck, Leo, Institute, B1
Bagby, Arthur Pendleton, correspondence, U6
Bainbridge, William (1774–1833), papers, N8
Baizerman, Saul, G1, M7
Baker, Ray Stannard (1890–1946), papers, P7
Bakhmeteff Archive of Russian and East European History and Culture, C8
Bakhmeteff glassworks, M2
Bakhmetev, Boris, O2
Bakst, Leon (1866–1924), F4, N24, N25, S7
Balanchine, George (1904–1983), correspondence, N25
Balieff, Nikita, N24
Ballet dancers, B1, F4, N23, N25, N26, N29
Ballet russe de Monte-Carlo, collection, M7, N25, S7
    (Jean Cocteau), N25
    (Irvin Deakin), N25
    (Serge Grigoriev), N25
    (*Reflections of a Dancer . . .*), N23
Ballet russe, Original (Irvin Deakin), N25
Ballets russes, C7, F4, N26
    (Mikhail Mikhailovich Fokine), N25
    (Vaslav Nijinsky), N25
Ballets Russes de Diaghilev, programs, M7, N25, S7
Baltic region, P1
    Church (Berlin Collection), Y5
    (Rockefeller Foundation), R5
Baratynskii, Evgenii Abramovich (1800–1844) (Mikhail Iur'evich Lermontov), C7

Baratz, Leon (b. 1871), papers, Y5
Barnum, Frederick Lee, diary (1919–1920), C8
Baron, Salo (Mendel Osherowitch), Y5
Barrois, Georges, collection, S1
Baruch, Bernard M. (1870–1965), papers, P8
Barons, K., *Latwju Duinos* (1915, 1922), N19
Barr, Alfred H., Jr., papers, M7
Baryshnikov, Mikhail, F4
Bates, John L., biography, R8
Battleship Potemkin (film, 1925), N23
Beaumont, Cyril W. (Mikhail Mikhailovich Fokine), N25
Becke, Archibald, F. (b. 1871), papers, P7
Bed and Sofa (film, 1926), N23
Bedacht, Max, book collection, R3
Beilis trial (Lucien Wolf), Y5
Beiträge zur Kenntnis der russischen Reiches (1839–1900), N19
Belknap, Sara Yancey (Mikhail Mikhailovich Fokine), N25
Bell, John, *Travels from St. Petersburgh in Russia, to Various Parts of Asia*, London (1788), N8
Bellaud, *Essal sur la Langue Arménienne*, Paris (1812), N15
Belogonov, Ivan, watercolors, N16
Belorussia. *See* Byelorussia
Belvedere Archive (General Headquarters of the Polish Supreme Command) (1918–1920), P1
Belyi, Andrei Nikolaevich (1880–1934) (Sergei Zalshupin), N14
    See also Bugaev, Boris
Belza, Ivan, composition, N26
Benois, Alexandre (1870–1960), N25, S3, S7
Berezowsky, Nicolai T. (1893–1954), papers, C7
Berg Collection, New York Public Library, N10
Berlin (1945–1947), R8
Berlin Collection (1931–1945), Y5
Berlin Crisis of 1961 (Society for the Prevention of World War III), C7
Berman, Eugene (George Balanchine), N25
Bernstein, Eduard (Daniel Charney), Y5
Bernstein, Herman (1876–1935), papers, Y5
Bertesgaden, Germany, Camp, S4
Bervinchak, Nicholas, N14, U1
Betancourt, Augustin de
    (Robert Fulton), N8
    (T.P. Shaffner), N8
Bettmann Archive, B2
Bible, A1, N19, P7
Bible societies in Russia, A1
    See also Russian Bible Society
Bibles
    Armenian, M3, N15, P7
    Ostrog, S1
    Russian, A1
Biblioteka dlia chteniia (1834–1865), N19
Big Three Conferences, R8
Bigelow, Poultney, sketchbooks and diaries (1891–1892), N18
Bilibin, Ivan Iakovlevich (1876–1942), N21
Bilinsky, B., collection, S7
Billy Rose Theatre Collection, N24
Bintel Brief, Y5
Birobidzhan (YIVO Vilno Collection on Russia and the Soviet Union 1845–1930s), Y5
Birth of Soviet Cinema (film, 1972), N23
Bishop, John Peale, correspondence, P7
Black Americans and Russia, N30
Blakeslee, Victor F., Mrs. (Irina Skariatina), P7

Blaumanis, Rudolf, N19
Blavatsky, H.P., N31, O1
Blind Bird (film, 1963), N23
Bliss, George (1830–1897), N8
Blok, Aleksandr Aleksandrovich (1880–1921), N24
    (Sergei Zalshupin), N14
Blume, Peter, M7
Bogoraz (Jochelson and Bogoraz Paleo-Siberian Collections), N19
Bogoslovskii vestnik, S1
Boguslavskaia, N17
Bohlen, Charles E., C7
    (John Foster Dulles), P7, P8
Bolm, Adol'f (Irvin Deakin), N25
Bolotowsky, Ilya, G1, M7
Book illustration, N21, N29
Bookplates, N14
Books, avant-garde, K2
Books, Russian rare book collection, K2, P7, R1
Bookstore, E3, K1, R11
Bordofsky, Ben, book collection, R3
Borenstein, Julius. *See* Julius Borenstein–Leah Eisenberg Collection, Y5
Boris Godunov, N24
Borisoff, W., oil painting, H3
Bornstein, Joseph. *See* Roth-Bornstein, Joseph
Borochov, Ber (Marc Ratner), Y5
Borodin, Alexander, F4
    (*Prince Igor'*), N23
Borodino, commemorative coins, P2
Borovka, Nina, Crimean Tatar folk songs and dances, N26
Boutique Fantasque (Leonide Massine), N25
Boy Scouts, Russian, P3, R8
Boyd, Louise, photographs, Polish countryside, A2
Bradish Papers, N8
Bragdon, Claude (1866–1946), papers, P7
Brandt, Willy (John Foster Dulles), P7, P8
Braun-Vogelstein, Julie, collection, B1
Brazol, Boris, N18
Breshkovsky, Catherine, correspondence, N18
Breviaries (Robert Garrett Collection), P7
Briffault, Herma Hoyt, N18
Briullov, K., paintings, T2
Brodsky, Joseph, A6
    (*Soviet Dissidents in Exile*), N23
Brodzki, Viktor (1825–1904), M2
Brookhaven National Laboratory, B3
Brooklyn Museum, Art Reference Library, B4
Brooklyn Museum, Costume Collection, B5
Brookwood Labor College (Edward Falkowski), N34
Brothers Cramer, Russian merchants (David Parish), N8
Brown, Neill S., N8
Bryan, Julien
    (*Poland*), N23
    (*Religion in Russia*), N23
    (*Russia*), N23
    (*Russian Peasant*), N23
    (*Soviet Union*), I1
    (*Soviet Union: A New Look*), N23
    (*Women of Russia*), N23
Bryan, Sam (*Soviet Union: A New Look*), N23

Bryun, Cornelis de, *Reizen over Moskovie, door Persie en Indie* ... (1711), M3
"Budushchee Teatra" (Evgenii Ivanovich Zamiatin), P7
Budushchnost' (1900–1904), N11
Bugaev, Boris (Alexander Bacherac), C8
    See also Belyi, Andrei Nikolaevich
Bukovsky, Vladimir *(Soviet Dissidents in Exile)*, N23
Bulatov, C14
Bulatov, Eric, S5
Bulgakov, Mikhail A., working scripts, N24
Bullard, Arthur (1879–1929), papers, P8
Bund. *See* Bund Archives of the Jewish Labor Movement and under particular topics
    or individuals
Bund Archives of the Jewish Labor Movement, B6
Bunin, Ivan Alekseevich (1870–1953) (Alexander Bacherac), C8
Burliuk, David Davidovich (1882–1967), F2, M7
Burliuk, Vladimir, F2
Butensky, Jules Leon (1871–1947), M2
Butovych, Mykola (1895–1961), N14
By the Law (film, 1926), N23
Byelorussia, P1, P4
Byelorussia, church, Y5
Byelorussian Congress Committee of America, B7
Byelorussian embroidery, B8
Byelorussian folk art, B8
Byelorussian Folk Dance Company "Vasilok," B8
Byelorussian folk music, B8
Byelorussian historical documents, B7
Byelorussian language, C5, N19
Byelorussian literature, N19, N22
Byelorussian Mission, UNRRA, U4
Byelorussian weaving, B8
Byron, Lord (Mikhail Iur'evich Lermontov), C7
Bystren, A. (Mikhail Iur'evich Lermontov), C7
Byzantine Catholic Diocese of Passaic, Episcopal and Heritage Institute Libraries, B9
Byzantine illuminated manuscripts, N20
Byzantine-Ruthenian bishops in the United States, B9

C

Cahan, Abraham (Mendel Osherowitch), Y5
    See also Kahan, Abraham
Campan, Madame de, M4
Campbell, George Washington (1769–1848), correspondence, N8
Cantonists, P2
Capra, Frank, *(Battle of Russia)*, N23
"Carl Reinecke" (Nikolai Topusov), N26
Carnegie Endowment for International Peace (Malcolm Waters Davis), C7
Carpathian region, famine and reconstruction (1919–1930), A7
Carpathian village *(Shadows of Forgotten Ancestors)*, N23
Carpatho-Ruthenians, hymns (Elias I. Tziorogh), N26
Carpatho-Ruthenians in Europe, B9
Carpatho-Ruthenians in the United States, B9, O2
    (Elias I. Tziorogh), N26
Carroll, Charles, papers, M4
Carroll, Donald Frederic (1899–1948), papers, U6
Carus Gallery, C1

Carvings, Eastern Christianity, B9
C.A.S.E. Museum of Russian Contemporary Art in Exile, C13
Catherine II, empress, H2, M2, M4, N19
    (Madame de Campan), M4
Caucasus (Viktor Adiassewich), N18
Caucasus, languages, C5
Cecchetti, E. (Oral Interviews with Dancers), N25
Cedar Vale, Kansas, William Frey commune, N18
Center for History of Physics, American Institute of Physics, Niels Bohr Library, A4
Central Children's Room, Donnell Library Center, N21
Central Yiddish School Organization in Poland, B6
Cesnola, Luigi Palmer di (1832–1904), correspondence, N8
Chagall, Marc (1898–1985), G1, M2, M7
        (*Marc Chagall*), N23
        (Daniel Charney), Y5
Chaikin, Sol C., correspondence, I2
Chaikovskii, Nikolai Vasil'evich (1850–1926) (Maxim Vinawer), Y5
Chaikovskii, Petr Il'ich (1840–1893), F4. *See also* Tchaikovsky, Pyotr Il'yich
    (Toscanini Memorial Archives), N26
Chaim Soutine (film, 1970), N23
Chaliapin, Fedor, F4. *See also* Shaliapin, Fedor
        (Mikhail Mikhailovich Fokine), N25
        (Manuel Rosenberg), C7
Charash, C., papers (1912–1918), Y5
Charney, Daniel (1888–1959), papers, Y5
Charushin, Eugene I., N14
Chasnik, Ilja G., artwork, G1
Chauncey, Henry, papers, E2
Chauve-Souris Company, N24
Chekhov, Anton Pavlovich (1860–1904), N23, N24
        (Herman Bernstein), Y5
Chekhov, Michael, tapes, N24
Chekhov Press, New York, Y6
Chertkov (Tchertkoff), Mrs. V.G. (Lev Nikolaevich Tolstoi), C7
Chemiakine Metaphysical Arts, C2
Chemienski, Jan V., H3
Chemistry, Soviet literature on, B3
Cheremnykh, Mikhail (Louis Cowan), C7
Cherepnin, Aleksandr Nikolaevich, composition, N26
        See also Tcherepnin Society, T3
Cherry Orchard, U.S. production, N24
Chervonyi shlyakh, N19
Chess Fever (film, 1925), N23
Chew Family, papers, N4
Children of Labor (film 1976), N23
Children's books, K2, N19, N21,
Children's Room, Donnell Library Center, N21
Chinese Eastern Railway Co. (Russia, Foreign Office), P7
Chinese Turkestan, A9
Chmielnicki uprising (Simon Dubnow), Y5
Choiseul-Gouffier (Wickham Hoffman), memoirs, N8
Choreography. *See* Dance
Chubar (Tschubar) (Sam Echt), B1
Chubaty, Nicholas, papers, S4
Chukchee, ethnography, A8
Chukovskii, Kornei Ivanovich (1882–1969) (Alexander Bacherac), C8
Church archives, collections, B9, H4, O2, P5, R9, R10, S1, S8, S9, S10

Church, Armenian, P5
Church ceremonies, pictures, N29
Church reforms, Orthodox (1905–1906), O2
Church, Russian Orthodox (Lithuanian Consistory of the Russian Orthodox Church), Y5
Church Slavonic, N19. *See also* Old Church Slavonic
    Apocalypse, M3, N20
    Apostol, U2
        (1591), R1
    Canticles and Chants, N20
    Damascenus, Johannes, Philosophia, N20
    18th century church books, T4
    (Robert Garrett Collection), P7
    Gospels, M3, N20
    Kniga Tzvetnik, manuscript, N20
    Matthew, manuscript, A1
    Missal, "Slavonic" manuscript (Robert Garrett Collection), P7
    Music books (Robert Garrett Collection), P7
    New Testament, L'viv, N16
    Ostrog Bible, N16, S1
    St. Basil the Younger, Life, N20
    St. John Climachus, The Ladder, N20
    St. Luke, manuscript, N20
    Service book (Robert Garrett Collection), P7
    Service books, Galician, B9
Churchill, Winston, C7
Chuvash, language, N19
Cina, N19
Cisho (Central Yiddish School Organization in Poland), B6
Citizen Exchange Committee, C15
Citizen Exchange Council, C3
Civil Rights Congress (Paul Robeson), N30
Civil War in Russia, C5, H2, H4, N19
Civilization. *See* Cultural history
Clark, James L., A9
Clay, Lucius, General, R8
Clippings. *See* Press
Coalition to Free Soviet Jews, C4
Cocteau, Jean (1889–1963), N25
        (Pablo Picasso), N25
Coggleshall, George (1784–1861), papers, N8
Cohen, Barbara (*Molly's Pilgrim*), N23
Coins. *See* Numismatics
Cold War (Harry Dexter White), P8
Collection de dessins lithographies (Aleksandr Osipovich Orlovskii), N14
Collectivization, Krynychanska Silska Rada (1929–33), S4
College Board and ETS, testing in Soviet Union, E2
Collier's, World War II correspondent (Irina Skariatina), P7
Columbia University
    Boris Bakhmeteff Archive of Russian and East European History and Culture, C8
    (Department of Slavic Languages), C8
    Libraries, C5
    Oral History Research Office, C6
    Rare Book and Manuscript Library, C7
    School of Library Service Library, C9
Combustion Engineering, C12
Combustion Engineering–Soviet Joint Venture, C12
Commendone, Cardinal Giovanni Francesco, Papal envoy to Poland, N18

Comenius, Johann Amos (*Lux in Tenebris*), N19
Committee for the Absorption of Soviet Emigres (C.A.S.E.), C13
Committee on Public Information in Russia (Arthur Bullard), P8
Committee on Un-American Activities (film, 1962), N23
    See also *Hollywood on Trial*, N23
Communism and communist parties, B6, C5, I2, N1, N19, N34, R3, Y4, Y5
    (Germany, Federal Republic), P8
    (Kalman Marmor), Y5
    ("Paix et Liberté"), P8
    (Pettis Perry Papers), N30
Conférence Politique Russe (Maxim Vinawer), Y5
Conrad, Joseph, *Poland Revisited*, N10
Contarini, Ambrotio
    Viaggio al re di Persia (1487), M3
    Viaggi fatti da Vinetia, alla Tana, in Persia... (1543), M3
Contemporary Russian Art Center of America, C14
Coq d'Or (*Russian Rooster*), N23
Cory, Constance, C15
Cory, David, photographs, Soviet Union (1970, 1978), C15
Cossacks
    Ethnography, A8
    History (Viktor Adiassewich), N18
Costumes, N19
    (Leon Bakst), N25
    (Alexandre Benois), N25
    Byelorussian, B8
    Jewish, Y3
    Russian peasant, B5
    Russian uniforms, H2
    (Pavel Tchelitchev), N25
    Ukrainian, U1
    Vestments, B9
Council of Foreign Ministers (John Foster Dulles), P7, P8
Council of National Defense (Bernard M. Baruch), P7
Council on Foreign Relations, C16
    (Geroid Tanqueray Robinson), C7
Counterpoint: The U2 Story (film, 1974), N23
Cowan, Louis, collection (1941–1945), C7
Cracow Union of Help for Political Prisoners in Russia (1914), N19
Craig, Edward Gordon (1872–1966), N24, N25
    (Irma Duncan Collection), N25
    (Natalie Roslavleva), N25
    (Francis Steegmuller), N25
Cramer, Brothers, Russian merchants (David Parish), N8
Cretan Sketch Book (Leon Bakst), N25
Crimean regional government (1918–1919) (Maxim Vinawer), Y5
Crimean Tatar folk songs and dances (Nina Borovka), N26
Crimean War, photographs, J1
    (Archibald F. Becke), P7
Cronstadt (Maltby Gelston), N8
Crosley, W.S., correspondence, H3
Cuevas, Marquis de (Sergei Ismailoff), N25
Cultural history
    Eastern Christianity, B9
    Eastern Europe, C8, N19
    Russian empire, B4, C5, C8, N19
    Soviet Union, C5, C8, N19
Cutrer, Emile (Siberian Expedition Photographs), U6
Czap, Father Michael, collection, S1

D

Dag Hammerskjold Library, United Nations, U5
Daily Worker, New York (Robert Minor), C7
Dallin, David J., papers, N18
Dana, Francis (1743–1811), correspondence, N8
    (Robert R. Livingston), N8
Dance, B8, N25, N26, S7
    Graph method of dance notation (Joseph Schillinger), N25
Dance Collection, Library and Museum of the Performing Arts at Lincoln Center, New York
   Public Library, N25
Danielian, L. (Oral Interviews with Dancers), N25
Danilova, Aleksandra Dionisievna (b. 1904), collection, N23, N25
Danzig, Jewish community, B1
Darlington, William (1782–1863), papers, N8
Dashkov (Dashkoff), Andrei Ia., N8
    (Albert Gallatin), N8
    (Randall J. LeBoeuf, Jr.), N8
    (Stevens Family), N4
Databases, A3, C11
Davidoff, Charles, correspondence, N26
Davidov (Mikhail Iur'evich Lermontov), C7
Davis, Benjamin J., Jr., book collection, R3
Davis, Malcolm Waters (1889–1970), C7
Deakin, Irvin (1894–1958), correspondence, N25
Debs, Eugene V. (1855–1926), personal library, N34
Decorations. *See* Numismatics
Decrees. *See* decrees and documents under country or ruler
DeDaehn, Alexander (Peter DeDaehn), C8
DeDaehn, Peter, papers, C8
Demetrius, Saint, "Letopis'," manuscript, N19
De Mille, Agnes (b. 1918), "Russian Journals" (1966, 1969), N25
Demography, Soviet Union, C5
Denham, S.J. (Sergei Ismailoff), N25
de Stael, Madame, B5
    (Albert Gallatin), N8
Deutsch, Babette, papers, N18
    (Harry Miller Lydenberg), N18
Deval, Jacques, working scripts, N24
Devyatkin, Dimitri (*Media Shuttle . . .*) (*Russian Soul*), N23
De Zirkoff, Boris, collection, O1
Diaghilev, Ballets Russes, programs, M7, N25, S7
Diaghilev, Sergei, F4, N25, S7
    (Gabriel Astruc), N25
    (George Balanchine), N25
    (Mikhail Mikhailovich Fokine), N25
    (Lincoln Kirstein), N25
    (Vaslav Nijinsky), N25
    (Oral Interviews with Dancers), N25
Diaspora, Armenian, P5
Dickson, Benjamin Abbot (1897–1975), papers, U6
Dicter, Misha (b. 1945), A6
Dietrich, Irene (Catherine Breshkovsky), N18
Dijeur, Ilya (Elias Tcherikower), Y5
Diplomacy and foreign relations, Soviet Union, C5, C16, N19
Dirksen, von (Sam Echt), B1
Displaced persons, P3, S4
Djindnihashvili, Nodar (*Last Journey*), N23

Dmitriev, Ivan (Mikhail Iur'evich Lermontov), C7
Dobreitzer, Doctor (International Health Board), R5
Dobuzhinskii (Dobuzhinsky), Mstislav Valerianovich (1875–1957),
   materials, N14, N18, N25, S3
Doctrinal theology, H4
Documents. *See under* country or names of rulers, etc.
Documents Relating to the Emancipation of the Serfs (1867–1868), N19
Dominique Jean Larrey, Baron, *Field Diary in Russia* (1812–1813), M3
Dondo, Karl, composition, N26
Donnell Library Center
   Central Children's Room, N21
   Media Center, N23
Dostoevskii (Dostoevsky), Fedor Mikhailovich (1821–1881), N24
   (Nikolai Vladimirovich Remizov), N24
Douglas, Norman, N10
Dovzhenko, Alexander (*Earth*), N23
Drakon (Evgenii Ivanovich Zamiatin), P7
Drama. *See* Theater and drama
Drawings. *See* Art and under individual artists
Dreizehn Steinzeichnungen (Alexander Archipenko), N14
Drevniaia rossiiskaia vivliofika, N19
Dubinsky, David, Russian artist, I4
Dubinsky, David, union leader, correspondence, I2
Dubinsky, Pinchas
   (A. Charash), Y5
   (Marc Ratner), Y5
Dubnow, Simon (1860–1941), papers, Y5
   (Daniel Charney), Y5
   History of the Jews in Russia and Poland, N11
   (Elias Tcherikower), Y5
Duchnovich, A.V. (Elias I. Tziorogh), N26
Dudinskaia, Natalia (Oral Interviews with Dancers), N25
Dukelsky, Vladimir, M3
Dulles, John Foster (1888–1959), papers, P7, P8
Duma. *See* Russia
Duncan, Irma
   (Irma Duncan Collection), N25
   (Allan Ross Macdougall), N25
   (Francis Steegmuller), N25
Duncan, Isadora (1877–1927), papers, N25
   (Edward Gordon Craig), N25
   (Mikhail Mikhailovich Fokine), N25
   (Irma Duncan Collection), N25
   (Allan Ross Macdougall), N25
   (Oral Interviews with Dancers), N25
   (Natalia Roslavleva), N25
   (Francis Steegmuller), N25
Duranty, Walter (Herbert Renfro Knickerbocker), C7
Duse, Eleanora (Irma Duncan Collection), N25
Dymov, Osip, working scripts, N24
Dziga Vertov (*Man With a Movie Camera*), N23

E

Earth (film, 1930), N23
Easter eggs, F1
   (*Pysanka, The Ukrainian Easter Egg*), N23

Eastern Christianity, B9
Eastern Orthodox Church, N19, N29
Echt, Sam, collection, B1
Economic and Social History of the World War (James Shotwell), C7
Ecumenical Institute, Edinburgh (Georges Florovsky), P7
Eden, Anthony (William Averell Harriman), C7
Eden, R. *The History of Trauayle in the West and East Indies, and Other Countries Lying eyther way . . . as Moscouia . . .*, London (1577), N8
Edison National Historic Site, E1
Edison, Thomas, correspondence with Russia, E1
Educational Testing Service (ETS), E2
Effect Publishing, E3
Eglitis, Anslvs, N19
Ehrenburg, Il'ia Grigor'evich (1891–1967), I4
Einstein, Albert (Mendel Osherowitch), Y5
Eisenberg, Leah. *See* Julius Borenstein–Leah Eisenberg Collection
Eisenhower, Dwight, General, R8
Eisenstein, Sergei Mikhailovich (1898–1948), M7, N23, N24
Eisenstein's Mexican Study Film (1930–31), N23
Ekstrom Collection, Parmenia Migel. *See* Stravinsky–Diaghilev Foundation Collection
El Lissitsky, E4, G1, M7, N20
Elfinger, Zenzl (Eric Muehsam), B1
Eliot, George, N10
Elizabeth I, Queen of England, H5
Elman, Mischa, collection, M1
Embroidery designs. *See* Art
Emes (1921–1935), N11
Emigration and emigres
    Byelorussian literature, N19, N22
    Eastern Europeans to Western Europe and United States, C8
    Finnish-Americans (*Children of Labor*), N23
    Gorky, R4
    Jews, A5, A6, B1, N18, Y2, Y4, Y5
    Latvian literature, N19
    Mensheviks, B6
    Publishing, E3, R11
    Russian, C5, E1, H2, H4, N18, N19, N22, R4, T4, Y6
        (Alexander Bacherac), C8
        (Boris Sapir), C8
    Soviet Union, T1
        (*Molly's Pilgrim*), N23
        (*Soviet Dissidents in Exile*), N23
    Ukrainian, N19, S4, U3
        (Berlin Collection), Y5
        (*Jaraslawa*), N23
    See also Displaced persons; Jewish history, American
Emma Goldman papers, N18
Emmons, George T., collection, A8
Enamels, M2
Endzelins, J. and Karlis Muelenbachs, *Letviesu Valodas Vardnica* (1923–56), N19
Engelbrecht, T.H., *Landwirtschaftliches Atlas des russischen Reiches in Europe und Asien*. Berlin (1916), A2
English for Foreign Students, E2
Epstein, Gershon, collection, Y5
Epstein, Lasar (b. 1886), A6
Errante, ballet (Pavel Tchelitchev), N25
Esenin, Sergei Aleksandrovich (1895–1925)

(Irma Duncan Collection), N25
(Allan Ross Macdougall), N25
Essai sur la lanque arménienne, Bellaud, Paris (1812), N15
Estonia, C5, C7, N19
    (American Joint Reconstruction Foundation), Y5
    Jews (Berlin Collection), Y5
Estonian language, C5
Etchings. *See* Art and under individual artists
Eternal Glory (film, 1972), N23
Ethnography
    Cossacks, A8
    Emmons, George T., collection, A8
    Even, A8
    Evenk, A8
    Evenki, A8
    Georgians, A8
    Gilyak (Nivkin), A8
    Goldi (Nanai), A8
    Itel'men, A8
    Jesup Collection, A8
    Jewish, Y3
    Kamchadal (Itel'men), A8
    Koryal, A8
    Lamut (Even), A8
    Nanai, A8
    Nivkin, A8
    North Pacific tribes, A8
    Peoples in Russia, M3, N13
    Russians in Siberia, A8
    Samoyed, A8
    Siberian coast, A8
    Tungus (Evenk or Evenki), A8
    Ukrainian arts and crafts, S8
    Yakut, A8
ETS. *See* Educational Testing Service
European Caravan (Aleksei Mikhailovich Remizov), P7
European Russia . . . Album . . . collected by George Kennan, N13
European travel reports about Muscovy (16th c.), H5
Even, ethnography, A8
Evenk, ethnography, A8
Evenki, ethnography, A8
Eversole, H.O., "Medical Education in Baltic states" (Rockefeller Foundation), R5
Evrei na voinie (1914?), N11
Evreinov, Nikolai N. *See* Yevreinov. . .
Evreiskie pogromy, 1918–1921, N11
Ex Libris, E4
Export-Import Bank (Max Rabinoff), C7
Exter, Alexandra, I4, N24
Ezhegodnik imperatorskikh teatrov, N19
Ezhemesiachnye sochineniia, N19

F

Faberge, Peter Carl, F1
Fabricant, Misha (Marc Ratner), Y5
Fadeev, Aleksandr Aleksandrovich (1901–1956) (Paul Robeson Collection), N30
Faiko, Aleksei M., working scripts, N24
Falkowski, Edward, collection, N34
Fall of the Russian Empire (Nikolai M. Khravrov), N18

Falz-Fein, von, family, A12
Farragut, Admiral D.G., N8
Farrelly, Theodore S. (1883–1955), papers, C7
Faryniak, S., correspondence, S4
Feder, Aizik, I4
Federal Writers' Project, W.P.A. (NYC unit), N7
Federation Internationale des Archives du Film (Paris) ("Filmographie russe, 1907–1932"), M7
Federation of Lithuanian Jews in New York (Mendel Sudarski), Y5
Federation of Russian Organizations in America (1918–1924), N18
Federation of Ukrainian Jews in America (Mendel Osherowitch), Y5
Fedorov, Ivan, N16, S1
Feinberg, Leon (1897–1969), papers, Y5
Feldman, Ronald, Fine Arts, R7
Feodor Chaliapin (Mikhail Mikhailovich Fokine), N26
Field, John, compositions, N26
    (Toscanini Memorial Archives), N26
Film. *See also* Film titles; Microfilm; Photographs; Slides; Videos;
  and under individual film titles
    Expeditions, A9
    "Filmographie russe, 1907–1932," M7
    (Leonid Massine), N25
    Polish, documentaries, P1
    Russian, N23
    Russian (1912–1970s), M6
    Russian, stills (ca. 1920–1985), M5
    Soviet, C3, N2, N23
    Soviet Union (1930s), I1
Film Stills Archive, Museum of Modern Art, M5
Film Study Center, Museum of Modern Art, M6
Film titles
    Afternoon with Gregor Piatigorsky (film, 1977), N23
    Alexander Nevsky (film, 1938), N23
    Battleship Potemkin (film, 1925), N23
    Bed and Sofa (film, 1926), N23
    Birth of Soviet Cinema (film, 1972), N23
    Blind Bird (film, 1963), N23
    By the Law (film, 1926), N23
    Chaim Soutine (film, 1970), N23
    Chess Fever (film, 1925), N23
    Committee on Un-American Activities (film, 1962), N23
    Counterpoint: The U2 Story (film, 1974), N23
    Earth (film, 1930), N23
    Eternal Glory (film, 1972), N23
    First Encounter: A Russian Journal (film, 1978), N23
    Free Voice of Labor—The Jewish Anarchists (film, 1980), N23
    Frogland (film, 1925), N23
    Galina Ulanova (film, 1964), N23
    Hollywood on Trial (film, 1976), N23
    Ivan the Terrible (film, 1944), N23
    Jaraslawa (film, 1975), N23
    Kremlin (film, 1963), N23
    Man With a Movie Camera (film, 1928), N23
    Marc Chagall (film, 1965), N23
    March–April: The Coming of Spring (film, 1967), N23
    Marx for Beginners (film, 1978), N23
    Meet Comrade Student (film, 1963), N23
    Mirror (film, 1974), N23
    Moiseyev Dancers (film, 1959), N23

Molly's Pilgrim (film, 1985), N23
Mother (film, 1936), N23
Navigator (film, 1934), N23
Nose, The (film, 1963), N23
October (film, 1927), N23
Olga: A Film Portrait (film, 1974), N23
One Day in the Life of Ivan Denisovich (film, 1971), N23
Point of Order (film, 1964), N23
Poland (film, 1965), N23
Polka Graph (film, 1953), N23
Prince Igor' (film, 1969), N23
Pysanka, The Ukrainian Easter Egg (film, 1975), N23
Raoul Wallenberg, Buried Alive (film, 1983), N23
Red Pomegranate (film, 1972), N23
Reds in Hollywood (film, 1948), N23
Reflections of a Dancer: Alexandra Danilova (film, 1981), N23
Religion in Russia (film, 1968), N23
Reminiscences of a Journey to Lithuania (film, 1971), N23
Revenge of the Kinematograph Cameraman (film, 1912), N23
Russia (film, 1958), N23
Russian Peasant (film, 1968), N23
Russian Rooster (film, 1975), N23
Shadows of Forgotten Ancestors (film, 1964), N23
Siberia: A Day in Irkutsk (film, 1967), N23
Soviet Union (film, 1930s), I1
Soviet Union: A New Look (film, 1978), N23
Stalker (film, 1979), N23
Stanislavsky: Maker of the Modern Theater (film, 1972), N23
Steppe in Winter (film, 1965), N23
Symphony of Psalms (film, 1976), N23
Tanya the Puppeteer (film, 1981), N23
Ten Days that Shook the World (film, 1927), N23
Train Rolls On, The (film, 1974), N23
Uncle Vanya (film, 1972), N23
War Without Winners (film, 1978), N23
Women of Russia (film, 1968), N23
Fine Arts, Russian empire, B4. *See also* Art
Finnish-Americans (*Children of Labor*), N23
Finno-Ugric languages, N19
Firebird (Leon Bakst), N25
Firestone Library, Princeton University Library, P6
Firestone Library, Rare Book, Manuscript, and Special Collections,
    Princeton University Library, P7
First Encounter: A Russian Journal (film, 1978), N23
First to Go Back (Irina Skariatina), P7
Fischer, Louis (1896–1970), papers, P8
Flanagan, Hallie, Russian theater scrapbook (1926), N24
Flea, The (Evgenii Ivanovich Zamiatin), P7
Fleishman, Edwin, E2
Fleming, Harold M., papers, N18
Fletcher, Giles, *Of the Russe Commonwealth* (1591), P7
Flora Rossica (Peter Simon Pallas), N14
Florimond, Joseph, duc de Loubat, *Narrative of the Mission to Russia, 1866, of the Hon.
    Gustavus Vasa Fox . . . From the Journal and Notes of J.F. Loubat*, New York (1873), N8
Florovsky, Father Georges, Library, St. Vladimir's Orthodox Theological Seminary, S1
Florovsky, Father Georges, papers, P7
Flynn, Elizabeth Gurley, book collection, R3
Fokine, Mikhail (Michel) Mikhailovich (1880–1942), F4, N25, N26

Fokine, Mikhail (Michel) Mikhailovich (1880–1942), F4, N25, N26
    (Lincoln Kirstein), N25
Folk costumes. *See* Costumes
Folklore, C5, Y4
    (Gershon Epstein), Y5
Folksongs. *See* Music
Forbes Magazine Galleries, F1
Foreign Committee of the Bund, papers, B6
Foreign Language Library, New York Public Library, N22
Foreign Relations. *See* Diplomacy and foreign relations
Forward Association, Y5
Foster, William Z., book collection, R3
Fox, Gustavus Vasa (1821–1883), papers, N8
Fraind (1903–1913), N11
Franko, Ivan, *Z vershyn i nyzyn: Zbirnyk Poezii*, 1887, S4
Franko, Sam
    (Mischa Elman), N26
    (Serge Koussevitzky), N26
Free Voice of Labor—The Jewish Anarchists (film, 1980), N23
Freidus, Ella, F2
Freland League for Jewish Territorial Colonization (Isaac N. Steinberg), Y5
Frey, William, papers, N18
Frick Art Reference Library, F3
Friedman, Phillip, collection, Y4
Friends of Soviet Russia (Kalman Marmor), Y5
Frisch, Efraim, archives, B1
Frisch, Fega Lifschitz (Efraim Frisch), B1
Frisek, B.A., composition, N26
Frogland (film, 1925), N23
Frueh, Alfred, caricature (Alla Nazimova), N24
Fulbright, James W. (John Foster Dulles), P7, P8
Fuld, James J., F4
Fulton, Robert, portfolio, N8
    (Randall J. LeBoeuf, Jr.), N8
    (T.P. Shaffner), N8
Futurism, E4, M7, N20, R1

G

Gabo, Naum, G1, M7
Gabrilowitsch, Ossip, correspondence, N26
    (Samuil Moiseyevich Maikapar), N26
Galina Ulanova (film, 1964), N23
Galitzin, Princess Eudosee, correspondence, M4
Gallatin, Albert, papers, N8
    (Levett Harris), N8
    (Christopher Hughes), N8
Gambler, The (Nikolai Vladimirovich Remizov), N24
Gamow, George (1904–1968), A4
Garrett, Robert, collection. *See* Armenian manuscripts
Gelston, Maltby, collection, N8
Geography, USSR, A2, C5
Geological specimens and minerals, A9
George, Henry (Lev Nikolaevich Tolstoi), N19
Georgia, C7, P2
Georgian language, C5, N15
Georgians, ethnography, A8
German, L. (Leon Baratz), Y5

Germany, Federal Republic, Anti-Communist Collection, P8
Gershoy Family papers, N18
Gide, Andre (1869–1951) (Alexander Bacherac), C8
Gilyak (Nivkin), ethnography, A8
Ginzburg, Alexander (*Soviet Dissidents in Exile*), N23
Ginzburg, Alfred de (Elias Tcherikower), Y5
Girl Scouts, Russian, R8
Glantz-Leyeles, Aaron (Mendel Osherowitch), Y5
Glazunov, Aleksandr Konstantinovich (1865–1936), F4, M3, N26
Glebov (Mikhail Iur'evich Lermontov), C7
Glezer, Alexander, C13
Gliere, Reinhold, F4
Glinka, Mikhail, F4, N26
        (Herbert Reynolds), N26
Godowsky, Jr., Leopold (b. 1900), A6
Goede, Ludwig, composition, N26
Gogol', Nikolai Vasil'evich (1809–1852), N24
        (*The Nose*), N23
Gold, Ben, book collection, R3
Goldi (Nanai), ethnography, A8
Goldin, Z. (Marc Ratner), Y5
Goldman, Emma (1869–1940), papers, N18
Goldovsky, Boris (b. 1908), A6
Golizowski, libretti, N25
Golschmann, Vladimir (Nicolai T. Berezowsky), C7
Goncharova, Natalie (1881–1962), G1, M2, M7, N14, S7
Gordin, Z. (A. Charash), Y5
Gordon, David, book collection, R3
Gorky, Maksim (1868–1936), N24, R4
        (Herman Bernstein), Y5
        (John Peale Bishop), P7
        (*Mother*), N23
        (Lev Nikolaevich Tolstoi), P7
Gorsky, Yitzchak (A. Charash), Y5
Gospels, A1, M3, N19, N20, P7
Gotbaum, Victor H. (b. 1922), A6
Gotchnag, New York (1910–), N15
Graduation Ball
        (Mstislav Valerianovich Dobuzhinskii), N25
        (David Lichine), N25
Graham, John D., M7
Grant, Ulysses S. (1822–1885), correspondence, M4
        (Andrew Johnson), M4
Graph method of dance notation (Joseph Schillinger), N25
Graphic arts, Russia and Soviet Union, C9, E4, N14
Graves, III, George C., A9
Graves, William Sidney (1865–1940), papers, U6
Grechaninov, Aleksandr Tikhonovich, C7, M3, N26
Grecke, Johan Adolph, metalwork, M2
Grenier, Alexander W., papers, C8
Griffin, Anthony J., correspondence, N18
Grigoriev, Boris (1886–1939), M2
Grigoriev (Grigorieff), Serge, papers, N25
        (Jean Miro), N25
Grigorii, Monk, "*Zhitie...*" (1888), N19
Grinberg, N. (Gregori Gurevitch), Y5
Gruenberg, Louis, compositions, N26
Guenzburg, Dmitri, Baron (Gabriel Astruc), N25
Guenzburg, Baron Horace (Naftali Herz) (1833–1909), Y5

Guggenheim Museum, G1
Gurevitch, Gregori (Gershon Badanes) (1852–1929), papers, Y5
Guselnikov, A. (Mikhail Iur'evich Lermontov), C7
Gypsies, Russian, photographs, N8

H

Ha-Goren (1898–1928), N11
Ha-Maggid (1856–1903), N11
Ha-Meliz (1860–1904), N11
Ha-zman, N11
Halliburton, Richard, photographs of Russia, P7
Hapgood, Elizabeth Reynolds, papers, N24
Hapgood, Isabel, papers, N18, N19
Hapgood, Isabelle, correspondence, N8
Harriman, Averell W., C7
    (John Foster Dulles), P7, P8
Harriman Institute for Advanced Study of the Soviet Union, C10, C11
Harris, Levett, correspondence (1804–1819), N8
Hauptmann, Aloysius, composition, N26
Haviland, Francis A. (Anna Pavlova), N25
Hawthorne, Nathaniel (Mstislav Valerianovich Dobuzhinskii), N14
Hayden, Levi, diary, N18
Haynt (1914–1919), N11
Hayrenik (1901–), N15
He-'avar (1917–1918), N11
Heartmann, Charles, collection (1770s–1870s), N8
Hebrew language, J2, Y4
Hebrew Union College–Jewish Institute of Religion, Klau Library H1
Heifetz, Vladimir, composition, N26
Heins, Vladimir Konstantinovich. *See* Frey, William
Hendricks Family, papers, N8
Hennin, Georg de, manuscript on Siberia (1735), N19
Hentz, Johann Bernhard (1834–1855), silversmith, M2
Herberstein, Sigismund
    Rerum Moscoviticarum commentarii, M3, N8
    Picturae variae quae . . . varias legationes obeuntem exprimunt, M3
Hermitage Museum (Cesnola, Luigi Palmer di), N8
Herter, Christian A. (John Foster Dulles), P7, P8
Hicks, Isaac (1767–1820), papers, N8
Hirsch, Moritz, Baron, B1
Hirsch of Gereuth Family, B1
Histoire Raisonée du Commerce de la Russie, J.B. Scherer, Paris (1788), N8
Historia i literatura zydowska, Lwow (1923–1925), N11
Historical Museum Rodina, H2
History
    Armenian, P5
    Armenian church, P5
    Byelorussian, N19, P6
    Church, B9, H4, S1, S10, U2
    Jewish, Y3
    Lithuanian, V1
    Polish, C5, N19, P6
    Russian, C5, N19, N28, N33, P6, S10
    Russian, rare book collection, P7, R8
    Russian-Jewish, H1
    Science (David Eugene Smith), C7
    Ukrainian, C5, N19, P6, S4

History of Socialism Project, oral history, C6
History of the Jews in Russia and Poland, Simon Dubnow, N11
*History of Trauayle in the West and East Indies, and Other Countries Lying eyther way . . .
  as Moscouia . . .*, R. Eden, London (1577), N8
Hnizdovsky, Yakiv, N14
Hodin, Joseph Paul ("Soviet Attitude to Art"), M7
Hoffman, Charles J., H3
Hoffman, Wickham (1821–1900), papers, N8
Hollywood on Trial (film, 1976), N23
Holocaust, material, Y4, Y5
Holubnychny, Lydia (1929–1975), papers, C7
Holy Synod, Russia, minutes and reports, S1
Holy Trinity Seminary Library, H4
Hopkins, Harry (William Averell Harriman), C7
Hordynsky, George Sviatoslav, N14
Hourwich, Isaac A. (1860–1924), papers, Y5
Hovey, E. O., Geological Expedition to Russia and Italy, A9
Hoyt and Meacham Families, correspondence, N8
Hrushevsky, Myhaylo, correspondence, S4
Hughes, Christopher (1786–1849), correspondence, N8
Human rights, Jews, A5
Hurok, Sol, N25
    (Irvin Deakin), N25
    (Mstislav Valerianovich Dobuzhinskii), N25
Huttenbach, Henry R., H5
Huzarska, Halina. *See* Isdebska, Halina (Huzarska)
Hymnals, M3, N20

I

IAA, A3
ICA (Jewish Colonization Association), B1
    (Hirsch of Gereuth Family), B1
Icons, B9, M2, R10
Igor (*Prince Igor'*), N23
Iliazd (I. Zdanevich), N20
Illuminated manuscripts. *See* Byzantine illuminated manuscripts
Illustration. *See under* individual topic (e.g., book) or artist
Imagerie Populaire, R1
    (Russkii Narodnyi Lubok), N14
Immigration. *See* Emigration and emigres
Immigration and Naturalization Service, N1
Imposter, The (J. Karnavicius), N26
Imprecorr, R3
In Siberia (Evgenii Ivanovich Zamiatin), P7
Information science, Russia and Soviet Union, C9
Ingerman, Sergius (1863–1943), papers, N34
Inkeles, Alex, E2
INS. *See* Immigration and Naturalization Service
Institut d'Études Slaves (Maxim Vinawer), Y5
Institute for Jewish Proletarian Culture (Alexander Pomerantz), Y5
Insurance business, Russia and Soviet Union, N9
Intellectual life, Soviet Union, C5, N19
International Aerospace Abstracts, A3
International Film Foundation, I1
International Ladies' Garment Workers' Union, B6
International Ladies' Garment Workers' Union, Archive, I2
International relations. *See* Diplomacy and foreign relations

International Research & Exchanges Board (IREX), I3
International, Second, B6
International socialist labor movement, B6
International, Third, B6
International Writers Congress, USSR (Paul Robeson Collection), N30
Iranian (Tajik, Ossetian), languages, N15
IREX, I3
IREX Update, I3
Irkutsk (*Siberia; A Day in Irkutsk*), N23
Irma Duncan Collection of Isadora Duncan Materials, N25
    (Edward Craig Gordon), N25
    (Isadora Duncan), N25
    (Natalie Roslavleva), N25
    (Francis Steegmuller), N25
Irving, Washington (Bradish papers), N8
Isadora: A Revolutionary in Art and Love (Allan Ross Macdougall), N25
Isadora Duncan in Russia (Irma Duncan Collection), N25
Isadora Duncan School in Moscow (Isadora Duncan), N25
    (Allen Ross Macdougall), N25
Isdebsky, Vladimir, materials, I4, M7
Isdebsky-Pritchard, Aline, I4
Ismailoff, Sergei (b. 1912), papers, N25
Itel'men, ethnography, A8
Ivan IV, tsar, H5
Ivan the Terrible (film, 1944), N23
Ivanov, I.I., K2
Ivy L. Lee and Associates (Ivy Ledbetter Lee), P8
Izdebska, Halina (Huzarska), I4
Izraelita. Pismo tygodniowe (1866–1913), N11

J

Jacobson, Jacob, collection, B1
Jakobson, Roman (Correspondence of . . .), C8
Jakowliv, Andriy, papers, S4
James Stokes Society Papers, Y6
Janet Lehr, Inc., J1
Japanese Peace Treaty (John Foster Dulles), P7, P8
Jaraslawa (film, 1975), N23
Jauna Gaita, N19
Javits, Jacob K. (John Foster Dulles), P7, P8
Jedność. Organ żydów polskich (1910–1911), N11
Jefferson School of Social Research, Library, R3
Jefferson, Thomas (1743–1826) (John Ledyard), N8
Jegers, Benjamin, N19
Jesup Collection, A8
Jesup North Pacific Expedition (1897–1903), A9
Jewelry, Russian, pictures, N29
Jewelry, tsarist Faberge collection, F1
Jewish Colonization Association (ICA), B1
    (American Joint Reconstruction Foundation), Y5
    (Baron Horace Guenzburg), Y5
Jewish community, Danzig, B1
Jewish Council for Russian War Relief (Louis Levine), Y2
Jewish cultural movements, B6
Jewish Daily Forward, Y5
Jewish Division, New York Public Library, N11

Jewish history, American, B6, Y4, Y5
Jewish Labor Bund, B6
    Congress, 1903 (Isaac A. Hourwich), Y5
Jewish Labor Committee, B6
Jewish labor movement, B6, Y4, Y5
Jewish Proletarian Culture, Institute for (Alexander Pomorantz), Y5
Jewish Socialist Workers' Party
    (Marc Ratner), Y5
    (Chaim Zhitlovsky), Y5
Jewish Territorialist Movement (Isaac N. Steinberg), Y5
Jewish Theological Seminary of America, J2
Jews
    Autobiographies (1932–1939), Y5
    Babi Yar (*Last Journey*), N23
    Baltic countries (Berlin Collection), Y5
    Beilis trial (Lucien Wolf), Y5
    Biographies, communal leaders, B6
    Blood libel trials
      (Simon Dubnow), Y5
      (Lucien Wolf), Y5
    Clipping files, A5
    Community records, *pinkeysim* (Simon Dubnow), Y5
    East European history, N11, Y4, Y5
      (American Joint Reconstruction Foundation), Y5
    Emigration, A5, A6, B1, N11, Y4, Y5
      (Julius Borenstein–Leah Eisenberg Collection on Early Jewish Migration), Y5
    Human rights, A5, A6, Y4
    Landsmanshaften, Y5
      (American Jewish Joint Distribution Committee), Y5
      (Louis Levine), Y2
    Minsk congregation (*Last Journey*), N23
    Moscow Synagogue (*Last Journey*), N23
    Oral history, A6
    Pogroms, B1, B6, J2, N11, Y4
      (Herman Bernstein), Y5
      (Central Archives of the Editorial Committee on Collection and Investigation of the Materials Relating to the Pogroms in the Ukraine, Y5
      (Simon Dubnow), Y5
    Poland, B6, N11, P4, Y4, Y5
    Political parties, Poland, B6
    Refuseniks, C4
    Riga ghetto (1941–1944), H5
    Russia and Ukraine, A5, J2, N11, Y1, Y4, Y5
      (American Joint Reconstruction Foundation), Y5
      Manuscript (1860–1917) (Union of Russian Jews), Y5
      Manuscript (1918–1961) (Union of Russian Jews), Y5
    Self-defense groups, B6
    Soviet Jewry, A5, A6, C4
    Synagogues, Russian Empire, S3
    World War II, B6
    Zionist organizations in Russia, Z1
Jews of Poland: a Social and Economic History . . . from 1100 to 1800, Bernard D. Weinryb, Philadelphia (1973), N11
Jobotinsky, Vladimir (Lucien Wolf), Y5
Jochelson and Bogoraz Paleo-Siberian Collections, N19
Jochelson, Vladimir (Waldemar), papers, A9, N18
John Reed Collection of Russian revolutionary posters, N19
Johnson, Andrew (1808–1875), correspondence, M4
Jonynas, Vytautas Kazys, N14

Journals
Aeronautical Engineering Review, A3
Af di Vegn zu der neier Shul (1924–1928), N11
Ahiasaf (1893–1923), N11
Akademiska dzive, N19
Apollon, N19
Beiträge zur Kenntnis der russischen Reiches (1839–1900), N19
Biblioteka dlia chteniia (1834–1865), N19
Bogoslovskii vestnik, S1
Budushchnost' (1900–1904), N11
Chervonyi shlyakh, N19
Cina, N19
Drevniaia rossiiskaia vivliofika, N19
Emes (1921–1935), N11
Evrei na voinie (1914?), N11
Ezhegodnik imperatorskikh teatrov, N19
Ezhemesiachnye sochineniia, N19
Fraind (1903–1913), N11
Gotchnag (1910–), N15
Ha-Goren (1898–1928)
Ha-Maggid (1856–1903), N11
Ha-Meliz (1860–1904), N11
Haynt (1914–1919), N11
Hayrenik (1901–), N15
Ha-zman (1903–1914), N11
He-'avar (1917–1918), N11
Imprecorr, R3
International Aerospace Abstracts, A3
IREX Update, I3
Izraelita. Pismo tygodniowe (1866–1913), N11
Jauna gaita, N19
Jedność. Organ zydów polskich (1910–1911), N11
Jutrzenka. Tygodnik dla izraelitów polskich (1861–1863), N11
Kamer fur'erski tzeremonial'nyi zhurnal (1695–1815), N19
Karogs, N19
Khristianskoe chtenie, S1
Kievskaia starina, N19
Krasnyi arkhiv: istoricheskii zhurnal (1922–1941), N19
Kultura, N19
Latvijas PSR preses hronika, N19
Liberator, R3
Likumu un ministru kabineta notukumu (July 1919–), N19
Lucifer, O1
Mainstream, R3
Masses and Mainstream, R3
Mickiewicz Blatter (1956–), N19
Morskiia zapiski, H2
New Masses, R3
Oktiabr' (1926–1935), N11
Otechestvennyia zapiski (1839–1884), N19
Perezhitoye (1909–1913), N11
Polymya, N19
Posledniya novosti (1920–1940), O2
Pravda (1912), N19
Pravitel'stvennyi vestnik (1869–1917), N19
Pravoslavnoe obozrenie, S1
Pravoslavnyi sobesednik, S1
Rahva haal, N19
Ratnbildung (1928–1936), N11

Razsviet (1879–1881), N11
Razsviet (1907–1913), N11
Riigi teataja (1918–1940), N19
Rossiiskii teatr', N19
Russian-American Orthodox Messenger (1896–1973), O2
Russkii yevrei (1879–1884), N11
Sbornik geograficheskikh, topograficheskikh i statisticheskikh materialov po Azii (1883–1914), N19
Sbornik istoricheskago obshchestva (1867–1916), N19
Scientific and Technical Aerospace Reports, A3
Sefer ha-shanah (1900–1906), N11
Sovremennik (1848–1865), N19
Starye gody (1906–1917), T2
Stenograficheskii otchet (Supreme Soviet) (1939–), N19
Svod vysochaishikh otmetok, annual of Alexander II, N19
Svod zakonov rossiiskoi imperii (1857–1916, 1906–1914), N19
Teatr', N19
Teatral'naia zhizn', N19
Tiesa, N19
Trudy Kievskoi Dukhovnoi Akademii, S1
Tserkovniya vedomosti (1891–1917), O2
Universitas, N19
Vedomosti (Supreme Soviet) (1930–), N19
Vera i razum, S1
Vestnik Evropy (1803–1826, 1866–1917), N19
Vesy, N19
Visti, N19
Vladibas nestnesis (1922–1940), N19
Voskhod (1886–1906), N11
Voskresnoe chtenie, S1
Vyriausybes zinios (1918–1940), N19
Wiadomosci literaki, N19
Yevreiskaya biblioteka (1871–1903), N11
Yevreiskaya letopis' (1923–1926), N11
Yevreiskaya zhizn' (1915–1917), N11
Yevreiskii mir (1909–1911), N11
Yidishe folksbibliotek (1888–1889), N11
Zapysky Naukovoho Tovarystva imeny Shevchenka (1892–), N19
Zhytya i revolyutziya, N19
Judaica manuscripts (Gershon Epstein), Y5
Judaizers, H5
Julius Borenstein–Leah Eisenberg Collection on early Jewish Migration (1868–1930), Y5
Jurzykowski, Alfred, Memorial Library, Polish Institute of Arts and Sciences of America, P4
Jutrzenka. Tygodnik dla izraelitów polskich (1861–1863), N11

K

Kabakov, C14
Kabakov, Ilya, S5
Kachalov, Vasilii Ivanovich (1875–1936), N24
Kadet Party (Maxim Vinawer), Y5
Kahan, Abraham, papers, Y5
   See also Cahan, Abraham
Kahn, Albert E. (Galina Ulanova), N25
Kalinin, Mikhail Ivanovich (1875–1946) (Sam Echt), B1
Kalinka, Valerian, N19
Kalmanovitch, Zalman (Sholom Schwarzbard), Y5

Kalmuck literature, N15
Kalmuk Resettlement Committee, papers, N34
Kamchadal (Itel'men), ethnography, A8
Kamchatka, N18, N20
Kamer fur' erski tzeremonial'nyi zhurnal (1695–1815), N19
Kamerny Theater, Moscow, N24
Kamkin, Victor, bookstore, K1
Kampelman, Max H. (b. 1920), A6
Kandelaki, Doctor (International Health Board), R5
Kandinskii (Kandinsky), Vasilii Vasil'evich (1866–1944), G1, L2, M7
Kaplan, Anatolii L'vovich, N14
Kapnist, Vasilii (Mikhail Iur'evich Lermontov), C7
Karlgof, Elizaveta Alekseevna, autograph album, N19
Karlhof (Mikhail Iur'evich Lermontov), C7
Karnavicius, J., N26
Karogs, N19
Karpovich, Michael M., O2
Karsavina, Tamara, F4
    (Jean Cocteau), N25
    (Oral Interviews with Dancers), N25
Kataev (Katayev), Valentin Petrovich (b. 1897), working scripts, N24
Katcherginski (Abraham Sutzkever–Shmerke Katcherginski Collection) (1806–1945), Y5
Katzman, Eugene A. (1890–1969), M2
Kautsky, Karl (Daniel Charney), Y5
Kazan Khanate, history (Western Americana Collection), P7
Kazin, Alfred (b. 1915), A6
Kemenov, Vladimir, "The Soviet Attitude To Art," M7
Kennan, George (1845–1924), N18, N13, N19
Kennan, George Frost (b. 1904), papers, P8
    (John Foster Dulles), P7, P8
Kerdimun, Boris, K2
Kerensky, Alexander (Mendel Osherowitch), Y5
Khachaturian, Aram Il'ich (1903–1978), F4
Khal'fin, Konstantin Ia., working scripts, N24
Khazars, P2
Khevra Mefitzei Haskolo (1909–1938), records, Y5
    (Baron Horace Guenzburg), Y5
Khlebnikov, Velemir (1885–1922), M7
Khlebnikov, *Zhizneopisanie . . . Baranova* (1835), N16
Khodasevich, Vladislav Felitsianovich (1886–1939) (Alexander Bacherac), C8
Khovansky, Aleksei (Mikhail Iur'evich Lermontov), C7
Khravrov, Nikolai M., papers, N18
Khristianskoe chtenie, S1
Khrushchev, Nikita Sergeevich (1894–1971), tapes, C6
    (American Civil Liberties Union), P8
Khyyl'ovyi, Mykola, N19
Kievskaia starina, N19
Kilims, U1
King, Rufus (1755–1827), papers, N8
Kinney, Troy (Anna Pavlova), N25
Kipnis, Alexander (b. 1891), A6
Kirgiz, Language, N15, N19
Kirov Ballet (Oral Interviews with Dancers), N25
Kirov Opera (*Prince Igor*), N23
Kirstein, Lincoln, N25
    (Jean Cocteau), N25
    (Sergei Diaghilev), N25
Kisling, Moise (1891–1953), M2
Kivko, John, Father, collection, S1

Klenenteva, K.A., N14
Knickerbocker, Herbert Renfro (1898–1975), papers, C7
Knipper-Chekhova, Olga, autographed photograph, N24
Koenigsberg, Rights of Jews (Jacob Jacobson), B1
Kogan, Moissey, N14
Kohlossian Matthew, manuscript, A1
Kolchak, P2
Kolchin collection of liturgical music, S1
Kollontai, Alexandra, Project, C6
Komar and Melamid, C14, K3, R7
Komar, Vitaly. *See* Komar and Melamid
Konenkov, Sergei Timofeevich (1874–1971), L1
Korbut, Olga (*Olga: A Film Portrait*), N23
Korvin-Krukovski, Piotr, working scripts, N24
Koryalk, ethnography, A8
Kosciuszko Foundation, K4
Kosorotow, A.J., working scripts, N24
Kostakis, George, collection, Russian and Soviet Avant-Garde art, G1
Kotzebue, August von, working scripts, N24
    (Maria Feodorovna), M4
Koulakov, K2
Koussevitzky, Serge (1874–1951), C7, N26
Kovenatsky, K2
Kovensky, Maxim, collection (1906–1913), Y5
Kowarski, Lew (b. 1907), A4
Kozlinskii (*Oktiabr' 1917–1918. Geroi i Zhertvy Revoliutsii*), N17
Kozlov, Ivan Ivanovich (1779–1840) (Mikhail Iur'evich Lermontov), C7
Krasnyi arkhiv: istoricheskii zhurnal (1922–1941), N19
Krasovskaia, Vera
    (Lillian Moore), N25
    (Francis Steegmuller), N25
Kremlin (film, 1963), N23
Kreutser Sonata (Lev Nikolaevich Tolstoi), P7
Krimchiks, P2
Kronstadt (Maltby Gelston), N8
Kruchenykh (Kruchenych), Aleksei, M7
Krychevsky, Vasyl, U1
Kuhn, Ernest (1864–1935), papers, U6
Kuindzhi, Arkhip Ivanovich (1841–1910), M2
Kuleshov, Lev Vladimirovich (1899–1970) (*By the Law*), N23
Kultura, N19
Kurakin, Prince, family records, N19
Kustodiev, Boris M. (1878–1927), M2

L

Labunski, W., composition, N26
Lampard, Marie Turbow, L1
Lamut (Even), ethnography, A8
Landsmanschaften Archives, Y5
Lang, Anders, silversmith (1843–1851), M2
Language(s)
    Altaic (Mongolic), N15
    Armenian, C5, N15, P5
    Azerbaijani, N15, N19
    Byelorussian, C5, N19
    Caucasian, C5
    Church Slavonic, N19
    Chuvash, N19

Estonian, C5
Finno-Ugric, N19
Georgian, N15
Hebrew, J2, Y4
Iranian (Tajik, Ossetian), N15
Kirgiz, N17, N19
Latvian, C5, N19
Lithuanian, C5, N19
Moldavian, C5
Mongolic (Altaic), N15
Ossetian, N15
Paleo-Caucasian, N15
Paleo-Siberian, C5, N19
Polish, C5, N19
Russian, C5, N19, N33
Soviet Central Asian, C5, N15
Tajik, N15
Tungus-Manchu, N15
Turko-Tataric, N15
Ukrainian, C5, N19, S4
Ural-Altaic, C5
Uzbek, N19
Yakut, N19
Yiddish, Y4, Y5
Lansing, Robert (1864–1928), papers, P8
Larionov, Mikhail, M7, S7
Larson, Arthur (John Foster Dulles), P7, P8
Laserson, Max Matthasia (1887–1951), papers, C7
Lassalette, Vincent (Jonathan Ogden), N8
Last Journey (film, 1981), N23
Last Year of the Tsars (film, 1971), N23
Latvia, N19, R5
    Church (Berlin Collection), Y5
    Jewish communities (American Joint Reconstruction Foundation), Y5
Latvian language, C5, N19
Latvian literature, N19
Latvian Social Democratic Party, B6
Latviesu Valodas Vardnica (1923–1956), N19
Latvijas PSR Preses Hronika, N19
Latvijas Valsts Bibliotekas Biletens, N19
Latwju Dainas, K. Barons (1915, 1922), N19
Law, Soviet Union, C5
Lazda, Zinaida, N19
League of Nations, Secretariat (Arthur Bullard), P8
Lebedeff, Jean, I4
Lebedev, Klavdy V. (1852–1916), M2
LeBoeuf, Jr., Randall J. (1897–1975), Robert Fulton Collection (1764–1857), N8
Lectionaries, Armenian, N15
Lednev-Schukin, S., M2
Ledyard, John (1751–89), papers, N8
Lee, Ivy Ledbetter (1877–1934), selected files, P8
Left Socialist Revolutionary Party (Isaac N. Steinberg), Y5
Legat, Nikolai, ballet caricatures, N25
Lelewel, Joachim, N19
Leo Baeck Institute, B1
Lepky, Bohdan, documents, S4
Lermontov, Mikhail Iur'evich (1814–1841), C7
    (Nikolai Platonovich Ogariov), N26
Leschetizky, Theodore, compositions, N26

Leskov, Nikolai Semenovich (1831–1895) (Mstislav Valerianovich Dobuzhinskii), N14
Lestchinsky, Jacob
    (Gregori Gurevitch), Y5
    (Mendel Osherowitch), Y5
Letopis' Hryhoriia Hrabanki (1854), S4
Letopis' Samovidtsa (1878), S4
Lettisches Lexicon, F.F. Stender (1789–1791), N19
Levin, Josef, I4
Levine, Louis, collection, Y2
Levitan, Isaak Il'ich (1835–1877), T2
Levitan, Michel (Marc Ratner), Y5
Levitoff, Alexander (Mikhail Mikhailovich Fokine), N25
Levitzky, D., T2
Levytsky, Myron, N14
Leyda, Jay (Sergei Mikhailovich Eisenstein), M7
Liadov, Anatolii Konstantinovich (1855–1914), composition, N26
Liapunov, Sergei Mikhailovich (1859–1924), composition, N26
Liberal Party (1944–1951) (Forward Association), Y6
Liberator, R3
Liberman, Alexander, G1
Library science, C9, N19, P6
Lichine, David, N25
    (Mstislav Valerianovich Dobuzhinskii), N25
Lifschitz, Fega (Efraim Frisch), B1
Likumu un Ministru Kabineta Notukumu (July 1919–), N19
Limon, Jose (George Balanchine), N25
Lincoln Center, Library and Museum of the Performing Arts
    Billy Rose Theatre Collection, Performing Arts Research Center, N24
    Dance Collection, N25
    Music Division, N26
    Rodgers and Hammerstein Archives of Recorded Sound, N27
Linguistics, Slavic and East Central European, C5, N19
Lipchitz, Jacques (1891–1973), A6, G1
Lipsky, Alexander, composition, N26
Literature
    Armenian, C5, N15, P5
    Byelorussian, N19, N22
    Georgian, N15
    Jewish, Y3
    Latvian, N19
    Polish, C5, N19, N22
    Russian, C5, N19, N22, N33, P6, P7, R1
    Third Wave, C5, N19
    Ukrainian, N19, N22, P6, S4
    Yiddish, N11, Y4, Y5
Lithographs. *See* Art and under individual artists' names
Lithuania, N19, N20 V1
    Church (Berlin Collection), Y5
    Famine relief and reconstruction (1919–1930), A7
    Federation of Lithuanian Jews in New York (Mendel Sudarski), Y5
    Jewish communities (American Joint Reconstruction Foundation), Y5
    (*Reminiscences of a Journey to Lithuania*), N23
Lithuanian Consistory of the Russian Orthodox Church, records (1807–1900), Y5
Lithuanian Jewish Communities, records (1844–1940), Y5
Lithuanian language, C5
Liturgical works, I4, N19, S1, S10
Litvinov, Pavel (*Soviet Dissidents in Exile*), N23
Litvinova, Ivy Low (Irma Duncan Collection), N25
Livet Reichard Company. *See* Sovart . . .

Livingston, Robert R., Family (1685–1885), papers, N8
(Francis Dana), N8
Livonian, New Testament translations, N19
Livshits, Benedict, F2
Lloyd W. Smith Collection, M4
London, Meyer, Library, N34
Long, Rose-Carol W., L2
Lopatnikoff, Nicolai (Nicolai T. Berezowsky), C7
Lopukhina, Varvara (Mikhail Iur'evich Lermontov), C7
Lortzing, Albert, working scripts, N24
Louire, Arthur, compositions, N26
Loukomski, George, wooden synagogues, pastels, S3
Lovestone Group (1918–1919), I2
Lubki, R1
(Russkii Narodnyi Lubok), N14
Luce, Henry (1898–1967) (John Foster Dulles), P7, P8
Lucifer, O1
Lumer, Hyman, book collection, R3
Lunacharskii, Anatolii Vasil'evich (1875–1933) (Irma Duncan Collection), N25
Lunz, Lev Natanovich, working scripts, N24
Lutov, Father Paul, collection, S1
Luts-Arumaa, Karin, N14
Lux in Tenebris (1657), N19
Lviv, Assumption Brotherhood church books, S8
L'vov, Aleksei, F4
Lydenberg, Harry Miller, correspondence, N18

M

*M. Mykhailo Drahomanov Pavlyk (1841–1895): Eho Iubilei, Smert',
Avtobiografiia i Spys Tvoriv* (1895), S4
McCarthy, Joseph (*Point of Order*), N23
Macdougall, Allan Ross (1893–1957), collection, N25
(Irma Duncan Collection), N25
MacInnes, Duncan Arthur (1885–1965), papers, R5
Mack, Nila (Alla Nazimova), N24
McLean, Henry C. (1887–1955), diaries, N8
Madison, James, M4
Magnus, Olaus, *Historia de gentibus Septentrionalibus . . .* (1555), M3
Maiakovskii, Vladimir Vladimirovich. *See* Mayakovsky . . .
Maikapar, Samuil Moseyevich, composition, N26
Mainstream, R3
Makletsov (*Oktiabr' 1917–1918. Geroi i Zhertvy Revoliutsii*), N17
Makovsky, Konstantin E. (1839–1915), M2, T2
Makovsky, Vladimir E. (1846–1920), M2
Malaria Conference, Pan-Russian (International Health Board), R5
Malevich (Malewitch), Kasimir Severinovich (1878–1935), G1, M7, N14, N20
Maliutsa, Antin (1908–1970), N14
"Man in Spanish Costume" (Leon Bakst), N25
Man With a Movie Camera (film, 1928), N23
Mandel'shtam, Osip Emil'evich (1891–1938), collection, P7
Manhattan School of Music, M1
Mani-Leib (Leon Feinberg), Y5
Manilevitsch, H. (A. Charash), Y5
Manuscripts. *See under* specific languages or names of individuals
Manuscripts and Archives Section, New York Public Library, N18
Maps, A2, P1, R1, R8
Marc Chagall (film, 1965), N23
March–April: The Coming of Spring (film, 1967), N23

Mari, Gospel translation (1821), N19
Maria Feodorovna, tsarina, correspondence and portrait (1789), M4
Markova, Alicia (Oral Interviews with Dancers), N25
Markushevich, A.I., E2
Marmor, Kalman (1879–1956), papers, Y5
Martianoff, Nikolai, collection, University of Rochester, Rush Rhees Library, R4
Martinoff, S. (Mikhail Iur'evich Lermontov), C7
Marx for Beginners (film, 1978), N23
Marxist literature in English, R3
Mashkov, I., M2
"Mask of God" (Vaslav Nijinsky), N25
Masonic manuscripts, K2
Masses and Mainstream, R3
Massevitch, A.G. (b. 1918), A4
Massine, Leonide (1896–1979), collection, N25
Master of Asia (Evgenii Ivanovich Zamiatin), P7
Materialy, Imperial Commission for the Study of Land Ownership
    in the Trans-Baikal Region (1898), N19
Masterkova, C14
Maude, Alymer (Lev Nikolaevich Tolstoi), C7
Maurina, Zenta, N19
Maxwell, John Stevenson (1817–1870), correspondence, N8
Mayakovsky, Vladimir Vladimirovich (1893–1930), M7, N17
Mazepa, Halyna, N14
Meacham family (Hoyt and Meacham Families), N8
Medallions. *See* Numismatics
Medals. *See* Numismatics
Media Center, Donnell Library Center, N23
Medicine, Russian, N6
Medvedkin, Alexander (*The Train Rolls On*), N23
Meet Comrade Student (film, 1963), N23
Meisch, N. (Gregori Gurevitch), Y5
Mekas, Jonas (*Reminiscences of a Journey to Lithuania*), N23
Melamid, Alexander, C14, K3, R7
Melikoff, Princess Alexandra, working scripts, N24
Menjou, Adolph (*Reds in Hollywood*), N23
Menologium, M3, P7
Mensheviks in emigration (1920s–1960s), papers, B6
Mentchinova, Vera, N24
Merezhkowskii, Dmitrii Sergeevich (1866–1941) (Maxim Vinawer), Y5
Metropolitan Museum of Art, M2
Meyer London Library, N34
Meyerhold, Vsevolod Emil'evich (1874–1940), N24
Michailoff, Helen (Mikhail Iur'evich Lermontov), C7
Mickiewicz, Adam (1798–1855), N19
Mickiewicz Blatter (1956–), N19
Microfilm and Microform. *See also* Film; Film titles; Photographs; Slides; Video
    Alaskan Russian Church, records, S1
    Aleksandra D. Danilova, scrapbooks, N25
    Archives for History of Quantum Physics, A4
    Judaica, N11, Y4, Y5
    Lithuania (15th–17th c.), documents, V1
    Muscovy, documents (16th c.), H5
    Sources for History of Modern Astrophysics, A4
    Soviet Union, R2
    World War II, C16
Mid-Manhattan Library, New York Public Library, N28
    Picture Collection, N29
Mikheev, engravings (1753), R8

Mikoun, Mika (1886–), M2
Mikoyan (Mikojan), Anastas Ivanovich (1895–1978) (Sam Echt), B1
Mili, Gjon (George Balanchine), N25
Milton, John (1608–1674), C7
Minor, Robert, C7, R3
Minsk
  Jewish Community Council, records (1825–1921), Y5
  Jewish congregation (*Last Journey*), N23
Miriam and Ira D. Wallach Division of Arts, Prints and Photographs, New York Public Library
  Art and Architecture Collection, N12
  Photographic Collection, N13
  Prints, N14
Miro, Jean (b. 1893), miscellaneous manuscripts, N25
Mirror (film, 1974), N23
Misha Elman (1891–1967), collection, M1
Mishagola (Russia) (Kalman Marmor), Y5
Misins, Janis, N19
Miskhovich, Bogan, collection, S1
Missal (Robert Garrett Collection), P7
Missionaries, correspondence, A1
Misticheskie obrazy voiny (1914) (Natalia Sergeevna Goncharovna), N14
Mlada, ballet (Nikolai Andreevich Rimskii-Korsakov), N26
"Modern Russian Theater" (Evgenii Ivanovich Zamiatin), P7
Moiseyev Dancers (film, 1959), N23
Moldavian language, C5
Molitoslov, U2
Molly's Pilgrim (film, 1985), N23
Molotov, Vyacheslav (William Averell Harriman), C7
Monety Tsarstvovanii, 1700–1890, A10
Money. *See* Numismatics
Mongolic (Altaic) languages, N15
Montenegro, Roberto, *Vaslav Nijinsky* (Vaslav Nijinsky), N25
Montferrand, Auguste Ricard de
  Église cathédrale de Saint-Isaac (1845), M3
  Plans et details du monument consacré à la memoire de l'empereur Alexandre (1836), M3
Moore, Lillian (1911–1967), papers, N25
Moore, Sonia, N24
Morden, William, A9
Morden–James L. Clark Asiatic Expedition (1926), A9
Morden–Graves Asiatic Expedition (1929–1930), A9
Mordvin, Gospel translation (1821), N19
Mordvinov, Count, family records, N19
Morgan, Pierpont, Library, M3
Morristown National Historical Park, M4
Morskiia zapiski, H2
Moscow (1850) (Neill S. Brown), N8
Moscow (1870–1880), photographs, J1
Moscow Art Theater, N24
  (*Stanislavsky: Maker of the Modern Theater*), N23
Moscow First Symphony Ensemble (Nicolai T. Berezkowsky), C7
Moscow Synagogue (*Last Journey*), N23
Mosolov, Nikolai Semionovich (1846–1914), N14
Mother (film, 1936), N23
"Mother Kemsky" (John Peale Bishop), P7
Motion pictures. *See* Film; Film titles; and under individual film titles
Moussorgsky. *See* Mussorgsky, Modeste Petrovich
"Movements for Ballet and Orchestra" (Balanchine, George), N25
Mowshowitch, David (Lucien Wolf), papers, 1890s–1950s, Y5
Muehsam, Eric, papers, B1
Muehsam, Zenzl Elfinger (Eric Muehsam), B1

Muelenbachs, Karlis and J. Endzelins, *Letviesu Valodas Vardnica* (1923–56), N19
Murals, R10
Murphy, Robert D. (John Foster Dulles), P7, P8
Muscovy, documents (16th c.), microfilm, H5
Museum of Modern Art
    Film Stills Archive, M5
    Film Study Center, M6
    Library, M7
Music, N26
    Ballet scores, S7
    Church choir, archives, S10
    Crimean Tatar folksongs and dances (Nina Borovka), N26
    Folk, B8, N19
    (Robert Garrett Collection), P7
    Jewish, Y3
    Mischa Elman, collection, M1
    Russian, F4, H4, S1
    Sheet music, U2, Y5
    Tcherepnin Archive, T3
    Yiddish, Y4, Y5
    ZIMRO (Petrogradskii Kamernyi Ansambl', Obshchestvo Evreiskoi
        Narodnoi Muzyki), Z1
Music Division, Library and Museum of the Performing Arts at Lincoln Center,
    New York Public Library, N26
Mussorgsky, Modeste Petrovich (1839–1881), F4
    (Toscanini Memorial Archives), N26
    (Maurice Ravel), M3
Mustel, E.R. (b. 1911), A4
My Life in Art (Edward Gordon Craig), N24
Myhocky, Dmytro, papers (1907–1971), C8
Mysticism, N19

N

Nabatov, A., working scripts, N24
Nabokov family, A12
Nabokov, Nicolas, composition, N26
Nadai, A.L., "Trip to Moscow" (Duncan Arthur MacInnes), R5
Nadelman, Elie, M7
Nadir, Moshe (Leon Feinberg), Y5
Nagorsky, N.N., N14
NALNET, A3
Nanai, ethnography, A8
Napiersky, Karl, N19
Narekatsi, Grigorius, complete works (1840), N15
*Narrative of the Mission to Russia, 1866, of the Hon. Gustavus Vasa Fox . . . From the Journal and
    notes of J.F. Loubat*, New York (1873) (Joseph Florimond, duc de Loubat), N8
NASA library network system, A3
National Archives—New York Branch, N1
National Board of Young Men's Christian Association (YMCA), Historical Library.
    See YMCA of Greater New York
National Council of American Soviet Friendship, N2
National Council of Jewish Women–Service for the Foreign Born (1939–1968), Y2
Naukove Tovarystvo imeny Shevchenka, zapysky (1892–), N19
Naval History Society, N8
Navigator (film, 1934), N23
Nawratil, Karl, musical autograph, N26
Nazi Collection, Y4

Nazimova, Alla, N24
Needleman, Gibby, book collection, R3
Neizvestny, Ernst, N3
Nemirovich-Danchenko, Vladimir Ivanovich (1858–1943), N24
Nepomnyashtchy, S. (Daniel Charney), Y5
Nesterov, Mikhail V. (1862–1942), M2
Neue Kunstlervereinigung, membership card, L2
Neumann, J.B. (Jsrael Bar), papers, M7
Newbold, George, papers, N8
Newsky, Pierre (Piotr Korvin-Krukovski), working scripts, N24
Newspapers. *See* Press
New Jersey Historical Society, N4
New Masses, R3
New Rochelle Historical Association, N5
New York Academy of Medicine, Library, N6
New York City Municipal Archives, N7
New York Herald (1917–1920) (Herman Bernstein), Y5
New-York Historical Society, N8
New York Life Insurance Company, Research Center/Archives, N9
New York Programming Center, Radio Free Europe/Radio Liberty, R2
New York Public Library
    Berg Collection, N10
    Jewish Division, N11
    Miriam and Ira D. Wallach Division of Arts, Prints and Photographs
        Art and Architecture Collection, N12
        Photographic Collection, N13
        Prints, N14
    Oriental Division, N15
    Rare Books and Manuscripts Division, N16
        Arents Collection, N17
        Manuscripts and Archives Section, N18
    Schomberg Center for Research in Black Culture, N30
    Slavic and Baltic Division, N19
    Spencer Collection, N20
New York Public Library, Donnell Library Center
    Central Children's Room, N21
    Foreign Language Library, N22
    Media Center, N23
New York Public Library at Lincoln Center
    Billy Rose Theatre Collection, Performing Arts Research Center, N24
    Dance Collection, N25
    Music Division, N26
    Rodgers and Hammerstein Archives of Recorded Sound, N27
New York Public Library, Mid-Manhattan Library, N28
    Picture Collection, N29
New York Theosophical Society, N31
    See also Olcott Library and Research Center
New York Times, Archives, N32
New York University, Elmer Holmes Bobst Library,
    Special Collections, N33
    Tamiment Collection, N34
Nicholas, Bishop of Alaska, N8
Nicholas I, tsar, M4, N6
Nicholas II, tsar, fundamental laws (1905–1906), O2
Nicholas Roerich Museum, R6
Nicols & Plinke, silversmiths (1829–1900), M2
Niels Bohr Library, Center for History of Physics, American Institute of Physics, A4
Niger, Shmuel (Daniel Charney), Y5
Nijinska, Bronislava (1891–1970), N25

(Sergei Ismailoff), N25
Nijinsky, Vaslav (1890–1950), F4, N25
    (Gabriel Astruc), N25
    (Jean Cocteau), N25
    (Lincoln Kirstein), N25
Nikifor, U1
Nikolai Martianoff Collection, University of Rochester, Rush Rhees Library, R4
Nikon, Sv., "Izvestie a rozhdenii . . . i o zhitii . . ." (ca. 1687) (Ivan Kornil'yevich Shusherin), N19
Nilov, General, "rodoslovnaia kniga," H2
1905 Revolution. *See* Revolution
Nivkin, ethnography, A8
Nixon, Richard M. (John Foster Dulles), P7, P8
Nordoff, Paul (Nicolai T. Berezowsky), C7
Norman Thomas Papers, N18
North, Joseph, book collection, R3
North Pacific tribes, collection, A8
North Russian expedition
    (Benjamin Abbot Dickson), U6
    (George Stewart Evans), U6
Norton Dodge Collection, Soviet sculpture, C14
Nose, The (film, 1963), N23
Novakivsky, Oleksa, U1
Novakovsky, Yehuda (Marc Ratner), Y5
Novelle collection de quarante-deux vues de Saint-Petersbourg et de ses environs (1826), M3
Novelles estraordinaires de divers endroits . . . (1766), M3
Novosti, publications, N2
Nuclear engineering, Soviet literature on, B3
Nuclear physics, Soviet literature on, B3
Nuclear war (*War Without Winners*), N23
Numismatics, A10, N16, P1, P2, U1
Nureyev, Rudolf (b. 1938–), F4

O

O dniakh bylykh, R8
Obolenskaia, Maria Tolstaia (Lev Nikolaevich Tolstoi), C7
Obolensky, Colonel S., O2
Obratsov, Sergei (*Tanya the Puppeteer*), N23
Obshchestvo Evreiskoi Narodnoi Muzyki, Petrogradskii Kamernyi Ansambl' (ZIMRO), Z1
October (film, 1927), N23
Odessa (Hoyt and Meacham Families), N8
Odezhdy russkago gosudarstva, watercolors, N16
Offrosimoff (Mikhail Iur'evich Lermontov), C7
Ogariov, Nikolai Platonovich, compositions, N26
Ogden, Jonathan, business records (1800–1824), N8
Oktiabr' (film). *See October*
Oktiabr' (1926–1935), N11
Oktiabr' 1917–1918. Geroi i zhertvy revoliutsii, N17
Olcott, H.S., N31, O1
Olcott Library and Research Center, O1
    See also New York Theosophical Society
Old Believers, Vyg Community, N19
Old Church Slavonic. *See also* Church Slavonic
    Lectionary (14th c.), N18
    Sluzhebnaia kniga (19th c.), N8
Olenets, "Kratkaia istoricheskaia zapisa . . ." (1887), N19
Olga: A Film Portrait (film, 1974), N23

Oliver Sayler collection on the Moscow Art Theater, N24
One Day in the Life of Ivan Denisovich (film, 1971), N23
Oppler, Ernst, B1
Oral history, A4, A6, C6, H5, I2, N25, P7, P8
Oral History Research Office, Columbia University, C6
Orbok, Attila, working scripts, N24
Ordono Rosales, Emanuelle (Lincoln Kirstein), N25
Original Ballet Russe (Irvin Deakin), N25
Orlovskii (Orlowski), Aleksandr Osipovich (1777–1832), N14
Orthodox Church in America, Archives, O2
Orthodox Church in America, (Russian) Orthodox Cathedral of the Protection
    of the Holy Virgin, R9
Orthodox Church in Russia (Lithuanian Consistory of the Russian Orthodox Church), Y5
Orthodox Eastern Church, materials, S1
Osherowitch, Mendel (1887–1965), N24, Y5
Oslinyi Khvost i Mishen, M7
Ossetian, N15
Ostroff, Israel (Sholom Schwarzbard), Y5
Ostrog Bible, N16, S1
Ostrovskii, Aleksandr Nikolaevich (1823–1886), working scripts, N24
Ostrovskii, Zalman Solomonovich, *Evreiskie pogromy, 1918–1921*, N11
Osvobozhdenie Truda, B6
Otechestvennyia zapiski (1839–1884), N19
Oukrainsky, Serge (Pavley-Oukrainsky Ballet Russe), N25
Our World (Arthur Bullard), P8
"Ovis Pole" ibex, A9
Owen family, New Harmony, Indiana, travel diary, southern Russia, (1869), N18

P

Pachulski, Henryk, composition, N26
Padalka, Ivan (1895–1961), N14
Paderewski, Ignace Jan (1860–1941), M3
Paduchak, O., papers, S4
Paik, Nam June (*Media Shuttle . . .*), N23
Paintings. *See* Art and under individual artists
"Paix et Liberté," files (1950–1952), P8
Paleo-Caucasian languages, N15
Paleo-Siberian Collections, Jochelson and Bogoraz, N19
Paleo-Siberian languages, C5, N19
Pallas, Peter Simon (1741–1811), N14
Pan-Russian Malaria Conference (ca. 1924/25) (International Health Board), R5
Pantuhoff, Oleg, Sr. (1882–1973), materials, R8
Parade (Pablo Picasso), N25
Parajanov, Sergei (*Shadows of Forgotten Ancestors*), N23
Parfanovych, Sophia, papers, S4
Paris Peace Conference (Herman Bernstein), Y5
Parish, David, letterbooks, N8
Parish life, B9, S9, S10
Parish registries, R9, S9
Pasternak, Leonid, B1
Patent materials, Russian, E1
Patriarch Tikhon, Archbishop of North America, O2
Patterson, William, book collection, R3
    (Paul Robeson Collection), N30
Paul I, tsar, documents, M4, N20
Paul Robeson Collection, N30
Pauli, Fedor Khristianovich, *Description ethnographique des peuples de la Russie* (1862), M3

Pavilion d'Armide, Le (Alexandre Benois), N25
Pavley-Oukrainsky Ballet Russe, records (1915–1950), N25
Pavlov, Ivan Petrovich (1849–1936), works, N6
  (Rockefeller University), R5
Pavlov, Vladimir (Rockefeller University), R5
Pavlova, Anna (1881–1931), materials, C7, F4, N25
  (Gabriel Astruc), N25
Pavlyk, M. Mykhailo Drahomanov. *See M. Mykhailo Drahomanov Pavlyk*...
Peerce, Jan (b. 1907), A6
Perchyshyn, Luba (*Pysanka, The Ukrainian Easter Egg*), N23
Perezhitoye (1909–1913), N11
Periodicals. For subjects *see* Press; for titles *see* Journals or under individual title entries;
  see also Newspapers
Perov, Vasilii G. (1834–1882), M2
Perovsky, Mikhail Mikhailovitch, Count, documents, N19
Perry, Pettis, Papers, N30
Persian Gulf Command, U.S. Army, R8
Peshkov, Aleksei Maksimovich. *See* Gorky, Maksim
Peter I, tsar, A10, C2
Peters, Roberta (b. 1920), A6
Petipa, Marius Ivanovich (1819–1910), miscellaneous manuscripts, N25
Petlyura, Simon (Sholom Schwarzbard), Y5
Petrogradskii Kamernyi Ansambl', Obshchestvo Evreiskoi Narodnoi Muzyki (ZIMRO), Z1
Petroleum industry in Russia (Viktor Adiassewich), N18
Petrov, Yevgenii Petrovich, working scripts, N24
Pettis Perry Papers, N30
Pevsner, Antoine (1886–1962), G1, M2
Peyton, Bernard, correspondence, N18
Philately
    Azerbaijan, P2
    Georgian, P2
    Polish, P1
    Soviet film industry (1969), N24
    Ukrainian, P2
    Unauthorized issues (1920s), P2
Philosophy
    Orthodox, H4, S1, S10
    Slavic and East Central European, C5, N19
Photographs. *See also* Film; Film titles; Videos; Slides
    Aksania Nova, A12
    American Expeditionary Forces, Siberia, U6
    Archival files, ETS, E2
    Carpathian region, famine relief and reconstruction (1919–1930), A7
    Churches and dioceses, H4, O2
    Cossacks, H2
    Crimean War, J1
    Danilova, Aleksandra Dionisievna, N25
    Diaghilev, Sergei, S7
    Expeditions, A9
    Gypsies, Russian (Alland Photography Collection), N8
    International Ladies' Garment Workers' Union, Archive, I2
    Irma Duncan Collection . . ., N25
    Isdebsky, Vladimir, I4
    Jewish life in Poland and Russia, Y3, Y5
    Lithuania, famine relief and reconstruction (1919–1930), A7
    Kadet Corps, H2
    Macdougall, Allan Ross, N25
    Massine, Leonid, N25
    Mischa Elman, and associates, M1

Moscow, J1
Nikolaevsk Cavalry Academy, H2
North Russian Expedition (1919), U6
Pavlova, Anna, N25
Poland, A2, P1
Romanov family, H2
Russia, C2, J1, N13, N19, P7, R1, R9
Russian-American Line (ca. 1916), N8
Russian avant-garde art, C2, G1
Russian Ball (1863), N8
Russian boy and girl scouts, R8
Russian emigres, H2
Russian military road, Caucasus, (ca. 1870), J1
Russian Revolution and Civil War, H2
Russian theater and theater personalities, N24
Russo–Japanese War, H2
   (Claude Bragdon), P7
   (Ernest Kuhn), U6
St. Petersburg, J1
Science and scientists, A4
Siberian Expedition Photographs, U6
Soviet artists, C14
Soviet avant-garde art, G1
Soviet Union, C15, P2, T1
Stock photo agency, B2, S6
Stravinsky, Igor, S7
Tsarist penal system (George Kennan), N19
Tsarist period, C2
Ukraine, famine relief and reconstruction (1919–1930), A7
Ukrainian archives, U1
Ulanova, Galina, N25
Valaam monastery, Finland, (Vidy), N19
Video disc of, Y5
World War I, H2
World War II archive, S4
Phylactery, C7
   (Robert Garrett Collection), P7
Physical sciences, N19
Physics, high energy, Soviet literature on, B3
Piatigorsky, Gregor (*An Afternoon with Gregor Piatigorsky*), N23
Picasso, Pablo (1881–1973), correspondence, N25
Picnic by the Roadside (Stalker), N23
Picture Collection, Mid-Manhattan Library, New York Public Library, N29
Pierpont Morgan Library, M3
Pil'niak, Boris Andreevich (1894–1937) (Alexander Bacherac), C8
Pilsudski Institute of America for Research in the Modern History of Poland, P1
Pioneers and Russian boy scouts, P3
Piramyz Albo Stolp' . . ., manuscript, S4
Pis'ma i Bumagi Imperatora Petra Velikago, N19
Platonov, Valerian, archives, P1
Pleasant, Richard (Bronislava Nijinska), N25
Pleskow, Martin, P2
Plieksans, Janis, N19
Plisetskaia, Maiaia Mikhailovna (b. 1925), materials, N25
Poale Zion, B6
   (Kalman Marmor), Y5
Pogedas, George A. de, painting of Moscow Art Theater, N24
Pogroms, B1, B6
Point of Order (film, 1964), N23

Pokhuznina, Nadezhda (Mikhail Iur'evich Lermontov), C7
Poland, M2, N18, N19, P1, P4
    (Berlin Collection), Y5
    (Jacob Jacobson), B1
Poland (film, 1965), N23
Poland Revisited, Joseph Conrad, N10
Polenov, Vasilii Dmitrievich (1844–1927), M2
Polish-American affairs, P4
Polish-American ethnic group, P4
Polish–Bolshevik War (Belvedere Archive), P1
Polish Diplomatic Services from Russia (Belvedere Archive), P1
Polish Institute of Arts and Sciences in America, Alfred Jurzykowski Memorial Library, P4
Polish labor movement, B6
Polish language, C5, N19
Polish literature, C5, N19, N22
Polish political parties, P4
Polish–Russian/Soviet Union relations, K4
Polish Socialist Party, B6
Polish–Ukrainian relations, P4
Polish uprising (1863), P1
Political movements, Russia and Soviet Union, C5, N19
Polka Graph (film, 1953), N23
Polnoe sobranie russkikh letopisei (1853–1922), N19
Polymya, N19
Pomerantz, Alexander (1901–1965), papers, Y5
Pontifico Seminario de S. Giosafat (Dmytro Myhocky), C8
Popov (Mikhail Iur'evich Lermontov), C7
Populist movement in Russia, B6
Posledniya Novosti (1920–1940), O2
Possev—USA, E3
Postage stamps. *See* Philately
Postcards, N19, P1, P2, R1
    Soviet underground postcards, P3
Posters. *See* Prints and Posters
Potemkin (*Battleship Potemkin*), N23
Potofsky, Jacob S. (b. 1894), A6
Potsdam, R8
Powers, Francis Gary (*Counterpoint: The U2 Story*), N23
Pravda (1912), N19
Pravitel'stvennyi vestnik, 1869–1917, N19
Pravoslavnoe Obozrenie, S1
Pravoslavnyi sobesednik, S1
Prelacy of Armenian Apostolic Church of America, St. Nerses Shnorhali Library, P5
Press
    Byelorussian, N19, R2
    Clipping files, C16, H2, M1, M6, N14, N19, N25, P8, R2, S10
        (Aleksandra Dionisierna Danilova), N25
        (Irma Duncan Collection), N25
        (George Kennan), N19
        (Ivy Ledbetter Lee), P8
        (Anna Pavlova), N25
        (Natalie Roslavleva), N25
    Estonian, R2
    Judaica, H1, Y4
    Latvian, R2
    Lithuanian, R2
    Polish, N19, P1, R2
    Religious–theological, R9, S1
    Russian, C5, N19, R2

Russian and Soviet art and culture, K3
Russian emigre (1914–51), H4
Russian medicine (early 19th c. to present), N6
Soviet, C5, N19, R2
Soviet Central Asian, C5
Ukrainian, N19, R2, S4
Prieth, Benedict (Lev Nikolaevich Tolstoi), P7
Prilucki, Noah (Sholom Schwarzbard), Y5
Prince Igor' (film, 1969), N23
Princeton University Library
Firestone Library, P6
Firestone Library, Rare Book, Manuscript, and Special Collections, P7
Seeley G. Mudd Manuscript Library, P8
Printing History, Russian, C9, N19
Prints and Posters
Anti-communism ("Paix et Liberté"), P8
Civil War, Russian (Harold M. Fleming), N18
Film posters, Russian, E4
Tamara Karsavina (Jean Cocteau), N25
Music (Joseph Schillinger), N26
Vaslav Nijinsky (Jean Cocteau), N25
Posters, Russian, pictures, N29
Prints, Russian, N14, R1
John Reed Collection of revolutionary posters, N19
TASS Windows Collective (Louis Cowan), C7
World War I, C7
World War II, C7
Progress, publications, N2
Prokofiev, Sergei Sergeevich (1891–1953), F4, M3
Proletariat, Polish labor movement group, B6
Protestants, correspondence, A1
Psalms (Armenian manuscripts), P7
Psalter (Robert Garrett Collection), P7
Puchkov, Sergei, composition, N26
Pudovkin, Vsevolod
(*Chess Fever*), N23
(*Mother*), N23
"Pulcinella," ballet (George Balanchine), N25
Pun', N17
Puppets, N24
(*Tanya the Puppeteer*), N23
Pushkin, Aleksandr Sergeevich (1799–1837), materials, C2, N24
(Mikhail Iur'evich Lermontov), C7
Put' russkogo bogoslaviia (Georges Florovsky), P7
Pysanka, The Ukrainian Easter Egg (film, 1975), N23

R

Rabbinica, Y4
Rabinoff, Max, C7, N26
Rabinovich, Alex, R1
Rachmaninoff, Sergei Vasil'evich (1873–1943), F4, M3, O2. *See also* Rakhmaninov, Sergei
Radio Free Europe/Radio Liberty, New York Programming Center, R2
Radio Liberty, oral history, C6
Radio scripts ("Paix et Liberté"), P8
Raduga, publications, N2
Rahva Haal, N19
Rakhmaninov, Sergei Vasil'evich (1873–1943), visiting cards, N26
See also Rachmaninoff, Sergei

Rand School of Social Science, records, N18, N34

Randall, Tony (b. 1924), A6

Randolph, John (William Turk), N8

Ranis, J., N19

Rankin, Edward E. (Russia, Foreign Office), P7

Raoul Wallenberg, Buried Alive (film, 1983), N23

Rare Book, Manuscript, and Special Collections, Firestone Library,
    Princeton University Library, P7

Rare Books and Manuscripts Division, New York Public Library, N16
    Arents Collection, N17
    Manuscripts and Archives Section, N18

Rasputin, correspondence, O2

Ratnbildung (1928–1936), N11

Ratner, Marc, papers (1906–1913), Y5

Ravel, Maurice (1875–1937), M3

Razsviet (1879–1881), N11

Razsviet (1907–1913), N11

Reavey, George (Aleksei Mikhailovich Remizov), P7

Recordings. *See also* Tape recordings
    Polish, P1
    Russian music, N27
    Russian sound recordings, E1
    Russian/Soviet plays, N24
    Ukrainian, U2

Red Pomegranate (film, 1972), N23

Reds in Hollywood (film, 1948), N23

Reed, John, N19, N24
    (*Ten Days that Shook the World*), N23

Reference Center for Marxist Studies, R3

Reflections of a Dancer: Alexandra Danilova (film, 1981), N23

Refuseniks, C4

Register of American Field Research on Eastern Europe and the USSR, I3

Reichsicherheitshauptamt, Einsatzgruppen "in the USSR," records, Y5

Reichskommisariat für das Ostland (Berlin Collection), Y5

Reichsministerium für Volkaufklaerung und Propaganda (Berlin Collection), Y5

Reisin, Zalman (Mendel Osherowitch), Y5

Religion in Russia (film, 1968), N23

Religious and ecclesiastical brochures, H4

Remington, Carl (1879–1919), papers, C7

Remington, Frederic (1861–1909), N18

Reminiscences of a Journey to Lithuania (film, 1971), N23

Reminiscences of Ten Years' Chaos in Russia (1916–1928), M3

Remizov, Aleksei Mikhailovich (1877–1957), papers, N18, P7
    (Alexander Bacherac), C8

Remizov, Nikolai Vladimirovich, photographs for *The Gambler*, N24

Repella, Archimandrite Anthony, library, S1

Repin, Ilya, S3, T2

Requiem Canticles (Igor Stravinsky), P7

Rerikh, Nikolai Konstantinovich. *See* Roerich, Nicholas

Research Program on the Communist Party in the Soviet Union
    (Geroid Tanqueray Robinson), C7

Respighi, Ottorini (1879–1936), M3

Retzvitan, Russian ship, altar cross, R10

Revenge of the Kinematograph Cameraman (film, 1912), N23

Revolution, Russian (1905), B6

Revolution and Civil War, Russia, H2
    (Norman Armour), P8

Revolutionary movements, Russia, B6, N19

Reynolds, Herbert, bibliography of Glinka (1935), N26

Rhana, Lisa (Rudolf Nureyev), F4
Riabouchinsky, Michael P., papers (1917–1960), N18
Riga, H5
    (George Coggleshall), N8
    (Edward Wyer), N8
Riigi teataja (1918–1940), N19
Rimsky-Korsakov, Nikolai Andreevich (1844–1908), F4
    (*Mlada*), N26
    (*Russian Rooster*), N23
Robbins, John Jacob, papers, N18
Robeson, Paul (Paul Robeson Collection), N30
Robinson, Geroid Tanqueray (1892–1971), papers, C7
Rochester, University, Rush Rhees Library, Nikolai Martianoff Collection, R4
Rockefeller Archive Center, R5
Rodchenko, Alexander Mikhailovich (1891–1956), E4, G1, M7
Rodgers and Hammerstein Archives of Recorded Sound, N27
Rodzinski, Artur (Nicolai T. Berezowsky), C7
Roerich, Nicholas (1874–1947), M7, R6, S7
Roerich, Nicholas, Museum, R6
Rogoff, Hillel (Mendel Osherowitch), Y5
Rokyta, Jan, N19
Roller coasters (Stevens Family), N4
Romanzoff, Comte N.P. de (Albert Gallatin), N8
Ronald Feldman Fine Arts, R7
Ronde, Jean Baptiste (fl. 1759–1764), M2
Room, Abram (*Bed and Sofa*), N23
Roosevelt, Franklin D. (William Averell Harriman), C7
Root, Joel (b. 1770), diary, N8
Rosales, Emanuelle Ordono (Lincoln Kirstein Collection), N25
Rose, Billy, Theatre Collection, N24
Rosen, Joseph A. (1887–1949), records, Y5
Rosenberg, Lev Samoilovich. *See* Bakst, Leon
Rosenberg, Manuel (1897–1967), drawings, C7
Rosenfeld, Leon (1904–1974), A4
Roslavleva, Natalia, papers, N25
    (Lillian Moore), N25
Ross, T.J. (Ivy Ledbetter Lee), P8
Rossiiskii teatr', N19
Rosta, N19
Rostovtsev, Mikhail Ivanovich (1870–1952) (Maxim Vinawer), Y5
Roth, Joseph, Austrian journalist. *See* Roth-Bornstein, Joseph
Roth-Bornstein, Joseph, B1
Rothermel, Doctor (International Health Board), R5
Rothko, Mark (1903–1970), G1, M7
Rubenstein, Anton, F4, M3, N26
Rubenstein, Ida (Gabriel Astruc), N25
Rueben, Helen, book collection, R3
Ruega, Eduard, N14
Rugs, Ukrainian (*kilim*), U1
Rural Russia Under the Old Regime (Geroid Tanqeray Robinson), C7
Russia. *See also* Muscovy (16th c.)
    Alexander I, tsar, collection, M4, N4, N8
    Alexander II, tsar, collection, M4, N19, O2
    Alexander III, tsar, correspondence, A12
    Alexei Mikhailovich, tsar (John Milton), C7
    Catherine II, empress, collection, H2, M4, N19
    Civil War, C5, H2, H4, N19
      (Benjamin Abbot Dickson), U6
      (Harold M. Fleming), N18

(George Evans Stewart), N18
Crimean War, J1
    (Archibald F. Becke), P7
Decrees (18th–19th c.), C8, H2, O2
Departament Politsii, Documents (1812–1913), C8
Documents Relating to the Emancipation of the Serfs, (1867–1868), N19
Duma, *Stenograficheskie otchety* (1906–1917), N19
Education, military, H2
Foreign Office, P7
Holy Synod, minutes and reports, decrees, O2, S1
Imperial Commission for the Study of Land Ownership in the Trans-Baikal Region (1898),
    Materialy, N19
Imperial Dancing Academy (Vaslav Nijinsky), N25
Imperial family, C2
    Collection, H4, M3
Insurance business, regulation, N9
Ivan IV, tsar, H5, N19
Junker Academy graduates, career records, H2
Marie, "wife of Alexander I," correspondence, M4
Military, Army, H2, N19
    (Peter DeDaehn), C8
    Regimental histories, C5, H2, N19
    Semenovsky regiment, history, C5, H2
Military history, C5, H4, N19
Military orders, Caucasian front, H2
Military road in the Caucasus (ca. 1870), J1
Military service records (1904–14), H2
Ministerstvo vnutrennykh del (1862, 1902–1907), N19
Ministry of Justice, documents (Simon Dubnow), Y5
Monarchy
    History, C5, H4, N19
    Portraits of monarchs, H2
Moscow
    (1850) (Neill S. Brown), N8
    (1870–1880), photographs, J1
Municipal histories, N19
Naval figures, portraits, H2
Naval history, H2, N4
Navy, manuscript list (1764), M3
Nicholas I, tsar, N8, M4
Nicholas II, tsar, fundamental laws (1905–1906), O2
Odessa (Hoyt and Meacham Families), N8
Orthodox Church (Lithuanian Consistory of the Russian Orthodox Church), Y5
Paul I, tsar, documents, M4, N20
Penal system, N19
Peter I, tsar, collection, A10, C2, M4, N19
Petroleum industry (Viktor Adiassewich), N18
Polish relations, P1, P4
Polnoe sobranie zakonov, N19
Pravitel'stvennyi vestnik (1869–1917), N19
Printing history, C9
Provincial governors, reports, N19
Revolution, H2, N19
"Rodoslovetz . . . velikikh kniazei rossiiskikh," N19
St. Petersburg, J1, R1, R8
    (John Quincy Adams), M4

(Neill S. Brown), N8
(Peter DeDaehn), C8
(John Stevenson Maxwell), N8
(George Newbold), N8
(Jonathan Ogden), N8
(David Parish), N8
(Joel Root), N8
(Edward H. Wright), N4
Senate, documents (Simon Dubnow), Y5
Serfdom, emancipation decree, O2
Ship models and histories, H2
Steamboats (Randall J. LeBoeuf, Jr.), N8
Svod zakonov rossiiskoi imperii (1857–1916, 1906–1914), N19
Trade
(Hendricks Family), N8
(T.P. Shaffner), N8
Trans-Baikal Region (Imperial Commission . . . *Materialy*), N19
Transcaucasia, P1
Weapons models, H2
YMCA in Russia (1900–1920s), Y6
Russia and Africa, N30
Russia and Afro-Americans, N30
Russia and Ukraine, Jews in, A5
Russia, childhood in (Irina Skariatina), P7
Russia, correspondence with Thomas Edison, E1
Russia (1774), description by Peter Alexander Allaire, N5
Russia (film, 1958), N23
Russia, southern, diary of travel (1869) (Owen Family), N18
Russia, Zionist organizations, Z1
Russian Academy of Sciences (Duncan Arthur MacInnes), R5
Russian-American Line, N8
Russian-American telegraph expedition (Herma Hoyt Briffault), N18
Russian Archeographic Commission, *Polnoe sobranie russikikh letopisei* (1853–1922), N19
Russian art. *See* Art and under individuals or movements
Russian art library, T2
Russian Artillery Commission in North America (1915–1917), N34
Russian Artillery Commission in United States (1917), N18
Russian avant-garde. *See* Art
Russian Ball, New York Academy of Music (1863), N8
Russian baths, New York, lithograph (1878–1879), N8
Russian Bible Society, A1, N19
Russian book, history, C9, N19, R1
Russian Boy and Girl Scout Archive, R8
Russian boy scouts and pioneers, P3
Russian Central Asia, A9
Russian children's books, K2, N19
Russian Division, U.S. Department of State (Arthur Bullard), P8
Russian films, N23, M5, M6
Russian Fleet in New York, collection (1863), N8
Russian Futurists. *See* Futurism
Russian illustrated books (1606–1920s), N20
Russian Imperial Army, Museum and Archive, H2
Russian Jewry. *See* Jews
Russian language, C5, N19
Russian Lawyers Association in the U.S.A., N18
Russian literature, C5, N19, N22

(Alexander Bacherac), C8
Russian loan question (1944–1945) (Harry Dexter White), P8
Russian Mennonite settlement, Kansas, N8
Russian music, recordings, N27
Russian Naval Museum, H2
Russian Organizations in America, Federation of, N18
Russian-Orthodox American Messenger (1896–1973), O2
(Russian) Orthodox Cathedral of the Protection of the Holy Virgin
 (Orthodox Church in America), R9
Russian Orthodox Church, New York, wood engraving, N8
Russian Orthodox St. Nicholas Cathedral, R10
Russian Pamirs (1926), A9
Russian Peasant (film, 1968), N23
Russian-Polish Zionist groups, B6
Russian Refugee Relief Association, London (Laura Spelman Rockefeller Memorial), R5
Russian relief operations (Commonwealth Fund), R5
Russian Revolution and Civil War, C5, H2, N19
 (Norman Armour), P8
Russian revolutionary movement (pre–1917), B6
Russian Rooster (film, 1975), N23
Russian royal family, ceremonies, C2, C5
Russian Social Democratic movement, B6
Russian soldier in China (1904) (Peter DeDaehn), C8
Russian sound recordings, E1
Russian–Soviet musical compositions, C5
Russian–Soviet plays, recordings, N24
Russian stage designers (Mstislav Valerianovich Dobuzhinskii), N25
Russian steppe (*Steppe in Winter*), N23
Russian Student Christian Movement, Y6
Russian Student Fund (Laura Spelman Rockefeller Memorial), R5
Russian Superior Technical Institute, Y6
Russian theater, N24
Russian Theological Academy, Y6
Russian theological literature, S1
"Russian war bride" case (American Civil Liberties Union), P8
Russian women (*Women in Russia*), N23
Russian Zemstvos Committee (Laura Spelman Rockefeller Memorial), R5
Russians in America, composition (Kurt Schindler), N26
Russians in Siberia, ethnography, A8
Russica/Sovietica Collection, Y4
Russkii yevrei (1879–1884), N11
Russkii Narodnii Lubok, N14
Russo–Japanese War (1904–1905)
 (Archibald F. Becke), P7
 (Claude Bragdon), P7
 (Ernest Kuhn), U6
 Pictures, N29
 (Carl Remington), C7
Russo–Turkish War (1877–1878), H2
 (Archibald F. Becke), P7
Rusthaveli, Shot'ha (12th century), N15
Ruthenberg, Charles E., book collection, R3
Ruthenberg Library, Workers School, R3
Ruthenian texts (17th–18th c.), B9
Ryska Socialistika Federative Sovjket-republikens Telegramyra, Stockholm, N19

S

S beregov Ameriki, H2
Sadan, Dov (Mendel Osherowitch), Y5
Safonoff, Vassily Ilyich, letters, N26
St. Albans (Georges Florovsky), P7
St. Basil's College, Library, S8
St. Catherine of Siena (Georges Florovsky), P7
St. Gregory the Illuminator (Robert Garrett Collection), P7
St. Innocent, Apostle to America . . ., O2
St. Nerses Shnorhali Library, Prelacy of Armenian Church of America, P5
St. Nicholas, Apostle to Japan, O2
St. Nicholas Ukrainian Catholic Church, S9
St. Petersburg, J1, R1, R8
    (John Quincy Adams), M4
    (Neill S. Brown), N8
    (Peter DeDaehn), C8
    (George Newbold), N8
    (John Stevenson Maxwell), N8
    (Jonathan Ogden), N8
    (David Parish), N8
    (Joel Root), N8
    (Edward H. Wright), N4
St. Petersburg (Sergei Zalshupin), N14
St. Sergius (Georges Florovsky), P7
St. Teresa of Avila (Georges Florovsky), P7
St. Theophan the Recluse, O2
St. Vladimir's Orthodox Theological Seminary, The Father Georges Florovsky Library, S1
    (Georges Florovsky), P7
Samaroff, Olga (Nicolai T. Berezowsky), C7
Saminsky, Lazare, compositions, N26
Samizdat, N19, R2
Samoyed, ethnography, A8
Sapir, Boris, correspondence (1974–1984), C8
Savrasov, Alexei K. (1830–1897), M2
Sayadian, Arutuin (*Red Pomemgranate*), N23
Sayler, Oliver (Oliver Sayler collection on the Moscow Art Theater), N24
Sbornik geograficheskikh, topograficheskikh i statisticheskikh materialov po Azii (1883–1914), N19
Sbornik istoricheskago obshchestva (1867–1916), N19
Scarloss, Walter, collection, S1
Schaufuss, Tatiana, correspondence, T4
Scheide, William, Library, P7
Scherer, J.B., *Histoire raisonée du commerce de la Russie*, Paris (1788), N8
Schillinger, Joseph, N26, S2
Schindler, Kurt, composition, *Russians in America*, N26
Schlesinger, Benjamin, correspondence, I2
Schley, Reeve, Sr., papers (1904–1944), N4
Schmidt, Adolf (Pavley-Oukrainsky Ballet Russe), N25
Schomberg Center for Research in Black Culture, New York Public Library, N30
Schroder, J.J., *Thesaurus Linguae Armenicae*, Amsterdam (1711), N15
Schuchaef, Wassily (1887–), M2
Schultz, General, Russo–Turkish War (1877–78), notebooks, H2
Schwab, George, A6, S3
Schwarzbard, Sholom (1886–1938), papers, Y5
Schwarzschild, Leopold, papers, B1
Scientific and Technical Aerospace Reports, A3
Scientific and technical literature, Soviet, A4, B3
Scott, Hugh Lenox (1853–1934), papers, P8
Scouts, Russian, P3, R8

Scribner publishing archive (Lev Nikolaevich Tolstoi), P7
Sculpture. *See* Art and under individual artists
Second International, B6
Second Moscow Art Theater, N24
Seeley G. Mudd Manuscript Library, Princeton University Library, P8
Sefer ha-shanah (1900–1906), N11
Semionov-Polonski, S., working scripts, N24
Sermons, Russian, M3
Serov, Vladimir (1910–1968), M2
Sevastopol', coat of arms, P2
Shabad, Theodore, collection, A2
Shabelsky, N.L. de, B5
Shachtman, Max, collection, N34
Shadows of Forgotten Ancestors (film, 1964), N23
Shaffner, T.P. (1818–1881), correspondence, N8
Shaliapin, Fedor Ivanovich (1873–1938). *See also* Chaliapin, Fedor
    (Gabriel Astruc), N25
    (Mikhail Mikhailovich Fokine), N25
Shapoval, Mykyta Iukhymovych, works, N19
Shattuck, Amos Blanchard (1896–1935), diary, U6
Shatzky, Jacob (Mendel Osherowitch), Y5
Shdanoff, George, working scripts, N24
Shevchenko Scientific Society
    Archeographic publications, U2
    Library and Archives, S4
Shidlovskii, Boris (Gabriel Astruc), N25
Shipovnik, N19
Shostakovich, Dmitry, F4
    (*Polka Graph*), N23
Shotwell, James (1874–1965), papers, C7
Shragin, Boris (*Soviet Dissidents in Exile*), N23
Shramshenko, P2
Shusherin, Ivan Kornil'yevich, N25
Siberia, A8, A9, N20
    (Herma Hoyt Briffault), N18
    (Georg de Hennin), N19
    (John Ledyard), N8
    (Amos Blanchard Shattuck), U6
Siberia: A Day in Irkutsk (film, 1967), N23
Siberian Expedition Photographs, U6
Siberian tiger, A9
Siberian tribes, A9
Sienkiewicz, Henryk, N19
Sigman, Morris, correspondence, I2
Sikes, Frederick G. (1893–1957), correspondence, P7
Silberg, Abel' Abramovich, composition, N26
Silberstein, Shmuel (Simon Dubnow), Y5
Simmons, Ernest (Correspondence of . . .), C8
Simonov, Konstantin Mikhailovich (b. 1915), working scripts, N24
Simonov, N. (Lev Nikolaevich Tolstoi), P7
Singaevsky, N. (Sergei Ismailoff), N25
Sisco, Joseph (b. 1919), A6
Skariatina, Irina (Mrs. Victor F. Blakeslee), papers, P7
Skorodumov, Gabriel (1748?–1792), N14
Skrebitzki, *Documents Relating to the Emancipation of the Serfs* (1867–1868), N19
Skyroad to Russia (Irina Skariatina), P7
Slavic and Baltic Division, New York Public Library, N19
Slavic illustrated manuscripts, N20
Sleeping Beauty (Leon Bakst), N25

Slides
     Citizen Exchange Committee, Soviet Union (1978), C15
     Russian and Soviet art and culture, K3
     Russian Empire (1895–1914), H3
     Russian Painters and the Stage, G1
     Stage Designs and the Russian Avant-Garde, G1
Slonimsky, Nicholas (Alexei Mikhailovich Remizov), N18
Sluzhebnaia kniga, Old Church Slavonic (19th c.), N8
Smith, David Eugene (1860–1945), papers, C7
Smith, Howard Alexander (1880–1966), papers, P8
Smith, Jessica, book collection, R3
Smith, Joseph A. (Rufus King), N8
Smith, Lloyd W., collection, M4
Smith, Thomas, *Sir Thomas Smithes voiage and entertainment in Rushia* (1605), M3
Smith, Timothy (Hoyt and Meacham Families), N8
Social Democrats, B6
     (Sergius Ingerman), N34
Socialist Party of America
     (Eugene Debs), N34
     (Sergius Ingerman), N34
Socialist Revolutionaries, Yiddish literature, B6
     (Isaac A. Hourwich), Y5
     (Maxim Kovensky Collection), Y5
     (Chaim Zhitlovsky), Y5
Socialist Territorialists, B6
Society for the Prevention of World War III, records, C7
Society for the Propagation of Enlightenment (Khevra Mefitzei Haskolo), Y5
     (Baron Horace Guenzburg), Y5
Soiuz russkikh S.D., B6
Sokoloff, S.V., murals, (1907), R10
Solennités du saint couronnement . . . 1899, N16
Solntsev, Fiodor Grigor'yevich (1801–1892), watercolors, N16
Solntsev, N. (Konstantin Sergeevich Stanislavskii), N24
Solotareff, Boris (1889–1966), M2
Solovii, Yurii, N14
Solov'iov, Vladimir S., working scripts, N24
Solzhenitsyn, Alexander (*One Day in the Life of Ivan Denisovich*), N23
Sotsialisticheskaya Yevreyskaya Rabochaya Partiya (Marc Ratner), Y5
Soutine, Chaim (*Chaim Soutine*), N23
Sovart, c/o Livet Reichard Company, S5
Sovetakar hayasdan, N15
Sovetskii Pisatel', contract (Osip Emil'evich Mandel'shtam), P7
Sovfoto/Eastfoto, S6
Soviet–American economic relations (Frank A. Vanderlip), C7
"Soviet Attitude to Art," by Vladimir Kemenov, M7
Soviet avant-garde. *See* Art
Soviet bibliographies, computerized index, C11
Soviet books, periodicals, newspapers, N2, K1
Soviet Central Asia, languages, C5, N15, N19
Soviet Dissidents in Exile (video, 1981), N23
Soviet films, M5, M6, N2, N23
Soviet Jewry. *See* Jews
Soviet of the Unemployed in Petersburg (1906–1907) (Wladimir S. Woytinsky), C7
Soviet poetry, C5, K2, N19, N33, P6, P7
Soviet Russia, American accounts (1918–1940s), N34
Soviet scientific and technical literature, A3, A4, B3
Soviet Union, C3, C5, N19, P1
     Archival access, surveys, I3
     Armenia. *See* Armenia

Cine-Trains (*Train Rolls On*), N23
Collectivization, Krynychanska Silska Rada (1929–1933), S4
Diplomacy and foreign relations, C5, C16, N19
Education (1950s–1970s), E2
   (*Meet Comrade Student*), N23
History, C5, N19, P1, P6
   (Robert Lansing), P8
   (1920s) (Denys Trefusis), C8
   (1930s), film, I1
   (1930–1937) (Edward Falkowski), N34
Imprisonment, T1
   (*Soviet Dissidents in Exile*), N23
Information science, C9, N19
Insurance business, regulation, N9
Library science, C9, N19, P6
Minister of Justice (Isaac N. Steinberg), Y5
Polish relations, P1, P4
Printing history, C9, N19
Programma II, state television, C10
Red Army
   (Berlin Collection), Y5
   (Vladimir Mikailovich Zenzinov), N19
Reichsicherheitshauptamt, Einsatzgruppen "in the USSR," records, Y5
Research on, I3
Rosta, inclusive file, N19
Supreme Soviet
   Stenograficheskii otchet (1939–), C5, N19
   Vedomosti (1930–), C5, N19
Television broadcasts, C10
Testing by College Board and ETS, E2
Ukrainian dissident movement (1960–), U3
YMCA in Russia (1900–1920s), Y6
Soviet Union (film, 1930s), I1
Soviet Union: A New Look (film, 1978), N23
Soviet unofficial artists, C13
Soviet writers, correspondence (Paul Robeson Collection), N30
Sovremennik (1848–1865), N19
Soyer, Moses, M7
Soyer, Raphael (b. 1899), A6, M7
Special Diplomatic Mission to Russia (Hugh Lenox Scott), P8
Special Envoy to Churchill and Stalin, 1941–1946 (William Averell Harriman), C7
Spencer Collection, New York Public Library, N20
Spessivtzeva, Olga (Oral Interviews with Dancers), N25
Stalin, Joseph (1879–1953) (William Averell Harriman), C7
Stalker (film, 1979), N23
Stanfield, Boris Michael (b. 1889), papers, C7
Stanislavski Method, The (Sonia Moore), N24
Stanislavskii, Konstantin Sergeevich (1863–1938), papers, N24
   (Edward Gordon Craig), N24
   (Elizabeth Reynolds Hapgood), N24
   (Sonia Moore), N24
"Stanislavsky and America," broadcast by N. Solntsev (1958), N24
Stanislavsky: Maker of the Modern Theater (film, 1972), N23
Stanitsin, V., N24
STAR, A3
Starkman, Moshe (Mendel Osherowitch), Y5
Starling, Ernest H. (Rockefeller University), R5
Staronosov, Peter, N14
Starye gody (1906–1917), T2

Statutes of Grand Duchy of Lithuania, B7
Steamboats in Russia (Randall J. LeBoeuf, Jr.), N8
Steegmuller, Francis, correspondence, N25
Stefansson, Vilhjalmur (Herma Hoyt Briffault), N18
Steffens, Lincoln (1866–1936), papers, C7
Steinberg, Isaac N. (1888–1949), papers, Y5
Stender, F.F., *Lettisches Lexicon* (1789–1791), N19
Stenograficheskii otchet (Supreme Soviet) (1939–), N19
Steppe in Winter (film, 1965), N23
Sterlete, Veronika, N19
Stettinius, Edward L. (William Averell Harriman), C7
Stevens Family, papers (1663–1959), N4
Stewart, George Evans (1872–1946), papers, U6
Stokowski, Leopold (1882–1977) (Nicolai T. Berezowsky), C7
Story magazine and Story Press (Mikhail Zoshchenko), P7
Stoughton, Mary, diary (1878–1879), N18
Straight, Willard (Claude Bragdon), P7
Stravinsky–Diaghilev Foundation Collection, Parmenia Migel Ekstrom Collection, S7
Stravinsky, Igor (1882–1971), F4, M3, N25, N26, P7, S7
    (George Balanchine), N25
    (*Symphony of Psalms*), N23
Stravinsky, Vera, painting, G1
Strimer, Joseph, compositions, N26
Struck, Hermann, B1
Strugatzky, Arkady and Boris (*Stalker*), N23
Struggling Russia (1919–1920), N8
Struve, Gleb (Alexander Bacherac), C8
Student Friendship Fund (Laura Spelman Rockefeller Memorial), R5
Stulberg, Louis, correspondence, I2
Subcarpathian Ruthenia, B9
Sudarski, Mendel (1885–1951) and Alta Sudarski, papers, Y5
Sudeikin, watercolors, S3
Sukhovo-Kobylin, W., working scripts, N24
Sun Yat-sen University (Chan-han Wu), C7
Suprematism, Russian, M7
Surguchev, Il'ya D., working scripts, N24
Sutzkever (Abraham Sutzkever-Shmerke Katcherginski Collection) (1806–1945), Y5
    (Mendel Osherowitch), Y5
Svinin, Chevalier (Randall J. LeBoeuf, Jr.), N8
Svod vysochaishikh otmetok, annual of Alexander II, N19
Svod zakonov rossiiskoi imperii (1857–1916, 1906–1914), N19
Symbolism (rare book collection), P7
Symphony of Psalms (film, 1976), N23
Syngalowski, Aron (A. Charash), Y5
Synod of Russian Bishops Outside Russia, Cathedral of the Sign, S10
Sytin, Ivan D., *Polveka dlia knigi*, autographed copy (1916), N19
Szajkowski, Zosa, collection, B1
Szajnocha, N19
Szujski, Josef, N19

T

Tairov, Aleksandr, N24
Tajik language, N15
Takh-Tat, Gzerot (Simon Dubnow), Y5
Tamiment Collection, Elmer Holmes Bobst Library, New York University, N34
Tanya the Puppeteer (film, 1981), N23
Tape recordings, E2, L1, P1, P2

(Georges Florovsky), P7
Tapestries, M2
Tarassuk, Leonid, archive, T1
TASS Windows Collective (Louis Cowan), C7
Tatlin, Vladimir, M7
Tatyana Gallery, T2
Tchaikovsky, Nikolai Vasil'evich (1850–1926) (Maxim Vinawer), Y5
Tchaikovsky, Pyotr Il'yich (1840–1893), M3. *See also* Chaikovskii, Petr Il'ich
Tchelitchev (Tchelitchew), Pavel (1898–1957), M7, N25
Tcherepnin, Alexander (1899–1977), music collection, T3
Tcherepnin Society, T3
Tcherikower, Elias (1881–1943), Y4, Y5
Tchertkoff (Chertkov), Mrs. V.G. (Lev Nikolaevich Tolstoi), C7
Teatr', N19
Teatral'naia zhizn', N19
Teheran, Big Three, R8
Ten Days that Shook the World (film, 1927), N23
Terry, Ellen (Irma Duncan), N25
Textiles, B5, B9, M2, U1, Y2. *See also* Costumes
Theater and drama, N18, N19, N24, N25, S3, S7, Y4, Y5
Theology, Orthodox, S1, S10
Thesaurus Linguae Armenicae, J.J. Schroder, Amsterdam, 1711, N15
Third International, B6
Third Wave literature, C5, N19
Thomas, Michael Tilson (b. 1944), A6
Thomas, Norman (1884–1968), papers, N18
Thomashevsky, Boris, collection, N11
Three Sisters (Vassily Ivanovitch Katchaloff), N24
Tiesa, N19
Todd, Charles S. (George Newbold), N8
Tokarzhevsky-Karasevych, Ivan, papers, S4
Tolokonzeff (Sam Echt), B1
Tolstaia, Alexandra (Lev Nikolaevich Tolstoi), C7
Tolstaia, Ol'ga (Lev Nikolaevich Tolstoi), C7
Tolstaia, Tat'iana (Lev Nikolaevich Tolstoi), C7
Tolstoi, Aleksei Konstantinovich (1817–1875), working scripts, N24
Tolstoi, Alexandra, papers, T4
Tolstoi, Leo L., M2
Tolstoi, Lev Nikolaevich (1828–1910), materials, C7, E1, M3, N19, P7
    (Herman Bernstein), Y5
Tolstoi, Sergius (Lev Nikolaevich Tolstoi), C7
Tolstoy Farm, archives, T4
Tolstoy Foundation, library and archives, T4
Tooke, William, *View of the Russian Empire . . .* London (1799), A2
Topusov, Nikolai, N26
Toscanini Memorial Archives, N26
Toumanova, Tamara (Irvin Deakin), N25
Tower, Charlemagne (1848–1923), papers, P7
Trade unions, Poland (1919–1939), B6
Train Rolls On, The (film, 1974), N23
Trans-Baikal region (Imperial Commission . . . *Materialy*), N19
Transcarpathia, history, B9
Transcaucasia, P1
Travels from St. Petersburgh in Russia, to Various Parts of Asia, John Bell, London (1788), N8
Trebnik (1713), U2
"Tree of Life," N3
Trefusis, Denys, manuscript, C8
Tret'yakov, Sergei M., working scripts, N24
Triod tsvetnaia (ca. 14th c.), N19

Triptych, metal and enamel (Western Americana Collection), P7
Trotsky, Lev Davidovich (1879–1940), C7, N19, N34
    (Julie Braun-Vogelstein), B1
Troubetskoi, Prince Paul (1866–1938), M2
Troubridge, Lady (Vaslav Nijinsky), N25
Trouhanova, Natasha (Gabriel Astruc), N25
Trudy Kievskoi Dukhovnoi Akademii, S1
Truman, Harry S. (1884–1972) (William Averell Harriman), C7
Trush, Ivan, U1
Tschubar (Sam Echt), B1
Tserkovniya vedomosti (1891–1917), O2
Tsvetaeva, Marina (Alexander Bacherac), C8
"Tuchki" (Nikolai Platonovich Ogariov), N26
Tumarin, Boris, working scripts, N24
Tungus (Evenk or Evenki), ethnography, A8
Tungus-Manchu language, N15
Tur, L., working scripts, N24
Turgenev, Ivan Sergeevich (1818–1883), M3, N10, N24
"Turgeniev Snovidetz" (Aleksei Mikhailovich Remizov), P7
Turk, William, papers (1824–1833), N4
Turkestan, Chinese, A9
Turkey. *See* Armenia
Turko-Tataric, N15
Tyumenev, Il'ya, compositions, N26
Tziorogh, Elias I., Carpatho-Ruthenian hymns, N26

U

UAW Local 365 (Edward Falkowski), N34
Ukaz. *See* Russia and under individual decrees
Ukhtomskii, Andrei G., N19
Ukraine, N19, P1
    (Viktor Adiassewich), N18
    (Berlin Collection), Y5
    (Central Archives of the Editorial Committee on Collection and Investigation of the
        Materials Relating to the Pogroms in the Ukraine), Y5
    Famine relief and reconstruction (1919–1930), A7
    Jewish communities (American Joint Reconstruction Foundation), Y5
    Liberation Movement (1918–1922), U2
    (Dmytro Myhocky), C8
    Revolutionary Committee (1919–1920), statutes, N19
Ukrainian Academy of Sciences, Kiev, Institute for Jewish Proletarian Culture (Alexander
    Pomerantz), Y5
Ukrainian Americans (Louis Adamic), P7
Ukrainian Autocephalic Orthodox Church in America, U2
Ukrainian Catholic Church, S8
    (Dmytro Myhocky), C8
Ukrainian Catholic University, Lviv, U2
Ukrainian children's books, K2
Ukrainian easter eggs (*Pysanka* ...), N23
Ukrainian famine (1932–1933), U3
Ukrainian immigration. *See* Emigration and emigres
Ukrainian Jews in America, Federation of (Mendel Osherowitch), Y5
Ukrainian language, C5, N19
Ukrainian literature, N19, N22, U2
Ukrainian Mission UNRRA, U4
Ukrainian Museum, U1
Ukrainian National Army, U3
Ukrainian National Ensemble, P2

Ukrainian National Republic (Aitol Vitoshynsky), S4
Ukrainian National Women's League of America, U1
Ukrainian passport (1920), P2
Ukrainian–Polish relations, P4
Ukrainian Research and Documentation Center, U3
Ukrainian textiles, U1
Ukrainian theater, N24
Ukrains'kyi Tekhnichno-Hospodar'skyi Instytut, N19
Ulanova, Galina, N25
Una (Vaslav Nijinsky), N25
Uncle Vanya
    (film, 1972), N23
    Moscow Art Theater production (1900), N24
Uniforms. *See* Costumes
Union of Russian Jews, records (1945–1960), Y5
United Hebrew Trades, B6
United Nations Relief and Rehabilitation Administration (UNRRA), records (1943–1949), U4
United Nations
    Archives, U4
    Atomic Energy Commission (Bernard M. Baruch), P8
    Dag Hammerskjold Library, U5
    General Assembly (John Foster Dulles), P7, P8
United States. *See also* American; U.S.
    Attorneys and marshals (1821–1983), N1
    Consul in Riga
        (Edward Wyer), N8
    Courts of Appeal, N1
    Department of State, Russian Division (Arthur Bullard), P8
    District courts (1685–1973), N1
    Immigration and Naturalization Service, N1
    Information Agency, N1
    Minister to Russia
        (Francis Dana), N8
        (Robert R. Livingston), N8
        (William Turk), N4
        (Gulian Crommelin Verplanck), N8
    Persian Gulf Command, Army, R8
    Secretary of Legation, St. Petersburg
        (Edward H. Wright), N4
    Senate Foreign Relations Committee (1946–1959) (Howard Alexander Smith), P8
    Special Diplomatic Mission to Russia (Hugh Lenox Scott), P8
    United States Military Academy, Library, U6
Universitas, Stuttgart, N19
UNRRA. *See* United Nations Relief ...
Ural-Altaic language, C5
Urvantsev, Lev N., working scripts, N24
U.S./U.S.S.R. Exchange Program in Higher Education (1974–1978), E2
Uzbek, N19

V

Vaad Hatzala (1940–1963), Y2
Vakhrameev, N. (Mikhail Iur'evich Lermontov), C7
Vakhtangov, Eugene B. (Sonia Moore), N24
Valaam, Finland, monastery, (Vidy), N19

Valkenier, Elizabeth Kridl (Louis Cowan), C7
Van Buren, Martin (Gulian Crommelin Verplanck), N8
Vanderlip, Jr., Frank A. (1864–1937), papers, C7
Vasa Fox, Gustavus (1821–1883), papers, N8
Vasilevskis, Stanislav (b. 1907), A4
Vasilieff, N14
"Vasilok," Byelorussian Folk Dance Company, B8
Vaslav Nijinsky (Vaslav Nijinsky), N25
Vatican (Dmytro Myhockij), C8
Velde, Janis, N19
Vera i razum, Kharkov, S1
Verdaro, Virgilia (Marc Ratner), Y5
Vereshchagina Albums (Mikhail Iur'evich Lermontov), C7
Vereysky, Georgi, N14
Verplanck, Gulian Crommelin (1786–1870), correspondence, N8
Vershinin (Vassily Ivanovitch Katchaloff), N24
Vertov, Dziga (1895–1954) (*Man With a Movie Camera*), N23
Vestments, Eastern Christianity, B9
Vestnik Evropy (1803–1826, 1866–1917), N19
Vesy, N19
Viardot-Garcia, Pauline, composition, N26
Vibbard, Chauncy (Miscellaneous Manuscripts), N8
Victor Kamkin Bookstore, K1
Video disc, photographs, Y5
Videos, C3, C4, C10, N23
Vihalemm, Arno, N14
Vilna Collection, Y4
Vilno
        (Abraham Sutzkever–Shmerke Katcherginski Collection) (1906–1945), Y5
        (Jewish Community Board in Vilno), records (1820s–1940), Y5
        (Rabbinical School and Teachers' Seminary, Vilno), records (1847–1914), Y5
        (YIVO Vilno Collection on Russia and the Soviet Union) (1845–1930s), Y5
Vinawer, Maxim (1862–1938), papers, Y5
        (Simon Dubnow), Y5
        (Lucien Wolf), Y5
Visti, N19
Vitoshynskyi, Aitol, papers, S4
Vladeck, Barukh (Daniel Charney), Y5
Vladibas Nestnesis (1922–1940), N19
Vogel, Vladimir Rudolfovich, composition, N26
Voice of America scripts, N1
Voliansky family, archives, S4
Vologodskaia Fabrika Soderzhatelia Toruntaevskogo (Western Americana Collection), P7
Von Loew, Karl, V1
Voskhod (1886–1906), N11
Voskresnoe chtenie, S1
Vstrecha s Rossiei (1945) (Vladimir Zenzinov), N19
Vyg Community, Old Believers, N19
Vyriausybes zinios (1918–1940), N19
Vyshinskii, Andrei Ianuar'evich (1883–1954) (William Averell Harriman), C7

W

W. Averell Harriman Institute for Advanced Study of the Soviet Union, C10, C11
Wague, George (Leon Bakst), N25

Wallenberg, Raoul (*Raoul Wallenberg, Buried Alive*), N23
Walsh, Edmond A., *The Fall of the Russian Empire* (Nikolai M. Khravrov), N18
War Industries Board (Bernard M. Baruch), P8
War Memoirs of Robert Lansing (Robert Lansing), P8
War Without Winners (film, 1978), N23
Watercolors. *See* Art and under individual artists
We (Evgenii Ivanovich Zamiatin), P7
Weaving, *See* Art
Webbe, Edward, *Rare and most wonderful things which Edw. Webbe ... has seene ... in the landes of ... Russia ...* (1590), M3
Weber, Max, M7
Weinreich, Max, collection, Y4
Weinryb, Bernard D., *The Jews of Poland: a Social and Economic History ... from 1100 to 1800*, Philadelphia (1973), N11
West Germany (Germany, Federal Republic of), P8
Westchiloff, Charles, M2
Western Americana Collection, P7
Western Mongolia, A9
Whistler, Anna McNeil, diaries (1843–1844), N18
White, Harry Dexter (1892–1948), selected papers, P8
Wiadomosci literaki, N19
Wieniawski, Henri, composition, N26
Wigman, Mary (Mikhail Mikhailovich Fokine), N25
Wiiralt, Edward, N14
Witonski, Ted. J., H3
Wolf, Lucien, papers (1890s–1950s), Y5
Women of Russia (film, 1968), N23
Woodridge, L.D., slides (1895–1914), H3
Workers School, Ruthenberg Library, R3
Workmen's Circle, B6
    (Louis Levine), Y2
World Council of Churches (Georges Florovsky), P7
World Union of Poalei Zion, B6
    (Kalmon Marmor), Y5
World War I, C5, C7, H2, N19
World War II, C5, C7, C16, N19, P3
    (Irina Skariatina), P7
Wortis, Rose, book collection, R3
Woytinsky, Wladimir S. (1885–1960), papers, C7
W.P.A. Federal Writers' Project (NYC unit), N7
Wrangel, P2
Wright, Edward H., correspondence (1850–1851), N4
Wu, Chan-han (fl. 1920s), C7
Wuralt, Edouard, I4
Wyer, Edward, papers (1813–1816, 1825–1838), N8

Y

Yakut, ethnography, A8
Yakut, language, N19
Yakutsk, pictures, N29
Yalta, Big Three Conference, R8
Yarmolinsky, Avrahm
    (Harry Miller Lydenberg), N18
    (Babette Deutsch), N18

Yeshiva University
    Archives, Y2
    Mendel Gottesman Library of Hebraica/Judaica, Y1
    Museum, Y3
Yevreinov, Nikolai N., working scripts, N24
Yevreiskaya biblioteka (1871–1903), N11
Yevreiskaya letopis (1923–1926), N11
Yevreiskaya zhizn' (1915–1917), N11
Yevreiskii mir (1909–1911), N11
Yevreyskaya tribuna (Maxim Vinawer), Y5
Ycvstafiev, Alexei Grigorevich, family papers (1829–1916), N18
Yiddish language, N11, Y4, Y5
Yiddish literature, N11, Y4, Y5
Yiddish material, B6, J2, N11, Y4, Y5
Yidishe folksbibliotek (1888–1889), N11
YIVO Vilno Collection on Russia and the Soviet Union (1845–1930s), Y5
YIVO Institute for Jewish Research, A5, Y4, Y5
Yizkor memorial books, N11, Y4
YMCA in Paris, archives, Y6
YMCA in Russia (1900–1920s), Y6
YMCA of Greater New York, Archives, Y6
YMCA of USA, Archives. *See* YMCA of Greater New York, Archives
YMCA Work in Paris for Emigre Russians, Y6
Your Isadora
    (Natalie Roslavleva), N25
    (Francis Steegmuller), N25
Youskevitch, I., manuscripts, N25
    (Oral Interviews with Dancers), N25
Yukaghir, ethnography, A8
Yunkers, Adja, G1, M7
Yur'yevich, Semion Alekseyevich, correspondence, N19

Z

Z vershyn i nyzyn: zbirnyk poezii, Ivan Franko (1887), S4
Zabytki historyczne zydow w Polsce, Warsaw, 1929, N11
Zadkine, Ossip (1890–1967), N14
Zale, Klara, N19
Zalshupin, Sergei, N14
Zamiatin, Evgenii Ivanovich (1884–1937), materials, P7
Zapysky Naukovoho Tovarystva imeny Shevchenka (1892–), N19
Zdanevich, I. (Iliazd), N20
Zenzinov, Vladimir Mikhailovich, letters, N19
Zhitlovsky, Chaim (1861–1943), Y5
    (Simon Dubnow), Y5
    (Marc Ratner), Y5
    (Maxim Vinawer), Y5
Zhizneopisanie . . . Baranova, N16
Zhukovskii, Vasilli Andreevich (1783–1852) (Mikhail Iur'evich Lermontov), C7
Zhytya i revolyutziya, N19
Zimmerman, Charles S., collection, I2
ZIMRO (Petrogradskii Kamernyi Ansambl', Obshchestvo Evreiskoi Narodnoi Muzyki), Z1
Zionist Archives and Library, Z1
Zionist Socialist Workers' Party (A. Charash), Y5
Zirkoff, Boris de, collection, O1

Ziskind, Alexander (Marc Ratner), Y5
Zoffer, Gerald, working scripts, N24
Zoshchenko, Mikhail Mikhailovich (1895–1958), materials (Archives of *Story* magazine and Story Press), P7
Zukunft, Y5
Zunser, Miriam Shomer, papers (1900–1907), N18
Zuskind, Chaim (Simon Dubnow), Y5

ROBERT A. KARLOWICH is associate professor in the Graduate School of Computer, Information and Library Sciences at the Pratt Institute in Brooklyn, New York. He was formerly Head of Slavic Acquisitions at Columbia University Libraries, and Slavic Bibliographer and Head of Slavic Acquisitions at the University of Illinois Library.

Professor Karlowich earned an M.S. and a D.L.S. in library service from Columbia University, and did graduate work at Yale University and at the Institute of Culture in Leningrad, USSR.

He is a member of numerous professional associations and committees. Among his other publications, Professor Karlowich edited *Libraries, Bibliographies, and Books in Russia in 1917–1935: A Preliminary Bibliography of Books and Serials on the Period Published in the Soviet Union, 1946–1985.*